T0341742

Special issue

Globalized Media Archaeologies

Edited by

Daniel Morgan

boundary 2

an international journal

of literature and culture

Volume 49, Number 1

February 2022

Duke University Press

boundary 2

an international journal of literature and culture

Founding Editors   Robert Kroetsch and William V. Spanos

Editor   Paul A. Bové
   Victoria Glavin, Assistant to the Editor

Managing Editor   Margaret A. Havran

Editorial Collective

Jonathan Arac, University of Pittsburgh
Anthony Bogues, Brown University and University of Johannesburg
Paul A. Bové, University of Pittsburgh
Arne De Boever, California Institute of the Arts
Nergis Ertürk, Pennsylvania State University
Leah Feldman, University of Chicago
Wlad Godzich, University of California, Santa Cruz
David Golumbia, Virginia Commonwealth University
Stathis Gourgouris, Columbia University
R. A. Judy, University of Pittsburgh
Kara Keeling, University of Chicago
Aamir R. Mufti, University of California, Los Angeles
Donald E. Pease, Dartmouth College
Bruce Robbins, Columbia University
Hortense Spillers, Vanderbilt University
Anita Starosta, Pennsylvania State University
Christian Thorne, Williams College

Editorial Board

Charles Bernstein, University of Pennsylvania
John Beverley, University of Pittsburgh
Rey Chow, Duke University
Colin Dayan, Vanderbilt University
Nuruddin Farah, Bard College
Margaret Ferguson, University of California, Davis
Anthony Grafton, Princeton University
Michael Hays, Independent Scholar, Pittsburgh, Pennsylvania
Fredric Jameson, Duke University
George Lamming, Barbados
Marcia Landy, University of Pittsburgh
Gayatri Spivak, Columbia University
Wang Hui, Tsinghua University, Beijing
Cornel West, Princeton University
Rob Wilson, University of California, Santa Cruz

Advisory Editors

Nancy Condee, University of Pittsburgh
Christopher L. Connery, University of California, Santa Cruz
Harris Feinsod, Northwestern University
Ruth Y. Y. Hung, Hong Kong Baptist University
Annette Damayanti Lienau, Harvard University
Nick Mitchell, University of California, Santa Cruz
Daniel Morgan, University of Chicago
Bécquer Seguín, Johns Hopkins University
Gavin Steingo, Princeton University
Q. S. Tong, University of Hong Kong
Henry Veggian, University of North Carolina, Chapel Hill
Lindsay Waters, Independent Scholar, Belmont, Massachusetts

Assistant Editors

Jason Fitzgerald, University of Michigan
Sierra Lomuto, Rowan University
Chris Taylor, University of Chicago

Contents

Editor's Note

Paul A. Bové

boundary 2 says goodbye to Meg Havran, the managing editor of this journal for more than thirty years. We are told no one is irreplaceable, but those who have worked with Meg know that is just not true.

A managing editor is a technician, an organizer, a mediator, and something of an artist. Each person's character, values, and imagination impress special qualities on all those roles. And collectively, we think no one could have done it with more skill, imagination, and care than Meg.

Meg and I have edited *boundary 2* as a team on which she was always the more important person. I have an entire vocabulary that has no purpose without her here working ahead of me. Any success *b2* might have had over this part of its nearly half-century-long history comes from her clarity and generosity. She managed Duke's saving of *b2* long ago and worked too hard to establish us as a quarterly publishing one thousand pages per year. And all those whose writing has appeared in those pages know the writing is better for her attention.

boundary 2 49:1 (2022)   DOI 10.1215/01903659-9615347   ©2022 by Duke University Press

Such a profound change in editing promises new futures, I am sure, although those futures will have had their measure set for them at the highest level. I suppose I will learn to suffer the loss—although I wish it hadn't come.

Managing Editor's Note

Margaret A. Havran

This issue will be my last as managing editor of *boundary 2*. If I have been successful, I have many people to thank for it. Chief among them is Paul Bové, who has been the leader the journal has needed for the last thirty-three years. He gave me free rein from day one to run my own show in the editorial office, giving me space to find my way and allowing me to do my work. Only the "supervised" know how important that is. He has always been my champion, recognizing me as an equal, honoring my value, and always giving me credit when it was due. For all that, I am infinitely grateful. He is my treasured friend.

While *b2*'s masthead has changed over the years, I have enjoyed immensely the relationships, indeed friendships, that developed through my work with the editorial collective, advisory editors, assistant editors, and the editorial board. They all, too, have valued my skills and acknowledged my contributions to the journal and have been unwavering in their support. I have learned a great deal from all of them, as well as from the hundreds of

boundary 2 49:1 (2022)   DOI 10.1215/01903659-9615361   ©2022 by Duke University Press

authors I've had the pleasure of working with during my thirty-two years with the journal. I am grateful for editors' and authors' cordiality and collegiality, which always tempered the challenging work of b2.

Two longtime colleagues at Duke University Press deserve special mention. Rob Dilworth, journals director, lent guidance and support that have sustained the journal in all ways. Cynthia Gurganus, b2's longtime production coordinator, shepherded our manuscripts and fielded my countless questions. My thanks to both, not only for their professional expertise but also for their friendship, which developed as an offshoot of working closely together. My collaborations with David Spratte and Emily Combs at HALO 22 were inspiring and gave me the chance to expand my right brain. I marvel at their creativity and special knack for capturing concepts and making stunning covers.

A special note of thanks to my husband, Ron Winkler, for loving me, for always standing by me, and for taking joy in my accomplishments. He was the hidden gem it was my good fortune to find many years ago.

As I move on to new opportunities, I will keep b2 close to my heart always. The journal is in very capable hands.

Introduction:
Media Archaeology and the Resources of Film Studies

Daniel Morgan

1

The emergence of film studies as a discipline in the 1970s and 1980s was marked by a recalcitrance to deal seriously with other media—even moving image media. Television was relegated to cultural studies, and video, along with the increasing presence of moving image works in gallery spaces, was taken up largely within art history. Discussions of precinematic media, from the magic lantern and the phantasmagoria to the phenakistoscope and the zoetrope, were either positioned within a teleological narrative that led to cinema or taken up by studies in the history of science and perception (see Manoni 2000; Crary 1990). Indeed, it wasn't until the rise of digital media became inescapable that the notion of media entered the field's general self-conception. The Society for Cinema Studies changed its name to Society for Cinema and Media Studies only in 2002, yet even within that framework, the term *media* was firmly—if implicitly— identified with the prominence of new media.

boundary 2 49:1 (2022)   DOI 10.1215/01903659-9615375   ©2022 by Duke University Press

During this period, however, an alternate framework for thinking about media arose, initially as a kind of "media theory"—exemplified by Marshall McLuhan and Friedrich Kittler—and then located within the domain of "media archaeology." Media archaeology emerged through an engagement with Michel Foucault's *Archaeology of Knowledge* (1969) as a way of telling alternate histories to dominant (often teleological) narratives about media. As Wolfgang Ernst notes, the term *archaeology* can be mistakenly thought of as a "digging out" of forgotten episodes of media, whereas its intention was to create "an epistemologically alternative approach to the supremacy of media-historical narratives" of progress and technological development (2013: 55).[1] This approach led to two large arguments. The first was to introduce media and technology into Foucault's archaeological method and to use that technical framework to rethink questions about subjectivity as well as epistemic excavations. The second was to displace cinema—and, to a lesser extent, television—from its centrality in media histories, thus allowing other possibilities from what Siegfried Zielinski has called the "secret paths in history" to emerge in its place (Zielinski 1996; see also Zielinski 1999 and 2006). Drawing on work by Kittler and, from a later generation, Zielinski, Bernhard Siegert, and Norbert Bolz, media archaeologists wove together strands of media theory with archival impulses in order to generate creative accounts of the different ways that media interacted with each other, with the perceptual capacities of the people who used them, and with wider social contexts.

There were certainly affinities between media archaeology and debates within film studies. The famous claim by Lev Manovich in his 2001 *The Language of New Media*, which posits cinema as a brief episode in a longer history of animation—one that is reinstated by the rise of digital technologies—is familiar to arguments in media archaeology.[2] Yet the connection between film studies and media archaeology did not become explicit until Thomas Elsaesser's 2004 article "The New Film History as Media Archaeology." There, Elsaesser drew a methodological connection between media

1. Ernst provides a helpful distinction of *media archaeology* from the other key Foucaldian term, *genealogy*: "Media archaeology is not a method of analysis separate from genealogy but rather complementary to it. Genealogy examines process, whereas archaeology examines the moment, however temporally extended that moment might be . . . a snapshot, a slice through the discursive nexus" (2013: 198).
2. "Born from animation, cinema pushed animation to its periphery, only in the end to become one particular case of animation" (Manovich 2001: 302).

archaeology and the way a new group of early cinema historians in the mid-1980s challenged the teleological formulations of traditional film histories. Rather than seeing early cinema as a precursor to classical Hollywood cinema, or a "primitive" version of it, these historians argued that it had an autonomous logic, meaningful stylistic traits, and modes of appeal to the spectator—what Tom Gunning termed the "cinema of attractions" (1986). Elsaesser thought that such work needed to be done across the history of media in the twentieth century, especially cinema, eschewing teleological models to open up a history of how different media functioned and what possibilities they enabled. To Elsaesser, media archaeology was

> intended to liberate from their straight-jackets all those re-positionings of linear chronology that operate with hard binaries between, for instance, early cinema and classical cinema, spectacle versus narrative, linear narrative versus interactivity. Instead, film history would acknowledge its peculiar status, and become a matter of tracing paths or laying tracks leading from the respective "now" to different pasts, in modalities that accommodate continuities as well as ruptures. We would then be mapping media-convergence and self-differentiation not in terms of either a teleology or a search for origins, but in the form of forking paths of possibility. (2004: 99)

Only by incorporating the tools of media archaeology, he suggested, could film studies adequately deal with the overlooked media of the twentieth century and the emerging media of the twenty-first. If the history of early cinema provided a paradigm for an understanding of postclassical cinema—what Wanda Strauven termed "the cinema of attractions reloaded" (2006)—this resembled the work done by media archaeologists to excavate the principles of historical media in order to bring those utopian ambitions to bear on the present.

By and large, the terms of Elsaesser's arguments have driven the interactions between the two. It has been a powerful framework, allowing the work of media archaeologists to enter a field that describes itself as cinema *and media* studies; the affinity that film history and media archaeology share for the archive as a site of conceptual innovations, as well as practice information, has enabled this connection to thrive. This is no small thing, providing comparative ballast to arguments about cinema and theoretical stakes for archival investigations.

Yet the affinity between film history and media archaeology has also produced a set of blind spots and methodological stagnation. What drove the connection was a challenge to linear models of historical development, but this has led to a problem. While producing a range of important methodological tools and conceptual models, media archaeology has also fallen into a trap of emphasizing only a few select traditions within the context of a global mediascape. Jussi Parikka makes the point explicit: "media archaeology . . . has for a long time neglected, for example, most Asian regions and their cultural histories, as well as, for example, the Arabic world, in addition to South America, Africa, and Australian indigenous people" (2012: 52). This exclusion, as I hope to show here, is not simply a matter of content but of method. While some recent developments in media theory have begun to fill this gap—for example, Patrick Jagoda's notion of network aesthetics (2016); Arjun Appadurai's explorations of the international flows of knowledge and culture (2011); Nick Dyer-Witheford's modeling of the international forms of labor and laboring bodies (2015)—such accounts are still preliminary and are only slowly moving into the terrain of media archaeology.

The essays in this special issue look to tackle this question by turning to one of the most important resources within cinema and media studies, namely its models for thinking about moving image media as *inherently international* phenomena. They do so in order to push against the geographic blinders that have emerged within media archaeology. As I'll argue in this introduction, the goal is not to promote one field or discipline over another. Yet if there is still a need to think about cinema as a medium among other media, there is an equal, perhaps even more pressing need to make sure that an archaeology of media thinks about space and geography as carefully as it does about time and history. The aim here is to set out new ways of thinking about the ways that media function within an international, and especially non-Western, context. It is to set the terms for a globalizing media archaeology.

2

The central orientation of media archaeology has been a relation to time.[3] It is an orientation that can be found everywhere, from the theoretical models on which media archaeology is built to the specific case studies

3. Parikka lists "media time that is recurring and based on topoi; the idea of deep times . . . ; the focus on microtemporalities that define technical media culture on the level of machines and technological processes; the recursive methodology of time and the expansions of new film history into media archaeology" (2015: 7).

that make up its operation. Distinguishing itself from traditional histories, which—on this criticism—tell a fairly straightforward linear history of progress, media archaeology looks to moments in a history and technology of media in which ruptures, or overlooked or forestalled innovations, occurred. Even more, many accounts of media objects turn them into a meditation on time. Wendy Chun's seminal study of software, for example, begins by announcing time as its theme: "New media, like the computer technology on which it relies, races simultaneously towards the future and the past." And she then rapidly identifies the key Kittlerian tropes, memory and storage, as crucial for thinking about digital media (2008: 148; see also McPherson 2005).

The focus on temporality, and on the dynamics of histories and historiography, shapes the kind of media that is discussed. Parikka emphasizes "an emphasis on the forgotten, the quirky, the non-obvious apparatuses, practices and inventions" and characterizes a prominent strand of media archaeology as "celebrating weirdness in media culture and its non-linear paths, and using that weirdness as a methodological guideline" (2012: 2, 45).[4] For Ernst, this is a "technique of remembering their past in a way that is radically alternative to historical discourse" (2013: 49). The aim of such diving into the past, and its forgotten pathways, is not simply to correct the historical record but to create "parallel" histories: putting past and present together without a teleological framework, such that neither is reducible to the other. What John Durham Peters labels "weird media theory" involves finding (hitherto unsuspected) resources with which to rethink central aspects of the present (2015: 29).

A method oriented toward history produces arguments about history and time. This is not news. Walter Benjamin, from whom media archaeology gains some of its redemptive charge, praised the ambitions of surrealists for their ability to grasp "the revolutionary energies of the 'outmoded'—in the first iron constructions, the first factory buildings, the earliest photos, objects that have begun to be extinct, grand pianos, the dresses of five years ago, fashionable restaurants when the vogue has begun to ebb from them" (1999: 210). And much of his monumental study of the Paris of the nineteenth century, especially in the fragments that constitute *The Arcades Project*, was designed to rescue the forgotten revolutionary energies from elements of the past: to use the overlooked and the outmoded to gain a new

---

4. Elsewhere Parikka talks about "lost ideas, unusual machines, and reemerging desires" (2015: 146).

purchase on the present. It is in no small way because of Benjamin's influence that, as Parikka acknowledges, many media archaeologists turned to the nineteenth century to mine it for technologies that would generate "possibilities for differing routes" around the dominant media of the twentieth century, namely cinema and television (2012: 64).

Yet it is precisely the *longue durée* of this model that creates a set of anxieties in and for media archaeology and that has begun to lead toward a kind of impasse. One is the worry of nostalgia. Elsaesser, invoking Zielinski, paraphrases this problem: it is about whether media archaeology "is to be more than the name of a nostalgic look back at a lost Eden of optical toys and vision machines, and [if new film history is to be] more than cinephilia turned necrophilia" (2016b: 56). This is the sense of a culture fetishizing the old and the outmoded, the handmade over the machinic—one of the symptoms of which, to take a recent example, is that the production of vinyl records outstripped production of CDs in 2019.[5] Beyond that, there are the political traps of nostalgia, the fetishizing of the out of date as a way of avoiding the present, much in the way that Theodor W. Adorno criticized Benjamin for the terms of his interest in the nineteenth century (see Adorno and Benjamin 1999: 104–14, 280–89).

A related worry is that of the utopian impulse itself. It is no coincidence that much of the interest within media archaeology concerns technologies that never succeeded, that never quite got off the ground, that flourished only within niche communities, or that remained only as plans and fantasies. Kittler's *Gramophone, Film, Typewriter*, for example, contains a range of media fantasies, including Rilke's speculation of what the grooves of a skull would sound like when played by a record needle (1999: 38–42). The very organization of Kittler's book, with short inserts and text that record the imaginations of the unrealized possibilities of media, is constructed around this aim. But there is a cost to this. One of the reasons that a moment like the Paris Commune of 1871 remains celebrated is that it never developed into a state, never withered away its romantic energy. (Hannah Arendt thought that this loss of energy was the inevitable afterlife of revolution, in which the open possibilities of the revolutionary moment—its utopian experience—decay into ossified bureaucracy [(1963) 1990].) Elsaesser worries about a correlate in the way media archaeologists can overlook cinema as a medium—precisely because its revolutionary

---

5. For information on sales, see https://www.riaa.com/u-s-sales-database/.

energy seemed to dissipate with its increasing commercialization. This is, he says, "a bias that echoes and confirms the diminished status of cinema" in a digital age and thus evacuates the ambitions—not only fantasized but realized—it contained (2016b: 56).

Behind all this, however, is a palpable anxiety that the energy of media archaeology is winding down. Parikka expresses it in terms of the need for an "act two" in which "new theories and practical ideas" come together to keep the method "exciting and fresh" (2012: 14). One of the new models he labels as a "media materialism" (2015: 3), which goes far beyond the standard debates about medium specificity or about the technological underpinning of media. It is a materialism invested in the "geophysical reality" that comprises media and that media depend on for their operation, a physical existence that includes not just the algorithmic processes within digital media but the dust that collects on their screens, the atomic infrastructure that binds the technology together, and the earth involved in the mining of material (2015: 87, 103, 139; see also Mattern 2017). It is a new media materialism, Parikka suggests, out of which new kinds of stories will be told and that will enable new kinds of creative practices.

But media reductionism carries its own risks, and knowing where to stop is no easy thing. Michael Baxandall's study of limewood sculptors in fifteenth- and sixteenth-century Germany may at times reduce the material of their medium to its cellular structure, but it does so in order to explain why limewood both enabled and required a certain model of relief and carving (1980: 27–93). In this vein, Yuk Hui cautions against a reductionist logic in media analysis:

> Why do we approach the existence of digital objects from the perspective of data? True, these objects appear to human users as colorful and visible beings, yet at the level of programming, they are text files; *further down* the operational system, they are binary codes, and *finally, at the level of* circuit boards, they are nothing but signals generated by voltage values and the operations of logic gates. How might we think about these voltage differences as being the substance of a digital object? *Searching downward*, we may end up with the mediation of silicon and metal. And *finally*, we could go into particles and fields. It would be possible to approach from these different layers, *but doing so may not be the most productive method.* (2017: 27–29)

Hui's point is not to return to a phenomenology of media, to the realm of experience, but rather to tarry with the object itself—and not to lose sight of it in the desire to get to new analytic projects.

It is not a trivial fact, I think, that at the same moment Parikka elaborates a reductionist model of media materialism, Peters produces one of the most all-encompassing accounts of media. "The old idea that media are environments can be flipped," he writes; "environments are also media" (2015: 3). Drawing on the tradition of media archaeology, yet pushing far beyond its limits, he asks readers to think about familiar natural phenomena such as clouds and oceans—and the creatures who live in them—as already themselves media, and as capable of generating media. The aim is to displace our familiar assumptions about the site of meaning and meaningfulness: "To posit media of nature is to deny the human monopoly of meaning" (280).

Does this mean that we should make a choice between theories of media that are expansive or reductive? Should we choose between models that move into the microprocesses of technology or that expand away from the human altogether? Each would create a new frame of reference, whether a microtemporality or a deep time of the natural world itself. But Hui's implicit question still hovers around. To what end are these productive methods for working with and thinking about media? Would either, for example, provide a different energy for Lisa Gitelman's excavation of the Xerox machine (2014: 83–110) or for Hannah Frank's reworking of that account to think about its use in animation practices (2019: 108–43)? Would either transform the "platform" model that Nick Montfort and Ian Bogost developed in relation to the outmoded Atari video game system (2009)?

I don't insist that they would not, or could not, merely that it is not yet clear how these frameworks differ dramatically from the methodological terms that structured the "first act" of media archaeology. Even Elsaesser (2016a: 200–201) finds himself caught. When he speculates over the ways that debates about cinema can get beyond impasses around the apparatus and the ontology of the image, he sees only two avenues. One is "the revival of phenomenology on a broad front . . . as it attempts to address the limits of the fixed geometry of representation." The other is the use of media archaeology to create "an alternate genealogy, which grounds the cinema differently." He writes, "I believe it should be possible to develop a media-archaeological account, from which analogue and digital cinema can be seen to be equally valid if differently weighted ways of understanding both the material basis of cinema and its different manifestations over time, so that apparent 'returns' . . . need not be plotted on a chronological timeline and therefore . . . appear as ever-present resources that film-makers and artists are able to deploy as options and possibilities." It is striking how little this formulation differs from the first wave of media archaeologists and their focus on time and counter-histories—perhaps the only difference is Elsaesser's long-standing insistence on keeping cinema at the center of debates.

If the temporal critiques in media archaeology have fallen into a conceptual rut, moving through familiar models for bringing the past into relation to the present—again, we know how such arguments go—there is a need for a different way of working with media in an expanded field. It is to augment time with space.

3

Space has been a vexed topic in media archaeology, when it appears at all. In distinguishing his approach from Foucault's, for example, Ernst writes, "Foucauldian archaeology and archivology remain somewhat centered on space, topologically 'other spaces.' Such analyses autopoetically refer to the alphabet-based world and the symbolic order of textual libraries." Against this, Ernst posits the "the age of so-called analog media such as the phonograph and cinematograph," in which "signs of or in time themselves can be registered"—before being dialectically subsumed within the orbit of digital media (2013: 30). What I want to draw attention to here is not just that Ernst is situating his version of media archaeology, focused as it is on a period beyond the dominance of the library, as oriented around temporal considerations. It is that even the conception of space he invokes is abstracted from the physical world; where "space" does appear, it is the "other space" outside the dominant logic of media, the zone of heterotopia. It is conceptual rather than geographic.

I want to stay with this point briefly, because it is crucial to see how closely tied work in media archaeology is to a logic of time and how firmly it buries sustained investigations of space. This theoretical turn may be familiar (see, for example, Doane 2002), but it is nonetheless strange to think that media—analog or digital—should be understood almost entirely in temporal terms. After all, the infrastructure that makes such media possible is inherently bound to spatial concerns. Alice Lovejoy (2019) has written about the way that the raw stock of film was already enmeshed within systems of geopolitical tensions, especially during World War II and the

Cold War. Marc Levinson has drawn attention to the transformations in the shipping industry and the move to a globally systematized logic of distribution (2006), which Erika Balsom has recently picked up to think about the logic of the ocean in contemporary cinema (2018)—including Allan Sekula and Noël Burch's film about cargo container ships, *The Forgotten Space* (2010). And Nicole Starosielski has described the network of cables, moving within and between nations, that makes the digital age possible (2015).

It has been curiously difficult to find these debates within the main texts of media archaeology. Perhaps it is the case that the focus on "weird objects" in media archaeology, on forgotten moments, somehow worked to remove the circulation of technologies and media from consideration. If they were not developed, how could they move and be moved? There are, to be sure, some significant exceptions. Hui's study of the idea of technology in the context of China, and philosophical traditions drawn from there, is one example (2016). Another is Xiao Liu's exploration of the introduction of digital technology—and fantasies about technology—within a Chinese context in the 1980s and the different ways that technologies were taken up and used (2016). Machiko Kushara has excavated a version of a zoetrope from Japan in the 1930s that could be played on a gramophone and shows how it weaves together (modern) Western technology with (traditional) Japanese cultural forms (2011). And there has been a range of recent works that draw on a tradition of Islamic discourses and artistic practices to rethink questions of image, technology, and representation.

It is in order to move beyond these cases to more general questions of the geographic stats of media, culture as well as space, that a turn to the domain of film studies matters. Because it is there that the most sophisticated approaches to thinking about how media cross borders have been developed, providing models for how media move internationally and how they are viewed, absorbed, and transformed in the context of their reception. Certainly, it is not only within film studies that questions about international or global influences are felt; this is a vital topic in art history, literary studies, and music. But it is particularly insistent when talking about cinema. Partly this has to do with the history of cinema itself and the extraordinary international spread of the medium after the first screening in Paris in December 1895. Within a little more than a year, films had been shown across the globe: in India, in China, in Japan, in Mexico, in Egypt, et cetera. And because of the construction of the Lumière cinematograph, which could be configured as both camera and projector, showing films in a given location meant that films could be made there. Cinema functioned, as Gunning has argued, as a way for people to see themselves on screen while also allowing for new representations to travel in multiple directions (2006).

Many of the models that film studies developed for thinking about cinema were thus predicated on its international spread. Yuri Tsivian, for example, argued that the very idea of a national cinema did not emerge from an exclusively national tradition—of literature, art, and culture—but was from the beginning defined within an international context (2004, 2014). Other scholars have shown how ideas of specific national cinemas took shape through a logic of borrowing and adaptation. Some of this was political necessity: an extensive project by Colin MacCabe and Lee Grieveson showed how the film practices of the British Empire both shaped and occasioned creative responses from within its far-flung reaches (2011). More broadly, Miriam Hansen developed the model of "vernacular modernism" to account for the way classical Hollywood cinema appealed to audiences as the height of the modern, providing not just compelling narratives but an image of a modern way of life—from clothing to design to gender roles and more. Hansen developed this model in particular through a reading of Shanghai cinema of the 1930s, but it has a more general application (1999, 2000). Michael Raine has delineated the operation of vernacular modernism in postwar Japanese commercial cinema (2007), and, more recently, Nilo Couret has used it to analyze how Latin American film comedy relies on what he calls a "mock classicism." As Couret puts it, "The identification of networks of film and media exchange prior to the 1960s challenges the diffusionist and center/periphery models that overdetermine understandings of cinema in that period. Circulation invites us to ask why do certain things travel? How quickly? How far? How long?" (2018: 21). These are models of thinking that govern discussions about the international constitution of cinemas and answers Natasa Durovicova and Kathleen Newman's question about "the limits of the nation-state paradigm as the basic film-historical unit" (2009: ix).

There are also analyses that do not depend on the flow of Hollywood cinema or that show the influence of other cinemas on the Hollywood model. Rochona Majumdar has argued that the very idea of art cinema emerges within Indian cinema through its absorption of a French cinematic framework, not just Satyajit's Ray's connections to Renoir but lectures by figures like Marie Seton, who helped set up ciné-clubs as she traveled

(Majumdar 2016; see also Galt and Schoonover 2010). Masha Salazkina has shown how emerging Indian film directors were often trained in Soviet film schools during the 1960s and 1970s, creating a line of technical influence that bypassed the Hollywood model (2010). Ling Zhang has traced lines of reciprocal influence between China and Japan in the 1920s and 1930s, a cosmopolitan vision of East Asian cinematic influences whose ideal would be belied by the war to come (2015). In a different direction, there are studies that elucidate international influences on Hollywood cinema: from the well-known stories of German émigrés arriving in Hollywood during the 1930s (see, for example, Germünden 2013) to the influence of martial arts cinema, especially from Hong Kong, over the past two decades (Yip 2017). This persists even outside Hollywood: Allyson Field has delineated the ways Latin American "third cinema" came to influence the emergence of a radical Black cinema in the 1970s (2018).

This is of course just a brief sketch of some of the main strands of thinking about cinema as an international phenomenon. Alongside this, there have been attempts to decenter the notion of the spectator implied by the cinematic spectacle by recasting *who* is doing the looking and from what form of experience. Some of this emerges from key texts by bell hooks (1991) and Fatimah Tobing Rony (1996), but it has also been the logic behind recent studies and collections of non-canonical film theories. Aaron Gerow (2010) and Naoki Yamamoto (2020) have written on earlier Japanese film theory, while Victor Fan (2015) has treated that period in Chinese film theory; Francesco Casetti, Silvio Alovisio, and Luca Mazzei (2017) have collected a trove of hitherto untranslated Italian writings on the first decades of film history; Jaroslav Andel and Petr Szczepanik (2008) published decades of pre–World War II Czech film theory and criticism; and Nicholas Baer, Michael Cowan, and Anton Kaes (2016) have put together a new history of early German responses to the cinema. In each case, and in other volumes that are currently being prepared—for example, on the history of Chinese film theory—the aim is to move the terrain of film studies from one dominated by the United States and Western Europe in order to see other models of cinema and theory that provide alternate accounts of what the medium is and can do. In their work, these new histories follow through on the challenge that Aamir Mufti posed for theories of world literature: "Could it be that the [Euro-American] is always at the 'center' of the discourse whenever we talk about world literature? What would a discourse look like in which that was not the case?" (2016: xi, 52). And yet the goal is to do so in a way that does not treat artistic traditions as essentially autonomous or isolated within a national paradigm. Indeed, each of Mufti's chapters starts away from the Western (and Anglo-American) model, but they invariably circle around it. The goal is not to ignore but to recalibrate, to reorient.

The essays that follow take this as their project. They focus largely on cinema but as one medium that exists within a wider field of media. Each essay takes as its focus a case outside of Western Europe and the United States, ranging in location from Eastern Europe to Cuba to Ghana to India to China—even though in many cases a Western context is the necessary interlocutor for the exchange, flow, and dialogue of and around media. The essays aim to use their internationalist perspectives as a way to reenergize debates on media, their history, and the historiography that emerges around them. Their goal is to absorb the lessons that media archaeology has taught film studies and to use the resources of film studies to decenter the examples and methods of media archaeology from its embeddedness in a Western framework.

Weihong Bao's essay takes up this challenge directly. Displacing debates over media theory to the landscape of a Chinese context, she argues that contemporary practices in independent Chinese documentary can provide a new—and differently grounded—impetus for what Bernhard Siegert called "cultural techniques." Exploring the work of filmmaker, critic, artist, and farmer Mao Chenyu, she shows how he develops an expanded notion of a medium that still remains bound to specific technical arrangements and practices. The resulting combination of technical devices and cultural resonances, especially that of a history of shamanism, results in what she describes as a "media communitarianism." This model, Bao argues, encompasses "techniques of space, time, and environment as well as human and non-human consciousness" and does so within a necessarily public context. In this way, Mao Chenyu explicitly negotiates a Western model of theory within a Chinese lineage, creating new resonances and possibilities for thinking media.

The question of what constitutes a medium gets a further expansion in Hannah Frank's posthumous essay on the recurrent, if little employed, fantasy of synthetic sound, the creation of sound cinema by the direct drawing of images on the celluloid film strip itself—a fusion of the Kittlerian modes of cinema and gramophone. Moving from the Soviet Union to France to the United States, Frank shows how this idea depends on differences in epistemic certainty between sight and sound. Arguing for synthetic sound as a fundamentally documentary mode, she shows how it can be used to create a more open epistemology of unheard sound—from the contours of objects to the sounds of ancient times to the intimations of the future.

Rochona Majumdar's discussion of the song-text within Indian cinema argues that stylistic features can themselves take on the qualities of a medium. Showing how the reception of songs from popular Hindi cinema removes them from their narrative context, circulating as autonomous units through radio, television, cell phone ringtones, and social media, Majumdar argues that this popular usage warrants a revised account of how these songs function. Focusing on key films, popular as well as art cinema, from the post-Independence years, she argues that these songs create a temporal rupture that allows for a non-teleological, nonlinear approach to history—one that takes part in and even anticipates many aspects of postcolonial historiography.

A pair of essays take up the dynamics of documentary cinema in the postwar era, seeing in the *idea* of the documentary an important medium in its own right. Joshua Malitsky looks at the way cinema functioned within and across the republics that made up Yugoslavia in the years immediately after its independence. This subnational address proved uniquely difficult: films were pitched toward specific republics, while also aiming—often through the figure of Tito himself—to create a general image of the nation. Malitsky turns to the creation of film programs, arguing that they were made, distributed, and consumed in a flexible operation, enabling local audiences to adapt to a newly emerging nation-state. Using the omnipresence of nonfiction types of cinema in these programs, he elucidates what he terms a "documentary imaginary" of a nation.

In the opposite direction, Alice Lovejoy traces the supranational history of the World Union of Documentary, an attempt by filmmakers located across Europe—both West and East—to bypass the hegemonic divisions of the Cold War and create a new model of an internationally produced, socially ambitious documentary. Drawing on institutional histories, Lovejoy analyzes why the internationalism of this idea was so crucial to the politics of its documentary ethos. She focuses on the complex reasons why the World Union failed, even as individuals involved in its establishment thrived, seeing in this history a way to understand how institutions—national and international—shaped the possibilities of documentary film politics in the early Cold War years.

Focusing on a different technology, Jennifer Blaylock traces the short-lived experiment of socialist television in Ghana. Begun in 1965 under the rule of Kwame Nkrumah, Ghana Television was directed by Shirley Graham Du Bois (the second wife of W. E. B. Du Bois), who had moved to Ghana after being expelled by the United States. Blaylock draws on extensive archival material to show how Du Bois sought to weave together national, indigenous models of communication with technological, aesthetic, and political assistance from countries around the world. Blaylock traces her travels to Britain, Canada, Italy, Czechoslovakia, and Japan as she sought models to formulate a model of Ghanaian television. Discussing both the fantasy and practical idea of Ghana Television, Blaylock shows how it models an Afrofuturist approach that bears affinity to, yet also differs significantly from, the terms of media archaeology.

The account of contemporary Cuban media offered by Laura-Zoë Humphreys also tracks the logic of circulation. Like Blaylock, Humphreys moves between the international and the national, showing how Cubans' desire for global media—for being culturally up to date—in the twenty-first century led to a unique form of media distribution in the 2010s. Partly because of poor internet connection on the island, entrepreneurs formed the *paquete seminal*, or weekly packet, a flash drive of illegally downloaded media—from magazines to songs to music videos to television shows to movies—that were then distributed through gray markets. Humphreys traces the ambiguous politics of the paquete to a larger history of how Cuban artists negotiated the terms of state censorship, creating a space for resistance that was nonetheless in accord with its general socialist ideals.

Jason McGrath also takes up digital media, though with a topic more familiar to debates in cinema and media studies. Discussing the rise of digital cinema, especially computer-generated animation, in China, he argues that its use emerged through a complex negotiation with national history and the international hegemony of Hollywood. McGrath shows how debates from nineteenth-century opera, especially an aesthetic of suppositionality that eschewed mimetic realism, not only shaped early debates about cinema in China but have returned in recent years to frame how both audiences and performers engage with digital technology. Looking to this lineage in criticism as well as films, he argues that the connection to theater provides the terms of an indigenous and deeply antirealist aesthetic of digital cinema—an aesthetic that is growing increasingly prominent on screens beyond China.

Despite the reach of these essays, this special issue does not aim to provide a *global media archaeology*, or even a global archaeology, of cinematic forms. There are far too many areas, from national cinemas to transnational movements, that are simply left out. Excluded, too, are innumerable media that warrant consideration. But the force of the issue lies elsewhere, in the gerund of its title: *globalizing*. The aim is not to be completist, in terms of either content or method, but to produce a new way of going forward. It is to create new methods for taking up questions of media history and circulation, and to bring the resources of how film studies thinks about cinema across and between national contexts to bear on our thinking about media, in its various and varied technological and historical forms.

References

Adorno, Theodor W., and Walter Benjamin. 1999. *The Complete Correspondence, 1928–1940*, edited by Henri Lonitz, translated by Nicholas Walker. Cambridge, MA: Harvard University Press.

Andel, Jaroslav, and Petr Szczepanik, eds. 2008. *Cinema All the Time: An Anthology of Czech Film Theory and Criticism, 1908–1939*. Prague: National Film Archive.

Appadurai, Arjun. 2011. "How Histories Make Geographies: Circulation and Context in a Global Perspective." *Transcultural Studies* 1, no. 1: 4–13. https://heiup.uni -heidelberg.de/journals/index.php/transcultural/article/view/6129.

Arendt, Hannah. (1963) 1990. *On Revolution*. New York: Penguin Books.

Baer, Nicholas, Michael Cowan, and Anton Kaes, eds. 2016. *The Promise of Cinema: German Film Theory, 1907–1933*. Berkeley: University of California Press.

Balsom, Erika. 2018. *An Oceanic Feeling: Cinema and the Sea*. New Plymouth, NZ: Grovett-Brewster Art Gallery.

Baxandall, Michael. 1980. *The Limewood Sculptors of Renaissance Germany*. New Haven, CT: Yale University Press.

Benjamin, Walter. 1999. "Surrealism: The Last Snapshot of the European Intelligentsia." In *Selected Writings, Volume 2: 1927–1934*, edited by Michael Jennings, Howard Eiland, and Gary Smith, 207–21. Cambridge, MA: Harvard University Press.

Casetti, Francesco, Silvio Alovisio, and Luca Mazzei, eds. 2017. *Early Film Theories in Italy, 1896–1922*. Amsterdam: Amsterdam University Press.

Chun, Wendy Hui Kyong. 2008. "The Enduring Ephemeral, or the Future Is a Memory." *Critical Inquiry* 35, no. 1: 148–71.

Couret, Nilo. 2018. *Mock Classicism: Latin American Film Comedy, 1930–1960*. Berkeley: University of California Press.

Crary, Jonathan. 1990. *Techniques of the Observer*. Cambridge, MA: MIT Press.

Doane, Mary Ann. 2002. *Cinematic Time: Modernity, Contingency, the Archive*. Cambridge, MA: Harvard University Press.

Durovicova, Natasa, and Kathleen Newman, eds. 2009. *World Cinemas, Transnational Perspectives*. New York: Routledge.

Dyer-Witheford, Nick. 2015. *Cyber-Proletariat: Global Labour in the Digital Vortex*. London: Pluto.

Elsaesser, Thomas. 2004. "The New Film History as Media Archaeology." *CiNéMaS* 14, nos. 2–3: 75–117.

———. 2016a. "Media Archaeology as Symptom." *New Review of Film and Television Studies* 14, no. 2: 181–215.

———. 2016b. *Film History as Media Archaeology: Tracking Digital Cinema*. Amsterdam: Amsterdam University Press.

Ernst, Wolfgang. 2013. *Digital Memory and the Archive*, edited by Jussi Parikka. Minneapolis: University of Minnesota Press.

Fan, Victor. 2015. *Cinema Approaching Reality: Locating Chinese Film Theory*. Minneapolis: University of Minnesota Press.

Field, Allyson Nadia. 2018. "Third Cinema in the First World: L.A. Rebellion and the Aesthetics of Confrontation." In *1968 and Global Cinema*, edited by Christina Gerhardt and Sara Saljoughi, 273–88. Detroit: Wayne State University Press.

Frank, Hannah. 2019. *Frame by Frame: A Materialist Aesthetics of Animated Cartoons*. Edited by Daniel Morgan. Berkeley: University of California Press.

Galt, Rosalind, and Karl Schoonover, eds. 2010. *Global Art Cinemas: New Theories and Histories*. Oxford: Oxford University Press.

Germünden, Gerd. 2013. *Continental Strangers: German Exile Cinema, 1933–1951*. New York: Columbia University Press.

Gerow, Aaron. 2010. *Visions of Japanese Modernity: Articulations of Cinema, Nation, and Spectatorship, 1895–1925*. Berkeley: University of California Press.

Gitelman, Lisa. 2014. *Paper Knowledge: Toward a Media History of Documents*. Durham, NC: Duke University Press.

Gunning, Tom. 1986. "The Cinema of Attractions: Early Cinema, Its Spectator, and the Avant-Garde," *Wide Angle* 8, no. 3: 63–70.

———. 2006. "'The Whole World within Reach': Travel Films without Borders." In *Virtual Voyages: Cinema and Travel*, edited by Jeffrey Ruoff, 25–41. Durham, NC: Duke University Press.

Hansen, Miriam. 1999. "The Mass Production of the Senses." *Modernism/modernity* 6, no. 2: 59–77.

———. 2000. "Fallen Women, Rising Stars, New Horizons: Shanghai Silent Film as Vernacular Modernism." *Film Quarterly* 54, no. 1: 10–22.

hooks, bell. 1991. *Black Looks: Race and Representation*. Boston: South End Press.

Hui, Yuk. 2016. *The Question Concerning Technology in China: An Essay in Cosmotechnics*. Falmouth: Urbanomic Media.

———. 2017. *On the Existence of Digital Objects*. Minneapolis: University of Minnesota Press.

Jagoda, Patrick. 2016. *Network Aesthetics*. Chicago: University of Chicago Press.

Kittler, Friedrich. 1999. *Gramophone, Film, Typewriter*, translated by Geoffrey Winthrop-Young and Michael Wutz. Stanford, CA: Stanford University Press.

Kushara, Machiko. 2011. "The 'Baby Talkie,' Domestic Media, and the Japanese Modern." In *Media Archaeology: Approaches, Applications, Implications*, edited by Erkki Huhtamo and Jussi Parikka, 123–47. Berkeley: University of California Press.

Levinson, Marc. 2006. *The Box: How the Shipping Container Made the World Smaller and the World Economy Bigger*. Princeton, NJ: Princeton University Press.

Liu, Xiao. 2016. "Magic Waves, Extrasensory Powers, and Nonstop Instantaneity: Imagining the Digital beyond Digits." *Grey Room* 63: 42–69.

Lovejoy, Alice. 2019. "Celluloid Geopolitics: Film Stock and the War Economy, 1939–47." *Screen* 60, no. 2: 224–41.

MacCabe, Colin, and Lee Grieveson, eds. 2011. *Empire and Film*. London: BFI.

Majumdar, Rochona. 2016. "Art Cinema: The Indian Career of a Global Category." *Critical Inquiry* 42, no. 3: 580–610.

Manoni, Laurent. 2000. *The Great Art of Light and Shadow: Archaeology of the Cinema*, translated by Richard Crangle. Exeter: University of Exeter Press.

Manovich, Lev. 2001. *The Language of New Media*. Cambridge, MA: MIT Press.

Mattern, Shannon. 2017. *Code and Clay, Data and Dirt: Five Thousand Years of Urban Media*. Minneapolis: University of Minnesota Press.

McPherson, Tara. 2005. "Reload: Liveness, Mobility, and the Web." In *New Media, Old Media: A History and Theory Reader*, edited by Wendy Hui Kyong Chun and Thomas Keenan, 199–208. New York: Routledge.

Montfort, Nick, and Ian Bogost. 2009. *Racing the Beam: The Atari Video Computer System*. Cambridge, MA: MIT Press.

Mufti, Aamir. 2016. *Forget English! Orientalisms and World Literatures*. Cambridge, MA: Harvard University Press.

Parikka, Jussi. 2012. *What Is Media Archaeology?* Cambridge: Polity.

———. 2015. *A Geology of Media*. Minneapolis: University of Minnesota Press.

Peters, John Durham. 2015. *The Marvelous Clouds: Toward a Philosophy of Elemental Media*. Chicago: University of Chicago Press.

Raine, Michael. 2007. "Modernization without Modernity: Masumura Yasuzo's *Giants and Toys* (1958)." In *Japanese Cinema: Texts and Contexts*, edited by Alastair Phillips and Julian Stringer, 152–67. London: Routledge.

Rony, Fatimah Tobing. 1996. *The Third Eye: Race, Cinema, and Ethnographic Spectacle*. Durham, NC: Duke University Press.

Salazkina, Masha. 2010. "Soviet-Indian Coproductions: Alibaba as Political Allegory." *Cinema Journal* 49, no. 4: 69–87.

Starosielski, Nicole. 2015. *The Undersea Network*. Durham, NC: Duke University Press.

Strauven, Wanda, ed. 2006. *The Cinema of Attractions Reloaded.* Amsterdam: Amsterdam University Press.

Tsivian, Yuri. 2004. "New Notes on Russian Film Culture between 1908 and 1919." In *The Silent Cinema Reader,* edited by Lee Grieveson and Peter Krämer, 339–48. New York: Routledge.

———. 2014. "Talking to Miriam: Soviet Americanitis and the Vernacular Modernism Thesis." *New German Critique* 41, no. 2: 47–65.

Yamamoto, Naoki. 2020. *Dialectics without Synthesis: Japanese Film Theory and Realism in a Global Frame.* Berkeley: University of California Press.

Yip, Man-Fung. 2017. *Martial Arts Cinema and Hong Kong Modernity: Aesthetics, Representation, Circularity.* Hong Kong: Hong Kong University Press.

Zhang, Ling. 2015. "Rhythmic Movement, the City Symphony and Transcultural Transmediality: Liu Na'ou and *The Man Who Has a Camera* (1933)." *Journal of Chinese Cinema* 9, no. 1: 42–61.

Zielinski, Siegfried. 1996. "Media Archaeology." *CTheory.net.* https://journals.uvic .ca/index.php/ctheory/article/view/14321/5097.

———. 1999. *Audiovisions: Cinema and Television as Entr'actes in History,* translated by Gloria Custance. Amsterdam: Amsterdam University Press.

———. 2006. *Deep Time of the Media: Toward an Archaeology of Hearing and Seeing by Technical Means,* translated by Gloria Custance. Cambridge, MA: MIT Press.

Archaeology of a Medium:
The (Agri)Cultural Techniques of a Paddy Film Farm

Weihong Bao

In recent years, media archaeology has arisen as an interdisciplinary field of research. Drawing its intellectual arsenal from Michel Foucault's archaeology of knowledge, new historicism, and new materialism, and conjoining insights from a number of disciplines—German media theory and history, early cinema, new media studies, art history, literary and cultural studies, and anthropology, to name a few—media archaeology strives to "construct alternate histories of suppressed, neglected, and forgotten media" (Huhtamo and Parikka 2011: 3) and focuses its energy on dead

This essay owes a debt to a fellowship at IKKM Weimar (2012) for introducing me to the critical interventions of cultural techniques and to the UC San Diego workshop The Tangled Dynamics of Independent Filmmaking in Contemporary China (June 16–21, 2014, organized by Zhang Yingjin and Paul Pickowicz) for my first exposure to Mao Chengyu's films. I thank Yuriko Furuhata for kindly sharing my essay at the Workshop on Post-X Politics at Leuphana University on November 22, 2017, and for valuable feedback. Conversations with Reinhold Martin and Bernard Geoghegan have greatly enriched the essay. I also thank Dan Morgan for his insightful editorial input and Mao Chengyu for generously granting me extensive interviews.

boundary 2 49:1 (2022)   DOI 10.1215/01903659-9615389   © 2022 by Duke University Press

ends, failures, and imaginary constructs escaping the teleological thesis and capitalist economy of technological perfection. A notable divide, however, seems to have developed between two major orientations in media archaeology: a politically oriented, cultural studies–informed approach largely situated in the British American academy attending to the entwinements of technological histories with institutional, political, and economical forces; and a German-brewed, philosophically poised, and technologically conscious approach, with attention to specificities of media technology and modes of operations (Huhtamo and Parrika 2011: 8–9; Parrika 2012: 66–67). Regardless of the methodological and ideological divide between the so-called Anglophone versus German school of media archaeology, media archaeologists across the field tend to position their politics largely on the material and formal specificity of technical media in different historical moments and contexts as a corrective to an essentialized, naturalized, and monolithic conception of media often predicated on its dominant format or mode of operation—in the case of cinema, the theatrical, large-format film exhibition. Perhaps for this reason, media archaeology is particularly invested in the politics of time as intervention into linear constructions of history while it counts on the alternative agency of media and objects for a new materialist critique of a human-centered notion of agency.

Yet if film studies is already poised to place cinema in a longer history of the senses and an expanded horizon of media, given its historical turn and the flourishing of early cinema studies since the 1980s—much of which sought to account for cinema in the perceptual challenges of industrial and technological modernity—what methodological purchase does a fully identified media archaeology provide? If the benefit is to decentralize and deterritorialize cinema by expanding the inquiry of the synchronic and diachronic interplay between media, what insight into culture, society, and subject does it bring us? Will a media archaeologically informed approach to film studies, despite its benefit of rescuing cinema from the shadow of obsolescence cast by digital media, become caught in the same dilemma between a politically oriented cultural studies approach, largely situated in British/American studies of media, and a German-brewed approach, technologically heavy and focused on specificities and operations?

The discussions of these issues have largely taken place in North America and Europe. In addition to dutifully *doing* media archaeology, and also testing its method in a cultural context outside the dominant focus on North America and Europe, I want to explore an opportunity to bring together the perceived polar oppositions between British/American and German approaches, particularly since the two sides have enjoyed a long history of cross-pollination. I believe a more fundamental rethinking of media can be exercised to incorporate the usual concerns of technological, aesthetic, and material investigations—but also go beyond it. Below I will consider how these three strands of analysis can be combined so as to refocus questions of culture, society, and the human subject in an increasingly globalized society in the age of the Anthropocene and the posthuman. I will further explore how our view of object and environment can be cast in a different light with a specific case from China. This is not to claim a Chinese exceptionalism but to benefit from the alternative perspective afforded by shifting centers. The inquiry into distant places and times is bound up with concerns of the present and interventions with dominant modes of thinking in dominant societies. In this sense, media archaeology could benefit from cultural anthropology's reflection on the construct of center and periphery.[1]

To do this, I explore a case in contemporary documentary film practice as an instance of media art that constitutes a branch of media archaeology. Yet this is a case that combines critical writings, aesthetic experiments, and alternative modes of exhibition in a way that blurs the boundary between media archaeology as a scholarly critical inquiry and media archaeology as artistic creative reflection. My point of entry is contemporary documentary filmmaker Mao Chenyu, who is also an organic farmer, a critical thinker and writer, and a film exhibitor. Mao provides an intriguing case of how ethnography, ecology, and cosmology intertwine; how media art can take the form of media activism by redefining its boundaries and exhibition space; and how media art can be rethought by replacing its usual focus on media as object with a focus on media as space, community, and social process. Media archaeology in Mao's case suggests a particularly reflexive archaeology of the medium in relation to history, religion, nature, and locality, mobilized by his inquiry of shamanism as bodily and mental/spiritual techniques and as social practice.

To further my inquiry, I turn to the notion of *cultural techniques* (*Kulturtechniken*), proposed as the second wave of German media history and theory, a revision of or true inheritor of media archaeology (depending on who defines it), using it to examine the disciplinary space it opens up as well

---

1. This conversation with cultural anthropology is still lacking, despite recent claims of an anthropological turn in media studies. For such claims, see Siegert 2007.

as its missed opportunity to engage media and society in a global context. Investigating the "post-hermeneutic" turn advanced by the proponents of German media theory, I consider the intellectual contexts that gave rise to the method of cultural techniques and its displacement of aesthetics and politics in its gesture to reconnect media and culture (Siegert 2007: 29). This will provide me the conceptual ground to consider Mao's film practice, which brings together archaeology and ethnography in addressing medium shamanism, local history, and social changes in post-socialist China as a way to reengage representation as "cultural techniques" of aesthetics and politics.

Beyond Mao Chenyu's filming, I will show that his film exhibition lends itself to "medium communitarianism," his reinvention of the notion of the medium as a subculture—here as an alternative to the existing subculture of Chinese independent documentary. Mao's subculture, I argue, has to be understood in terms of a rather unique ecology of the medium. This ecology pushes the boundary of the medium beyond media technology to articulate a distinct vision and practice of the public by recasting the dynamic between body and technology, and between archaic and new media, to reconnect the divine and the secular, the local and the global. Key to this distinct ecology is Mao's medium shamanism. By reinvesting in the shamanistic—the archaic notion of the medium as human conduit between the living and the dead—but foregrounding the social space it generates and mediates, Mao reintegrates documentary cinema in rural life through an exhibition practice that repositions the technical medium of cinema in relation to the shamanistic sphere of influence. This ecology of the medium articulates a public sphere of exchange and transformation that enacts a new documentary subculture, one that aspires toward local sustainability. Mao's medium communitarianism thus allows us to explore a medium's plural dimensions as techniques of space, time, and environment, as well as human and nonhuman consciousness. In the end, it will point toward a different way of conceiving the implications of post-humanity, one in which the entwinement of technology and humanity recognizes the agency of animals, nature, and objects without privileging the a priori of technology and operations as the programmability of society.

From Media Archaeology to Archaeology of the Media:
The Post-hermeneutic Turn and Cultural Techniques

Perhaps the most profound epistemological shift that characterizes yet potentially bridges the "German" versus "Anglophone" debate is the response to the "post-hermeneutic" turn in the humanities. The term *post-hermeneutic* was coined by David Wellbery in 1990 in reference to Kitt-ler's working method, an approach premised on assumptions of exteriority, mediality, and corporeality whose impact on the humanities has been pal-pably felt in fields such as media archaeology.[2] The idea was that it sus-pended semantic interpretations of representation in favor of inquiries into the material constituents of the signifier and symbolic systems. Yet the term is now given a more specific historical association (Wellbery 1990; Gum-brecht 1994). Bernhard Siegert, a student of Kittler and a proponent of cul-tural techniques as the second wave in German media theory, narrates this new approach as involving a geopolitical framework (2015).[3] He considers the postwar parallel development of German and Anglophone approaches to media so as to situate cultural techniques as the "end of the intellectual postwar era" (2013) in German media theory, which coincides with the end of the Cold War and converges with the most recent developments in post-humanities in the United States.

For Siegert, both German and Anglo-American postwar approaches to media, as carried out in media studies, communication studies, and soci-ology, were haunted by the specter of social enlightenment under the rubric of the public sphere. Under the shadow of the abuse of media during the Second World War, media studies treated mass media as a threat to indi-vidual autonomy and authentic experience, hence the emphasis on "com-municative reason" built on the semantics of meaning through the self-present, rational subject. Dominated by critical theory's "technophobia," as Siegert sees it, media scholars split meaning and non-meaning into a

2. To some extent, this post-hermeneutic approach is indebted to Marshall McLuhan's notion of medium as message at the height of cybernetics in rejecting any semantic content of media in favor of a quantifiable "mathematical model" of communication. This engineering model of communication, developed at the end of World War II, is central to the emerging field of media studies, encompassing new media studies, media archaeol-ogy, and communication studies, to name a few, culminating in Alexander Galloway and Eugene Thacker's claim that "there is no content" (2007: 144). For my reflections on this legacy, see Bao 2015a: 249–97.

3. For its "American" migration, see Winthrop-Young, Iurascu, and Parikka 2013.

struggle between the positive "public sphere" and the negative horizon of "war," pitting the rational, conscious, autonomous subject in control of mass media for meaningful communication against the unconscious, involuntary subject caught in the abyss of non-meaning overtaken by the otherness of mass media.

The rise of German media theory in the 1980s, Siegert clarifies, thus needs to be understood against the "hegemony of meaning" advanced within these debates. Because of this, instead of concerning itself with the theory and history of individual media, "media" for German media theory serves as a frame of reference to launch an "anti-hermeneutic" polemic against the intellectual postwar dominated by critical theory and the hegemony of reason and meaning. Originating in literary studies rather than media studies, media is less the focus than "a frame of reference for other things"; it suggests both a change in the usual subjects of humanities and "a paradigmatic replacement of both psychoanalysis and discursive analysis (thus affirming an indebtedness to and a technologically informed distancing from Lacan and Foucault)" (Siegert 2015: 2).

Pitting "Freiburg" against "Frankfurt,"[4] Siegert accounts for the rise of German media theory into two stages: first, the anti-hermeneutic stage in the 1980s set against the interpretive paradigm of critical theory and its enlightenment hegemony of meaning; second, the post-hermeneutic stage in the 1990s, when the fall of the Berlin Wall reintroduced cultural studies approaches from the German Democratic Republic and enabled the shift in critical framework from "media" to "cultural techniques." Although Siegert does not fully explain the difference between *post-hermeneutic* and *anti-hermeneutic*, and the two terms continue to be used interchangeably by a number of scholars (along with the term *non-hermeneutic*), giving *post-hermeneutic* a temporal association serves to foreground *cultural techniques*, which marks a revision against the historical politic of "medium" and the parameters of Kittlerian technocentric analysis. The term *cultural techniques*, Siegert explains, is derived from a nineteenth-century reference to agricultural engineering that later connotes literacy skills of reading, writing, and arithmetic. It thus allows for analysis of more mundane, incon-

4. Siegert identifies Freiburg as the cradle for the development of German "media theory" against "critical theory" and associates scholars such as Kittler, Klaus Theweleit, Manfred Schneider, Wolfgang Hagen, and Norbert Bolz with the movement; the rise of cultural techniques also finds philosophical underpinnings in Martin Heidegger, who taught at Freiburg in postwar Germany.

spicuous, and basic techniques in order to usher in more durable cultural forms or systems—in the way, for example, that agriculture shapes culture by cultivation of the land "as chains of operations that link humans, things, media and even animals" (Siegert 2013: 48). Media is no longer a historical given, grounded in technical form or hardware. Instead, cultural techniques "shift the analytic gaze from ontological distinctions to the ontic operations that gave rise to the former in the first place" (48).

Central to the shift undertaken with cultural techniques is the realignment of cultural history with media history. On the one hand, this opens up concrete practices and symbolic operations such as ritual acts, religious ceremonies, and scientific data generation (Siegert 2007: 31); on the other hand, anthropology is reintroduced in media studies to make inquiries regarding humanity. For Siegert, the post-hermeneutic turn thus generates a renewed interest in the human as always already technologically mediated.[5] Notably, as Siegert observes, a similar reconception of the human occurred in Anglophone approaches to posthumanities at the turn of the millennium. There, the earlier understanding of humanity as increasingly hybridized with technology gave way to a more fundamental rethinking of humanity as mediated by the nonhuman in the first place. This shared deconstruction of anthropological difference across the Atlantic, Siegert argues, incited a renewed interest in reconceiving historical anthropology in relation to cultural techniques as "anthropotechnics" (2015: 7).

This realignment of culture and media in cultural techniques bears several implications for my project here. First, the focus of cultural techniques shifts the inquiry of media archaeology, with its emphasis on the history of media, to "an archaeology of a cultural system of meaning" (Siegert 2015: 3)—or "an archaeology of media."[6] This debunking of established media concepts and forms to inquire into "operations or operative sequences that historically and logically precede the media concepts generated by them" opens media histories to cultural histories involving broader questions of the body, technology, and society (27). In this sense, the method of cultural techniques sets itself apart from institutionalized media histories that adopt the label of "media archaeology" for their "tamed" version of alterna-

5. This notion of technological constitutions of the human very much resonates with Stiegler (see Stiegler 1998).
6. As Bernard Geoghegan explains, its methodological emphasis on the configurations of instruments, practices, and signs "that comprise the a priori of a given technical and cultural system" makes cultural techniques "not media archaeology but rather an archaeology of media" (2013: 70).

tive media histories (Siegert 2007: 28–29). Yet a simultaneous closing off of the world is implied with the conflation of culture and techniques without questioning our own positioning or, as Reinhold Martin points out, without questioning the (human) power struggle that underlies the media-technical operations (2016: 111).[7] In that sense, the softer "techniques" do not so much serve as viable alternatives to the hardware-heavy "technologies" but rather retrofit the latter. Their rules and principles of operations are now paraded as new sources of epistemic determinants.

Second, the reintroduction of anthropology in media studies might have cross-cultural promise, but its emphasis is not on productions of cultural but anthropological differences. Inquiries into "anthropotechnics" assume certain anthropological constants as a result of technical formation but do not question the universality of such conditions. What Siegert means by "plural cultures" is explicitly not multiculturalism but "a posthumanist understanding of culture that no longer posits man as the only, exclusive subject of culture" (2015: 11). Tellingly, Siegert relies heavily on social anthropologist Bronisław Malinowski, who, despite his immersive mode of ethnography, falls squarely into a functionalist approach to culture (see Siegert 2015: chaps. 1, 4). The extent to which the shift to anthropotechnics has bracketed the question of anthropology/ethnography itself as an imperialist science, to my mind, needs to be addressed by placing it in dialogue with cultural anthropology's "hermeneutic approach" to culture. Based on rigorous reflections on culture, the role of the ethnographer, and the act of writing and narration entangled in histories of colonialism and economic and cultural imperialism, there is an important theoretical and methodological lesson in the anthropological model.

Third, if those who employ cultural techniques claim to end the postwar intellectual deadlock of "public sphere" versus "war," for the posthermeneutic approach, the question of the public remains a rather silent subject or uncharted territory. If humanity is given renewed interest in terms of its technical formations, we are still pressed to account for humanity in terms of social groups and collectives, or the positioning of them as such in specific geopolitical situations, without privileging the human in changing orders of the world that entangle humans with animals, things, and technology.

I will carry out inquiries into these three areas, questions that chal-

7. Martin provides a powerfully subtle critique of cultural techniques by pitting media politics against Foucauldian biopolitics and Gilles Deleuze and Félix Guattari's political project underlying their nomadology.

lenge claims about cultural techniques reconnecting media and culture, by engaging Mao's film and social practice. Mao's work will allow me first to examine the concept of cultural techniques in their originary agricultural sense while still entangled in local and global systems of knowledge and exchange; second, it will address a missed encounter between cultural anthropology and the anthropotechnics of humans, showing how specific techniques of locality and local identity become caught in a tense negation with plural histories and geopolitics; third, by tackling Mao's tenacious and intricate account of the public, the essay will end with a tentative proposal regarding the public sphere as a political ecology.

A final question, a remainder of sorts, concerns the status of the hermeneutic after the post-hermeneutic turn in media theory and history: is it simply left behind, or is it still haunted by the turn? More broadly, what is the status of representation? If anti-hermeneutic insistence on the materiality and externality of signifiers reifies the distinction between external and internal, while cultural techniques allow us to revisit the mutual constitution between the material and the symbolic, to what extent can we rethink representation in terms of techniques? How do concerns for symbolic techniques, the strong version of cultural techniques with self-referential capacities, allow us to consider cinema not only as a technical but also an aesthetic and representational medium? In the end, I argue that the recursive and retrospective aspect of cultural techniques needs to be reinvested in the inquiry between "representation" and its material constituents.

A Minor Cosmos and Archaeology of the Future: Medium Shamanism and Local History

Among emerging documentary filmmakers in China, Mao has a distinct profile. Born in 1976 in a rural village of Hunan's Yueyang county, where his family practiced shamanism and medicine, Mao was one of the first farmers in his village to receive a college education. He studied civil engineering at one of the most prized architecture schools in China, Tongji University in Shanghai, but found his true passion in cinema, writing online film criticism and producing short films. After graduating from college, he decided to pursue a film career. Mao's rural background with an early immersion in shamanism and later training in civil engineering provide him a rather unique perspective on filmmaking. Mao has stayed close to the subject of rural and religious life in inland China, taking on a strong ethnographic interest with a spirit of reflection and experimentation.

Bumming in Beijing briefly as the usual rite of passage for aspiring artists, Mao started a short-lived artist studio, tried his hand at state television production, and shot an unsuccessful film in Shanxi. In 2003, one year after Mao returned to Shanghai and began making a meager living as a book reviewer and film critic, an opportunity came up when a real estate developer in the suburbs of Shanghai wanted to establish a Truthful Film (Zhenshi dianying) art studio to cultivate "cultural taste." Mao went to the sparsely populated Shennongjia Nature Reserve in Hubei and made the documentary Linshan (Soul Mountain), adopting the title of Nobel Prize laureate Gao Xingjian's novel based in the same area. Dwelling in the mountainous region where the ancient folklore epic about creation, Heian zhuan (Tale of Darkness), was discovered and still chanted, Mao seasoned myth with reality and documented the daily dealings of a Daoist priest and his family of three generations caught in the struggle against poverty and their encounter with religion, death, and transcendence.

Soul Mountain proved to be a breakthrough for Mao's career, winning him the highest prize at the Conceptual Art Festival (Gainian yishujie) organized by Downstream Garage (Xiahe micang), a prominent underground performance venue in Shanghai.[8] Supported by the sponsors of the studio, Mao went on to make a series of documentary and ethnographic shorts based in the multiethnic regions of Guizhou, where he experimented with the idea of "second text" (di'er wenben).[9] By second text, Mao sees filmmaking as supplementary to the filmed subject as the primary or first text—the second text becomes a reflective and constructive process that simultaneously acknowledges and bridges the gap between filmmaking and the filmed subject in a process of mutual othering. The second text thus entails an open attitude to the film text and the filmed subject based on the ethnographic method of fieldwork. Giving up the desire for control and scripting, the filmmaker tries to follow the logic of life orchestrated by the daily rhythms, distribution of labor, and social relationships among the filmed subjects. The result is an open text that exceeds the documentary subject or the design of any film text.[10]

8. Downstream Garage was forced to shut down in 2013. For more on Downstream Garage, see Leibenluft and Wang 2014.

9. All his films henceforth bear the logo "2nd text laboratory."

10. Mao's process-oriented filmmaking focusing on rural life reminds one strongly of Ogawa Shinsuke's filmmaking practice, which Mao admires. For a rigorous study on Shinsuke, see Nornes 2007.

If Mao describes second text as a reflective ethnography in a narrow sense in his Guizhou experiment, he turned it into a general ethics of "writing difference" (*xiezuo chayi*) when he returned home to the regions dominated by the Han majority. Second text, which became the logo for all his future films, asserts his politics of filmmaking informed by both ethnography and engineering, a materialist and technical process of recording, analysis, and transformation.[11] In 2008, Mao made the documentary *Shenyanxiang* (*Ximaojia Universe*) about his own village in Yueyang county, a rice farming town in the Dongting Lake area on the mid-Yangtze River.[12] *Ximaojia Universe* has been recognized as an innovative documentary, receiving special mention at the prestigious Yamagata Documentary Film Festival in 2009, further solidifying Mao's status as an independent filmmaker. The idea of a second text is put into creative practice here, this time not simply by allowing the documentary subject and its world to rewrite the filmmaker's intention and design; instead, Mao sought to recover and reconstruct a minor history through creative acts of rewriting by simultaneously tapping into and intervening in the village's daily life. He reconstructs the local universe of the Mao clan (Ximaojia) village, made up of eleven families, concentrating on their daily practices organized around farming, gambling, and living with the dead through shamanic practices, local myth, folk religion, and fragmented personal memories. Mao plays the triple role of an observer, participant, and intervener in the village's religious and secular life, marking himself as both an insider and an intruder carrying on a subtle negotiation with the village's daily life and sense of history.

Although text and writing have served as consistent metaphors for Mao's conceptions of filmmaking, *Shenyanxiang* is particularly interesting when seen as a piece of media archaeology. If Mao performs a reflective ethnography by zooming in on his own village and acknowledging his triple role in writing a local culture and history, he twists it with a strong desire for an experimental and alternative archaeology. Archaeology for Mao is not simply a way to uncover the hidden history of the village but to reconstruct

11. Mao has emphasized this double method of ethnography and engineering in his recent exegesis on second text. See http://www.paddyfilm.org/2nd.text_lab.html, accessed January 25, 2020.

12. According to Mao, *Shenyanxiang* was a rewriting of an earlier film he made in 2004, *Ximaojia yinyangjie* (*The Liminal Space of Ximaojia*). Although I was not able to see this earlier film, from descriptions and images of the film available online, it seems to have served as a draft that Mao reworked to make *Shenyanxiang* (pers. comm., August 31, 2015).

Figure 1 A ceramic figure Mao made of a beast between a tiger and a leopard, which he placed in an "archaeological site," a newly dug-out pit in the woods. Film still, *Shenyanxiang* (Ximaojia Universe, dir. Mao Chenyu, 2008).

its multiple threads and ambiguous origins through creative acts. This alternative archaeology is embedded in the very beginning of the film, which opens with a long shot and long take of an "archaeological site," a newly dug-out pit in the woods in which he plants an ambiguous object (Figure 1). This is a ceramic figure Mao himself made, as the film reveals later, of a beast between a tiger and a leopard at the center of a mythical encounter of his ancestors, according to Granny Liu's contradictory tale that accompanies the opening shot. What this opening shot does is establish archaeology as speculative reconstruction, and it functions as Mao's response to a quote from Jean-François Lyotard that he inserts at the end of the opening credits: "Let us wage a war on totality, let us be witnesses to the unpresentable. Let us activate the differences and save the honor of a name" (1984: 82). Mao supplements Lyotard's quote with one of his own, "Wherever I am, there is history," from his fictional book titled *A Nonconsecutive Road* (*Fei lianxu de daolu*). This complex array of quotations and images acknowledges a highly situated knowledge that involves mobile contexts and Mao's own role in writing that history.

This model of archaeology, between fact and fiction—reality and imagination—is realized on and across the screen through a series of aesthetic experiments involving various materials and media. The film interweaves documentary footage, writing, and color ink drawings through constructive editing; within the documentary footage, Mao himself appears as a villager and artist at work with ceramic, wood, and iron. Mao's reflective ethnography is thus punctuated by the presence of experimental and performance art. Playful ink drawings often provide caricatured doubles of the previous scene, sometimes stand in as history's absence, sometimes serve as illustrations and recaps of historical tales, and sometimes function as a close-up, a zooming in, a highlight, or a distancing totality. Mao constructed on-site art installations, for example, building and half burying a sinking boat in the rice fields and burning ceramic totem fragments using the family's kiln. In addition, Mao frequently interrupts a scene with written commentaries that reenact the intertitles of silent cinema, either explicitly acknowledging his method or providing poetic narration. A highly reflective and experimental piece of ethnography and archaeology heightened by constructive editing, the film reconstructs the Mao family genealogy and religious universe in order to reflect on the interpenetration between history and the present, the secular and the religious, myth and reality in rural daily life—all the while acknowledging the filmmaker's own role in such reconstruction.

The film thus performs an unusual media archaeology. First, as a piece of contemporary work, we can see it as an instance of media art as archaeology, both in terms of the art installations that Mao constructs as homage and reflections of history and, more uniquely, in terms of his resorting to documentary as a means of recording and exhibiting such ephemeral art. Compared to an art gallery or a museum as the usual space for media art that emphasizes art as object, Mao's documentary provides an alternative archive and exhibition space with the advantage that allows him to record his media art as a process in the making. Mao's media art thus differs from the museum-hosted media art for its "archaeological" value mainly due to its experiments with technical processes in mediating human perceptual experience and modes of temporality in a general sense. Rather, Mao's art installations alter our sense of temporality and history by producing a process-based but site-specific reflection on the intermixing of myth, religion, and minor history. This space involves the dynamic interactions of the villagers who take part in shaping his art or whose indifference makes a subtle commentary on his interventions. But the film goes beyond faithful recording and display; like the archive and the museum, it plays an active role in shaping its collection and artwork, as Mao readily acknowledges through his constructive editing discussed above.

Second, and more strikingly, Mao's media archaeology can be seen as an "archaeology of media"—not in the usual sense of uncovering dead ends or seeking alternative routes of historical technical media but by contemplating the notion of the medium as operative chains that make us rethink the matter of nature, body, and technology in relation to a cosmic and secular sense of history and society. In this sense, Mao's approach is closer to that of cultural techniques in reconnecting media and culture and their anthropological implications. This alternative sense of the medium helps us move away from the primary concern for technical media as a product of modernity, instead tapping into both the deeper history of media and a minor social history.

This is where Mao's film gains its real force. That history first of all concerns shamanism in the upper and mid-Yangtze River region. As a practice of religion, medicine, art, and music, shamanism stands as the long-repressed origin of Chinese poetry. It enjoyed a particularly strong hold in the region where Yueyang, Mao's hometown, is located. Yueyang also borders the sacred burial site of Qu Yuan (340–278 BC), the famed poet and politician during the Warring States period who was exiled to the region and committed suicide in the Miluo River. Qu's celebrated poems were considered texts for shamanistic chanting (Sukhu 2012) and religious performance. In the twentieth century, shamanism was suppressed in the anti-religion and anti-superstition modernizing discourse during the Republican (1912–1949) and People's Republican (1949–) periods[13] as a discredited mode of knowledge, belief, and communication, although it never died away in local practice.

Mao's film adopts the structure of the *Nine Songs* by Qu Yuan, yet instead of reclaiming the iconic myth, Mao seeks to reconstruct a minor his-

---

13. In the early twentieth century, the impact of shamanism on poetry and literature was recognized by scholars under the influence of cultural anthropology, including the celebrated poet Wen Yiduo, who studied at the Art Institute of Chicago in the 1920s. This anthropological account, though contributing to the modernizing discourse in displacing shaman practice to a practice of the past and relegating it to a minor religion still practiced by ethnic minorities and in the hinterland, was suppressed during the Second Sino-Japanese War (1937–1945) under the discourse of patriotism. Wen himself changed his perception of Qu Yuan from a shaman practitioner to the "poet of the people."

tory much closer to home. The Earth Temple in the Mao clan village hosts the Earth Bodhisattva, one of the most common folk gods blessing the local area, yet it also enshrines two local gods that dwarf the Earth Bodhisattva in actual size: General Yang Si and Senior General Mao—Mao's grandfather, who was posthumously elevated to a god in recognition of his virtue as a shaman and who serves as Yang's medium. Later, Mao identifies a more specific source of the folk religion—the Water God General Yang Si is a tribute to the peasant uprising leader Yang Yao (1108–1135) during the Southern Song dynasty, who held his six-year resistance in the Dongting Lake region (1130–1135) and committed suicide upon defeat (Mote 2003: 301–2). The local people deified him under the guise of Yang Si, instead of Yang Yao, his recognized name.[14] In contrast to Qu Yuan, who allegedly threw himself in the Miluo River and became immortal after his death, Yang Yao was not killed after throwing himself in the water and thus gained the status of a water god and continued to lead the uprising (he later killed himself by a sword). Yang Yao and his fellow rebels built an enormous following by their experiments with land reform and their demands to improve the peasants' treatment. They also advanced farming techniques and managed to win major battles with their astonishing shipbuilding techniques and tactics for water battle, hence occupying a special place in the histories of military combat and science and technology in China.[15] Yet the rebellion, considered a major threat to the Southern Song government, was demonized for its practices of shamanism and other secret religions.[16]

By evoking such a minor history, Mao can be read as binding popular religion to a history of power and powerful resistance by means of integrated techniques of nature—water and earth—and people. Shamanism is the means through which such material becomes part of a cultural technique. Historically, the peasant uprising maintained its power through a local form of governance by conjoining agricultural techniques of farming, naval technology, and cult religion to tap into water, earth, and people as sources of energetic operations. In contemporary times, shamanism serves

14. Yang Yao's real name is Yang Tai. He assumes the name Yang Yao as *yao* signifies "the youngest," referring to him as the youngest among the leaders of the uprising.
15. Joseph Needham has discussed their shipbuilding techniques and speculated that the large fleet boat for Yang Yao was the first execution of a paddle wheel boat with twenty-two wheels. See Needham 1995: 310–20; see also Needham 1965: 418–22.
16. Scholars have debated the specific religion practiced by Yang Yao and his predecessor Zhong Xiang but identified local shamanism and Manichaeism originated from Iran as the most possible practices. See Ma 1956; Lu 1996; Lu 1999.

as a remainder and a reminder of that history through its mediation of local everyday life. Mao treats shaman practice as the medium between the realms of the dead (*ying*) and the living (*yang*), between god and human. Melding a liminal space (*yingyangjie*) between human, god, and ghosts, Mao imagines this space as "narrow, flat, thin as a leaf but infinitely extendable and spreadable, looking like fog at night."[17] The shamanistic medium retains one of the oldest uses of the term *medium* across a number of cultures. A medium, in this sense a select human as the communicative conduit bridging the spiritual and human worlds, has garnered considerable attention in media archaeology, especially regarding the historical cross-fertilization between spiritualist/cult mediums and modern media technologies (Sconce 2000; Andriopoulos 2008). The emphasis for Mao, however, is not the human mediums or their technological extensions alone but the social space they help generate.

Mao draws our attention to this social space by situating shamanism in a world of plural gods addressing mundane and secular concerns. Indeed, both Mao's grandfather and father are well respected shamans, or "horse feet" (*majiao*) (as they are locally called), running between the two realms. Gods, humans, and ghosts are paid equal tribute from the beginning of the film. Starting with the mythical tale of the ancestors injured by a tiger/leopard, the film will introduce three gods and a funerary procession. Inside the Earth Temple (*tudimiao*), the three "gods" share an altar: the Earth Bodhisattva, General Yang Si, and Old General Mao. A funeral procession involving Daoist priests chanting is followed by older women expressing concerns on the care for the elderly, and the gods are "bribed" to mitigate the forces of capitalism when villagers pray for a drop in the price of fertilizers and speculate on gilding the Earth Bodhisattva statue to bring better fortune. A gambling table gathers men and women, young and old, to woo fortune in a game of chance, and shamans are said to have participated in the guessing game, evoking the godly force for the wrong cause and often failing in such attempts.[18] Gambling later takes the form of a lottery, with the family watching a TV broadcast for the results—the television set becoming the new gambling table, which reconfigures the social space.

With shamanism fully integrated into everyday life, conjoining farm-

17. See http://www.paddyfilm.org/film/yinyangjie.html, accessed December 28, 2015.
18. See Chinese film critic and curator Wang Xiaolu's insightful blog (2010). Wang writes that Mao's own father had used spirit writing to seek winning lottery numbers.

ing, ritual ceremonies, and gambling in answering updated wishes and worries, Mao turns his attention to the actual operation of shamanism as a highly technical and multimediated affair. The technical ensemble of spirit writing, or *fuji*, consists of several simple objects and two or more people: a sand table; sand, which serves as the medium for writing; and two people who hold the stylus, sometimes with an additional person adding and flattening the sand and another person who interprets and copies down the message.[19] (Instead of sand, Mao explains, people in the Dongting Lake area have used ground rice husks on the sand table. By way of the rice husks, writing reconnects with eating and the tilling of the fields.) The spirit writers spell the message word by word, thus slowing down the process of writing, reading, and interpreting the message. For the people present and the film audience, the mode of spirit writing initiates a different temporality, the liminal time where *ying* and *yang* meet, executed by the technical ensemble involving multiple agents and the techniques of spirit writing.

Remarkably, the sand table of spirit writing is framed similarly to the gambling table as a site of social communion and communication. With the camera looking slightly downward, the spirit writing agents are kept off-screen. Instead, we are shown only the automatic writing on the sand table by the V-shaped stick made of mahogany branches functioning as a stylus held by two people, one possessed by the spirit known as the *majiao* and the other as the assistant (Figure 2).[20] With the camera looking down from above, we get a total view of the *fuji* spirit writing set: a sand table, a bowl of rice husk and a bowl of water, a stack of yellow paper, and three people resting around the table. A motorcycle resting by the wall reminds one of the contemporary setting of the spirit writing. All three people look relaxed, with the one preparing the yellow paper holding a cigarette in his mouth.

As the villagers arrive, spirit writing quickly turns into live theater. The camera cuts to a frontal long shot from behind the sand table set, creating a proscenium stage with the villagers making an entrance from the doors. Women and children are included; later, an elderly woman also appears at the *fuji* table with the sand assistant. A man emerges from the far end

19. According to Mao, the fuji ritual in the region involves at least two people, who carry out both the writing and the interpretation of the spirit message. Additional people are used depending on needs and occasions, and a copyist is needed if the spirit writing involves a medicinal prescription. WeChat interview with Mao Chengyu, January 7, 2016.
20. Interviews with Mao Chengyu, December 18, 2014, Shanghai; April 14, 2016, Shanghai.

Figure 2 The *fuji* spirit writing set with the two agents holding the mahogany branch as the stylus. Film still, *Shenyanxiang* (Ximaojia Universe, dir. Mao Chenyu, 2008).

dressed in a black T-shirt; he is identified as Mao Jianjun, a *majiao*. As the *majiao* and his assistant form a writing pair, wielding the planchette stylus with force, the film blacks out with an intertitle asking about the Mao family's vision of history. One family member, Mao Dezong, comments, "History is the bridge between matter and soul. These two contradict but also inter-act with and transform each other. The middle ground is the liminal space between *yin* and *yang*." As the camera gazes down at the sand table at length, the sand table occupies the full screen and turns into a white canvas that bears the ephemeral writing as erasure amidst the dust of rice husks, turning it into an abstract landscape but also a rice field for tilling. Writing itself becomes drawing and pounding on the surface, gaining a particularly haptic rapport with the audience. With the villagers gathering around the sand table just as they do at the gambling table, shamanistic ritual provides the middle ground between matter and soul as a vehicle of living history.

It would be useful to revisit this middle ground from discussions of cultural techniques, by way of the curious figure of the parasite. The para-site, for Siegert, is a key trope to conceive of cultural techniques in terms of the figure of the "third," or media, as the interface between the real and the cultural order to "process the observation, displacement, and differentiation of distinctions" (2007: 31). Drawing from Jacques Derrida's earlier writing and Michel Serres's negotiation with communication-information theory and anthropological linguistics, Siegert considers the parasite, which in French also connotes disruption and noise, not as a by-product but as the a priori, the ground that produces the distinction itself and any relation in terms of an exchange (33). In other words, the parasite is what precedes and enables the binary distinction that produces culture and enables communication as a dialogue. "The third precedes the second. That is the beginning of media theory—of any media theory" (33).

Mao's archaeology of media intimates the logic of the parasite to excavate minor histories, as he explores phenomena such as names to open new conceptual space. The difference, as in Lyotard's quote that starts the film, indeed lies in the name and the shamanistic-cinema medium's witnessing the unpresentable. The peasant upriser Yang Yao is called Yang Si, since *yao* means the youngest and *si* refers to the fourth sibling, both of which apply to Yang. As we hear Mao speak off-screen to "interview" Yang Si through the shamanistic-cinema medium, the *fuji* writing spells out the word *si* 泗 with the water radical to mark Yang Si as the water god. Yet when Mao inquires to clarify which *si* character (with or without the water radical) it was, the water god responds with an equivocal "both." The intertitle explains the folk wisdom: by deliberately confusing Yang Si the peasant uprising leader and the legendary patriotic hero Yang Silang (the fourth of General Yang's children) from the aristocratic martial family, popular belief is able to seek refuge in nationalist ideology and the hegemonic discourse of power. Yang Si thus takes parasitic residence in history in the confusion of a name.

If the water radical in the Chinese character *si* is the means by which Yang Si the peasant hero seeks parasitic refuge via cacography, bad writing through which folk memory is embedded in history's master narrative, to conceive of it as a cultural technique is not to see it as an added symbol a posteriori but to see how Yang Si the antihero enables Yang Silang the fictional hero to be projected back to an earlier moment of history in the first place.[21] By maintaining that ambiguity while hosting an unstable,

---

21. The stories of the aristocratic and martial Yang family in fiction and drama, though attributed to the actual Yang family of Northern Song (tenth century), were not created until the seventeenth century. In this sense, Yang Yao's story indeed proceeded that of Yang Silang.

secret difference (through the gap between writing and speaking, as *si* with and without the water radical are homophones), such a parasitic third both activates and disrupts internal differentiation through shifting strategies of inclusion and exclusion. In a similar way, shamanism serves as an analogous and enabling medium of the parasite, as the middle ground that does not so much operate between *yin* and *yang*, the dead and the living, but produces such distinctions to start with. Shamanism is the ritual technique that activates not only a sign but a whole social field. Through writings on rice husks as erasures and repetition in difference, this minor history is enlivened not simply in the name but also in the mode of sociality as a shamanistic complex.

The presence of cinema, however, makes the question of the third, the intermediating medium, sticky. Introducing the water god General Yang Si over a black screen, an intertitle asks: "Are you Yang Silang or Yang Yao?" The camera thus turns itself into an interlocutor's assistant so that the black screen becomes either the talking head of the god or the extension of the sand table. Yet what is the mediating third here? The body of the *majiao*, his assistants, the filmmaker, or the camera? Is it realized by writing on the sand or the screen, live or mediated sound, image, or performance? Instead of the singular body of the technical medium, the medium here is an ensemble of high and low, old and new technology, conjoining the human, spirit, and technological media in which the documentary film participates but also mediates and reflects on. By watching the film, we become part of the social gathering in communicating with the dead and recovering a minor history that, with its plural agents and multimediated process, becomes a gamble of history itself.[22]

In this sense, it is no longer possible to draw a boundary between film and a host of mediating agents, nor to draw a clear distinction between filmic representation and the archaeology of the media seen through shamanistic practice. In other words, shamanism should not merely be understood as the "content" of filmic representation; instead, cinema has become

22. By "gamble of history," I evoke Siegfried Kracauer's "all-out gamble of history," which sees cinema and photography, as Miriam Hansen points out, as critical agents of history in enabling the chance to reshuffle the fragmented time and lost collective memory through capitalist modernity and make them accessible again. See Hansen 1991: 109. The emphasis here, though, is less on the "go for broke" ethics enabled by a singular media technology as the privileged product and antidote of modernity. Rather, the reshuffling of time and memory is constituted by the multimediation between ancient (including human) and new technology, which is part of the gamble.

a part of this process as an important element—but only an element—of mediation and reflection. Yet if filming and shamanistic writing are both symbolic techniques capable of self-reference, shamanism does not so much reflect on its role of the mediating third as imbricate cinema as its extension. By contrast, Mao's documentary camera tries to perform an archaeology of media by making bare the shaman practice that makes its mediation invisible and possible. Indeed, the reflexive function of cinema would qualify it as a cultural technique in its stronger version, or second-order technique. Cultural techniques, Thomas Macho (2013: 30) argues, "should be strictly limited to symbolic techniques" whose ability to thematize themselves distinguish them from first-order techniques such as cooking or field tilling.

This distinction between first- and second-order techniques, however, is problematized by Mao self-consciously aligning his film and art installation with the context of agriculture. Heeding the belief that the insurrection army built a "thriving boat" (*feihuang tengda zhou*) for Yang Si (in their dream of assuming power), which sunk to the bottom of Dongting Lake after the army's defeat, Mao built a sinking boat in the rice paddy field to evoke its spirit (Figure 3). In a series of long shots of the boat in the paddy field, alternating with a few closer shots of different profiles of the boat—edited using the "antiquated" technique of a wipe—Mao documents the lapses of time. This happens both within the individual shot—the waving movements of the rice crop, distant smoke from household cooking, the sound of a rooster, a bird flying across the sky, fog lifting—and between the shots, when the ellipsis of time is captured by changing seasons and light of the day or the crops turning from green to gold (Figure 4). When the rice crop is harvested, the boat exposes itself, with ducks swimming across, creating an impression of a boat on the river. This is intercut with Mao painting a ceramic object red (a leopard) and mounting it on the boat. The symbolic monument of the sinking boat ages with the crops in the field, its status as a monument subverted by two ducks quietly swimming across the field.

In this scene, Mao aligns cinema with the forces of nature and agriculture as technics of (natural) time—its editing technique mirrors the changing seasons and time of the day corresponding with farming activities—while acting upon them as a reflexive technique. Such positioning of cinema as both first- and second-order cultural techniques parallels Mao's art installation of the boat as both material and symbolic techniques whose status as a mutable monument is realized only by situating itself in the rice field and receiving the forces of agricultural engineering.

Figure 3 A "sinking boat" Mao installed in the rice field to evoke the spirit of the "thriving boat" built by the peasant insurrection army led by Yang Yao. Film still, *Shenyanxiang* (Ximaojia Universe, dir. Mao Chenyu, 2008).

Figure 4 Time lapse captured by the crops turning from green to gold. Film still, *Shenyanxiang* (Ximaojia Universe, dir. Mao Chenyu, 2008).

The last section of the film takes Mao and his father to revive an old kiln so as to make ceramic objects as tribute to the Mao clan with memory and imagination. Mao and his father burn a picture as sacrifice to the newly built kiln, which he shows to be a human body lying naked with breasts and toes, and lips colored with dye. Mao's father comments, "Pigs and cows used to be the sacrifice; now it's the image, which has gained the status of flesh and life." The film documents the whole process of building the kiln and firing the pottery figurines, as Mao and his father move the objects in, pile up the bricks, and leave space to add tree branches to adjust the temperature of the fire. The film then cuts to the inside of the kiln, with the red light of the fire saturating the full screen, superimposed with Mao's intertitle: "The camera gives me the privilege to write history. We reanimate the ordinary faces buried in the grass: heads, hands, inner organs, and breasts. High temperatures fire various gods; thus Ximaojia's fragmented memories become remnants of history." By aligning cinema as the kiln, the camera turns into the furnace that fires history. The final comment sums up Mao's vision of his documentary as a reenactment, an archive, and an archaeology: "The members of the Ximao clan will all die, and cinema will become an animated history for the future. My action becomes an archaeology of the future. Film naturally stores the rubbings of the living rhythm of Ximaojia village."

The Culture of Techniques, or Reorienting the Anthropological Turn in Media Archaeology

The year 2012 marked a significant departure in Mao's career, as independent documentary in China entered a new phase. Dissatisfied by the notion of "independent" film and the power dynamic orbiting around film critics' discourse and international film festivals, Mao and his fellow filmmakers started a film criticism journal of their own, *Dianying zuozhe* (*Film Auteur*), inspired by and modeled after the French journal *Cahiers du cinéma*. This new vehicle sought not simply to resurrect the notion of the film auteur since the French New Wave but to carve out a discursive and interactive space for a different practice of cinema that recasts the dynamic among film criticism, film production, and film exhibition in an effort to contribute to local social and political life.

This connection is seen concretely in the Paddy Film Farm (Dao dianying nongchang) Mao also started in 2012, designed to create a subculture (*yawenhua*) integrating a new forum for film production and discussion with an alternative mode of farming. Resisting industrialized production for both film and farming, Mao calls for a return to outmoded means of farming, by reviving the agricultural techniques before the use of pesticides, chemical fertilizers, and genetically modified products. Mao's desire ironically matches an emerging market niche in organic farming. His efforts to sell the organic product through the Chinese e-commerce platform Taobao, despite its meager success, remind us of the intricate imbrication between the global and the local in post-socialist China and offer evidence of the interpenetration between old and new cultural techniques.

By framing cinema in the operative chain of (agri)cultural techniques of farming, Mao does not simply parallel but interweaves organic farming with film production, the circulation and consumption of his farming products—rice and wine—with film exhibition through virtual and local platforms. By such an absorption of cinema into the agricultural and consumptive organization of life—and he is not ignorant of or immune to the gift and exchange economy—Mao enacts an ambitious agenda: "Paddy Film Farm does not simply explore a healthy organic farming culture but seeks a means of social construction through culture. The goal to farm rice is to farm society. To some extent, this can also be seen as an experimental exchange between [Joseph] Beuys' idea of 'social sculpting' and medium communitarianism."[23]

Art curator Dong Bingfeng, in a recent exhibition at THEROOM featuring Paddy Film Farm, calls the farm a "concrete medium to explore rural society in China" and an example of "artistic activism."[24] From a comparative perspective, though, what Mao means by *culture*—as a vehicle of social construction by conjoining agricultural farming techniques with techniques of filming, editing, and exhibition—strikes a stronger resonance with the analytical method of cultural techniques. In two extended interviews I conducted, and in his online discussions, Mao reflects on his training in civil engineering and identifies paddy films with engineering in terms of method and attention to material.[25] Conscious of the ethnographer's external position as the other, and the intimate relationship between engineering and material, Mao values how the product enters a field of ethics and cultural interactions and considers himself and his coworkers "engineers who involve themselves in producing rubbings of cultural systems with engineering methods—the current instances of reality might be cultural relics of local history and geography."[26]

Mao's "cultural techniques," however, stem from intellectual and political contexts rather different from German media scholars' post-human and post-hermeneutic agenda. Rather than rethinking/reengaging anthropology at the level of anthropotechnics and theorizing binary opposition itself as a cultural technique in general terms, Mao draws directly from more recent and reflexive findings in cultural anthropology that he mixes with an eclectic range of intellectual sources dominated by post-structuralist and postmodern theory, philosophy, historiography (Lyotard, Derrida, Foucault, Giorgio Agamben, Jacques Rancière) and, more recently, philosophies of technology (Stiegler and Catherine Malabou).[27] Drawing on cultural anthropology's

23. See http://mini.eastday.com/a/160730064831966-3.html, accessed August 5, 2016. An exhibition of Beuys's works took place at the Central Academy of Art in 2013 featuring works purchased by a Chinese independent gallery, the Hao Gallery.
24. See http://mini.eastday.com/a/160730064831966-3.html. Mao's films were exhibited and discussed in THEROOM, Beijing, from July 30 to September 25, 2016.
25. Interviews with Mao Chenyu, December 18, 2014, Shanghai; April 14, 2016, Shanghai.
26. See http://www.paddyfilm.org/2nd.text/lab.html, accessed August 12, 2015.
27. Stiegler's recent tour of Chinese universities, including Tongji University, Mao's alma mater, has boosted interest in Stiegler's work in China. Stiegler's *Technics of Time* has been translated into Chinese from French.

own reflection on culture in relation to histories of imperialism, comparative cosmologies and epistemologies, and capitalist economy, Mao resituates questions of cultural distinctions, local culture, and epistemologies in the changing geopolitical landscape and world order.

Mao is particularly drawn to the works of Sidney Mintz and Marshall Sahlins, both of whom relativize cultural distinctions by reconceptualizing the dynamic between the center and the periphery. Whereas Mintz (1985) reevaluates the notion of the world system by recounting how local negotiations on the periphery constitute the very center of the world system, as in the case of the production and consumption of sugar, Sahlins (1996) conducts a "reverse anthropology," focusing on the West as his object of anthropological inquiry refreshed by the wisdom of comparative cosmologies. He thus similarly rethinks the center from the margins in his archaeology of "native anthropology of the west" (Sahlins 1996: 395).

Drawing on Mintz's and Sahlins's insights, Mao aspires toward an indigenous anthropology that remains critically reflexive and walks a tightrope to maintain a delicate balance in complex, entwined, and competing systems of power and knowledge. Skeptical of postcolonial charges of Eurocentrism that end up reproducing Western systems of knowledge in the name of the indigenous, Mao is particularly critical of a nationalist China-centered approach endorsed by the state's consolidation of domestic and international power.[28] In response to the call for a "China model" in constructing a self-differential, national knowledge system encompassing culture, economy, and politics, Mao makes the sober remark: "How a 'human' self is established under the China model is itself a process of epistemological transformation. This is nothing but a historical process, not a beaming ray of thought. From the perspective of politics, this is a process of identity transformation and the continuous consolidation of the regime of power."[29]

By questioning the binary construct of center-periphery, and following Mintz and Sahlins, Mao is interested in exploring the realm of difference mapped by "games of identity reversal."[30] Such difference lies in the terrain eclipsed by essentialist accounts of a particular system of knowledge that reconfirms the system by a constitutive other. For this reason, Mao is inter-

28. Mao refers to the "China model" as discussed in a forum held at Beijing University in 2008 by prominent Chinese intellectuals, the result of which was published in a book. See Pan and Ma 2010.
29. See http://www.paddyfilm.org/study/MCD.html, accessed July 10, 2015.
30. See http://www.paddyfilm.org/study/MCD.html, accessed July 10, 2015.

ested in subcultures situated in the fissures of binary cultural distinctions as sites for articulating possible differences (based on a revisionist history) and oriented toward an alternative future. Independent documentary in China, for Mao, is precisely an instance of such a subculture.

In this sense, Mao's reflexive indigenous anthropology serves as an alternative to a nationalist epistemology camouflaged as "local knowledge"; equally important, it complements the German school of cultural techniques that often stops short of cross-cultural analysis to account for the other side of the story. Bernard Geoghegan, who remains sensitive to this limit, astutely points out an oversight shared by cultural techniques and Kittlerian media archaeology in their tendency to "identify cultural differentiation with the respectable officials of *Wissenschaft*, the state and engineering" (2014: 424).[31] On such a map, "barbarians are produced yet never producing. A history of the nomad and barbarian as producers of territories and maps transversal to the state would constitute an important extension of contemporary research in cultural techniques" (424).[32] If we shift this critique from within a culture to a cross-cultural situation, Mao's Paddy Film project opens up this self-enclosed space and provides a provocative example to consider how the method of cultural techniques—an inquiry into the operative chain that constitutes a medium—could be repurposed and expanded to reconnect film and (agri)cultural techniques in mediating the dynamics of environment, land, state, and global capitalism. It is in this sense that a general inquiry of "anthropotechnics" could yield to more specific inquiries of how the "human" is constituted by geopolitically situated techniques and technologies (including bioengineering). Correspondingly, the anthropological turn in media archaeology toward cultural techniques can be seen as an opportunity to reinvent ethnography to encompass an archaeology, ecology, and cosmology of a culture. The stakes are as large as the status of nature and culture, technology and spirituality.

31. I thank Geoghegan for generously sharing this essay.
32. My subsections titled "The Culture of Techniques" and "The Techniques of (Agri)-Culture" borrow from Geoghegan's section titles to solicit further dialogue on how these terms are negotiated in Mao's case.

The Techniques of (Agri)Culture:
Consumption, Exhibition, and an Alternative Subculture

Mao's delineation of documentary in China as a subculture should be understood in three distinct but interconnected developments. First, independent documentary has been one of the fastest growing film cultures since the early 1990s. From underground circulation in semipublic spaces in colleges, cafes, and households to film festivals based in Beijing, Nanjing, Yunnan, and Chongqing, independent documentary has attracted both domestic audiences and international attention, leading to increased presence at major film festivals in Venice, Berlin, Rotterdam, and Tokyo; documentary festivals such as the Reel China Film Festival in New York and the Yamagata International Documentary Festival; and curated film series in various film venues in Toronto, London, New York, and Paris. The impressive quality, volume, and diversity of independent documentary from China has garnered substantial attention in film exhibitions as well as film scholarship, making these films increasingly integrated into the college curriculum in and outside China.[33] These films and their domestic and international circulation have created a critical subculture of documentary that weaves together enthusiasm and censorship but also global commodification.

Second, an expanded exhibition and museum culture spurred by the growth of creative industries, real estate and urban development, and state capitalism has reframed still and moving images in the neoliberal cultural landscape of display.[34] Reviving the tradition of world expos, cities such as Shanghai, Hangzhou, and Chongqing have taken the stage as hosts of variously themed expositions attracting immense tourist traffic and large numbers of artworks; urban renewal and development-oriented preservation projects have ushered in museum, gallery, and historic living quarters as spectacles of transnational architecture and manicured zones of nostalgia.[35] Documentaries have developed in tandem with but increasingly intersect with such an exhibition culture. As documentary films seek refuge and support in contemporary art centers, they also risk being neutralized

---

33. For major volumes on contemporary independent documentary, see Zhang and Pickowicz, 2006; Berry, Xinyu, and Rofel 2010; and Zhang and Zito 2015.

34. On the growth of China's creative industries, see Pang 2012; Wong 2014; Chumley 2016.

35. One such example is the town of Wuzhen in Zhejiang province, which has recently been entirely "restored" and expanded to serve as a major stage for international avantgarde theater, contemporary art, and tourism. For the case of Shanghai, see Ren 2014.

in the state's systematic conversion of artist villages on urban fringes to art districts that embody the marriage between neoliberal appropriation of creativity and governmental control.[36]

Third, the countryside has undergone drastic changes, not only physically but in its conceptual space. Urban development has resulted in a progressive recession of land and depletion of labor, aggravating the struggle with poverty, lack of education, and health care, among other issues. In this, the rural has been framed in the triadic issues of *sannong* (three aspects of rural)—agriculture (*nongye*), the countryside (*nongcun*), and farmers (*nongmin*)—by Chinese politicians and intellectuals. Meanwhile, overindustrialization and its by-products—pollution; food safety issues; environmental, economic, and health consequences of bioengineered farming—have provoked growing ecological consciousness alongside a nostalgic turn to the countryside, spurring pursuit of alternative lifestyles in dwellings, organic farming, and tourism, as well as utopian rural art projects (such as Ou Ning's Bishan Project) that evoke both a presocialist and a socialist past and have led to debates about further commodification of the countryside.[37] For independent documentaries, how to engage the changing status and problems of the countryside poses a particularly poignant challenge. Although filmmakers such as Wu Wenguang have invested in collective filmmaking by giving cameras to farmers and students visiting their home villages, the postproduction editing and screening of these films outside the filming site raise questions about their effect on rural life in the places they focus on.

Mao has engaged the subculture of independent documentary in all three of these contexts through domestic and international circulation of his films, through initially resisting but increasingly entering the art space and museum culture and, to a larger extent, through returning to the countryside. While he is searching for his own roots, he is also sharing his social nostalgia and utopian project to inspire social change. More specifically, he wants to create a "sub-" or alternative culture based in Hunan and other rural areas through a simultaneous location and dislocation—by creating the city in the country and the country in the city. His investment in such a

36. On the imbrication of art, urban renewal, and state control, see Ren and Sun 2012.
37. For a report on the Bishan Project, see Wainwright 2014. The project was shut down in 2016. Such utopian rural projects can be traced back to presocialist experiments, most prominently embodied by Y. C. James Yen from the 1920s onward. See Yen 1929; Hayford 1990.

subculture shuttling between the local and the global, the country and the city, despite its connotation of cultural brokering, or as a parasite, in Siegert's sense, is better understood as an interest in reinventing the public by means of a locally based ecology of nature, society, and media within a mass medium—a public sphere.

A hint of this was seen at a unique film festival Mao participated in. In spring 2013, a small-scale local film festival was put together in Peitian, Fujian, on the southeast China coast facing Taiwan across the narrow Taiwan Strait. The festival was unique in terms of its intimate size and focus on rural issues. The festival showcased only six films and had an audience largely comprised of environmentally conscious filmmakers and artists from both sides of the strait—the intention was to carry on a dialogue with local residents and, to a lesser degree, with local tourism bureaucrats and representatives from a think tank on agriculture research.[38] Convened at the Spring Ploughing Fair, recently revived to attract tourism to the ancient village of Peitian (known for its eight-hundred-year history and well-preserved vernacular architecture), the Peitian film festival provided an alternative venue to the more prominent Yunfest (Yunnan Multiculture Visual Festival), which had just been shut down by the government, thus serving as a modest forum for independent documentary in the context of a shifting dynamic of art and politics.

If the subculture of independent documentary in China has increasingly oriented the local for global consumptions, Mao and his fellow filmmakers are more invested in a subculture of the local that explores a different economic and aesthetic order. Reframing agriculture as culture—the Chinese translation of "agricultural heritage" is literally "agricultural cultural heritage" (nongye wenhua yichan)—the festival participants tapped into the recently institutionalized recognition of agriculture as an integrated cultural system involving nature, culture, and society.[39] The Peitian discussion thus

---

38. The festival was partly funded by the local tourist bureau and the Institute of Advanced Studies on Sustainable Development based at People's University in Beijing. Mao was invited to show his film.

39. This is informed by the United Nations Food and Agriculture Organization's Globally Important Agricultural Heritage System initiative since 2002, which identifies agricultural heritage as agroecology, a complex coevolution and adaptation between the countryside and its environment that forms the land use system and agricultural landscape endowed with biodiversity to sustain local social, economic, and cultural development. See http://www.fao.org/giahs/en/, accessed August 10, 2016. For Globally Important Agricultural Heritage System in China, see Sun et al. 2011; Fuller et al. 2015.

challenges a preservationist imperative toward the natural environment and cultural relics at the expense of local everyday life; instead, it explores a locally based subculture built on a more sustainable and evolving ecology of nature, rural economy, and social change. Drawing on the success of Taiwanese environmental activists and filmmakers and Japanese agroecological models of *satoyama* and *satoumi*, the festival participants reconsidered the village of Peitian in terms of an integrated agricultural system incorporating farming, forestry, historic vernacular architecture, cultural aesthetics, and politics to create a more generative dynamic between ecology, society, and culture.[40] Within such a frame, filmmakers reflected on documentary's role to record and disseminate knowledge of rural life—like a Xerox or fax machine, as Taiwanese filmmaker Ke Jinyuan suggested—as well as the filmmakers' own aesthetic innovations (Deng, Deng, and Yu 2013: 27). Mao (2013: 64) points out the inescapable question of politics: "But the question of environment is first of all a question of politics—if we discuss *fengsu dianying* [local customs/heritage films, a subgenre of ethnography Mao identifies emerging in contemporary Chinese documentary] without a social study of the politics of the local customs/heritage, we are forsaking the fundamental questions in our pursuit" (2013: 64).

It was in this context that Mao screened his new documentary *Yongyou, Xin Zhongguo nongmin zhanzheng — xiucixuede zhengyi* (*I Have What? Chinese Peasants War: The Rhetoric of Justice*) (2012), a scathing critique of rural development in the socialist and postsocialist eras. A highly charged experimental documentary that juxtaposes newsreel and feature film footage with varied modes of writing—diagrams, written commentaries, mathematical formulae—alternating with visual imageries of still and animated drawings, paper cutouts, and photographs, the film places the rural history of the People's Republic under trial. Although it slows down after the first fifteen minutes of dense commentary to usher in the filmmaker's own investigation through lengthy, largely observational interviews of farmers from Hunan, the film persists in its formal recalcitrance and inscriptive impulse. *Yongyou* periodically breaks into visual and acoustic collage through psychedelic rhythmic editing of pop art, ink drawings, writings, and diagrams underscored by a musical medley of rock, flamenco, and Chinese folk tunes.

Yongyou is a fascinating experimental documentary oscillating between a visual thesis, a call to arms (*xiwen*), a sermon, (counter)propaganda, and

40. On *satoyama* and *satoumi*, see Duraiappah et al. 2012.

a post-human database of cinema juggling a number of media (including internet video) in its archaeology of "rhetoric" as a cultural technique in which propaganda documentary plays a role.[41] Within the limited space here, I will only dwell on the scene of exhibition, which provides glimpses of the aspirations of the alternative subculture Mao sought to create, with its different emphasis from the more general subculture of contemporary independent documentary in China. The film exhibitors at the festival were highly conscious of this effect:

> Film exhibitions shape the subject-object relationship with the mere division by a screen. Considering the tight controls of various media under the current circumstances, on-site exchanges provide the best possible means for open and free interactions. Despite cinema's existence of barely over a century, it has already become an old medium compared with trendy interactive design and display monitors of various scales. Especially since the act of film viewing is situated in a dark enclosed space allowing no information influx but a unidirectional reception and decoding, the site may create a *fetish of the present*. Film screening is not confined to the area of the screen; instead, it becomes the river that cannot be crossed twice. (Long 2013: 105; emphasis added)

Evoking the outdoor film screenings at Shenzhen's Fringe Festival and the Bishan Project, the film exhibitors point out how the choices and constructions of the sites of film exhibition create different fields of exchange (Figures 5 and 6). The films were screened at the main family hall of the oldest residential building Yanqingtang (The Hall of Extensiveness), a piece of six-hundred-year-old wooden vernacular architecture that Peitian is known for (Figure 7). Whereas the majestic hall framed and dwarfed the portable projection screen with its high ceilings, aged horizontal beams, and vertical columns decorated with calligraphy and lanterns, its rigid order and awe-inspiring spatiality were negotiated by the audience sitting on wooden benches, chairs, and plastic stools or standing around, simultaneously attentive and casual—a "fetish of the present," indeed.

In addition to the film screenings, artists constructed site-specific environmental art to evoke a sense of absent presence and the mutual

---

41. Guo Xizhi (2013: 140) has criticized the film's unreadability given the extremely fast speed and excessive writing on the screen, which Mao deliberately evokes to create dyslexia (*yuedu zhangai*).

Figure 5 Outdoor film screening at Shenzhen's Fringe Festival. Source: *Dianying zuozhe*, special issue, no. 1 (2013): 105.

Figure 6 Outdoor film screening at the Bishan Project. Source: *Dianying zuozhe*, special issue, no. 1 (2013): 68.

Figure 7 Film exhibition at the ancestral Hall of Extensiveness, a portion of the six-hundred-year-old wooden vernacular architecture. Source: *Dianying zuozhe*, special issue, no. 1 (2013): 104.

penetration between nature and culture, past and present. In a series of artworks titled *Qingming Project: A Memorandum*, painted imageries of the socialist era haunt empty rooms with a ghostly presence.[42] Whereas culture projects itself onto nature with installations of a classic scholar's desk with ink, paper, and calligraphy occupying various natural settings, nature crawls back as a force of erosion and regeneration onto effigies of the past, with plants and microorganisms thriving as time-based media filling up empty spaces and containers—a bed frame in the open air, a canvas messenger bag, a wooden basin, picture frames along with other empty vessels such as a vase and a bird cage (Figure 8). By practicing film and art in rural and local sites, both the film exhibition and the art installation recall a long history of projecting an elitist agenda of mass education and mobilization onto

42. My translation of the subtitle as "a memorandum" is only approximate. Instead of using *beiwanglu* (memorandum), the artists actually replace *bei* (preparation) with the Chinese character *she* 畬, which refers to the ancient agricultural technique of burning the grass to prepare the land for planting. This ingenious title thus evokes forgetting and remembering, destruction and regeneration.

Figure 8 One of the art installations for *Qingming Project: A Memorandum*. Plants and microorganisms thrive as time-based media filling up empty spaces and containers against walls painted with imageries of the socialist era. Source: *Dianying zuozhe*, special issue, no. 1 (2013): 192.

the countryside through traveling film projection conjoined with art practice and theatrical performance.[43] Yet by reframing the rural local site as the very center and coauthor of creativity rather than a blank canvas for projection, such a subculture injects a healthy dose of the local not simply as place but as agentive in producing meaning and experience.

Shown as one of the centerpieces at the festival, *Yongyou* attracted heated responses at an unusual gathering of local farmers, environmentally conscious filmmakers, artists, bureaucrats, and political analysts.[44] Questions were raised regarding the issues of film form, rural issues and land politics, and the self-reflective critique of the institution of the documentary

43. For an example of such a conjoined film and art project for mass mobilization, see Bao 2015b: chap. 5.
44. Filmmaker Long Miaoyuan suggests that, in addition to database cinema and algorithm cinema, community film (*shequ yingxiang*) is the best means of artistic production that negates the notion of an auteur (*qu zuozhe hua*) (2013: 117).

and the film author himself. But the gathering also provided a forum for the farmers to reflect upon their memories of land reform and to share their contemporary experience of land and social deprivation. The discussions generated enthusiasm, resonance, as well as sharp criticism.[45] Although the scholarly and artistic communities remained relatively separate, ignoring each other's respective activities of academic symposiums and film screenings, the film screening and discussion in Peitian brought artists together with local residents in approximating an ideal of an alternative documentary subculture. Such a subculture does not pride itself on the relative autonomy of independent documentary but integrates documentary in the production of more sustainable local culture and artistic creations.

Medium Communitarianism: A Political Ecology

Mao's alternative subculture is better understood in terms of what he calls "medium communitarianism" (*meijie shequnzhuyi*), which reconsiders the question of the public (sphere) in relation to a critical rethinking of the medium. We can put this more polemically in conversation with *Kulturtechniken* and see medium communitarianism as reconceiving the medium as a cultural technique of the public sphere. In Peitian, Mao described his paddy film as his vision of a documentary subculture that reframes the technical medium of film in relation to a semireligious notion of the medium as a sphere of influence, as well as a notion of the public sphere as a social space of exchange and change while releasing individual and collective creativity (Deng, Deng, and Yu 2013: 19). In defense of his highly interventional approach to the film form that seems simultaneously subversive and didactic if not outright baffling, Mao unabashedly compares his artistic practice to a kind of "brainwashing" (*xinao*), which achieves a semireligious effect but also creates an extension of the medium/sign with qualitative difference: "I think brainwashing will produce some religious significance. With the passage of time the art will manifest significance beyond the work itself and through the individual spectator's body extend itself into something metaphysically or materially different. At the least, it becomes the extension of the signs" (Deng, Deng, and Yu 2013: 20).

Although artist Kong Delin responded to the film literally with signs made of six images of his artwork created for the festival, what Mao meant

---

45. See the highly critical account by Guo Xizhi, who describes Mao's film as an incomprehensible postmodern "visual thesis" without a logic (2013: 141).

by "signs" or medium should be seen in light of his complex notion of the medium that grounds his theory and practice (Kong 2013). In this, Mao explicitly negotiates with Habermas's notion of the public sphere, with cultural anthropology, and with communications theory to achieve an "indigenous anthropology" (*bentu renleixue*) that redefines "medium" to account for both contemporary mass media and the changing mechanism of social exchange and organization in China. Building on Melvin DeFleur's communication notion of the medium as any single or a series of organized carriers to disseminate human consciousness, Mao expands it to account for a broad range of phenomena that attend to China's specific situation and its changing media landscape. But there is a significant departure. Mao holds an anthropological interpretation of the medium that stems from the broadest notion of human communication and exchange, taking account of the object, social space, and means of organization. In this light, he situates what we understand as mass or communication media, including the retrospective account of traditional modes of exchange in writing, only at the end of this extended media inventory.

For Mao, medium, as the vehicle of human consciousness, encompasses four major categories:

1. An enlightenment model of the public sphere based on conscious communication, which he calls the "political public sphere," consisting of public opinion, social discourse, and cultural production.

2. A local public sphere comprising natural or subcultural organizations based on marriage, blood relationship, clan membership, shared interests, and regional power divisions.

3. Gift exchange and contract-based civilizations, including tribal and commercial/market societies, and cases such as China where the field of exchange is a conglomerate of political, economic, social, and cultural components.

4. Mass communication, including retrospectively recognized traditional modes such as reading clubs, writing, the notepad, radio, television, the telephone, satellite terminals, the internet and Web 2.0, and optical and electric communication.

Beyond these four categories, Mao stakes his belief on a medium built on its specificity or otherness that grounds an alternative notion of an inclusive public that turns human and animal consciousness on its head:

If possible, I hope it is nothing but a carrier of information, a code. Whether this medium disseminates information or not, its function of self-recognition and marking only applies to itself. Whether it is human or animal consciousness, whether it belongs to nature or supernature, whether it is orderly or chaotic, contains value judgment or is judgment free, is linguistic or nonstructural, I want to open up this space of inclusion and make it amenable to time so that its infinitely encompassing space and time gradually weaken the principles that regulate publicness, and henceforth one can no longer categorize and differentiate, thus increasingly approaching the medium's own world.[46]

In this rather challenging passage, Mao seems to start from one point and arrive at its exact opposite. Departing from the seemingly familiar notion of medium as transparent vehicle of information that suppresses its own materiality and organizational principles, Mao returns to this domain as the very site of possibility, a site whose openness in its spatial and temporal axes is defined by its otherness beyond a distinct group identity. The material and semiotic markers of a medium, what we conventionally understand as its categorical specificities, are deployed as the very means to defy categories and distinctions, using otherness as the basis for openness so as to exceed what defines publicness as the binding law for a specific group, however heterogeneous. By returning to the world of the medium beyond the claim of a particular subject, the medium defies distinction itself and offers an alternative notion of publicness. This is realized by the force of time and the medium's reflexive and recursive perpetuation of self-differentiation, which erodes boundaries and categorical distinctions. Yet perhaps even more surprisingly, instead of considering human or animal consciousness as the self-same subject of communication, Mao places consciousness on the same plane as an objective notion of the medium and extends it to nature and supernature. By turning consciousness on its head, or beheading the self-same subject of communication, Mao's vision of a medium-oriented public is clearly different from Habermas's notion of a public sphere based on communicative reason. Yet by insisting on the relevance of the public in relation to the medium, which he calls medium communitarianism, he explicitly places a notion of the public at the center of his practice.

To some extent, Mao has pushed the notion of medium to a limit

46. See http://www.paddyfilm.org/study/MCD.html, accessed August 16, 2015.

reached by media archaeologists and theorists, conceiving of medium as a versatile and inclusive/ubiquitous category that covers a broad spectrum ranging from media objects/technology to the human body, nature, and the environment broadly construed in its cosmic sense (air, earth, water, clouds, light)—or, in John Durham Peters's words, "elemental media" (2015). For Mao, the medium refers to shamanism in conjunction with the technological ensemble of spirit writing, cinema, writing, and organic farming. In other words, he has stretched the limits of *medium* to the point of its potential breakdown or uselessness. Does Mao share our obsession with the notion of the medium, or is his a changing frame whose reference remains unknown? Is this a post- or nonhuman notion of the medium?

I would suggest that this medium communitarianism proposes an ecological model of the public as practiced in his paddy film and the Peitian Film Festival. Mao does not so much push the limit of the medium to pointlessness as to the point of social interaction and intervention; we can even say that his is a post-human notion of the medium/public that relies on the otherness of the medium and its nonhuman or subjectless nature as the basis of an inclusive, open system. This would reside beyond the Enlightenment notion of a public sphere dictated by human consciousness and a correspondingly passive conception of the medium. Mao's medium can be conceived as a cultural technique in terms of its liminality; its ability to mediate, connect, and intervene; its self-recognizing, recursive nature; and its function to defy distinction or precede distinction in the sense that subculture itself is not a subcategory of culture but what precedes and remains outside of it and also carries the power to disturb it to the point of "*de*culturation" (Siegert 2007: 31). Yet where "cultural techniques" leave the question of the public unaddressed, Mao's medium communitarianism points to a possible public built on a new collectivity as the medium of social change. That collectivity is not exclusively human but the conjoint action of agents big and small that define a political field in terms of an assemblage of distributed agency (see Bennett 2010). Mao's medium-oriented public thus reshuffles and reconnects nature and technology, the rural and urban, archaic and new media through (agri)cultural techniques to revive and renew plural forms of social interaction—through artisan modes of farming and film production, communal rituals of multimediated shamanism, site-specific film exhibition, and critical discussions across live, print, and virtual platforms.

Coda: Archaeology, Allegory, Ecology—
What Are the Cinematic Good(s) For?

In a recent reflection on media archaeology, Thomas Elsaesser considers it to be less a method than a "symptom" and placeholder in response to a set of crises facing the dominance of digital culture (2016b).[47] Identifying the epistemic shifts from linearity to multiplicity/probability and from symbolic systems to technological automatism/algorithms, Elsaesser suggests that the rise of media archaeology refracts the very crises of causality and representation accompanying the digital age. Elsaesser cautions that media archaeology's preference for a heterogeneous, multidimensional, and multidirectional account of the emergence of cinema comprises an epistemological model that duplicates the postwar scientific model of data processing and control and thus "carries within itself the very principles it is supposed to investigate" and reflects "the prejudices and preferences of our present age" (191). Media archaeology's poetics of obsolescence, Elsaesser alerts us, could in turn serve as the ideology of the digital by fetishizing memory, objecthood, and the old—and thereby reconfirming the claim for the ephemerality and newness of the digital. To counter such a model of rupture and rivalry, Elsaesser traces a dual genealogy of cinema, using light as an instance of geometric and physiological optics, to propose cinema's compatibility with and continuing relevance to the digital.

By focusing on film history as media archaeology with its multiple genealogies, Elsaesser provides a pointed response to the Kittlerian and post-Kittlerian homage to the digital that promises to complete the process of critiquing the humanities and Enlightenment humanism (2016b: 207). Against this, he proposes to consider the allegorical function of media archaeology as materially and technologically mediated history that recognizes the mutual compatibility and constitution between the human and the machine. Whereas cinema lies at the heart of a digital culture that extends its geometric and physiological optics, cinema's supposed inoperativeness and uselessness, Elsaesser speculates, ready it for the status of art as an allegorical archaeology premised on a modernist notion of autonomy and freedom from circulation. Media archaeology, then, helps usher cinema's artistic dream by enabling its migration to museums and galleries. This is a tantalizing alternative to cultural techniques' post-hermeneutic and post-human claims. By recognizing the human in the machine, which in turn

---

47. The essay also serves as the epilogue for his book (Elsaesser 2016a).

interprets the human, Elsaesser sees media archaeology's ambiguity as a "placeholder (of the human)" with the potential to both deconstruct but also reconstruct the human (207). By considering cinema's status as art de facto in the twenty-first century, he gestures toward an allegorical archaeology with a possible revisit to representation and aesthetics.

Yet perhaps cinema is not the only thing at stake in this competition between the analog and the digital. Nor is the human, for which—on Elsaesser's terms—the question of cinema serves as a surrogate. If Elsaesser suggests that we enlarge our context and horizon to overcome the binary divide between the analog and the digital, perhaps we have not broadened our scope enough to question the universality of humanity, however technologically mediated. Nor can the artistic status of cinema guarantee its autonomy and freedom—museums and galleries and arthouse theaters are chains of commodity circulation different in space but not necessarily in kind from those of television and the internet. Elsaesser's question, "What is cinema (good) for?," relying on cinema's uselessness for its artistic virtue, in effect reaffirms the binary logic of digital/analog as both a technological and a qualitative difference.

By shifting the context to the subculture of independent documentary in China and using Mao as a case study, I have attempted to explore a different constellation that recasts the questions of human and technology, hermeneutics and meaning. To some extent, the phenomenon of Mao is a symptom of China's post-socialist condition, in which the question of cinema, facing technological, infrastructural, and ideological transformations, is inextricably bound up with issues of rural/urban development and the future of a mass-mediated public. It remains to be seen to what extent such a subculture serves as an alternative to the global circulation and consumption of the moving image space. In this sense, this essay harbors no desire to revive auteurism in late cinema. Whereas media archaeology habitually confronts a medium's technological and aesthetic transformations and its plural histories tied to our own institutional concerns, Mao has positioned cinema to fold back questions of culture, society, and politics.

These questions are no longer simply the "content" or mere matters of filmic representation. By breaking down the notion of the medium into operative chains of cultural techniques, Mao's film practice can be considered an experiment with media archaeology on three levels that bind the writing of alternative histories with the reshaping of the public sphere. First, Mao's focus on shamanism as a medium of memory and sociality illustrates how living religion actually operates as a technical ensemble and process to animate alternative histories that continue to produce locality. In this process, cinema serves as a recursive technique as it observes, participates in, and intervenes in the ritual process of spirit writing. Second, Mao's Paddy Film Farm can be seen as a perversion of "What is cinema (good for)?" to "What are the cinematic *good(s)* for?," turning cinema's uselessness on its head by reintegrating cinema into the agricultural techniques of organic farming and commodity exchange as an attempt, however meager and flawed, at "social sculpting." Third, through film exhibitions in rural communities such as Peitian, Mao and his fellow filmmakers exercise a "medium communitarianism" by reinvesting in the rural as the site of a possible subculture and alternative future, thus repositioning cinema and art in relation to agricultural heritage as sustainable cultural techniques of the environment and public sphere.

This threefold archaeology of the medium as cultural techniques—alternative histories, circulations, and a political ecology—effectively pushes the limit of cultural techniques' claim to reconnect media and culture. Whereas proponents of cultural techniques break down medium in terms of a priori techniques that deconstruct the human as anthropotechnics without challenging its anthropological constant, Mao's film practice and critical writing allow a more reflective investigation on culture outside the black box of media histories as histories of techniques/technologies. Instead of simply deconstructing familiar binaries as cultural techniques, he invests cinema in the analysis and production of a subculture in terms of both alternative histories and a possible future. This subculture is not simply a subcategory of culture but what constitutes it in the first place with the capacity for its mutation and dissolution. In this sense, Mao repositions independent documentary from a subculture of the neoliberal creative industry to an actionable good and a creative agent in constructing the local as an ecology of agricultural heritage, artistic techniques, and social organization. In this new model of the public sphere as an evolving ecology, the stakes of the human are high; they are tied to the question of technology in the production of locality. To consider such an ecological model of the medium and the public is not simply to affirm the agency of the object. It is to move away from the selfsame histories in which media become mere surrogates for the human subjects of history with their own rationales and teloi.

References

Andriopoulos, Stefan. 2008. *Possessed: Hypnotic Crimes, Corporate Fiction, and the Invention of Cinema*. Chicago: University of Chicago Press.

Bao, Weihong. 2015a. "The Art of Control: Hong Shen, Behavioral Psychology, and the Technics of Social Effects." *Modern Chinese Literature and Culture* 27, no. 2: 249–97.

———. 2015b. *Fiery Cinema: The Emergence of an Affective Medium in China*. Minneapolis: University of Minnesota Press.

Bennett, Jane. 2010. *Vibrant Matter: A Political Ecology of Things*. Durham, NC: Duke University Press.

Berry, Chris, Lu Xinyu, and Lisa Rofel, eds. 2010. *The New Chinese Documentary Film Movement: For the Public Record*. Hong Kong: Hong Kong University Press.

Chumley, Lily. 2016. *Creativity Class: Art School and Culture Work in Post-Socialist China*. Princeton, NJ: Princeton University Press.

Deng, Bochao, Deng Shijie, and Feng Yu, eds. 2013. *Dianying zuozhe*, special issue, no. 1.

Duraiappah, Anantha Kumar, Nakamura Koji, Takeuchi Kazuhiko, Watanabe Masataka, and Nishi Maiko, eds. 2012. *Satoyama–Satoumi Ecosystems and Human Well-Being: Socio-Ecological Production Landscapes of Japan*. Tokyo: United Nations University Press.

Elsaesser, Thomas. 2016a. *Film History as Media Archaeology: Tracing Digital Cinema*. Amsterdam: University of Amsterdam Press.

———. 2016b. "Media Archaeology as Symptom." *New Review of Film and Television Studies* 14, no. 2: 181–215.

Fuller, Anthony, Qinwen Min, Wenjun Jiao, and Yanying Bai. 2015. "Globally Important Agricultural Heritage Systems (GIAHS) of China: The Challenge of Complexity in Research." *Ecosystem Health and Sustainability* 1, no. 2: 1–10.

Galloway, Alexander, and Eugene Thacker. 2007. *The Exploit: A Theory of Networks*. Minneapolis: University of Minnesota Press.

Geoghegan, Bernard. 2013. "After Kittler: On the Cultural Techniques of Recent German Media Theory." *Theory, Culture & Society* 30, no. 6: 66–82.

———. 2014. "Untimely Mediations: On Two Recent Contributions to German Media Theory." *Paragraph* 37, no. 3: 419–25.

Gumbrecht, Hans Ulrich. 1994. "A Farewell to Interpretation." In *Materialities of Communication*, edited by Hans Ulrich Gumbrecht and K. Ludwig Pfeiffer, 389–402. Stanford, CA: Stanford University Press.

Guo, Xizhi. 2013. "Xunzhao tudi de jingshen" (In search of the spirit of the land). *Dianying zuozhe*, special issue, no. 1: 138–42.

Hansen, Miriam. 1991. *Babel and Babylon: Spectatorship in American Silent Film*. Cambridge, MA: Harvard University Press.

Hayford, Charles W. 1990. *To the People: James Yen and Village China*. New York: Columbia University Press.

Huhtamo, Erkki, and Jussi Parikka, eds. 2011. *Media Archaeology: Approaches, Applications, and Implications.* Berkeley: University of California Press.

Kong, Delin. 2013. "Guan *Yongyou* biji liuze" (Six notes on viewing the film *Yongyou*). *Dianying zuozhe*, special issue, no. 1: 143–45.

Leibenluft, Michael, and Maja-Stina Johansson Wang. 2014. "Spiritual Farming: Performance at Shanghai's Downstream Garage." *Drama Review* 58, no. 1: 25–41.

Long, Miaoyuan. 2013. "Kuisi chunri minxi tuyouji" (A visual journey of West Fujian in spring 2013). *Dianying zuozhe*, special issue, no. 1: 92–137.

Lu, Shi'e. 1996. "Yetan Nansong chunian Zhong Xiang, Yang Yao qiyi suo liyong de zongjiao paixi wenti" (On the religious sectors during the Zhong Xiang–Yang Yao uprising in early Southern Song). *Wuling xuekan* no. 1: 58–61.

———. 1999. "Yang Yao lugeng shuizhan de zhanlue jishu" (Yang Yao's techniques of farming and water battles). *Changde shifan xueyuan xuebao* 24, no. 4: 75–78.

Lyotard, Jean François. 1984. *The Postmodern Condition: A Report on Knowledge*, translated by Geoff Bennington and Brian Massumi. Minneapolis: University of Minnesota Press.

Ma, Shaoqiao. 1956. "Guanyu Nansong chu Zhong Xiang, Yang Yao qiyi de zongjiao paixi wenti de shangque" (A discussion on the religious sectors in the Zhong Xiang and Yang Yao uprising of early Southern Song). *Wenshizhe* no. 8: 61–64.

Macho, Thomas. 2013. "Second Order Animals: Cultural Techniques of Identity and Identification." *Theory, Culture & Society* 30, no. 6: 30–47.

Mao Chengyu. 2013. "Xianzai de huanjing shouxian shi zhengzhi wenti" (The question of environment is first of all a question of politics). *Dianying zuozhe*, special issue, no. 1: 63–64.

Martin, Reinhold. 2016. "Unfolded, Not Opened: On Bernard Siegert's Cultural Techniques." *Grey Room* 62: 102–15.

Mintz, Sidney. 1985. *Sweetness and Power: The Pleasure of Sugar in Modern History.* New York: Viking-Penguin.

Mote, Frederick. 2003. *Imperial History 900–1800.* Cambridge, MA: Harvard University Press, 2003.

Needham, Joseph. 1965. *Science and Civilization in China.* Vol. 4. Cambridge: Cambridge University Press.

———. 1995. *The Shorter Science and Civilization in China: 5*, abridged by Colin Roland. Cambridge: Cambridge University Press.

Nornes, Markus. 2007. *Forest of Pressure: Ogawa Shinsuke and Postwar Japanese Documentary.* Minneapolis: University of Minnesota Press.

Pan Wei, and Ma Ya, eds. 2010. *Renmin gongheguo liushi nian yu zhongguo moshi* (*Sixty Years of the People's Republic and the China Model*). Beijing: Sanlian.

Pang, Laikwan. 2012. *Creativity and Its Discontents: China's Creative Industries and Intellectual Property Right Offense.* Durham, NC: Duke University Press.

Parikka, Jussi. 2012. *What Is Media Archaeology?* Cambridge: Polity.

Peters, John Durham. 2015. *The Marvelous Clouds: Toward a Philosophy of Elemental Media*. Chicago: University of Chicago Press.

Ren, Xuefei. 2014. "The Political Economy of Urban Ruins: Redeveloping Shanghai." *International Journal of Urban and Regional Research* 38, no. 2: 1081–91.

Ren, Xuefei, and Meng Sun, 2012. "Artistic Urbanization: Creative Industries and Creative Control in Beijing." *International Journal of Urban and Regional Research* 36, no. 3: 504–21.

Sahlins, Marshall. 1996. "The Sadness of Sweetness: The Native Anthropology of Western Cosmology." *Current Anthropology* 37, no. 3: 395–428.

Sconce, Jeffrey. 2000. *Haunted Media: Electronic Presence from Telegraphy to Television*. Durham, NC: Duke University Press.

Siegert, Bernhard. 2007. "Cacography or Communication? Cultural Techniques in German Media Studies," translated by Geoffrey Winthrop-Young. *Grey Room* 29: 26–47.

———. 2013. "Cultural Techniques, or the End of Intellectual Postwar Era in German Media Theory." *Theory, Culture & Society* 30, no. 6: 48–65.

———. 2015. *Cultural Techniques: Grids, Filters, Doors, and Other Articulations of the Real*. New York: Fordham University Press.

Stiegler, Bernard. 1998. *Technics and Time, 1: The Fault of Epimetheus*. Stanford, CA: Stanford University Press.

Sukhu, Gopal. 2012. *The Shaman and the Heresiarch: A New Interpretation of the Li Sao*. Albany: SUNY Press.

Sun, Yehong, Myriam Jansen-Verbeke, Qingwen Min, and Shengkui Cheng. 2011. "Tourism Potential of Agricultural Heritage Systems." *Tourism Geographies* 13, no. 1: 112–28.

Wainwright, Oliver. 2014. "Our Cities Are Insufferable: Chinese Artists Go Back to the Land." *The Guardian*, December 2.

Wang, Xiaolu. 2010. http://wxiaolu999.blog.163.com/blog/static/135334147201011255219784/. February 12, 2010. Accessed December 20, 2015.

Wellbery, David. 1990. "Foreword." In *Discourse Networks, 1800/1900*, by Friederich Kittler, translated by Michael Meteer and Chris Cullens. Stanford, CA: Stanford University Press.

Winthrop-Young, Geoffrey, Ilinca Iurascu, and Jussi Parikka, eds. 2013. "Cultural Techniques." Special issue, *Theory, Culture & Society* 30, no. 6.

Wong, Winnie. 2014. *Van Gogh on Demand: China and the Readymade*. Chicago: University of Chicago Press.

Yen, James Y. C. 1929. *China's New Scholar-Farmer*. Dingxian, China: Chinese National Association of the Mass Education Movement.

Zhang, Yingjin, and Paul G. Pickowicz, eds. 2006. *From Underground to Independent: Alternative Film Culture in Contemporary China*. Lanham, MD: Rowman and Littlefield.

Zhang, Zhen, and Angela Zito, eds. 2015. *DV-MADE CHINA: Digital Subjects and Social Transformations after Independent Film*. Honolulu: University of Hawai'i Press.

The Hitherto Unknown:
Toward a Theory of Synthetic Sound

Hannah Frank

And you yourselves—how many times have you wondered about mankind's destiny, or asked the old questions: "Where are we going? Like the unheard music that lies latent in a phonograph record, where are we until God orders us to be born?"

—Adolfo Bioy Casares, *The Invention of Morel*

A wax cylinder embalms a sonic moment. A sound scratches the record's surface, leaving an incision that can be transformed back into sound—that particular sound, not just any sound. There is a one-to-one cor-

Special thanks to Jacob Blecher, Daniel Morgan, and Yuri Tsivian for their detailed comments on earlier drafts of this essay. Thanks also to Matt Hauske, Ian Bryce Jones, Tien-Tien Jong, Jim Lastra, Andrew Ritchey, and participants in the Mass Culture and New Media Workshops at the University of Chicago. [*This essay is based on a draft Hannah Frank (1984–2017) wrote in June 2017; I have completed it using material from an earlier draft and following indications from correspondence. I am grateful to Amy Skjerseth for her work in compiling the references.* —*Daniel Morgan*]

boundary 2 49:1 (2022) DOI 10.1215/01903659-9615403 ©2022 by Duke University Press

respondence, an indexical relationship, between the original acoustic event and its inscription. Without a phonograph player, however, the record's grooves resist interpretation. The inscription cannot be deciphered, let alone read. To paraphrase Charles Sanders Peirce, all we know is that *something* left such a mark—perhaps a clap of thunder, perhaps a rap on the door—"though we may not know precisely what the event was" (1955: 108–9).

Yet this very impenetrability awakens us to knowledge we had not known was possible. Suddenly, anything with a fissure or a striation becomes potentially playable: a corduroy jacket, a scar, or even, as Rainer Maria Rilke observed in 1919, the coronal suture of the skull: "What variety of lines, then, occurring anywhere, could one not put under the needle and try out? Is there any contour that one could not, in a sense, complete in this way and then experience it, as it makes itself felt, thus transformed, in another field of sense?" (1999: 41). These are the questions that drive the discipline of archaeophony, or acoustic archaeology, which seeks to excavate ancient tones. In 1969, Richard Woodbridge reported that sounds had been recorded in wheel-thrown clay pots and in brushstrokes on canvas. When played, a blue streak yielded the word *blue*, uttered in the painter's voice (1969).[1] In 2014, a technology called Irene (Image, Reconstruct, Erase Noise, Etc.), devised by a group of particle physicists, extracted sounds out of the damaged phonograph cylinders of two of Thomas Edison's talking dolls (Cowen 2015). "Now I lay me down to sleep," one of them shrieks—her very first words after decades of slumber.

The phonograph record changes our relationship to the past but also to the present and the future. As the music historian Douglas Kahn posits, "the phonograph might decode the inscriptions of the visible world," enabling us to "become sumptuously immersed in the sonorized secrets of all lines" (1999: 94). Commonplace things—cracks in a sidewalk, the rings of a tree—take on a resonance they didn't have before, for we now know that there exists a sound to which every object corresponds. But what we don't know is *how* each of these marks will sound. A potential sound lies suspended, as yet unheard. Rilke, for one, thought the skull contained a "primal sound without a name, a music without notation, a sound even more strange than any incantation from the dead for which the skull could have been used" (1999: 41). Other artists, writing around the same time as Rilke, contemplated generating their own impressions in order to produce sounds beyond the realm of human experience. In 1916, the Russian composer Arseny Avraamov read the fortune foretold by the phonograph's

---

1. I refrain from making any claim about the truth of Woodbridge's findings.

grooves. He speculated that, through the close, almost chiromantic, analysis of a record's lines, one could learn to "to create synthetically . . . even the most fantastic sounds by forming a groove with the appropriate structure of shape and depth" (quoted in Alarcón 2008; see Avraamov 2007: 175–98). In a similar fashion, the Bauhaus artist László Moholy-Nagy imagined that the phonograph could be turned from a technology of reproduction into one of production. Its grooves could be "incised by human agency, without any external mechanical means, which [could] then produce sound effects which would signify—without new instruments and without an orchestra—a fundamental innovation in sound production (of new, hitherto unknown sounds and tonal relations) both in composition and musical performance" (Passuth 1985: 289; see also 291–92). Both Avraamov and Moholy-Nagy envisioned the phonograph as a musical instrument capable of playing the scores drawn directly on—into—its surface. Significantly, however, they framed the aesthetic potential of these synthesized sounds in epistemological terms. What would make the music so wonderful was, indeed, *wonder*: the phrases these statements hinge on are, respectively, "the most *fantastic* sounds" and "new, *hitherto unknown* sounds and tonal relations" (emphasis added). The phonograph becomes an instrument of revelation.

Of course, this is the promise held out by all forms of new media—to "give us sense organs to perceive old things that were never, and always, there before," as John Durham Peters has put it (2004: 194). León Theremin's eponymous electrical instrument was said to harness the ethereal; we can tune into the radio waves emitted by Saturn's auroras and catalog the chirps of both blackbirds and black holes; the stethoscope enables us to pathologize our "hitherto inaudible" internal rattles and crackles.[2] Even the driest of trade and technical journals cannot resist imagining the unimaginable. In a short report from 1931 on advances in the optical printer, a machine that facilitated filmic special effects, a cinematographer concludes, "There are endless possibilities to the different devices which may be constructed and used advantageously with it: but still more boundless are the possibilities which must be latent in the minds of those who utilize it" (Knechtel 1931: 270).

What was particular about the phonograph, however, was the one-to-one correspondence between the groove and the sound. The relationship between a cause (a sound) and its effect (the groove) is palpable.

2. For more on the stethoscope as a sonic medium, see Sterne 2003: 87–136. There are also Moog synthesizers and a range of other instruments for producing new sonic phenomena.

Consequently, the phonograph is at its most seductive as an instrument of potential knowledge—that is, of the unknown—when either the cause but not the effect is known (e.g., when Avraamov or Moholy-Nagy incises the record directly in order to produce fantastic melodies), or the effect but not the cause is known (e.g., when ordinary cracks and ridges, such as the coronal suture of the skull, are reconceived as the physical traces of sounds as yet unheard). A record solicits us to examine it. "What does *this* sound like?" we ask, running a finger along a groove. Or we put the record on, and wonder aloud: "What does *that* sound look like?"

By the end of the 1920s, Avraamov and Moholy-Nagy were able to put their speculations to the test through a new technology of sound reproduction, what was then called *sound-on-film* but later came to be known as the *optical soundtrack*. Printed on the edge of the filmstrip, parallel to the frames of the image, the optical soundtrack enabled the synchronization of sound and moving images. It also demystified the relationship between the acoustic event and its transcription. The grooves of the phonograph record had proven too minuscule for the kind of analysis Avraamov and Moholy-Nagy wanted, but the patterns traversing the optical soundtrack were visible to the naked eye: through a photoelectric process, sounds were transcribed as a series of waveforms (in the variable-density system) or of parallel lines of varying thickness and opacity (in the variable-area system). One needed only a magnifying glass and a ruler to measure the length and frequency between each of the undulating contours or the spaces between black-and-white horizontal striae. By studying these patterns and the sounds to which they corresponded, one could learn to imitate them with simple pen and ink—and thus synthesize sound without the intervention of a microphone.

In fact, anything that could be photographed could be transferred onto the optical soundtrack. This might include simulated waveforms, as well as any kind of graphic inscription—an idle doodle, say, or a letter of the alphabet—not to mention the objects that populate everyday life. The Hollywood director Rouben Mamoulian, for example, claimed to have photographed the light of a flickering candle onto the optical soundtrack. All these techniques produce rather than reproduce sounds through the direct manipulation of the optical soundtrack; together they constitute what I will refer to throughout this article as *synthetic sound*.[3]

3. By contrast, Gregory Zinman (2012) includes live sound in his historical survey of synthetic sound, and Maurizio Corbella and Anna Windisch (2013) incorporate the Theremin into their discussion of synthesized sound and Hollywood cinema.

The fantasies of producing sound out of images are not new, nor is a reckoning of their importance for thinking about media. When he develops his arguments about the cultural and political stakes involved in media of recording and reproduction, for example, Friedrich Kittler draws precisely on such fantasies by Rilke and others to articulate the episteme of audio recording (1999: 38ff.). Synthetic sound, however, marks a qualitatively different ambition. Kittler isolated the models of recording into three different regimes, only coming together in the world of the computer, of electronic media. Yet even here they remain analytically separate: "The historical synchronicity of cinema, phonography, and typewriting separated optical, acoustic, and written data flows, thereby rendering them autonomous. That electric of electronic media can recombine them does not change the fact of their differentiation" (14). Media specificity persists. What the history of synthetic sound shows, by contrast, is that a fusion between the heard and the seen, between phonography and cinema, was always present in an age of media production. It is a media fantasy that operates across forms and materials.

· · · ·

In 1878, E. W. Blake, a professor of physics at Brown University, devised a method of photographing sound. Consisting of a telephone mouthpiece, a heliostat, a vibrating disc, and a sensitized plate, the apparatus yielded visual records of such spoken phrases as "How do you do?" and "Brown University." Although Blake acknowledged his invention's technical limitations—it required the brightest sunlight, and even on a cloudless day proved insensitive to elements of audible speech—he was nonetheless impressed by the visual aesthetics of the patterns it produced. As sonic transcriptions they might fall short, but as photographs they were *beautiful* (Blake 1878: 54).

The decades following Blake's experiment boasted such inventions as A. Manuelli's "photophonic machine," patented in France in 1908, and F. D. Pudumjee's "photophonograph," patented in Great Britain in 1911 (Sponable 1947: 235, 246). Unlike Blake, these scientists regarded photography merely as a means for sound recording, not as an end in and of itself. Whatever *visual* properties photographic sound records might possess were subordinate to the photograph's primary function as a record of *sound*: the clearer the image, for example, the greater the ease with which its elements could be subjected to analysis. Photography also afforded certain practical advantages over rival processes like phonography. As Ernst

Ruhmer reported in *Scientific American* in 1901, the films produced by his "photographophone" were highly compact, such that even an "interminable" song or speech could be stored in a small space (1901). Moreover, by the 1880s, photographs had acquired legal standing: they could serve as evidence in judicial proceedings. Charles Fritts's 1890 patent for a "photophonographic apparatus" (filed the same year as Alexander Graham Bell's proposal for a "photophone") goes so far as to contend that his device's reproduction of "a dying man's deposition" might serve "as positive proof of the exact tenor of the message sent or received in any court as a photograph recording any event or scene" (1916: 15). In other words, if a photograph had evidentiary value, then so too could a photophonograph.

Most of these inventions led nowhere; that we remember them at all has largely to do with a use Ruhmer teases at the end of his essay: "It is my intention to employ the photographophone in connection with the cinematograph and to ascertain whether it be possible to record the movements of bodies and of sounds . . . upon the same film" (36). Ruhmer was followed by, among others, Eugene A. Lauste, who in 1906 filed a patent on a "method and means for simultaneously recording and reproducing movements and sounds" (Lauste 1907), and Elias Ries, whose 1913 patent application aimed to photograph sound in order to create a "photo-phonoscope film record" (Ries 1923).[4] Ruhmer's, Lauste's, and Ries's inventions were, in short, precursors to the *sound-on-film* or optical soundtrack. In standard projection, the optical soundtrack is hidden from view, its visual patterns instead translated back into sound: lips move on-screen, and we hear them say, "How do you do?" or "Brown University." The function of the optical soundtrack was, in effect, to be heard and not seen.

In the late 1920s, as sound-on-film was becoming the standard for synchronizing sound and moving images, filmmakers across the globe began attending to the graphic contents of the optical soundtrack and thinking of how that could be modified. Some were perfectionists, intent on fixing mistakes in the initial recording process by making minute changes to the patterns that had been transcribed. As the director Josef von Sternberg recalls in his memoirs, he occasionally "corrected faulty pronunciation and sibilants that disturbed [him] by the use of pen and ink on the sound track that runs sixteen frames away along the edge of the emulsion" (1965: 100–101). Others realized that *any* graphic trace might produce a

---

4. The quote about Ries's invention comes from Anon 1930: 32. For a more detailed account of the connections between these two patents, see Adams 2012: 215–19.

Figure 1 Boris Yankovsky's caricatures of himself and Arseny Avraamov, to be printed in place of waveforms on the optical soundtrack. From V. Solev, "Absolute Music by Designed Sound," *American Cinematographer*, April 1936.

sound, whether a blip or a thrum, a glissando or a fugue, and went even further, making up their own patterns and printing them directly onto the optical soundtrack. Under the direction of the Russian composer Arseny Avraamov, the animator Boris Yankovsky used facial caricatures in place of waveforms (Figure 1) (Solev 1936: 146–48, 154–55); the German animator Oskar Fischinger created bands of stars and circles (Moritz 2004: 181); John Cage, writing in 1937, imagined a new way of listening to Beethoven: repeating a portrait of the composer "fifty times per second on a sound track" (Cage 1967: 4).[5] In one of his reflections, Avraamov recalls a colleague asking, "If you were to trace an Egyptian or ancient Greek design on the soundtrack—would we hear some hitherto unknown archaic music?" (1939: 70; quoted in Izvolov 2014).[6]

Indeed, anything that could be photographed could be transferred onto the optical soundtrack. This might include simulated waveforms, idle doodles, hieroglyphs, geometric forms—and the objects that populate everyday life.

5. For information on other practitioners of synthetic sound, see Kahn 1999; Levin 2003; Smirnov 2013.
6. Oskar Fischinger is said to have found that a snake-shaped hieroglyph produced a hissing sound (Levin 2003: 73n41).

Figure 2 Sensual images run like a mill-race through Jekyll as he transforms into Hyde. *Dr. Jekyll and Mr. Hyde* (dir. Rouben Mamoulian, 1931).

Moholy-Nagy famously joked to a friend, "I wonder how your nose will sound," a cheeky reference to the artist's own *Sound ABC* (*Films Tönendes ABC*, 1932), the soundtrack of which consisted of silhouetted profiles and fingerprints as well as geometrical and typographical inscriptions (quoted in Kahn 1999: 93; Zinman 2012: 55). Through the direct manipulation of the optical soundtrack, all these techniques produce—rather than reproduce—sounds, and together they constitute the domain of *synthetic sound*.

In *Dr. Jekyll and Mr. Hyde* (1931), Rouben Mamoulian employs synthetic sound in order to represent Jekyll's first transformation into Hyde. First, we see Jekyll transform physically, through trick photography; then, we experience Jekyll's psychological transformation. In order to capture cinematographically the vertiginous sensations Jekyll undergoes, such as the "current of disordered sensual images running like a mill-race in [his] fancy" described by Robert Louis Stevenson, Mamoulian created a kaleidoscopic series of superimpositions set against the rapid and repeated rotation of the camera (Figure 2) (Stevenson 2004: 78). The soundtrack that accompanies this swirl of images is no less disorienting. Jekyll's "head noises," as

Mamoulian called them (Scheuer 1932), consisted of the sound of a gong (the impact of which had been cut off), his own heartbeats, and photographs of "light frequencies of varying intensity from a candle" (Higham and Greenberg 1969: 135). As Mamoulian later recounted, his goal was to produce an "incredible reality," which could only be achieved by "concoct[ing] a mélange of sounds that do not exist in nature, that a human ear cannot hear" (Atkins 1973: 42).[7]

Early theorizations of synthetic sound pick up this refrain: sonic experimentation will expand human experience. We hear it echoed in Moholy-Nagy's desire to "to enrich our aural experience sphere by giving us entirely unknown sound values" (Passuth 1985: 314), in Fischinger's dream of conjuring "new perceptions that until now were overlooked and remained neglected" (Avraamov 1932: 46), and in a commercial patent filed in 1929 by the American animation director Dave Fleischer, in which Fleischer affirms his invention's ability to "produce a sound which has never heretofore been produced" (Fleischer 1932) (Figure 3). The aural perceptions engendered by synthetic sound are intimately linked not just to how we hear but also to how we think, feel, and understand. By broadening the horizons of sensorial experience, these experiments promise to reshape human knowledge of the world and everyday life. Synthetic sound thus serves a radical epistemological function.

In what follows, I write an alternative history of synthetic sound: a counterfactual history, you might say, or what Thomas Elsaesser has opted instead to call a "possibilist history," whereby one thinks "into history all those histories that might have been, or might still be" (1999: 66). It is a history that is not causally linked but moves roughly from east to west, across different cinematic practices. Ultimately, synthetic sound amounted to mere novelty, finding its primary home in films like Sergei Eisenstein and Grigori Aleksandrov's avant-garde short *Romance Sentimentale* (1930), animated cartoons like Ub Iwerks's *Village Barber* (1930),[8] and genre pictures like

7. For more information on the film's soundtrack, see Lerner 2009: 55–79.

8. As reported by the London Film Society, which screened the film on February 8, 1931: "It is of special interest to note that certain loud and crashing effects in [*Village Barber*] are achieved by painting contrasting lines of black and white on the sound-track of the film, and are therefore, strictly speaking, not recorded at all, but edited into the film." See *Film Society Programmes* 1972: 178. Throughout the early 1930s, the London Film Society routinely showcased synthetic sound experiments, including Oskar Fischinger's experiments (screened on both May 21 and December 10, 1933) and Moholy-Nagy's *Films Tönendes ABC* (screened on December 10, 1933). Even earlier, the society had presented demonstrations of "sound projected backwards" and uncovered the portion of the screen "usually masked during projection . . . in order that the soundtrack may be observed" (160–61).

Figure 3 Illustrations demonstrating the synthesis of variable-area sound. Dave Fleischer, "Method of Marking Films for Producing Sound Effects," US Patent 1,888,914 (1932).

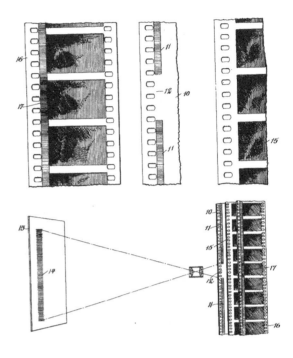

Mamoulian's *Dr. Jekyll and Mr. Hyde*—the margins of mainstream narrative cinema. Avraamov, for his part, treated synthetic sound as a mode of musical expression, one that built on his earlier forays into musique concrète and polytonal rhythm; Moholy-Nagy soon turned his attention to other artistic media; and later experiments by filmmakers such as Norman McLaren, John and James Whitney, and Barry Spinello remain largely curiosities, the peripheral practices of peripheral practitioners. Against this history, I posit a history in which synthetic sound reasserts the photographic basis of the optical soundtrack, a history in which we know every photograph to have a corresponding sound, a history in which synthetic sounds are *facts*.

Of course, photography is many things and serves many functions, and the medium's use in sound recording and reproduction would, if anything, seem to be indicative of as much. As the brief history I have sketched above suggests, that the optical soundtrack reproduces recorded sound photographically was largely a matter of convenience: yes, the optical soundtrack consists of photographs, but it is not photography per se—or, if it *is* photography, it is photography in the tradition of Étienne-Jules Marey's or Frank Gilbreth's motion studies, images that offer nothing aesthetically or psychologically, images that are instrumental and nothing more (or less). While André Bazin's "Ontology of the Photographic Image" begins by placing photography within a lineage of *visual* practices, sculpture and painting among them, an analogous genealogy of photographic sound would emphasize its *sonic* progenitors, beginning perhaps with hieroglyphs and cuneiform (both modes of converting oral speech into graphic inscription) and continuing onward to sound-reproduction technologies like the telephone, the loudspeaker, and the radio (all of which depend on a transducer, which, as Jonathan Sterne [2003: 22] notes, "turn sound into something else and that something else back into sound" [see also Butler 2015]).

But synthetic sound emerges in the 1920s, contemporaneous with new and often radical theorizations of the evidentiary capacities of photography and, by extension, cinematography. In keeping with what Devin Fore (2006: 129) has called the decade's "documentary episteme," avant-garde artists of the period repeatedly asserted that photographic media possess the unique power both to make visible the hitherto unseen and to fix facts precisely and objectively. To write my possibilist history of synthetic sound, I draw in particular on the work of the Soviet documentary filmmaker Dziga Vertov. While he in fact vehemently criticized at least two films that did utilize synthetic sound, he nonetheless provides the theoretical resources for imagining the technique's evidentiary potential, a documentary capacity that *might have been*. After all, as he explained in 1935, he first turned to filmmaking because of an experience he had had at a train station: "There lingered in my ears the sighs and rumble of the departing train . . . someone's swearing . . . a kiss . . . someone's exclamation . . . laughter, a whistle, voices, the ringing of the station bell, the puffing of the locomotive . . . whispers, cries, farewells." Hearing these disparate noises, trying to make sense of them, Vertov told himself, "I must . . . *photograph these sounds*" (1985: 40). In suggesting that synthetic sound might be incorporated into his cinematic enterprise, Vertov offers a radical media epistemology, extending the claims of documentary far beyond its familiar contours.

· · · ·

There are many things we cannot see unaided—some are too small or too large, others too far away or too abstract or too fleeting. We cannot see the future. We cannot see sounds or ultraviolet rays or philosophy. For Vertov, it is cinema that can be mobilized to enable us to see such objects, concepts, and processes for the first time. Vertov called his ideal cinematic apparatus the Kino-Eye, a technological prosthesis that would function not just as a motion-picture camera but also as an X-ray machine, microscope, television, and remote control. No cinematic technique was considered off-limits; in order to render "the invisible visible, the unclear clear, the hidden manifest, [and] the disguised overt" and to turn "falsehood into truth" (Vertov 1985: 41), the Kino-Eye might exploit rapid montage, superimposition, multiple exposures, freeze frames, and cutout animation. By deploying this battery of techniques, the Kino-Eye could visualize everything from complex mechanical operations to modes of production, from states of inebriation to global communism, from the routine to the magical. Through careful match cuts, workers scattered across the globe appear to meet one another's gaze; reverse motion brings a slaughtered bull back to life; scenes staged from extreme angles reconfigure space. Installments in Vertov's early newsreel series *Film Week* (*Kino-nedelya*, 1918–19) and *Film Truth* (*Kino-pravda*, 1922–25) recontextualize found footage in order to destabilize the source material's original intent, and his late silent masterpiece *Man with a Movie Camera* (*Chelovek s kinoapparatom*, 1929) contains stroboscopic sequences that erupt temporal relations both within the film and between the film and the viewer.

Advocating for the "sensory exploration of the world through film" (14), Vertov thought his camera could reveal a world that might not resemble at all the one we perceive. Writing in 1923, he ventriloquized the camera's perceptual abandon: "Now and forever, I free myself from human immobility, I am in constant motion, I draw near, then away from objects, I crawl under, I climb into them. I move apace with the muzzle of a galloping horse, I plunge full speed into a crowd, I outstrip running soldiers, I fall on my back, I ascend with an airplane, I plunge and soar together with plunging and soaring bodies" (17). The camera allows us to see the hitherto unseen. It can go places the human body cannot and can capture events that escape the human eye. These even include the thoughts of the people it shows: the camera can make visible the ultimate unknown, the minds of others.

Vertov anchors his theory of documentary in a very curious and, indeed, somewhat perplexing definition of the word *fact*, one that is as challenging conceptually as his films are perceptually. For Vertov, every frame of film that successfully captures life "unawares" is the representation of a fact. The truthfulness of the photographic image arises from the manner in which it was shot; while his contemporaries in the Soviet Union often worked with scripted and staged footage, Vertov's crew instead left the studio behind, assembling their films out of images "wrested from life" (88).

Thus, a filmic frame comes to constitute a fact because of conditions external to the represented content, namely, the conditions under which the content was captured. A photographic image attests not only to what is immediately visible to the film's spectator but also to all the information available to the cameraman at the moment of its original capture. Even though such a "fact taken from life" might not have its "name, date, place, and number . . . inscribed on the film," it nonetheless retains the specific *who, what, when,* and *where* of the thing depicted. Vertov offers an example of what he means: "A dog running by on the street is a visible fact, even if we don't catch up with it to read what's on its collar" (57).[9] The viewer, watching this footage months or even years after it was photographed, might be unable to determine the direction in which the dog was running or the precise breed or sex or age of the dog in question, but the image indexes—photographically and linguistically—this information.

Vertov here goes beyond a claim Christian Metz would make four decades later in his attempt to codify the language of cinema: "A close-up of a revolver does not mean 'revolver' (a purely lexical unit)," Metz writes, "but in the very least and without speaking of the connotations, it signifies 'Here is a revolver'" (1974: 67). In Vertov's schema, a close-up of a revolver would represent a specific fact: "Here is *this* revolver." Footage of a dog is of *that* dog. A shot of a person is of *that* person. Consider, for instance, a shot that appears in Vertov's *One-Sixth of the World* (*Shestaya chast mira,* 1926). A man, framed from the waist down, such that only his legs, snowshoes, and an expanse of white snow are visible, walks away from the camera, which gradually tilts upward to reveal the line of the tundra's horizon. The man is joined a couple seconds into his journey by a dog; the two of them then trudge into the distance, their shadows stretching out behind them. The image offers clues as to when and where it was shot, as the length, opacity, and relative position of their shadows suggest that dusk is approaching and that they are heading toward the occident. Moreover, their behavior leads us to take the man and beast to be companions, their bond distinctive and authentic. This moment has been captured from life, and not just any life, and not just any moment—its documentary value resides in its ability to

9. Vertov penned "The Same Thing from Different Angles" in response to Osip Brik, who had argued that Vertov's editing practices destroyed his films' "documentary quality." According to Brik, a "newsreel fact" might begin as "an individual, unrepeatable document" possessed of a "specific name, place, and time," but montage turns it into little more than "a blank space" (quoted in Tsivian 2005: 275–78).

present to us the irreducible, unvarnished, brute fact of *that* man, *that* dog, *that* tundra, *that* burgeoning twilight.

Such an account of photography seems naively indexical, indeed reductively so. It neglects to consider both the sorts of contextual clues (e.g., intertitles or voice-over narration) that might delimit how we are to interpret a visual fact and, as Metz suggests, the potential connotations that open up the image to generic and symbolic readings.[10] Many of Vertov's contemporaries, including Eisenstein and Osip Brik, criticized his films for exactly this reason.[11] Moreover, the casual viewer has no means of knowing the exact time or place this shot was filmed, nor any facts about, for instance, the dog itself. In a review of *One-Sixth of the World* written in 1926, Viktor Shklovsky complains the "factual nature of the shot" has all but disappeared from Vertov's work: "In this film we learned with interest that in one place they bathe sheep in the sea's breakers, and in another they bathe them in the river. This is very interesting, and the breakers are well shot, but where they are shot is not precisely established" ([1936] 1988: 153). In spite of these objections, Vertov would nonetheless contend that the shot retains all of this information, even if it is not communicated to the audience.

However, the intertitle that precedes the shot in question would seem to totally evacuate the image of superfluous information. An apostrophizing poem repeatedly punctuates the documentary footage of *One-Sixth of the World*, its fragmentary phrases often directly addressed to the facts we see on screen. In this instance, the prefatory intertitle introduces the man as, "someone, disappearing into the icy unknown distance." In other words, there is no mention of the dog, and the "someone" goes unidentified—and so, too, do the precise coordinates of the "distance." The image assumes a poetic power, speaking in generalities—indeed, in uncertainties—of the unknown and even the unknowable. This person's documentary meaning is divorced from the particularities of the reality from which his image was wrested. Practice betrays theory.

As this example from *One-Sixth of the World* demonstrates, Ver-

10. For a detailed (but still not exhaustive) breakdown of a single photograph's manifold meanings, see Branigan 2006: 66–67.
11. As Sergei Drobashenko writes, "Eisenstein accused Vertov's films of having insufficient purposeful intention in commenting upon the filmed event" (1972: 65). Brik criticized *The Eleventh Year* for its lack of "motivation for the film material . . . shots unravel, reach out towards their basic pieces of footage, and the intertitle dangles over them without uniting them at all" (quoted in Tsivian 2005: 310–11).

Figures 4a and 4b A visible fact as it appears twice in *One-Sixth of the World* (dir. Dziga Vertov, 1926). The second instance is at least one print generation removed from the first, as evidenced by its higher contrast.

tov's belief in the facticity of the photographic image is ultimately untenable, particularly insofar as it fails to account for meanings external to the individual photographic image. That a slightly different version of the same shot then reappears later in the same film would seem only to compound matters. The two shots derive from the same footage, but they differ in three key respects (Figures 4a and 4b). The second iteration is preceded by an extended sequence showcasing antiquated religious practices and totems (rosaries, shamans, ritual sacrifices), and a pair of intertitles then reinforces the shot's metaphorical function: "The old [ways] depart slowly . . . / like you who departs into the icy unknown." The shot as it then appears begins several frames before the first one did, with the man's legs closer to the camera, and concludes several seconds earlier, well before the camera tilts up high enough to reveal the line of the horizon. Finally, it is clear that the second version is at least one print generation removed from the first. Its blacks are blacker, its whites whiter, its grays obliterated, and with this higher contrast comes a loss in detail: no longer visible are the pockmarks in the snow, the snowshoe's straps on the man's thighs, the lighter patches of the dog's fur. This is a rephotographed image, its salient content degraded; it has not been wrested from life but instead from an earlier photograph.

I do not point this out in order to claim that Vertov is wrong. Rather, I wish to highlight the consistent epistemological challenge the Kino-Eye poses to its viewers. The ostensible indexicality of the image, its irreducible oneness with the reality it captures, is constantly obfuscated, unmoored, ravaged by the Kino-Eye's radical reimagining of the world. It is possible, of course, that Vertov's logic is simply inconsistent, if not downright incoherent. Can Vertov really believe that photographs maintain a necessary connection to their referent if he elsewhere boasts of splicing together "twelve walls shot . . . in various parts of the world" (1985: 17) into a single coherent room? Why harp on the individual shot's facticity if he ultimately seeks to construct a fictitious space out of discrete spaces, a false whole out of factual fragments? But the virtuosity of the Kino-Eye in the end is not at odds with the brute facts it exposes—quite the opposite. Formal manipulation has its own revelatory capacity, one that springs from but eventually exceeds the strict indexicality of the photographic image. And although Vertov's dense, prolix compositions might seem at first obscure or puzzling, the Kino-Eye treats such epistemological overload as the very object of its inquiry; it confounds human vision in order to augment human knowledge.[12] For Vertov, the image is an index because it focuses our attention—one of the very definitions offered by Charles Sanders Peirce ("Anything which startles us is an index," as he puts it [1955: 108–9]). Indeed, the Kino-Eye startles us, shocks us, incites us to wonder about cause and effect—what does *this* have to do with *that*?

One of the most indelible images of *Man with a Movie Camera* is a superimposition that places the titular cinematographer inside a mug of beer (Figure 5). The image plays with the parameters of cinematic representation: scale (has the man shrunk or the mug grown?), surfaces (is he inside the mug or behind it?), synchronicity (is this a single moment in time or two discrete moments that we happen to be looking at simultaneously?), and so on. It is a funny image, as well as a profound and surprising one, an image only the Kino-Eye is capable of. "I decipher in a new way a world unknown to you," one of Vertov's early manifestos declares. The Kino-Eye not only deciphers an unknown world, it deciphers it in a new way, a way that, too, is unknown: uncertainty is Vertov's radical epistemology. The Kino-Eye intends to disarm the audience, to confuse, to overwhelm. In the words of Annette Michelson, it inaugurates "*a crisis of belief*" (Michelson 1975: 108). What are we seeing? *How do we know?*

• • • •

Now imagine printing that footage of the man and dog from *One-*

12. For the definitive account of Vertov's "theory of film as epistemological inquiry," see Michelson 1975.

Figure 5 The man with a movie camera in a mug of beer. *Man with a Movie Camera Camera* (dir. Dziga Vertov, 1929).

Sixth of the World on the optical soundtrack. When run through a projector, the sounds that series of frames would produce would not sound *like* a man or *like* a dog. Instead of barking or howling or whimpering, for instance, the film would let loose a terrifying, unnameable cacophony—blasts emanating from an unknown distance. If we did not know how the soundtrack had been produced, we would be unable to name the source of the sound— certainly not man or beast, we'd think. We'd lack more than just the inability to read the dog's collar or distinguish between its gray and black patches— we would not be able to sense the dog at all. But, if Vertov is right, then the viewer's knowledge, or absence thereof, does not alter the bald truth of the sound. Whether we know it or not, we are hearing *that* dog.

This example returns us to the central aim of this article: to explore the documentary potential of synthetic sound, and the crisis of reference it entails—one which bears resemblance to what happened with digital photography decades later. To hear a soundtrack we know to have been synthesized inaugurates a crisis in belief analogous to that produced by the

Kino-Eye: *What are we hearing?* The effect is strange, the cause unknown. What is epistemologically troubling is that this question can be asked even of synthetic sounds that simulate known sounds—for example, those that operate like traditional sound effects. *Sure*, we think, *that certainly sounds like a dog. But* is *it a dog?* Such questions lead us to doubt the veracity of not just synthetic sound, but all filmic sound. *How do we know?*

As it turns out, *all* film sound, no matter its origins, fundamentally exploits our credulity: we believe what we hear. The uncertainty to which synthetic sound exposes us betrays a larger crisis: the ambiguity inherent to any recorded sound. Sound speaks in generalities, not specifics, a problem clearly articulated by the film theorist Béla Balázs: "A farmhouse may at a pinch be represented by voices of animals. But even then the listener will not be able to say whether the mooing of cows, neighing of horses, crowing of cocks, cackling of hens, barking of dogs is a sound picture of some bucolic farm or of a livestock market. Even recognizable sounds merely indicate the generality of the things they stand for" (1970: 204). The art of foley, not least, depends on such constitutive ambiguity. Sound, whether recorded in the street or in the studio, tells us only broad facts. We cannot be sure of the specifics of what we are hearing: a person, maybe *that* person, but where? And when? Should we somehow recognize the sound of someone's voice in a recording, perhaps detect a hint of sadness or the roar of an airplane overhead, even the most discerning ear would be hard pressed to identify anything else about what the recording represents.

A listener would thus be right to doubt her ears. A significant subset of sound experiments was devoted to analyzing preexisting soundtracks in order to produce voices that had never been uttered. Here the desire was to produce a recognizable effect, indeed, an effect so recognizable as to be indistinguishable from actual—factual—voices. Both Josef von Sternberg and Rouben Mamoulian worked for Paramount Studios in the 1930s, and in all likelihood they learned of synthetic sound from the American animation producers Max and Dave Fleischer, the brothers behind Betty Boop, Popeye, and Superman. Dave Fleischer had discovered the technique in late 1920s, independently of his contemporaries in Germany and the Soviet Union, and filed a patent for the process.[13] In an interview conducted in the late 1960s, he offered a version of his eureka moment:

13. According Leslie Carbaga, a historian of the Fleischer Brothers, Dave showed off his invention to the producers of Paramount, who subsequently "bought the patent for a large sum" (1976: 52).

I looked at the film and saw that the sound track was nothing but photographic striations. I wondered, "Why can't I draw sound?" So I [drew] a man saying, "What is it?" I copied that from a piece of film—but I didn't trace it. Then I photographed it and when I ran the film through a Moviola, it spoke. So it actually was *a drawing that was speaking*; it was not the original voice that was put on film. So I patented that. However, that patent is probably useless until maybe five hundred years from now, when they'll be able to analyze the values of those striations. If they know what each striation means, they can write a whole orchestra without hiring anybody. (Fleischer 1969; emphasis added)

For commercial producers like Fleischer, as well as for Hollywood directors like Sternberg and Mamoulian, synthetic sound offered a simple solution to critical economic concerns. An article in *Popular Mechanics* on Fleischer's process noted that it would allow the studio to dispense "with paid entertainers, costly orchestras, [sound recording] studios and elaborate machinery," saving a tremendous amount in overhead costs (see Anon 1931). A mere stroke of the pen would give Betty Boop her voice. The listener, meanwhile, would be none the wiser. Fleischer's plan capitalizes on the fallibility of our hearing in order to present "false" sounds as true. Synthetic sound thus tests the limits not only of cinematic epistemology but also of the human sense organs, particularly our ears.

• • • •

With these limitations in mind, most filmmakers of the period resisted treating sound as radically as they did the image. In the hierarchy of the senses, they held sight to have primacy. "The human eye is capable of perceiving, easily and immediately, the content of a succession of visual shots," Vsevolod Pudovkin acknowledges. "The ear," on the other hand, "cannot with the same immediacy detect the significance of alterations in sound" (1949: 167). We can see cuts, we can see rapid montage, but we cannot hear the sutures in a soundtrack; we can recognize animated cartoon characters as animated cartoon characters, but when we hear graphic inscriptions on the optical soundtrack, we have no idea what we are hearing; we can distinguish between a dachshund and a collie filmed running down the street, but the bark of one could easily stand in for the bark of the other.

Vertov did not recognize such limitations. Importantly, he maintained that "audible facts" have the same one-to-one correspondence with their source as visible facts do with their referent. In that respect, he departs significantly from his peers. In several essays and speeches, he explicitly argues for treating sound exactly as he does the image—an equation that would entail a profound equivalence between the knowledge afforded by sight and the knowledge afforded by hearing. A camera can rove in one direction, the microphone in the opposite; their disparate movements might then be yoked on a filmstrip with an optical soundtrack. Who knows what we might see? Who knows what we might hear? Vertov promoted his first sound film, *Enthusiasm: Symphony of the Donbass* (*Entuziazm: Sinfoniia donbassa*, 1931), as "the first freeing of the microphone from its immure-ment within the studio walls, and the leading of it into the actual hustle and bustle of the open" (*Film Society Programmes* 1972: 194). Believing, as John MacKay has argued, in the "potential comprehensibility of all sound" (2005: 7), no matter how noisy, Vertov sent his microphone to parades and rallies, under trains, and up coal elevators. The soundtrack, like the filmstrip, can and should be subjected to manipulation: reversed, sped up, edited frame by frame. The two components might synch up, or they might not; men might be given voices, but so might statues. Many commentators, taking Vertov at his word, have affirmed that he treats vision and hearing as analogous, even interchangeable: the Kino-Eye can readily fuse with the so-called Radio-Ear to become the *Radio-Eye*.[14]

The making of *Enthusiasm* was predicated on this belief. As he explained in one speech, he aimed to turn each of its audience members into "the worker in the Donbass, [for whom] every sound has a specific meaning; for him there are no 'noises'" (quoted in MacKay 2005: 4). But to teach an audience to hear—and to *know* through hearing—is no easy task. Most of Vertov's contemporaries in the Soviet Union were dismayed by the industrial cacophony he orchestrated in *Enthusiasm*. Among them was Avraamov, who had his own vision for what the documentary should have sounded like. "*The Symphony of the Donbass* should and can be written," he wrote, "not by documenting clanks and creaks or the deafening roars of 'industrial noise,' but with the new palette of timbres" (1932: 46). The timbres

14. Lucy Fischer, for instance, states that "Vertov's conception of Cinema-Eye [*sic*] applies exactly to his notion of Radio-Eye; what holds for his theory of cinematic visuals applies to his theory of cinematic sound as well" (1985: 250). Oksana Bulgakowa, mean-while, describes *Enthusiasm* as rewiring "the circuits of perception" such that the "eye and the ear exchange places" (2008: 151).

Avraamov had in mind were those afforded by synthetic sound. Another of Vertov's adversaries, the Soviet film critic Ippolit Sokolov, argued that documentary films should privilege sonic intelligibility over supposed fidelity. For Sokolov, the audience must immediately understand what they are hearing. This means they must be able to follow both the cadences and the content of the spoken word, as well as to name the putative source of a given sound—even if the source is, in fact, staged or synthetic. To assure that the sonic event is recorded without interference, then, Sokolov declared that "scientific films [should] be produced not in the lap of nature, not in the noise of the streets, but within the soundproof walls of the film studio, where no outside sound can penetrate" (quoted in Kahn 1999: 143).

But Sokolov's proposal is trickery, at least according to Vertov's criteria. Its sounds are not wrested from life but manufactured in the studio. The sounds of *Enthusiasm* might be unintelligible—"a cat concert," "chaos," "plain nonsense," "colossal nothing"—but that does not make them meaningless.[15] Vertov intended for *Enthusiasm* to demand the fullest concentration of his audience: he wanted to startle them into attention. Forced to make sense out of sonic disarray, they would learn to understand through hearing. By experiencing the noises that steelworkers and coal miners hear every day, his listeners would come to know these sounds as the audible facts they are: the din of a faraway factory would become as familiar as one's own breath, the bleats of a power plant as natural as a beating heart.[16]

What Vertov does not account for, however, is that there seems to be a limit to even the most specialized knowledge. Is it possible to train the ear to recognize a sound's *specific* source? A worker in the Donbass might be able to diagnose a particular clank or creak, but can he tell which *particular* machine it emanated from? A 1933 profile of a Hollywood sound technician points to the outer bounds of what sound alone reveals: "Owls hoot differently in various parts of the country, the whistle of a San Francisco ferry sounds nothing like the blast of a North River boat; the heavy roar of a tri-motored bomber does not resemble the staccato whine of a pursuit plane to the educated ear; the sound of footsteps in the snow varies greatly according to the snow's temperature, and so on, *ad infinitum*" (Ergenbright 1933: 33). What goes unstated in this litany is that the whistle of one San Francisco ferry will do just as well as the whistle of another, and that the whine of

---

15. These phrases were included in the promotional material for *Enthusiasm*'s screening at the London Film Society (*Film Society Programmes* 1972: 194).
16. I am here paraphrasing Vertov (2004: 136).

any given pursuit plane is sufficient to denote the general category of "pursuit plane." Furthermore, "the sound of footsteps in the snow"—supposedly so specific to the snow itself—can in fact be accurately replicated by treading on "a large leather sack with a compound of alum and cornstarch" (78), which is just what the sound technician is described as doing later in the same article.

Perhaps this is the ultimate failure of our powers of hearing, making us easy prey for fakery conjured up in the studio—or equally in postproduction. In that case, Vertov's implicit criticism of Sokolov and Avraamov would be correct: synthetic sound would be no different from traditional sound effects. Perhaps, then, synthetic sound cannot be documentary sound.

We have reached, it would appear, the limit of sonic epistemology. But Vertov himself holds that such limits must be tested—and, in so testing them, there might then emerge a case for synthetic sound's documentary function. For instance, take Sokolov's condemnation of the distortions produced by the indiscriminate microphone. "A fly buzzing too close to a microphone drowns out an express train," he writes. "A lump of sugar dropping into a teacup produces the impression of an exploding shell" (Sokolov 1929). What Sokolov perceives to be the microphone's failings could instead be interpreted as its very powers: much as the microscope and the telescope reveal surprising affinities between cellular structures and the cosmos, so the microphone lets us "enlarge" the sound of a fly such that we are able to hear its resemblance to the locomotive. Sound technology uncovers homologies we would not attend to otherwise. Walter Benjamin remarks that the close-up photographs of plants by Karl Blossfeldt "[reveal] the forms of ancient columns in horse willow, a bishop's crosier in the ostrich fern, totem poles in tenfold enlargements of chestnut and maple shoots, and gothic tracery in the fuller's thistle" (1999: 512); similarly, the microphone reveals the sugar cube in the bombshell and the cornstarch in the snow. The knowledge we obtain through sound technology is specialized in its own way, enabling us to hear sonic affinities that defy how we had previously organized the world. This had always been the promise of the Kino-Eye: "the creation of a fresh perception of the world" (Vertov 1985: 18).

Still, where synthetic sound fits in this scheme is not immediately obvious. After all, Vertov would himself reject the practice, criticizing Eisenstein and Aleksandrov's *Romance Sentimentale* for its "delicate, Western, flowery" sounds (quoted in MacKay 2005: 4) and expressing disdain for Avraamov's synthetic score for Abram Room's (now lost) documentary *Plan for Great Works (Five-Year Plan)* (*Plan velikikh rabot [Piatiletka]*, 1930)—he was perturbed by how it "squeezed" documentary sounds "inside the prison of an acoustically isolated studio," where editors then "tattooed it with artificial toy-sounds" (Vertov 1930; see Smirnov 2013: 167). In part, synthetic sound presents a direct challenge to the listener, who cannot readily determine what she is hearing. This was the very challenge that the Kino-Eye presented for the viewer; this, too, was the challenge of *Enthusiasm*'s "nonsensical" soundtrack.

Of course, synthetic sound is even more epistemologically fraught than the dissonance of *Enthusiasm*. All the listener knows for sure is that *something* produced what she is hearing. Yet despite Vertov's rejection of synthetic sound, his theories of the Kino-Eye and of documentary facts together give us the tools for discussing synthetic sound's documentary value. In searching for that something, in trying to determine what she is hearing, the listener is forcibly reminded that every technologically reproduced sound, be it synthetic or recorded, corresponds to a mark, just as every mark corresponds to a sound. The sound is an index, and as an index, it indicates—it specifies. This, in turn, unsettles our perception of sound's generality: all the sounds we hear, no matter how alien, have a potential and particular referent. A sound, any sound, is a fact, even if we don't know it yet.

. . . .

Synthetic sound, like the phonograph record before it, awakens us to the world around us, a world pregnant with sound, as well as to the sounds that reproduce that world. The question remains, however, what we can learn from synthetic sound. How can its facts, such as they are, reshape our experience? Here Jean Epstein's writings on sound provide the bridge between sonic experimentation and the audience's aural experience.

Like Vertov, Epstein did not dabble in synthetic sound, but his writings on what he called "slow-motion" sound share important sympathies with the theories of Avraamov and Moholy-Nagy. Epstein initially sought a sonic analogy to the cinematographic close-up, through which, he believed, "the most alluring falsehoods lose their force while the truth bursts forth on first sight, strikes the spectator with the unexpectedness of the evident, and arouses an aesthetic emotion, a sense of infallible wonderment and pleasure" (Abel 1993, 1:192). This wonderment is key. By slowing down sound, the filmmaker grants the listener a new understanding of the world:

"In detailing and separating noises, creating a sort of close-up of sound, sonic deceleration may make it possible for all beings, all objects to speak. The mistranslation of Latin scholars, who had Lucretius say that things cry, will thus become an audible truth. We can already see, we will soon hear the grass grow" (Keller and Paul 2012: 382). Epstein's invocation of the "audible truth" attests to the documentary function he invests in slow-motion sound. But just as significant is his faith in cinema to expose sounds that have been all around us all along. Epstein's theory of slow-motion sound provides a variation on the daydreams of Rilke, Moholy-Nagy, and Avraamov, in which sound technology provides unprecedented access to everyday phenomena. As early as 1930, he fantasized about making the unknown known:

> Now, we want to hear what the ear doesn't hear, just as through the cinema we see what eludes the eye. Let nothing be silent any more! Let thoughts and dreams be audible! There are murmurs which trouble the eardrum and cries which sing out that we cannot grow tired of. Let the secrets of their eloquence be wrenched from the foliage and the waves; let them be torn to pieces so that we can reconstruct them into voices more true to life than natural sounds! . . . We will uncoil cyclones in the cradle, and every child will hear the grass growing. (quoted in Abel 1993, 1: 67–68)

There is poetry and humor here, coupled with the poignancy that underlies any utopian fantasy. His final statement—"every child will hear the grass growing"—anticipates not only his later essay but also the mysticism of the American avant-garde filmmaker Stan Brakhage, who would famously wonder, "How many colors are there in a field of grass to the crawling baby unaware of 'Green'?" (2001: 12). Both filmmakers imagine a realm of knowledge unconstrained by set categories. A chestnut shoot contains a totem pole; flies and express trains buzz in unison. Even the senses are no longer divided into separate modes of perception. Things cry and thoughts speak. Vertov, too, spoke of the possibility of recording human thought through synaesthetic means: the "montage of visible-audible facts" would lead toward "the montage simultaneously of visible-audible-tangible-olfactory and so on facts," and from there "to the filming unawares of human thoughts" (quoted in Tsivian 2005: 319). What constitutes a fact, or a potential fact, is seemingly limitless.

• • • •

Synthetic sound enlarges the possibilities that had once been sought in the phonograph, in part because it broadens the field of experimentation. Filmmakers could readily proceed through trial and error: What will *this* sound like? And what might *that* sound like? Synthetic sound was experimental for audiences, as well, who did not have access to the visible inscriptions on the optical soundtrack. In other words, they could not see the sound before hearing it. For such an audience, the question is not "How will this sound?" but rather "What is *that* sound?" Here the etymological connection between *experimental* and *experiential* is pertinent, in that the audience is experiencing a sound they have never heard before and then trying to determine its source. This, again, is wonder—the same wonder as that engendered by Avraamov's "most fantastic sounds" and by Moholy-Nagy's "new, hitherto unknown sounds and tonal relations," a wonder that moves between fascination and fantasizing, between insight and inspiration.[17] Synthetic sound, like the phonograph record before it, awakens us to the world around us, a world pregnant with sound, as well as to the sounds that reproduce that world. As the narrator of Adolfo Bioy Casares's fantastic novel *The Invention of Morel* suggests, perhaps every sensory perception is primarily spatial, not temporal, and thus "somewhere the image, the touch, and the voice of those who are no longer alive must still exist" (1964: 78). The repeated invocation of the "hitherto unknown" becomes the germ of an unrealized history. In it one discovers, as Tom Gunning has said of early cinema more broadly, "the shards of a future discarded or disavowed," a future rich with untapped potential (1995: 467).

Let us remember, too, the central role of photography in the creation the optical soundtrack: whether a hieroglyph or a body part, an object must first be photographed in order to be heard. While Rilke had dreamed of playing the skull itself, in turn inviting us to think of *things* as sonic containers, the optical soundtrack gives us instead the sounds of *images*; it treats all patterns as graphic inscriptions. On the optical soundtrack, the line is the same as a circle, a circle is the same as a vase, a vase is the same as the ancient hieroglyph impressed on its surface, an ancient hieroglyph is the same as a letter of the alphabet, a letter of the alphabet is the same as the waveform that corresponds to the articulation of that letter of the alphabet. The optical soundtrack is unprejudiced. It just as easily turns abstraction (the marking on the soundtrack) into representation (a recognizable sound)

---

17. It is not a coincidence that Avraamov's experiments were guided by the synaesthetic writings of the Russian Futurist Velimir Khlebnikov, who referred to his poetry as *zaum*; through acts of linguistic creation and exploration, Khlebnikov wanted to reach *through rationality* or *beyond sense*. For more on the relationship between Avraamov and Khlebnikov, see Izvolov 2005: 130–41.

as it does representation (a photographic image) into abstraction (an unfamiliar noise). Moreover, it maintains the sneaking suspicion that we are now and have always been surrounded by unheard sounds, but it also brings with it all the powers ascribed to the medium of photography.

Its photographic basis means that Epstein's wish to hear the sound of grass growing can be cleverly fulfilled: just print a time-lapse photographic sequence of the growth of grass on the optical soundtrack. As with the hypothetical dog—the visible fact cited by Vertov that we can turn into an audible fact by rephotographing it onto the soundtrack—this form of synthetic sound is fundamentally synaesthetic. The optical soundtrack, as its name promises, has made sound visible, and we use it in order to hear images.

Mamoulian, for one, employed this particular mode of sonic synthesis in the sequence from *Dr. Jekyll and Mr. Hyde*. Just as Vertov purports to show "that which the eye doesn't see," so *Dr. Jekyll and Mr. Hyde* reverberates with what the ear cannot hear (1985: 41). In both cases, epistemological uncertainty is taken not as constraint but as an unexplored frontier. That "immediate reality" he produced did not discriminate between recorded sound and synthetic sound. Both are equal on the optical soundtrack, which flattens all sounds, regardless of their origins, into a single pattern. The optical soundtrack likewise homogenizes what we might think of as two discrete categories of synthetic sound: graphic or drawn sound (such as Moholy-Nagy's letters of the alphabet or Fleischer's "What is it?") and photographic sound (such as Mamoulian's flickering candle). One is manual, the other mechanical; one is constructed, the other represents. This amounts to the ontological differences between paintings and photographs or between animation and cinema, as it is commonly rehearsed: as Sean Cubitt succinctly phrases it, "Photographic frames reproduce, but animated frames produce" (2004: 92).

A media difference again suggests itself. Yet what I've been arguing is for a kind of convergence: both categories of synthetic sound are *documentary* sound.

• • • •

This is what Vertov grasped, that even the most abstract photograph could constitute a fact. "Long live *dynamic geometry*, the race of points, lines, planes, volumes," Vertov writes in one of his early manifestos, implying he has in mind something like the abstract animated films of Hans Rich-

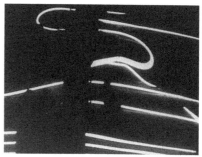

Figures 6a and 6b Representation turns into abstraction in *Enthusiasm: Symphony of the Don Basin* (dir. Dziga Vertov, 1931).

ter, Viking Eggeling, or Walter Ruttmann (1985: 9).[18] While the Kino-Eye takes from it life, it ultimately realizes "what cannot be realized in life" (9). It makes animate—it *animates*. Vertov would chase the clarity of geometric shapes in motion throughout his career. Several passages in *Enthusiasm* become plays of pure line; multiple exposures turn a view of railroad tracks into a cascade of diagonals, and high-contrast cinematography obliterates the human form from the image, leaving in sight only a glowing, snaking rod of molten steel (Figures 6a and b).

Most often, however, Vertov fulfills the call for dynamic geometry through animated titles, which function both graphically and linguistically. Their simplified forms and concentrated slogans underline what might otherwise go overlooked and clarify what might otherwise be murky. Animation allows Vertov to illustrate concepts (i.e., generalities). He reduces an idea to its essence while also expanding it into a maxim. Thus, we understand the hinged paper cutouts in the anti-alcohol exhortation in *Kino-Eye* (1924) as representing not specific characters but rather general "types"; likewise, the animated diagram of a radio receiver in the same film represents not one receiver in particular but rather the general workings of a category of receiver. That is, Vertov does not treat animation as he does photography. The latter is specific, the former generic. Yet the two modes share a revelatory capacity, and it is this capacity that is most salient: animation and photography both show us what we cannot see. A survey of animation techniques, written in 1926 by two American filmmakers, touches briefly on

18. Richter's *Rhythmus 21* (1921), for instance, is composed solely of rectangles of black and white.

this aspect of the form's documentary power: "The operation of machinery can be shown as by no other means. Drawings of interiors of blast furnaces, steam engines, flow of electric current, the operation of the vacuum tube, astronomical theories, Einstein's theory and hundreds of other things screened from human eyes and the understanding of most humans have been depicted in animation" (Leventhal and Norling 1926: 61). Animation and photography alike make the invisible visible. The authors' mention of Einstein's theory of relativity is especially telling: Vertov says of the Kino-Eye that it is "the theory of relativity on screen" (1985: 41). The knowledge animation provides might differ in kind from that provided by photography, but the two are united in service of the Kino-Eye's larger epistemological project.

Imagine, then: Vertov could have stippled on the soundtrack the "race of points, lines, planes, volumes" he pursued in his animated images. Through multiple exposures, he could have turned documentary images ("facts") into abstract zigzags and then transposed this photographic source material onto the optical soundtrack. Instead of using a telegraph and asynchronous sound-image editing to make a miner bleat Morse code, as he does in *Enthusiasm*, he could have drawn those dot-dot-dashes directly onto the optical soundtrack.[19]

In the 1910s, Vertov had attempted to transcribe the sounds he heard issuing from a sawmill. "In the beginning I used words to record the sounds, but then I attempted to capture all of these different noises with letters," he later remembered. But he had come up short. "The existing alphabet did not suffice to write down all of the sounds that you hear in a sawmill" (quoted in Bulgakowa 2008: 145). With the optical soundtrack, he could have slowed down the unchartered world of the sawmill's sounds and heard the multiplicities that reside within a single second. He could have studied the visual transcriptions of those sounds and created his own alphabet of waveforms. He could have written down all the sounds he heard in the sawmill and then all the sounds he heard when this transcription was played back to him: a truly dynamic geometry.

. . . .

What is now silent will be heard. What is now noisy will be understood. All around us is as yet unknown sound. Some of it we do not com-

---

19. For an analysis of the use of sound in this sequence, see Fore 2010.

prehend—it clanks, it creaks. Some of it distorts the familiar—a sugar cube explodes against the side of a teacup. Some of it we now can only see—a dog, a man, an icy expanse. Some of it lies in abeyance, inaudible until the snow melts or the skin around the skull decomposes.

These are examples of what Peirce would call "buried secrets," remote considerations that seem to make no practical difference in how we live our lives. Another such secret that fascinates Peirce involves the way that Aristotle spoke: while it is a commonly held belief, affirmed by several biographers, that Aristotle had rhotacism—the inability to pronounce his R's—this belief does not quite qualify as *knowledge*, in that we cannot test its veracity for ourselves. Even so, Peirce does not want to surrender this belief. He still holds out the expectation that it might one day be proven: "Give science only a hundred more centuries of increase in geometrical progression, and she may be expected to find that the sound waves of Aristotle's voice have somehow recorded themselves" (1978: 383).[20] Peirce imagines—*believes in*—a future in which the past will be revealed, and hence he lives in a present redolent with expectation.

Is it a fact that Aristotle spoke like Elmer Fudd? Can we ever know whether a particular flower bloomed and died even if no one smelled it or whether a stone glistens at the very bottom of the ocean? But Peirce wants to, needs to, *does* imagine that all these secrets only *probably* make no difference; he cannot foreclose the possibility "that that stone *may* be fished up tomorrow":

> Do these things not really exist because they are hopelessly beyond the reach of our knowledge? . . . Who can be sure of what we shall not know in a few hundred years? Who can guess what would be the result of continuing the pursuit of science for ten thousand years, with the activity of the last hundred? And if it were to go on for a million, or a billion, or any number of years you please, how is it possible to say that there is any question which might not ultimately be solved? (1955: 39–40)

Synthetic sound poses these same riddles. What is hidden will be made manifest and what is buried will be unearthed. Flowers and stones will cry. A synthetic voice asks, "What is it?" And one day—now, soon, in five hundred years—we will have an answer. We will know the hitherto unknown.

20. John Durham Peters reflects beautifully on this passage in several essays. See Peters 2004: 194; 1999: 162; and 2003.

References

Abel, Richard, ed. 1993. *French Film Theory and Criticism: A History/Anthology.* 2 vols. Princeton, NJ: Princeton University Press.

Adams, Mike. 2012. *Lee de Forest: King of Radio, Television, and Film.* New York: Springer.

Alarcón, Miguel Molina, ed. 2008. *Baku: Symphony of Sirens; Sound Experiments in the Russian Avant-Garde.* London: ReR Megacorp.

Anon. 1930. "Ries Sound-Film Patent Is Basic, Claimed." *Motion Picture News* 42, no. 1: 21, 30–33.

———. 1931. "With the Unpaid Stars of the Movies: How Artificial Voices Are Given Film Funnies." *Popular Mechanics* 56, no. 1: 8–12.

Atkins, Thomas R. 1973. "Dr. Jekyll and Mr. Hyde: An Interview with Rouben Mamoulian." *Film Journal* 2, no. 2: 36–43.

Avraamov, Arsenii. 1932. "Sintonfil'm" (Synth-Sound film). *Proletarskoe Kino* 7 (July).

———. 1939. "Sinteticheskaia muzika" (Synthesized music). *Sovestkaia muzika* 8.

———. 2007. "Griaduschaia muzikalnaia nauka i novaia era istorii muziki" (The future musical science and a new era of music history). In *Ars Novyi*, edited by Sergei Rumiantsev. Moscow: Deka-VS.

Balázs, Béla. 1970. *Theory of the Film: Character and Growth of a New Art,* translated by Edith Bone. New York: Dover.

Benjamin, Walter. 1999. "Little History of Photography." In *Selected Writings, Volume 2: 1927–1934,* edited by Michael W. Jennings, 507–30. Cambridge, MA: Belknap Press of Harvard University Press.

Bioy Casares, Adolfo. 1964. *The Invention of Morel.* New York: New York Review of Books.

Blake, E. W., Jr. 1878. "ART. VII.—A Method of Recording Articulate Vibrations by Means of Photography." *American Journal of Science and Arts (1820–1879)* 16, no. 91: 54–59.

Brakhage, Stan. 2001. "Metaphors on Vision." In *Essential Brakhage: Selected Writings on Filmmaking,* edited by Bruce McPherson, 12–71. Kingston, NY: McPherson.

Branigan, Edward. 2006. *Projecting a Camera: Language-Games in Film Theory.* London: Routledge.

Bulgakowa, Oksana. 2008. "The Ear Against the Eye: Vertov's Symphony." *Kieler Beiträge zur Filmmusikforschung* 2: 142–58.

Butler, Shane. 2015. *The Ancient Phonograph.* New York: Zone Books.

Cage, John. 1967. *Silence: Lectures and Writings.* Middletown, CT: Wesleyan University Press.

Carbaga, Leslie. 1976. *The Fleischer Story.* New York: Crown.

Corbella, Maurizio, and Anna Windisch. 2013. "Sound Synthesis, Representation and Narrative Cinema in the Transition to Sound (1926–1935)." *Cinémas: Revue d'études cinématographiques* 24, no. 1: 59–81.

Cowen, Rob. 2015. "Ghostly Voices from Thomas Edison's Dolls Can Now Be Heard." *New York Times*, May 4, 2015.

Cubitt, Sean. 2004. *The Cinema Effect*. Cambridge, MA: MIT Press.

Drobashenko, Sergei. 1972. *Fenomen dostovernosti* (Phenomenon of authenticity). Moscow: Akademiia nauk SSSR.

Elsaesser, Thomas. 1999. "'Le cinéma d'après Lumière': Rereading the 'Origins' of the Filmic Image." In *The Practice of Cultural Analysis: Exposing Interdisciplinary Interpretation*, edited by Mieke Bal and Bryan Gonzales, 60–74. Palo Alto, CA: Stanford University Press.

Ergenbright, Eric. 1933. "You Can't Believe Your Ears." *New Movie Magazine* 8, no. 3: 32–33, 78–79.

Film Society Programmes, 1925–1939. 1972. New York: Arno.

Fischer, Lucy. 1985. "Enthusiasm: From Kino-Eye to Radio-Eye." In *Film Sound: Theory and Pratice*, edited by Elisabeth Weis and John Belton, 247–64. New York: Columbia University Press.

Fleischer, Dave. 1932. "Method of Marking Films for Producing Sound Effects." US Patent 1,888,914, filed 1929, and issued November 22, 1932.

———. 1969. Interview by Joe Adamson. Box 11, folder 98–99, John Canemaker Animation Collection, MSS 040. Fales Library and Special Collections, New York University.

Fore, Devin. 2006. "The Operative Word in Soviet Factography." *October* 118: 95–131.

———. 2010. "Dziga Vertov: The First Shoemaker of Russian Cinema." *Configurations* 18, no. 2: 363–82.

Fritts, Charles E. 1916. "Recording and Reproduction of Pulsations or Variations in Sounds and Other Phenomena." US Patent 1,203,190, filed October 22, 1880, and issued October 31, 1916, pp. 1, 15.

Gunning, Tom. 1995. "Animated Pictures: Tales of Cinema's Forgotten Future." *Michigan Quarterly Review* 34, no. 4: 465–85.

Higham, Charles, and Joel Greenberg. 1969. *The Celluloid Muse: Hollywood Directors Speak*. Chicago: Angus and Robertson.

Izvolov, Nikolai. 2005. *Fenomen kino: istoriia i teoriia* (The phenomenon of cinema: History and theory). Moscow: Materik.

———. 2014. "From the History of Graphic Sound in the Soviet Union; or, Media without a Medium." In *Sound, Speech, Music in Soviet and Post-Soviet Cinema*, edited by Lilya Kaganovsky and Masha Salazkina, translated by Sergei Levchin, 21–37. Bloomington: Indiana University Press.

Kahn, Douglas. 1999. *Noise, Water, Meat: A History of Sound in the Arts*. Cambridge, MA: MIT Press.

Keller, Sarah, and Jason Paul, eds. 2012. *Jean Epstein: Critical Essays and New Translations*. Amsterdam: Amsterdam University Press.

Kittler, Friedrich. 1999. *Gramophone, Film, Typewriter*, translated by Geoffrey Winthrop-Young and Michael Witz. Stanford, CA: Stanford University Press.

Knechtel, Lloyd. 1931. "Optical Printing." *Cinematographic Annual* 2: 267–70.

Lauste, Eugene A. 1907. "A New and Improved Method of and Means for Simultaneously Recording and Reproducing Movements and Sounds." British Patent 18,057, filed August 11, 1906, and issued August 10, 1907.

Lerner, Neil. 2009. "The Strange Case of Rouben Mamoulian's Sound Stew: The Uncanny Soundtrack in *Dr. Jekyll and Mr. Hyde* (1931)." In *Music in the Horror Film: Listening to Fear*, edited by Neil Lerner, 55–79. London: Routledge.

Leventhal, J. F., and J. A. Norling. 1926. "Some Developments in the Production of Animated Drawings." *Transactions of the Society of Motion Picture Engineers* 10, no. 25: 58–66.

Levin, Thomas Y. 2003. "'Tones from out of Nowhere': Rudolph Pfenninger and the Archaeology of Synthetic Sound." *Grey Room* 12: 32–79.

MacKay, John. 2005. "Disorganized Noise: *Enthusiasm* and the Ear of the Collective, sec. 4: No Noise." *KinoKultura* 7. http://www.kinokultura.com/articles/enthusiasm-nonoise.pdf.

Metz, Christian. 1974. *Film Language: A Semiotics of the Cinema*, translated by Michael Taylor. New York: Oxford University Press.

Michelson, Annette. 1975. "From Magician to Epistemologist: Vertov's *The Man with a Movie Camera*." In *The Essential Cinema*, edited by P. Adams Sitney, 95–111. New York: New York University Press.

Moritz, William, ed. 2004. *Optical Poetry: The Life and Work of Oskar Fischinger*. Bloomington: Indiana University Press.

Passuth, Krisztina, ed. 1985. *Moholy-Nagy*. London: Thames and Hudson.

Peirce, Charles Sanders. 1955. *Philosophical Writings of Peirce*. Edited by Justus Buchler. New York: Dover.

———. 1978. *The Collected Papers of Charles Sanders Peirce: Pragmatism and Pragmaticism and Scientific Metaphysics*. Vols. 5–6. Cambridge, MA: Harvard University Press.

Peters, John Durham. 1999. *Speaking into the Air*. Chicago: University of Chicago Press.

———. 2003. "Space, Time, and Communication Theory." *Canadian Journal of Communications* 28, no. 4: 397–411.

———. 2004. "Helmholtz, Edison, and Sound History." In *Memory Bytes: History, Technology, and Digital Culture*, edited by Lauren Rabinovitz and Abraham Geil, 177–98. Durham, NC: Duke University Press.

Pudovkin, Vsevolod. 1949. *Film Technique and Film Acting*, translated by Ivor Montagu. New York: Lear.

Ries, Elias E. 1923. "Method of Reproducing Photographic Sound Records." US Patent 1,607,480, filed May 21, 1913, and issued November 16, 1923, pp. 21, 30–33.

Rilke, Rainer Maria. 1999. "Primal Sound." In *Gramophone, Film, Typewriter*, by Friedrich Kittler, translated by Geoffrey Winthrop-Young and Michael Witz. Stanford, CA: Stanford University Press.

Ruhmer, Ernst. 1901. "The 'Photographophone.'" *Scientific American*, July 20, 36.

Scheuer, Philip K. 1932. "A Town Called Hollywood." *Los Angeles Times*, January 3 B11.

Shklovsky, Viktor. (1936) 1988. "The Cine-Eyes and Intertitles." In *The Film Factory: Russian and Soviet Cinema in Documents*, edited and translated by Richard Taylor. Cambridge, MA: Harvard University Press.

Smirnov, Andrei. 2013. *Sound in Z: Experiments in Sound and Electronic Music in Early 20th Century Russia*. Cologne: Fundacion Proa.

Sokolov, Ippolit. 1929. "Kakoi tip zvukovoi fil'my nam nuzhen" (The type of sound film we need). *Kino i zhizn'* 3.

Solev, V. 1936. "Absolute Music by Designed Sound." *American Cinematographer* 17, no. 4: 146–48, 154–55.

Sponable, Earl. 1947. "Historical Development of Sound Films." *American Cinematographer* 28, no. 7: 235.

Sternberg, Josef von. 1965. *Fun in a Chinese Laundry*. New York: Mercury House.

Sterne, Jonathan. 2003. *The Audible Past: Cultural Origins of Sound Reproduction*. Durham, NC: Duke University Press.

Stevenson, Robert Louis. (1886) 2004. *Strange Case of Dr. Jekyll and Mr. Hyde*. Edinburgh: University of Edinburgh Press.

Tsivian, Yuri, ed. 2005. *Lines of Resistance: Dziga Vertov and the Twenties*. Bloomington: University of Indiana Press.

Vertov, Dziga. 1930. "Mart [*sic*] radioglaza" (March of the Radio-Eye). *Kino i Zhizn* 20.

———. 1985. *Kino-Eye: The Writings of Dziga Vertov*, edited by Annette Michelson, translated by Kevin O'Brien. Berkeley: University of California Press.

———. 2004. "Zvukovoi marsh (iz film'a *Simfoniia Donbassa*)" (Audio march [from the film *Symphony of the Donbass*]). In *Iz naslediia, Vol. 1, Dramaturgicheskie opyty*. Moscow: Eizenshtein-tsentr.

Woodbridge, Richard. 1969. "Acoustic Recordings from Antiquity." *Proceedings of the IEEE* 57, no. 8: 1465–66.

Zinman, Gregory. 2012. "Eradicating the Psychic Space between Eye and Ear: Synthetic Film Sound's Challenge to the Index." *Animation Journal* 20: 51–84.

Song Time, the Time of Narratives, and the Changing Idea of Nation in Postindependence Cinema

Rochona Majumdar

A considerable body of research has been devoted to understanding the distinctiveness of Indian cinema in terms of the ubiquity of its song and dance interludes. The integral role of the song in this cinema, viewed both historically and in the present, remains indisputable. Scholars have explained the centrality of songs in terms of early Indian sound film's continuities with other performance traditions such as *nautanki*, *lavani*, *jatra*, and theater (both the early Parsi ones and the later socialist-minded Indian People's Theater versions) (Chatterjee 2005; Gupt 2005; Mishra 2000). Others have challenged this argument by focusing on the significance of the technically produced disembodied voice or on the "overwhelming" importance of song and dance in the marketing and financing of films as modern commodities (Ganti 2012: 253–59; Morcom 2007; Booth 2011; Majumdar 2009). From a different vantage, scholars interested in questions of globalization and cin-

My deepest thanks to Dan Morgan, Gerard Siarny, and Dipesh Chakrabarty for their careful reading and critical suggestions on multiple drafts of this essay.

boundary 2 49:1 (2022)   DOI 10.1215/01903659-9615417   ©2022 by Duke University Press

ema have accounted for the centrality of musical numbers by mapping their protean circulation in other media forms such as cell phones, television, music videos, and reality shows (Gopal and Moorti 2008: 1–60). Recent writing, while conceding the musical number's "aesthetic relocation" in the new Bollywood cinema, does not challenge its importance to this cinematic mode (Gopal 2015: 806). Notwithstanding their differences, these views establish popular film music—Hindi film song and dance in particular—as a crucial, and by no means exhausted, field of inquiry for those interested in thinking about film history as media archaeology within the context of Indian cinema.

While the arguments mentioned above constitute an important background for the analysis that follows, the primary question motivating this essay takes a step back from the contemporary moment that is abuzz with discussions about the rapid proliferation of media technologies and their consequent impact (or the lack thereof) on the cinema. Breaking out of a matrix determined by the physical properties of media, their similarities and differences (for instance, between radio, film, and television), this essay asks: What changes in our understanding of Indian films when we treat the song sequence as a separate medium situated both within and outside the film text? To anticipate what follows, the distinctiveness of the song, I will argue, is embedded in its construction of temporality. Through a close reading of some select song sequences from both popular and art cinema in India, I demonstrate how songs may be read as allegories of particular temporal sensibilities that are often at odds with the temporality presented in the main narrative of the film. Analyzing the specificities of this temporal sensibility help us see the utopian—or dystopian—imagination in film songs. It is this intertwining of aesthetics and politics, I argue, that explains the power of the song sequences both within and outside the film. They generate affective registers for thinking the new nation as both history and myth.

The Problem

Much loved by consumers, the film song has been an object of controversy in South Asian scholarship over the years. Many have argued that songs break up the narrative continuity of the film, making them ponderous and convoluted. Lip-synced songs with no tonal perspective, often set in exotic locales, emphasized the spectacular at the expense of the realistic. As observed by one commentator, it makes little difference to the depth of the sound as to whether the person singing on-screen is near or far away from the camera (Dasgupta 1991: 62). Intelligibility seemed to be the preferred mode over fidelity, to put it in James Lastra's words, with reference to Hollywood cinema (2012). Songs existed as prefabricated parts that were later brought together to create a final product, the film. They were even retailed separately. The origins of the songs were varied: oftentimes they were composed for specific films; in other cases they preexisted the films as poems or songs by important authors such as Rabindranath Tagore, Nazrul Islam, Mohammad Iqbal, Faiz Ahmad Faiz, and many others.[1] Economic liberalization and the advent of new media have undoubtedly increased the disaggregation of these sequences in Indian cinema, but the structural continuities run deep in the history of film songs (Gopal and Moorti 2008; Ganti 2012).[2]

Their apparent lack of pedigree likely had further consequences, causing these popular songs, particularly those from Hindi films, to be regarded by early postcolonial leaders as parvenus in the cultural arena and thus to be treated with disdain by the leaders of the new nation. To give one example, in 1952, B. V. Keskar, the minister of information and broadcasting of the newly established government of India, took it upon himself to institute certain rules that resulted in the disappearance of Hindi film songs from All India Radio, the only existing radio station at the time. Popular songs, argued Keskar, appealed to none other than "raw and immature people like children and adolescents" (quoted in Sen 2008: 90). His policies reflected his judgment.[3] Championing the cause of "classical" music instead, Keskar moved to reserve for it half of the time slots available on national radio. Not surprisingly, the radio public was far more insouciant than Keskar imagined. His ruling led to an en masse defection on the part of listeners to Radio Ceylon, which continued to broadcast Hindi film songs. Bowing to the pressure of popular demand, the government of India launched a new channel

1. For an analysis of Urdu poems used in Hindi film lyrics, see Mir 2000.
2. The autobiography of the filmmaker and owner of the production house Dharma Productions, Karan Johar, offers important insights into the precarious but sovereign character of Hindi film songs (Johar 2017: 122, 128).
3. Barnouw and Krishnaswamy cite evidence from the July 1952 issue of the *Journal of the Film Industry* that reported that Keskar banned the practice of announcing the names of the films to which the songs belonged at the time of broadcast as he regarded it as "advertising." Film producers, who were the copyright owners of the songs, decided to register their protest by discontinuing the licenses under which All India Radio had been broadcasting film songs (1980: 208–9).

in 1957, Vividh Bharati, dedicated to playing "popular music and light entertainment" (Sen 2008: 90).

This brief background registers the autonomy of the Indian *filmigeet*. Belonging to the domain of cinema, its circulation, from very early on,
was not dependent on the viewing of films and took place independently,
from radio to television to social media. Not tied to one physical format, it
achieved the status of a medium all its own. That a number of blockbusters—
Kabhie Alvida na Kehna (dir. Karan Johar, 2006), *Bachna ae Haseeno* (dir.
Siddharth Anand, 2008), *Jab Tak Hai Jaan* (dir. Yash Chopra, 2012), *Ae
Dil Hai Mushkil* (dir. Karan Johar, 2016)—in the new millennium take their
names from lyrics of memorable songs from the 1950s–70s is testimony
to the autonomous nature of the song text.[4] Viewers today may or may not
have knowledge of the films to which these songs originally belonged. But
the lyrics invoke an ambience that gives to contemporary films titled after
these songs a retro-modern feel. There are more unusual cases of the use
of Hindi film songs by filmmakers like Jia Zhangke that also point to the
independence of the song sequence as a medium.[5]

Early governmental disdain had many parallels among filmmakers.
For those who defined their work against the norms of the average Hindi
film, it was important to eschew the song sequence in order to achieve
greater realism. Others, while appreciative of the creativity they embodied,
declared it an impossible endeavor to "find room for six songs in a film that
is expressly not a 'musical'" (Ray 1976: 73).[6] These attitudes persist to this
day and have been discussed at length. For our purposes, it is sufficient
to recall that in all genres that comprise popular Indian cinema—social,
mythological, devotional, historical, stunt, costume, fantasy, horror, urban,
and nonresident Indian film—songs remain ubiquitous. But the question
still remains: How do we understand and analyze the fact that the song has
power not only within the film but also independently of it?

---

4. "Kabhie Alvida na Kehna" is the refrain of a song in the film *Chalte Chalte* (dir. Sunder
Der, 1976), "Bachna ae Hasino" is from the song beginning with these same words in the
film *Hum kissi se kum nahin* (dir. Nasir Hussain, 1976), "Jab Tak Hai Jaan" from a song
in *Sholay* (dir. Ramesh Sippy, 1975), and "Ae Dil Hai Mushkil" is from a song from *C.I.D.*
(dir. Raj Khosla, 1956), discussed later in this essay.
5. See Sangita Gopal's discussion of songs such as "Awara Hoon" and "Jimmy Jimmy"
in Jia Zhangke's films *Platform* (2004) and *The World* (2004), respectively (2015: 805–6).
6. Nimai Ghosh decided to do away with song numbers in his film *Chhinnamul* (*The
Uprooted*) in order to develop a new realist aesthetic. For more details, see Biswas 2004.

The song text, I propose, is a complex thing, operating simultaneously on multiple levels. On the one hand, it is a medium with its own existence across platforms, providing it an appeal in a variety of audio and audiovisual forms. On the other, its content—formal and thematic—functions as a profound challenge to progressive and historicist (by which I mean developmental) ideas of modernity, often to be found in official statements, school and undergraduate textbooks, and of course in popular media such as the cinema. These ideas portray the present as a time of transition, in however complicated ways, connecting premodern and colonial pasts to a fully realized modern future. Songs in films have a way of condensing into simultaneous but multiple registers of affect a heterogeneous variety of distant and immediate pasts, thereby collapsing a palimpsest of past experiences and possible futures into a singular experience, the present. This is true, I argue, not only of popular film songs but also of those in Indian art films; the narrative of a transition to modernity, or at least fragments of such a narrative, is common to both varieties of filmmaking in the postindependence moment.

Given the connection of the song to the "deep structure" of popular cinema in India, all too often, attempts to define an "alternative cinema" tend to see this kind of filmmaking as one that must necessarily do away with the song number.[7] Even a passing familiarity with the body of films designated as art or parallel cinema, however, demonstrates the fallacy of such views. Songs play a powerful role in films by Satyajit Ray, Ritwik Ghatak, Mani Kaul, and M. S. Sathyu—to name just a few noted exponents of this stream of Indian cinema.[8] Labeled "Indian" on the festival circuit both at home and abroad, these films never eschewed their regional roots, forming an alternative to Hindi cinema's "national" address. But what is common, surprisingly, to both *filmigeet* and songs in art films is a refusal to chart the progression of a homogeneous, developmental, historical time. Put differently, if the time of a given film narrative is one that can be situated at a definite moment in history, the songs often take us out of the historical into

7. For a succinct summary of such views, see the introduction of Gopal and Moorti 2008.
8. Music, both instrumental and vocal, is crucial to any consideration of films as varied as *Jalshaghar* (*The Music Room*, dir. Satyajit Ray, 1958), *Goopy Gayen Bagha Bayen* (*The Adventures of Goopy and Bagha*, dir. Satyajit Ray, 1969), *Hirak Rajar Deshe* (*The Land of the Diamond King*, dir. Satyajit Ray, 1980), *Charulata* (*The Lonely Wife*, dir. Satyajit Ray, 1964), *Meghe Dhaka Tara* (*Cloud Capped Star*, dir. Ritwik Ghatak, 1960), *Siddheshwari* (dir. Mani Kaul, 1989), *Ghasiram Kotwal* (dir. Yukt collective, 1976), and *Garam Hawa* (*Hot Winds*, dir. M. S. Sathyu, 1973).

the realm of the mythic and the poetic. They puncture the realist narrative temporality of the film and transport the viewer, through their music and lyrics, to temporal moments that merge the present with elements that are "eternal" in Indian sensibilities.

Richard Dyer's discussion of musicals offers a useful way to develop this thought (2002: 19–36). The principal thrust of Dyer's argument about "musicals" as "entertainment"—the latter defined as "a type of performance produced for profit, performed before a generalized audience (the 'public'), by a trained, paid group . . . which have the sole (conscious) aim of providing pleasure" (19)—is to illustrate the utopian dimensions of such entertainment. Musicals work as entertainment, argues Dyer, precisely because they are utopian. People see and feel their desires come to life in song and dance in ways that are impossible in their quotidian existence. Distinguishing his notion of utopianism from the "classic utopias" of Thomas More and William Morris, Dyer writes that the musicals present "head-on as it were, what utopia would feel like rather than how it would be organized." Musicals, in his argument, work "at the level of sensibility" as "an affective code that is characteristic of, and largely specific to, a given mode of cultural production" (20). Importantly, however, he qualifies that "responding to a performance is not spontaneous—you have to learn what emotion is embodied before you can respond to it." Thus, "modes of experiential art and entertainment correspond to different culturally and historically defined sensibilities" (20).

This last point is masterfully illustrated by Dyer with the example of tap dancing, a dance form that involves "hard, short, percussive, syncopated sounds arranged in patterns and produced by the movement of feet" but that acquires different meanings in jazz, minstrelsy, and vaudeville (to name a few different entertainment contexts). This is what interests me in Dyer's discussion—that one can analyze the aesthetic pleasure of songs in Indian films as a "history of signs" shaped by "culture and history" (24). And yet, Dyer's emphasis on the historicity of utopianism is also a reminder that it is necessary to part ways with the details of the analyses he provides. The different utopian possibilities that he delineates in the musicals he analyzes have one commonality: they are all situated in and are products of an advanced capitalist society. This capitalist context accounts for the critical gaps and inadequacies that musicals point the viewer's attention toward as well as for the remedies they propose. In his words, "At our worse sense of it, entertainment provides alternatives *to* capitalism which will be provided *by* capitalism" (27).

What happens to this explanatory grid when we are dealing with songs and films that do not emerge out of contexts that are emphatically capitalist? To rephrase the question using some of Dyer's own categories, how do we read songs in a context where the hegemonic common sense does not necessarily translate notions of "abundance" into "consumerism," or "energy and intensity" into norms of "personal freedom and individualism," and "transparency" into freedom of speech (27)? That is the guiding question of this essay.

Indian cinema, particularly after the coming of sound in 1931, was constantly negotiating, both formally and historically, questions of (national) servitude and freedom. The complexity of expectations associated with cinema became more acute in the immediate postindependence period, during its so-called golden age in the 1950s. The government of the day as well as personnel associated with the film industry tasked cinema with the lofty ideals of nation-building and citizen formation, generating national pride, and articulating ideals of communal harmony in the aftermath of the tragic and violent partition of 1947 that accompanied the formation of the sovereign Indian nation-state. Such idealism was often in conversation and competition with considerations of profit by producers, directors, and stars—all of whom strove to evolve formulas that would guarantee box office success. There was also acute anxiety on the part of directors and producers to appear as respectable in the eyes of a state that was yet to give cinema formal recognition as an industry. Many post-independence leaders were critical of the purely "entertainment" aspects of films, especially when they were developed at the expense of the medium's pedagogic potential.

The myriad expectations foisted upon cinema in the era of decolonization were not peculiar to India alone. The account of an encounter between President Sukarno of Indonesia and a group of Hollywood executives offers a telling snapshot of the place of cinema in postcolonial imaginary in general. Together with India's first prime minister, Jawaharlal Nehru, Egypt's President Abdel Nasser, Yugoslavia's President Josip Tito, and Ghana's President Kwame Nkrumah, Sukarno tried to forge a bloc of "nonaligned nations" that were critical of Western imperialism and committed to social development programs and national modernization. At his meeting with Hollywood executives, Sukarno hailed them, "to their surprise and perhaps discomfiture," as "fellow revolutionaries and thanked them for their aid to the national revolutions of postwar Asia." As if echoing Miriam Hansen's arguments about Hollywood cinema as "vernacular modernism," he lauded these executives for depicting material prosperity on-screen, as it

inculcated a consciousness among "ordinary people" of "the sense of deprivation on man's birthright." These films were motivational for an impoverished people driving them to seek similar comforts for themselves. "That is
why I say you are revolutionaries, and that is why I salute you" (Barnouw
and Krishnaswamy 1980: 167; Hansen 2011). According to Barnouw and
Krishnaswamy, a survey of Hindi films undertaken in the 1950s showed a
penchant for "motoring, motorcycling, speedboating, skiing, . . . lavish background, radiant health, laughter" amidst an array of consumer goods (Barnouw and Krishnaswamy 1980: 166–67). It thus might appear that there are
enough similarities to align Indian cinema's utopias to Dyer's model. But a
deeper analysis of this cinema reveals aspects that trouble these putative
commonalities. In particular, the song sequence throws a veritable spanner
in the works in these progressive and developmental renderings of Indian
cinema history.

I take a cue from film critic and director Chidananda Dasgupta's discussion of the song in his essay "Why the Films Sing." Dasgupta's general
understanding of Indian popular cinema is as an object in "the midst of a
transition to an industrial age." As he noted, "certain themes" such as "problems of tradition and modernity, East and West, city and village, family and
state, feudalism and democracy, individual and society" that are "constantly
explored behind the façade of entertainment" constitute the staple of Indian
cinema (1991: x). It is "only the songs" that give a "transcendental quality" to
this cinema. He describes the songs as being "full of philosophy, passion-
ately felt and ably expressed, however trite they may be in their generaliza-
tions" (xi). The song turned "the present tense of the camera eye into the
past and the future" (59). Aside from providing philosophical expositions,
the song "proposes inductive and deductive syllogisms on the truths of individual life in relation to the social universe; explains hidden meanings; comments, like a chorus, on the worth or consequences of an action, besides
providing aural enchantment to the otherwise music-less urban world at
its rural grassroots" (60). While there is much to quarrel with in Dasgupta's
description of popular cinema as being rather like a "variety show of disparate elements rather than a unified whole," born as it was amid "clashes
of faith" that were "unable to come to terms with a technological mode of
apprehending reality," there remains something important to retrieve and
take forward in his observation that "what gives this form its only significant
core is the song" (65).

His subsequent lines affirm the earlier point I made about treating
the song as a medium that is apart from and yet within the film. He writes,

"Belonging to a different cultural level from the rest of the film, dismissing the demands of dramatic continuity and defying the inbuilt realism of the medium, the song acquires an autonomous presence rising above the disparateness of the other elements in a film. . . . There is a tacit agreement between the filmmaker and the viewer that the song is for transcendence" (65–66). By what means does the song achieve this transcendence from the medium that contains it to become something autonomous? While he repeatedly remarks on this feature, Dasgupta does not push this key insight into the role of the song in Indian cinema far enough. That is what I attempt to explain in the following analysis by exploring how these songs denote an experience and a politics of time—and the aesthetics that result from such denotation.

Anti-historicist Song Times

History, whether written by professional historians, public intellectuals, or nationalist leaders, is about posing a distance between the past and the present. Equally, it is about suggesting or documenting pathways of development or transition, how the subject of the modern nation-state, in this instance India, moves from the past to the future. Seen thus, Indian cinema negotiates questions of history through its exploration of binary oppositions: between the modern and the premodern, city and country, monarchy and democracy, and so on. In the song, by contrast, it is as though the time of the present is created by a number of isolated and self-contained points, arranged serially but never adding up to a narrative of transition from premodernity to the state of being modern (even if the larger story of the film may indeed intend to depict such transition). Through its successful combination of image, rhythm, beat, and cadence, the popular film song, whose essence of success inheres in the viewer's capacity to hum/sing it, presents every moment of experience as an assimilated whole. But those fragmentary moments do not add up to a grand narrative of the nation coming into its own.

My use of the category *experience* is indebted to Hansen's use of the concept that was in turn drawn from her reading of Alexander Kluge and Oskar Negt. Challenging the "empiricist" understanding of the word that implied "perception and cognition based on stable subject-object relations and directed towards instrumental uses of science and technology," Hansen uses experience as that "which mediates individual perception with social meaning, conscious with unconscious processes, loss of self with self-reflexivity." Emphasizing the "discursive" nature of experience, she saw it as "the capacity to see connections and relations" and as "the matrix of conflicting temporalities, of memory and hope, including the historical loss of these dimensions" (Hansen 1991: 12–13). Understood thus, the experience embodied in the song simultaneously entails a dehistoricization of the past in order to repackage it as the viewer/listener's present.

To establish this claim in its entirety would call for a larger exercise than can be conducted here. What I will do here is demonstrate, through a close reading of some select song sequences from popular Hindi cinema in its golden age, the manner in which a hybrid, pan-Indian "present" is established in these musical numbers. While the lyrics are rendered in Hindi, the national language espoused by the Indian Constitution, it is important to remember that the Hindi compositions of Bombay film songs were deeply inflected with Urdu. This was unlike the chaste Hindi spoken on All India Radio, not least because many important songwriters of the Hindi film industry were Urdu poets (Gopal and Moorti 2008: 22; Petievich 2004: 124; Kesavan 1994: 244–57; Roy 1998: 168). Furthermore, there is little in the picturization, musical scores, or mise-en-scène of these sequences that grounds them in any particular region of the country. Arriving onto the scene at the time of the birth of the new nation-state, the song sequences anoint that entity as simultaneously mythical and modern. That is to say, in the compressed utopian time of the popular Hindi film song, the nation appears as a unity, as if unscathed by the trauma of territorial disruptions and social divisions of caste, creed, and religions. It is also a site of modern, democratic citizenship, presented without any acknowledgment of the difficult paths that needed to be charted in order to transition into such an order.[9] Through a play with time, the song sequence, unlike many of the films that contain them, stands out as a radical instance of anti-historicism.

My use of *historicism* in this context is indebted to Dipesh Chakrabarty's analysis of the term. While acknowledging its highly debated nature, Chakrabarty deploys *historicism* in a way that speaks to the contestation around ideas of modernity and modernization in non-Western contexts. "Historicism," he argues, refers to a mode of thinking that "tells us that in order to understand the nature of anything in this world we must see it

9. By comparison, in Indian art cinema, the song often highlights the dystopic aspect of the present. Much like their popular counterparts, however, songs in art films also evoke heterotemporality as a means of distancing themselves from the time of the film's narrative.

as an historically evolving entity, that is, first as an individual and unique whole—as some kind of unity in potential—and second, as something that develops over time" (2008: 89–90). Defying such historicist logic, the film song instead collapses many temporalities and sensibilities to generate a kind of affect of plenitude. The collapsing of multiple temporalities makes the present of the song not a culmination of the empty, homogeneous time of history but a conjoining of a multiplicity of affective temporalities: of myths and of gods, the past and the future.

Song of the Citizen

I turn now to a close reading of one of the best-known song sequences in Indian cinema, "Mera Joota Hai Japani" (My Shoes Are Japanese) from *Shree 420* (*Mr. 420*, dir. Raj Kapoor, 1955). The song takes place some six and a half minutes into the film. It features the film's protagonist, a role essayed by actor Raj Kapoor (who was also the film's director). Raju/Ranbir (although we are yet to learn his name when the song occurs), a Chaplinesque, tramp-like figure with shades of Monsieur Hulot in his body language, is on a road that has something of a "yellow brick road" quality to it. Paved at some parts, winding, dusty, and desert-like at others, it leads to unnamed cities featuring ornate gateways reminiscent of some magical monarchical periods in Indian history before it dissolves into a crowded modern crossroad in a teeming metropolis that can be recognized as Bombay. All manner of people—and even some animals—appear as the protagonist walks and skips along the long road. One would be hard-pressed if they sought realist counterparts to the variety of people he encounters. For example, the four women shown sashaying across the frame, their bodies swaying to the rhythm of the song, act like a direct citation of many commonplace Indian nationalist statements about the supposedly idyllic charm and simplicity of rural life.[10] Seemingly unconcerned about the heavy loads on their heads, these village women smile happily as the singing protagonist skips by them. Their lack of urbanity comes through in the way they wear their saris hitched up to the knee and so without a blouse, an artifact introduced by the British as a mark of moral and sartorial modernization during the late nineteenth century. Likewise a moving caravan of elderly and young people, on foot or on camels, that appears out of nowhere on a des-

---

10. For an example of an Indian nationalist description of rural masses, see Nehru 1985: 67–68.

ert landscape and that the singing hero joins. This is reminiscent of images seen during the murderous partition of 1947, when thousands of refugees trekked across the border from one newly formed nation to another. Taken together with the elaborately decked out elephant, the snake that appears on the hero's path, religious figures smeared with ash and sandalwood paste, these myriad images offer a snapshot of Indian diversity—actual and mythical.

It should be noted that even before the song plays, viewers are familiarized with its tune as the background music for the film's title credits. The tramp figure, too, is familiar to them, having made his first on-screen appearance in exactly the same get-up in the film *Awaara* (*Vagabond/Tramp*, dir. Raj Kapoor, 1951). Four years later, he shows little change except in his shoes, which are now riddled with holes. By the time "Mera Joota Hai Japani" begins, the association of the tramp's charm with the melodious soundscape creates the anticipation of something that will be of anthem-like proportions. We know today that the song did not disappoint, but we need to analyze the factors that catapulted it to that status.

It is noteworthy that the song comes quite early in the film; very little of the story has unfolded at the time it occurs. Raju appears on the horizon in a long shot, like a tiny dot, and walks rapidly down the road until we get a good glimpse of his face looking up quizzically at a road sign that points in two directions, one toward Baghra Tawa (five miles from where he is standing) and another toward Guram Khedi (seven miles away). Situated near the Malwa plateau in the state of Madhya Pradesh, both names are unfamiliar enough to sound like non-places, though a search of the Indian Railways timetable reveals that they are in fact small stations in central India. The oddly dressed tramp tries in vain to hitch a ride on the deserted road, but three cars whiz past him showing no signs of slowing down. Desperate, he lies down on the road pretending to have passed out, when a big car stops and picks him up. It is owned by a wealthy gentleman, who is introduced as Seth Sonachand Dharmanand and who will later emerge as an important character in the film. At this point, he announces that he wishes to do good to the poor and needy and therefore instructs his driver to take the supine figure to a nearby hospital. The younger of the two women who are accompanying him rubs eau de cologne on the tramp's forehead in an effort to revive him, while the older one looks on with suspicion. As the tramp hears the wealthy man utter the word *hospital*, he sits up and confesses that he was only putting up an act in order to get a ride. He had in effect been forced to lie because, as he explains, he had no money for a train ticket and was really tired.

The truth only earns him a lecture from the big man, who calls him a "420"—everyday shorthand for a con man, the nomenclature referring to Section 420 of the Indian Penal Code that deals with crimes related to cheating and property fraud—and unceremoniously dumps the tramp from the car. So even before we learn his name, the vagabond is christened as a criminal type. He protests that honesty never got one anywhere (as demonstrated by the experience we just witnessed); pretending to be sick actually got him into the big car and the tender care of a young woman. Cutting through his protests, the car drives off, and we catch the plate number, which is BMZ 840, the number prefiguring the major thematic of the film: who is more deserving of the label "420"? Is it the poor vagabond on the long, lonely, dusty stretch of road who tells little lies because he is left with no option if he is to continue on his life's journey? Or is it the wealthy man who, for all his claims about doing good by the needy, is in fact the bigger con—twice over, to be precise? Frustrated in his efforts to get a ride, the poor tramp looks up at another road sign that now points one way in the direction of Shajapur, sixteen miles from where he is standing, and another toward Bombay, 420 miles away. His eyes light up as he reads aloud "Bombay 420." Looking down at his peep-toe shoes, which he refers to as "beta japani" (my Japanese son), thereby personifying them, the tramp begins walking as the prelude music of the song starts to play.

A signature of the composer duo Shankar Singh Raghuvamsi and Jaikishan Dayabhai Panchal, or Shankar-Jaikishan as they were better known, the song begins with a prelude that leads to the opening lines, or *mukhda*. Each paragraph of the song that takes the viewer to different locales the protagonist passes through is followed by an interlude of instrumental music performed by an orchestra. The sound is an imaginative and hybrid blending of musical instruments, including the harmonium, piano accordion, mandolin, percussion instruments, and mouth organ—as well as the recorder that the tramp is shown playing. Gayatri Chatterjee notes that starting with *Awara*, Raj Kapoor had begun to blend different elements into the musical soundtrack of his films. These included Goan and Uttar Pradesh folk music, Western classical music and Russian folks songs, Indian classical music, and the Indian People's Theater Association choral style (Chatterjee 1992). "Mera Joota Hai Japani" is no exception to this mélange of influences. I present below a rough translation of the lyrics, along with the different scenes that occur over the course of the song.

(On the road)
My shoes are Japanese,

These pants are English
On my head is a red Russian hat
But this heart is Indian for all that

(Going past the women)
I am out on the open road with my chest wide open
Only God knows which destinations I will stop at
I surge forward like a stormy river
(refrain: on my head . . . Indian for all that)

(Caravan)
Up above and down below
Life rolls on like a wave
He who sits on the edges seeking
The way to the homeland is naïve
Moving on is the story of life; to pause is death
(refrain)

(Atop an elephant)
There may be kings and sons of kings
But I am a prince with an unruly heart
Who ascends the throne whenever he so determines
The familiarity of my face leaves people puzzled
(refrain)

The song has an element of celebration despite, or perhaps because of, its wholehearted embrace of its singer's poverty. The latter is cataloged in the way he announces his composite costume: Japanese shoes, English pants, and a red Russian hat. While the frayed clothing is a sign of their age or even that they may have been hand-me-downs, the invocation of their varied origins seems to be a comment on the wearer's cosmopolitanism. All these varied influences, however, add up to the last line of the refrain, which states that his heart is Indian. The lyrics draw attention to the fact that Hindustani/Indian is not reducible to national particulars but can be "infinite ways of being."[11] Indeed, Hindustani as a linguistic construct flags

11. For a discussion of cosmopolitanism, not just as an idea whose history can be traced back to the Stoics or to Immanuel Kant but more in terms of lived and archival plenitude, see Breckenridge and Pollock 2002: 1–15. For a recent debate about the difference between Hindustan and Hindusthan, the latter marked by a Hindi-Hindu ethos, see Asif 2020: 9–13.

the confluence of Hindi and Urdu, of Hindavi and Persianate idioms, which were rendered marginal in post-partition Indian history (King 1994; Nijhawan 2016).

One way of reading these lines would be to suggest that being Indian is not a matter of external accoutrements. Nor is it a matter of "becoming" Indian, realizing a potential, as claimed in nationalist and historicist narratives. Being Indian, in this song, is a disposition, a matter of affective belonging that remains untouched by exterior trappings. Another more compelling reading would be to suggest that being Indian is to embrace difference. Seen thus, the quality of being Indian is an agglomeration—sometimes absurd and comic in its self-presentation—of varied elements, none complete in and of themselves but adding up to something that constitutes a fulsome or plenitudinous present. They echo the spirit of Nehru when he wrote, "It was India's way in the past . . . to welcome and absorb other cultures" (1985: 563).

Further, while a viewer familiar with Chaplin would likely see his shadow in our protagonist, for those not aware of him the tramp-like figure is simply a ragtag image of an impoverished everyman in the city. The tramp is actually an educated, unemployed young man trying to make his way from a small town to the city in search of a livelihood. This journey to the big city would have been significant in the 1950s popular Hindi cinema. India was on a course of economic modernization and urban development. Raj is no displaced peasant, but someone unmoored by the processes of modernization. Caught in the precarious years of post-independence turmoil, the labeling of the poor tramp trying to make his way to the big city as a 420 would have likely struck a sympathetic chord with most viewers. The big city was a zone of allure and ambiguity, of many bigger 420s as it were, like the rich man in the car. Yet it was also the desired destination for millions of newly anointed citizen subjects in search of livelihoods who saw their conditions mirrored in the curious figure of the tramp.

Coming a few years after independence, and following a period of high nationalism and partition, the song functions as something of a postcolonial "[re]discovery of India." Both M. K. Gandhi and Nehru had, immediately after their return to India from sojourns in the West or Western countries, engaged in traveling across India. Such travels were not only gestures of getting to know the country. Traveling was a way of enacting in their lives what many patriots had described as the historical ability of Indian civilization to assimilate to its own self all that diverse cultures contributed to it. An entire genre of writing, comprising books, poems, and essays by nationalist and immediate postnationalist intellectuals, leaders, and professional historians, sought to understand what it meant to be Indian. Most notably, Nehru, Rabindranath Tagore, and Sarvapalli Radhakrishnan, to name a few, upheld the idea of pluralism and diversity by tracking a history of assimilation at work in Indian history. Emphasizing the need to be open to others, Nehru wrote that it "is much more necessary today, for we march to the one world of tomorrow where national cultures will be intermingled with the international culture of the human race. We shall therefore seek wisdom and knowledge and friendship and comradeship wherever we can find them, and co-operate with others in common tasks, but we are no suppliants for others' favors and patronage. Thus we shall remain true Indians and Asiatics, and become at the same time good internationalists and world citizens" (1985: 566).[12]

The violence that accompanied the partition of the country in 1947 actually showed how unresolved—in spite of all that was written and said by Gandhi, Nehru, or Tagore—the question of Indian identity remained even at the end of the struggle for freedom from British rule. The creative genius of "Mera Joota Hai Japani" lay in resolving the contradictions thrown up by a dense and conflict-ridden history as an already accomplished fact of being Indian/*Hindustani* to its viewers. Shedding the gravitas of written histories, it humorously and ironically coupled the idea of being an Indian and a sovereign citizen-subject with that of being a vagabond, a petty criminal, a 420. Put differently, the song—sung by an ordinary, unexceptional tramp-like figure—registers the need to suture ethical values culled from the past to an uncertain and open-ended future through a creative revision of age-old ideas.

Combining a foot-tapping and almost folksy rhythm, the song presents a series of images that we can now read allegorically. For example, the four women mentioned above may be read as what Nehru described as "ideals, more based on the ineluctable facts of today, . . . the . . . proletarian ideal" that would have to be fused with the nationalist and international-

---

12. The lyrics also echo some of Nehru's more philosophical ruminations about the wonders of living and his attitude toward death, for example, when he cites William Butler Yeats's poem "An Irish Airman Foresees His Death": "I want to experience again 'that lonely impulse of delight' which turns to risk and danger and faces and mocks at death. I am not enamored of death, though I do not think it frightens me. I do not believe in the negation of or abstention from life. I have loved life and it attracts me still and, in my own way, I seek to experience it, though many invisible barriers have grown up which surround me; but that very desire leads me to play with life, to peep over its edges, not to be a slave to it, so that we may value each other all the more" (1985: 22).

ist ideals of the past and present "if we are to have a world equilibrium and a lessening of conflict" (1985: 53). The caravan that the protagonist joins may be read, and probably was by viewers in the 1950s, as reminiscent of the mass exodus across borders when the two nation-states of India and Pakistan were created. With its emphasis on movement as the pulse of life and the futility of asking questions about *watan*, or homeland, the song deterritorializes national identity at the same time as it elevates an idea of national belonging. Finally, the ornate gates that flit across the frame before the song ends in the busy thoroughfares of Bombay as well as the elephant the protagonist rides like a king dissolve the present "into the distant past" and assume "its immobile, statuesque appearance" (23). Bombay, in effect, becomes a magic kingdom where everybody enters with hope, an ironic comment on the world of Bollywood itself. The panorama, and not progression, of Indian history constitutes a democratic present in the song when the tramp proclaims himself as a prince, not by virtue of wealth, nor by the avowed principles of political representation, but through his claiming a sense of sovereign personhood that allows him to ascend the throne whenever he so chooses. His face leaves beholders puzzled, for he is not one born to distinction. His anonymity makes him an everyman. Like millions of poor people in the country, he is nonetheless a sovereign subject albeit caught in the struggle for survival. With a trick or two up his sleeve, his arena of action is the road and the street.

In other words, "Mera Joota Hai Japani" presents us with a new postcolonial common, one that is grounded on the road that leads from the country to the streets of the city. This new common, a complete rupture from a colonial past of servitude, is in turn the site of play, of personhood, and of jouissance. In condensing history into a series of allegorical snapshots, the song departs from a nineteenth-century sense of the discipline of history that emphasized facts, dates, development over time, and a philological commitment to the archive as the mode of knowledge production. Though part of the film, enabling the protagonist's journey from the country to the city, the song does not have a direct role in the diegesis. Yet it incontrovertibly establishes an ambience, as much for the film as for the film's context (see Figures 1–3).

In celebrating a figure that is one of the "mass" or the "common," the song taps into the mood of democracy that swept across the world in the post–World War II, decolonization era. It should come as no surprise that this is also one of the most well-traveled songs in Indian film history, a widely used text in postcolonial cinema and literature. Some well-known

Figure 1 Raju, the tramp (*awaara*; Raj Kapoor, *Shree 420*, 1955).

Figure 2 Raju in the caravan (Raj Kapoor, *Shree 420*, 1955).

Figure 3 Raju, the citizen as king (Raj Kapoor, *Shree 420*, 1955).

examples of its use in contemporary cinema are in the film *Gravity* (dir. Alfonso Cuarón, 2013), *Phir bhi dil hai hindustani* (dir. Aziz Mirza, 2000), and *Mississippi Masala* (dir. Mira Nair, 1991). Interestingly, none of these make any reference to *Shree 420*, the original film that contained the song. Nor does Kiran Desai's novel *The Inheritance of Loss* (2005), where the song is a signifier of home for an Indian immigrant.

The song's most memorable afterlife, however, is in Salman Rushdie's novel *The Satanic Verses* (1998), when the protagonist Gibreel Farishta sings the first stanza of the song during his fall into England from the exploded plane. He sings it, though, in English rather than in Hindi "in deference to the uprushing host nation" (5). In this, as in its other and repeated deployments, the original sense of the intertwining of past and present is absent. Instead, the song stands in for a more expansive understanding of personhood, hope, travel, hybridity, courage, and even postcoloniality, a sensibility that travels across media.

The idea of a postcolonial common featured in "Mera Joota Hai Japani" also animates other songs from the same period. Many of them depict the street as the domain of the underprivileged, a domain that despite overcrowding and squalor allows for play and agency. The song "Bombay

Meri Jaan" (*C.I.D*, dir. Guru Dutt, 1958) is another example that affords similar possibilities for intertextual and intermedial readings. Performed by two relatively marginal characters in the film, it nonetheless registers their sense of ownership and place in the paradigmatic Indian city, Bombay. Like "Mera Joota Hai Japani," it brings to fruition a certain romantic and national-ist, if dehistoricized, idea of the "people." But it expands the category of the "people" even further than "Mera Joota Hai Japani" by introducing a play-ful inversion of gender roles. The refrain of the song, performed mainly by the male playback (sung by Mohammad Rafi), asserts that "it is difficult to live in this place [Bombay]." The female voice, for the most part saying very little, compensates for her brevity by the power of her interjection in the last refrain. When we expect her to repeat that Bombay is a difficult place to survive in, she says the unexpected: "My love, it is easy to live here." Her lines are sparkling with wit and irony; as one commentator has observed, her interjection is a triumph of the composing technique. She affirms her confidence by calling the man her "mister" and "bandhu" (friend). It is the female voice that establishes "Bombay Meri Jaan" as part of an "aesthetic structure" that, Sudipta Kaviraj argues, was "a cultural combinatory of the modern sensibility which managed to find a strangely joyous description of the grim city while recognizing its sordidness" (Kaviraj 2004: 66).[13]

Kaviraj's discussion of "Bombay Meri Jaan" is instructive in this con-text. While he argues that the song belongs to the closed narrative con-text of the film, its link to that narrative context, much like "Mera Joota Hai Japani," was tenuous at best. More important is what Kaviraj describes as "a second structure of meaningfulness," which pertains to "the aesthetic perception" about urban life in a newly democratic and independent coun-try. Thus he notes,

> This song formed part of an entire repertoire of popular songs, mostly taken from films, in which each song with its idiosyncratic sequencing of words, internal economy of images, mood became a supporting neighbor to others of a similar kind. This poetry and these songs were not from the same films, or from identical narra-tives or composed by the same poets. But taken together, each of them advanced by slow and peculiar steps an aesthetic description and elaboration of the experience of modernity, and at its center, of the taste of city life. (66)

13. Similarly, Aarti Wani has recently discussed the centrality of songs in conceptualizing romantic love in the urban space with reference to 1950s Hindi cinema (2016).

"They were linked," argues Kaviraj, through the listening practices of viewers. Together, cinema-going and the auditory reception of film songs outside the cinema created a new sense of the world. The linkage was not "as parts of a single narrative, but rather of a single aesthetic." It was an aesthetic that gave a new vocabulary of pleasure and of politics to "people who lived rather impoverished lives." Rendered in music, this was a "new lilting language" with little questionable links to the real and the historical that thereby "achieved a miraculous transfiguration of the commonplace" (2004: 66).

While I recognize the commonplace assumption about the integral relationship of the song to the Hindi film, my goal has been to demonstrate the autonomy of the song as a medium unto its own. The multiple temporalities songs invoke, and the spaces—regional, local, and national—they imagine, are integral to the fantasy generated by the song that is quite distinct from the fantasy of the film. It also explains why songs from the 1950s–70s enjoy a life well into the present, long after many of the films they belonged to have disappeared from public memory.

Songs and Indian Art Cinema

In the remainder of this essay, I will focus on a song sequence from Ritwik Ghatak's 1960 film *Meghe Dhaka Tara* (*Cloud Capped Star*) in order to consider the role of song in the so-called art cinema and to demonstrate some of the differences between songs of this genre and those of the *filmigeet*. Even though an absence of songs is often equated with the art of parallel cinema in India, there are important exceptions to this tendency. The role of music in the films of Ray, Ghatak, and later avant-garde filmmakers such as Kaul and Kumar Shahani await more in-depth analyses. My intent in introducing this discussion of song in art cinema is to demonstrate, albeit provisionally, the varied and dense sedimentation of time and experience in these numbers in ways that are different from the above examples from popular cinema. It is also to emphasize the central argument of this essay, namely that songs, including those in art films, offer a parallax view of history through the creation of their own aesthetic universe that opens up within the film itself.

A crucial fact to note is that the songs from art cinema had little commercial circulation outside the films as *film* songs. A notable exception is *Goopy Gyne Bagha Byne*. *Goopy Gyne Bagha Byne*, noted Ray, had become a "part of popular culture" in his home state, West Bengal. Writing to the British critic Marie Seton a few months after the film's opening, he reveled in the fact that "there isn't a single child in the city who does not know and sing the songs" (quoted in Robinson 1989: 182). Such popularity, however, was not the fate of most songs from art cinema, unless they happened to be compositions by the poet laureate Rabindranath Tagore (1861–1941)—in which case they enjoyed a wide circulation in the Bengali educated public sphere both prior to and following their filmic use. Their inclusion in cinema may have popularized them, but such *rabindrasangeet* (songs by Tagore) were already a crucial component of Bengali sonic worlds. So also with classical music, which is the central thematic in films such as Ray's *Jalsaghar* and Mani Kaul's modernist biographical feature film *Siddheshwari* (1989). Training in the different schools of Indian classical music, and an active cultivation of such music in concerts and in private, formed the context for its use in cinema.

While the use of classical music and *rabindrasangeet* may sometimes be explained as giving the films a periodicity, the role of song in art cinema is more problematic when the films in question are not period pieces. The song I wish to focus on in the remainder of this essay is one that is neither classical nor *rabindrasangeet*, but rather the genre of a folk song. *Meghe Dhaka Tara* has a total of five musical interludes: two Indian classical ragas, one *rabindrasangeet*, and two folk songs. One of the latter belongs to the genre of *baul* songs.[14] The other song is associated with the last day (*bijaya*) of the five-day Bengali festival Durga puja (the festival that celebrates the worshipping of the mother-goddess Durga). It is to this one that I turn my attention in order to analyze the role played by songs in Ghatak's deployment of archetype and mythology, two tenets that were central to his understanding of Indian cinema, history, and culture. This will return us to the question of temporality in the song sequence that goes to the heart of this essay.

A few explanatory remarks will help in explaining the context of the song. The plot of *Meghe Dhaka Tara* revolves around a family evicted from east Bengal (then East Pakistan, now Bangladesh) trying to eke out a living in a refugee colony in Calcutta.[15] The family consists of a father, an idealistic, ex-schoolteacher who spouts Wordsworth and Yeats and is uncomfortable about his sons joining the market as "laborers." There are two broth-

14. A *baul* is a syncretic, religious itinerant, and a vast repertoire of music is associated with the *baul* tradition in Bengal. For a cultural history of *bauls*, see Openshaw 2002.
15. For more details on *Meghe Dhaka Tara*, see Dass 2020.

ers: Montu, whose skill in soccer gets him a job in a factory, and Shankar, who aspires to be a classical singer and eventually succeeds. The women are Nita, the film's protagonist; her anxious, poverty-hardened, and worldly mother; and her narcissistic and flirtatious younger sister Gita. Nita, who is described at one point in the film as "Sindbad the sailor," goes to great lengths to satisfy the desires and wants of the entire family. So dependent are they on her labors that the mother connives to have Gita married off to Nita's long-time suitor Sanat so as not to lose the money Nita earns from her job. Beaten down by the lack of care and poverty, exacerbated by a series of accidents suffered by the father and Montu, Nita succumbs to tuberculosis.

In an essay entitled "Human Society, Our Tradition, Filmmaking, and My Efforts" (originally published in Bengali in 1963), Ghatak observed that all great art produces "aesthetic relish" that courses through it in "multiple layers." At the primary level of the narrative, there are incidents that give rise to joy, sorrow, laughter, and other emotions. If one goes deeper, there are "political and social connotations at play." Probing further takes the viewer to "philosophical insights" and into the heart of the "artist's self-reflection." And finally, there are those "momentary feelings that cannot be expressed in words . . . moments [that] take him close to something unknowable" (Ghatak 2015: 13). "At this point," argued Ghatak, art "has a lot in common with divine worship." The latter, in turn, "is concerned with "worldly transactions with the gods at the first level, while at its deepest point lies the ineffable" (14).

Given this arc of thinking, it is not entirely surprising that comparative mythology and the concept of the archetype therein molded Ghatak's thinking about the way mythohistorical factors shaped the contemporary. His cinema weaves the past into the present, but it was a past mediated through his particular understanding of mythology and the archetype. "Myth—and therefore civilization," he noted, citing Joseph Campbell, "is a poetic, supernormal image, conceived like all poetry in depth, but susceptible of interpretation on various levels. The shallowest minds see in it the local scenery: the deepest the foreground of the world" (16). Like Campbell, Ghatak, too, was one in a long "line of twentieth-century artists and critics who came under the influence of C. F. Jung" (Biswas 2015: 12–13). As Moinak Biswas has noted, the notion of the archetype, so central to Jungian ideas of the collective unconscious, served as a "useful tool for him [Ghatak] to formulate and explain his method of what, in an Eisensteinian vein, he called 'throwing overtones' in his films" (12–13).

We witness a repeated return to the archetype of the mother in Ghatak's cinema, whom he describes as a central figure in mythology, Hinduism preeminent among them. He wrote,

> This Great Mother continues to haunt the consciousness of many races in the world. It has two aspects—the one promising benediction, the Sophia, and the other striking terror, much like the goddess Kali or Chandi. Our Puranas have visualized this deity in the two forms as part of a single entity in the "Devisukta." And this mother archetype has penetrated out society in its every pore. All the songs of Agamani and Bijaya from Bengal, the deeper aspects of our folktakes, bear witness to this. (Ghatak 2015: 15)

The preeminence of this archetype, a central component in the Bengali collective unconscious, he argued, "has a crucial role to play in the methods of filmmaking." Expanding its scope, he went so far as to assert that this unconscious happened "to be the pan-Indian aspect of our cinema, setting the criteria against which films should be ultimately measured" (15).

Referring to *Meghe Dhaka Tara* in the same essay, Ghatak observed,

> The Uma symbology used there should be clear. . . . I conceived her as a symbol of the daughters married off as part of the tradition of "gauridaan" for centuries in Bengali households. She is born on the day the goddess Jagaddhatri is worshipped. And she dies as she is united with the hills, which stand for Mahakaal [literally, Great-time, or an embodiment of Time itself]. When the first hint of her death comes through her tuberculosis, unknown voices start singing the lament of Menaka heard during Bijaya. (16)

History and myth thus come together in the fractured archetype of Nita as Uma in the film to produce a searing critique of contemporary conditions. This happens most effectively during the song sequence, where Ghatak merges the "time of history" and the "time of Gods" by inviting the viewer to see the goddess Uma in the very human and "modern" working girl Nita.[16]

The song in question takes place soon after Shankar has returned from Bombay as a successful singer and has discovered his beloved sister

16. For a critical discussion of the problems inherent in the ways in which a secular subject like history handles practices having to do with gods, spirits, or the supernatural as agentive forces in the world, see "Translating Life-Worlds into Labor and History" in Chakrabarty 2007: 72–96.

Nita's illness. Meanwhile, Gita, the younger sister now married to Sanat, is back in her paternal home expecting her first child. Citing the baby's health as the reason, her father walks into Nita's room during a night of torrential rain and lightning and asks her to leave home (as other family members fear her infection could affect the baby's health). Stricken and tearful that he has to throw out his beloved elder daughter from her home, he nonetheless carries out the family's verdict in the interest of the soon-to-be-born child. "You were successful," he tells her for bearing the burden of the entire family on her fragile shoulders. But now, he declares in utter helplessness, she has been reduced to a "burden" herself. "They are dreaming of two storys," he mutters referring to the mother's earlier wish to the successful singer Shankar for a bigger and better house. They believe that her "breath contains poison." As Nita picks up her spare belongings and a cherished framed photograph of her and Shankar taken in the hills, the plaintive notes of the song start playing on the soundtrack. Unlike in the songs discussed earlier, or even the songs we have heard thus far in *Meghe Dhaka Tara*, the lyrics of this one are indistinct. Even so, we can tell, as Ghatak's statement above also makes clear, that it is a song meant for Uma (another name for the goddess Durga) being beckoned by her mother Menaka to leave her marital home and visit her parents.

Agamani and *bijaya* songs—"the former sung in anticipation of Uma's coming and the latter in grief over her departure" (McDermott 2001: 4)— have a long tradition in Bengal, dating back at least three hundred years. As argued by Rachel McDermott, from the eighteenth century onward, there developed a tradition of composition of songs and poems devoted to Kali, Uma, and Durga, who were considered different aspects of the mother goddess in the vernacular Bengali language (as opposed to the courtly language of Sanskrit). While many of the better-known exponents of such poetry, such as Ramprasada Sen and Kamalakanta Bhattacharya, wrote songs about Kali, her softer and gentler counterpart Uma received the attention of many lesser-known authors. As noted by McDermott, "Menaka's piteous pleas for her daughter's safe return at the autumnal Puja Festival, Uma's marital problems with her husband Siva in Kailasa, and the events of her three-day reunion with her parents in the Himalayan kingdom provide ample scope for artistry" (275).

Ghatak's use of an *Uma-sangeet* at this climactic moment in the film not only recalls this long history of goddess devotion in Bengal but also serves to turn that tradition on its head by demonstrating the abuse suffered by one aspect of the goddess Uma/Nita. Ironically, much of the abuse comes from "Gita . . . the sensual woman [and] their mother [who] represent . . . the cruel aspect" (Ghatak 1982: 49). Nita, Gita, and their mother each represent different aspects of the archetype of the mother goddess, and their respective dispositions provide the driving motive of the film. Apart from the irony inherent in playing an *Uma-sangeet* for a consumptive woman who shall remain a spinster, Ghatak appears to be commenting on the continuing cruelty of a tradition that practiced *gauridaan* (the gift of a child-daughter). (He remarks elsewhere on the enthusiastic adoption of the practice of marrying off girl-children, thereby separating them from their "familiar playground[s]" in order for them to journey to "an unknown village, an unknown home, where the frowning faces around her would frighten her, and she would hanker for her own home" [50].) The modern conditions of scarcity and want in an urban, postcolonial, refugee colony culminated in a different *gauridaan* for Nita that was no less cruel.

Two song sequences in the film, not just the *Uma-sangeet* but the earlier *rabindrasangeet* as well, enable the braiding of myth and the present. In both sequences, Nita's face is shown in a series of tight, frontal close-ups. The gleam in her eyes, her curly hair streaming down her shoulders, and finally her upward gaze toward the stormy sky is reminiscent of Durga idols as they are immersed in the holy Ganges after the festival (Figure 4). Elsewhere, I have written about the significance of the inclusion of such mythic and folk elements in Indian art cinema (Majumdar 2016). Here, I want to emphasize the importance of the song in conveying Nita's destiny and in delineating the historical as well as mythical dimensions of her plight. In the *Uma-sangeet*, Nita's visage carries the signs of her fatal illness. On the face of the modern Uma, one who will never be married, we see splatters of blood instead of the vermillion (on the parting of the hair and on the forehead) that would have been the sign of a Hindu woman's marital status. As she picks up the childhood photograph of herself with Shankar in the hills, her desire to return to that spot of childhood bliss is once more established, except in this instance it will be a final union with *Mahakal* that is eternity. The song is the site for the enactment of a physical and psychic longing for Nita.

We get a premonition of this fate in the earlier *rabindrasangeet* that she requested Shankar to teach her on the eve of her sister's upcoming *bashor* (wedding night), during which a storm arises. The lyrics of that song make the storm outside an allegory for the pennant of the divine, who by the end of the song is standing before the devotee. The lines "When the morning came / I looked up to find you standing before me" prefigure Nita's death later in the film. The "you" in the above line refers to a non-idolatrous God.

Figure 4 Nita as Uma (Ritwik Ghatak, *Meghe Dhaka Tara*, 1960).

For most of the song, the two figures of Nita and Shankar are shown in a long shot sitting with their backs to one another in a darkened room (Figure 5). By the time these last lines occur, a cut shows Nita's face in an extreme close-up, her face tilted upwards. The close-up that invokes the feeling of a dramatic overture coincides with the lyrics of the song dissolving into sounds of whiplash, as if to reflect the repeated assaults upon her by her loved ones. This manner of framing the female face, tilted and looking upward, is reminiscent of Hindu idol immersion. It would become Ghatak's signature in later films such as *Titas Ekti Nadir Naam* (*A River Called Titas*, 1974). In *Meghe Dhaka Tara*, the lyrics of an *Uma-sangeet* and *rabindra-sangeet* combine with the close-ups of Nita's face to produce the effect of merging mythic time with the time of the contemporary. It is the song sequences that convey most powerfully the ironic but powerful presence of the archetype in contemporary society even as it is fractured into multiple aspects. By merging myth into the now, it jolts viewers into an awareness of the present as dystopia.

Across this essay, I have sought to demonstrate, if only provisionally, the manner in which experiences of time and space are condensed in the brevity of a song sequence. Like the Bakhtinian chronotope in literary

Figure 5 Nita and Shankar singing a duet (Ritwik Ghatak, *Meghe Dhaka Tara*, 1960).

analysis, the song sequence presents viewers with layers of experience that mediate the history of the present. The songs of popular cinema I have discussed here affirm the contemporary, thereby elaborating on the pleasures and the myths of the modernizing nation and of the modern Indian city. The ones from art cinema, by contrast, offer a critique of the present through the creation of alternate temporal registers. In both cases, the song sequence works by transporting the viewer to experiences of time and space that cannot be aligned with the deployment of progressive and developmental time that underlay both nationalist and Marxist/socialist historical narratives of the nation. *Shree 420*, for instance, ends with a suggestion of Nehruvian socialism finding fruition through the efforts of the protagonist. In *Meghe Dhaka Tara*, the plight of a working woman in a refugee colony tells us that we are in a difficult and disenchanted moment of transition from the semifeudal hierarchies of the traditional family to a modern structure that both allows and exploits women's employment and forces them into a subaltern status. The song sequences, however, puncture the linearity of these narratives of modern progress and development by introducing viewers to a heterotemporality that re-enchants the present with gods, myths, and a sense of self-contained plenitude. It is this quality, I claim, that gives them their nondevelopmental sense of time.

In a manner that parallels Chakrabarty's discussion of poetry in the production of a nationalist imagination, the song in postcolonial Indian cinema—although situated in the middle of the everyday—allows the viewer or listener to inhabit a sense of time that escapes the developmental history of modernization and the emergence of the nation-state. While the films' narratives remain in the realm of this account of transition, the songs use their particular conjoining of rhythm, language, and cadence to become a medium of personal/political affect in contemporary Indian lives. They survive on their own, often functioning as scripts of present-day desire and grief. Defying the covenant of narrative, history, and development, there is an unruliness to the songs' circulation. "Songs are," as the American activist and folk singer Pete Seeger remarked at a 1967 concert in Atlanta, "sneaky things . . . [that] can slip across borders. Proliferate in prisons. Penetrate hard shells. The right song at the right time can change history" (quoted in Dunaway 2008: 426). Untethered from the films to which they belong, film songs are taken up by each generation who gives them new and unanticipated meaning. The use of the lyrics of songs from the 1950s–1970s as the titles of blockbuster hits in the last ten years is just one testimony to the fact that the film song transfigures historical time by crisscrossing it with other modes of apprehending temporality. In so doing, it remains an independent medium that functions as the script of the libidinal economy of postcolonial India.

References

Asif, Manan Ahmed. 2020. *The Loss of Hindustan: The Invention of India*. Cambridge, MA: Harvard University Press.

Barnouw, Erik, and S. Krishnaswamy. 1980. *Indian Film*. 2nd ed. New York: Oxford University Press.

Biswas, Moinak. 2004. "The City and the Real: *Chhinnamul* and the Left Cultural Movement in the 1940s." In *City Flicks: Indian Cinema and the Urban Experience*, edited by Preben Kaarsholm, 40–59. Calcutta: Seagull Books.

———. 2015. "Two Articles by Ritwik Ghatak." *Cinema Journal* 54, no. 3: 11–13.

Booth, Gregory. 2011. "Preliminary Thoughts on Hindi Popular Music and Film Production: India's 'Culture Industry(ies),' 1970–2000." *South Asian Popular Culture* 9, no. 2: 215–21.

Breckenridge, Carol, and Sheldon Pollock, eds. 2002. *Cosmopolitanism*. Durham, NC: Duke University Press.

Chakrabarty, Dipesh. 2007. *Provincializing Europe: Postcolonial Thought and Historical Difference*. Princeton, NJ: Princeton University Press.

———. 2008. "In Defense of Provincializing Europe: A Response to Carola Dietze." *History and Theory* 47, no. 1: 85–96.

Chatterjee, Gayatri. 1992. "Music in Awara." In *Awara*, 127–40. New Delhi: Wiley Eastern Limited.

———. 2005. "Icons and Events: Reinventing Visual Constructions in Cinema in India." In *Bollyworld: Popular Indian Cinema through a Transnational Lens*, edited by Raminder Kaur and Ajay Sinha, 90–117. New Delhi: Sage.

Dasgupta, Chidananda. 1991. *The Painted Face: Studies in India's Popular Cinema*. Delhi: Roli Books.

Dass, Manishita. 2020. *The Cloud-Capped Star (Meghe Dhaka Tara)*. London: Bloomsbury BFI Classics.

Dunaway, David King. 2008. *How Can I Keep from Singing? The Ballad of Pete Seeger*. New York: Villard.

Dyer, Richard. 2002. *Only Entertainment*. London: Routledge.

Ganti, Tejaswini. 2012. *Producing Bollywood: Inside the Contemporary Hindi Film Industry*. Durham, NC: Duke University Press.

Ghatak, Ritwik. 1982. *Cinema India*, edited by Shampa Banerjee. New Delhi: Directorate of Film Festivals.

———. 2015. "Human Society, Our Tradition, Filmmaking, and My Efforts," translated by Moinak Biswas. *Cinema Journal* 54, no. 3: 13–17.

Gopal, Sangita. 2015. "The Audible Past or What Remains of the Song Sequence in New Bollywood Cinema." *New Literary History* 46, no. 4: 805–22.

Gopal, Sangita, and Sujata Moorti, eds. 2008. *Global Bollywood: Travels of Hindi Song and Dance*. Minneapolis: University of Minnesota Press.

Gupt, Somnath. 2005. *The Parsi Theatre: The Origins and Development*, translated and edited by Kathryn Hansen. Kolkata: Seagull Books.

Hansen, Miriam. 1991. *Babel and Babylon: Spectatorship in American Silent Film*. Cambridge, MA: Harvard University Press.

———. 2011. "The Mass Production of the Senses: Classical Cinema as Vernacular Modernism." In *Critical Visions in Film Theory*, 326–39. Boston: Bedford/St. Martin's.

Johar, Karan. 2017. *An Unsuitable Boy*. New Delhi: Penguin.

Kaviraj, Sudipta. 2004. "Reading a Song of the City: Images of the City in Film and Literature." In *City Flicks*, edited by Preben Kaarrsholm, 60–82. Calcutta: Seagull Books.

Kesavan, Mukul. 1994. "Urdu, Awadh, and the Tawaif: The Islamicate Roots of Hindi Cinema." In *Forging Identities: Gender, Communities, and the State in India*, edited by Zoya Hasan, 244–57. Boulder: Westview.

King, Christopher. 1994. *One Language, Two Scripts: The Hindi Movement in Nineteenth Century North India*. Bombay: Oxford University Press.

Lastra, James. 2012. "Fidelity versus Intelligibility." In *The Sound Studies Reader*, edited by Jonathan Sterne, 248–53. London: Routledge.

Majumdar, Neepa. 2009. "The Embodied Voice: Song Sequences and Stardom in Bombay Cinema." In *Wanted Cultured Ladies Only*, 173–202. Urbana: University of Illinois Press.

Majumdar, Rochona. 2016. "Art Cinema: The Indian Career of a Global Category." *Critical Inquiry* 42, no. 3: 580–610.

McDermott, Rachel. 2001. *Mother of My Heart, Daughter of My Dreams: Kālī and Umā in the Devotional Poetry of Bengal*. New York: Oxford University Press.

Mir, Raza. 2000. "Voh Yaar hai Khusboo ki Tarah / Jis ki Zubaan Urdu ki Tarah: The Friendly Association between Urdu Poetry and Hindi Film Music." *The Annual of Urdu Studies*. Center for South Asia, University of Wisconsin–Madison. https://minds.wisconsin.edu/bitstream/handle/1793/18165/18mir.pdf.

Mishra, Vijay. 2000. *Bollywood Cinema, Temples of Desire*. New York: Routledge.

Morcom, Anna. 2007. *Hindi Film Songs and the Cinema*. London: Ashgate.

Nehru, Jawaharlal. 1985. *The Discovery of India*. New Delhi: Oxford University Press.

Nijhawan, Shobhna. 2016. "Hindi, Urdu or Hindustani? Revisiting 'National Language' Debates through Radio Broadcasting in Late Colonial India." *South Asia Research* 36, no. 1: 80–97.

Openshaw, Jeanne. 2002. *Seeking Bauls of Bengal*. Cambridge: Cambridge University Press.

Petievich, Carla. 2004. "Rekhti: Impersonating the Feminine in Urdu Poetry." In *Sexual Sites, Seminal Attitudes*, edited by Sanjay Srivastava, 123–46. New Delhi: Sage.

Ray, Satyajit. 1976. "Those Songs." In *Our Films, Their Films*, 72–75. Calcutta: Orient Longman.

Robinson, Andrew. 1989. *Satyajit Ray: The Inner Eye*. London: I. B. Tauris.

Roy, Parama. 1998. *Indian Traffic: Identities in Question in Colonial and Postcolonial India*. Berkeley: University of California Press.

Rushdie, Salman. 1988. *The Satanic Verses*. New York: Penguin Viking.

Sen, Biswarup. 2008. "The Sounds of Modernity: The Evolution of Bollywood Film Song." In *Global Bollywood: Travels of Hindi Song and Dance*, edited by Sangita Gopal and Sujata Moorti, 85–104. Minneapolis: University of Minnesota Press.

Wani, Aarti. 2016. *Fantasy of Modernity: Romantic Love in Bombay Cinema of the 1950s*. New Delhi: Cambridge University Press.

The Documentary Imaginary of Brotherhood and Unity: Nonfiction Film in Yugoslavia, 1945–51

Joshua Malitsky

In the late 1940s, citizens of the Socialist Federal Republic of Yugo-slavia viewed state-sponsored newsreels and documentary films in a mul-titude of ways. A woman living in Zagreb, Croatia, might go to the local cinema and in one program see a *Filmske Novosti* (federally produced) newsreel detailing progress made in the Belgrade-Zagreb highway, images of Tito visiting Ljubljana, Slovenia, and an international dignitary visiting Belgrade, Serbia. Accompanying the federal newsreel would likely be a Croatian-produced *Pregled* (monthly film journal) that, perhaps, highlighted the growth of the coal industry—demonstrating the process of production, distribution, and uses of coal across Croatia at the time. That issue might even be followed by a documentary on folk culture produced in Croatia, or even one produced in a different republic (though that was less likely), prior to the screening of an animated film and the eventual feature film, perhaps from the Soviet Union. A man working and living in a new industrial timber

Unless otherwise noted, all translations are my own.

boundary 2 49:1 (2022)   DOI 10.1215/01903659-9615431   ©2022 by Duke University Press

town in Montenegro might have a related but different nonfiction film experience. At his local education center, he might be introduced to a documentary on the philosopher-poet Petar II Petrovic-Njegos, followed by a Montenegrin monthly on training youth about aerospace concepts through gliders and scientific efforts to expand agricultural yields through new technological discoveries. On the same day, a rural coal miner in Puračić, Bosnia-Herzegovina, might be waiting in the town square with three hundred comrades for a mobile screening of a *Filmske Novosti* following the movement of Tito's *stafeta* across Yugoslavia, a Bosnian monthly film journal on Muslim women "freeing themselves from the bonds of slavery" by publicly removing their veils, a documentary on the importance of rural literacy, and a feature film from Czechoslovakia.

These experiences indicate how governmental representatives of the federation, and of each republic, mobilized nonfiction film in the postwar era to project, model, and instill visions of Yugoslavia and of each republic to these citizens. At one level, there was considerable thematic and structural overlap across the multiple newsreel and documentary forms. And any of them might have addressed directly youth brigades rebuilding decimated infrastructures or an exposition dedicated to new national products. They might have addressed directly the need to think across republics as Yugoslav citizens. But at the same time, there were some key differences. While some Montenegrin monthlies focused intensely on intranational cooperation, Bosnian monthlies mentioned Yugoslavia and its leadership infrequently. Yugoslav citizens saw federally produced archival footage-based histories of the War of Liberation, and they saw republic-produced stories of rural populations whose traditional ways of life had been altered in the name of national progress. Nonfiction film was part of the broader media project that both built and sustained Yugoslavia's political structures, but it was one in which identity building and collectivity shaping were particularly ripe with ambivalences. Citizens would have been correct to wonder whether these films suggested that their Yugoslav identities took precedence over their national-republic identities—or the other way around. Might a Montenegrin be more likely to take the former as the lesson and Croatians the latter? And what about Macedonians? They were likely pleased to be addressed as Macedonians, even if that in itself was an identity newer in understanding. By necessity, citizens had to make decisions on how to situate the importance of one nonfiction film form over another. And they had to negotiate those understandings in relation to those of other nonfiction media forms realized through mass communications and journalism.

This essay explores how nonfiction film in postwar Yugoslavia (1945–51) expresses a fundamental ambivalence that negotiates a desire for and image of a unified nation-state (supranationalism) with that of one made up of multiple nations (nationalism). To be sure, it is not just articulated as ambivalence, as the ambivalence is mediated by the figure of leader Marshal Tito, who can subsume and resolve it in his body and personage. The broader image and idea of *revolution* likewise mediates the problem of ambivalence in nation-building. Revolution here exceeds either alignment (supranational or national) but in the process opens up its own set of ambivalences between the intranationalism of the Yugoslav Federation and the internationalism of communism. Indeed, the entire postwar nonfiction Yugoslav film project diagrams this tension and offers a set of relations that mirror the ambivalence—this is what makes it particularly valuable for any attempt to understand the postwar period and its legacies. It does so through the sites of its textualities, its industrial organization, its methods of production and circulation, and its organization of exhibition. The social lives of these films, in this way, laminates their internal poetics and thematics—a necessary component for a film project that asks its citizens not just to see but to act.

The Supranational and the National

The idea of imagining the people of Croatia, Slovenia, and Serbia as unified under a single national idea—indeed the very idea of Yugoslavia itself—was not a completely new undertaking in the years following World War II. Intellectuals as far back as the 1830s and 1840s had clearly articulated a vision of a united South Slavic community. The popularity of the idea waxed and waned in the latter half of the nineteenth century and throughout the twentieth century until a considerable lack of support led to the Yugoslav wars, which caused the breakup of the state in the late 1980s and early 1990s (Wachtel 1998: 128–72).

The victory of the Yugoslav Communists in the aftermath of World War II saw this long-standing idea take on a new form. Expanding beyond the "three-named people concept" (Croats, Slovenes, Serbs) that dominated royalist thinking in the first half of the century, the Yugoslav Communists, or Partisans, created a more inclusive system, recognizing Macedonians right away and Bosnian Muslims by the 1960s. More than that, the Socialist Federal Republic of Yugoslavia sought to reach beyond ethnicity and provide a new basis for unity through its political philosophy (Haug

2012: 115–32). The challenge of achieving the balance between the simultaneous recognition and respect for ethnicities and nationalities while envisioning a transethnic, transnational, class-based unity was evident from the start and was informed by both internal and external factors.

As in the Soviet Union after the Bolshevik Revolution, the Partisans struggled to balance their socialist revolutionary aspirations and their dreams of a unified (in this case, Yugoslav) identity with the particular national identities. The context of World War II made it quite challenging. Joseph Stalin and the Comintern emphasized during the war that the Partisans were to aid groups in liberating themselves from the tyranny of fascism—not to make a revolution. One of the major reasons for this is that they did not want to anger the British, who were supporting Draža Mihailović and his Cetnik royalist/nationalist movement. The Partisans, though loyal to the USSR, had their own agenda and followed this advice selectively. They used international revolutionary slogans, symbols, and principles when they saw fit. They also established what they referred to as "liberated territories" that showcased socialist life, such as the Užice Republic in Western Serbia, when they were feeling confident. If the Bolsheviks could rely on the "fight for 'mother Russia'" and work nationalist slogans into their revolutionary rhetoric (Haug 2012: 68–72), the Partisans were constantly balancing popular liberation and revolutionary aspirations. They knew that securing national rights garnered them support, but they also knew it could make things more fractious during this period of heightened hostilities. Moreover, they knew that fighting for unity meant, to some, securing power for Serbia, and they did not want to appear to be supporting Serbian hegemony and maintaining the policies of the Karađorđević dynasty. The national question, therefore, was always front and center for the Partisans, but it was also a complex topic.[1] The Yugoslav revolution was transnational *at its basis*, and, from the start, institutions, policies, alliances, and principles were established in relation to how it was addressed.

After the war, the Partisans' foremost means to resolve this question was to create a supranational "universal" culture fully reconcilable with the individual national cultures (Serbian, Croatian, Montenegrin, Macedonian, Bosnian, and Slovenian). Supranational culture expanded beyond the national to the ideological, overarching and connecting the national cultures rather than eschewing them. The goal, asserted continually and explicitly,

---

1. The centrality of the national question for the Partisans throughout their rebellion and in their governing is the central argument of Haug 2012.

was to fight for the "brotherhood and unity" ("bratstvo i jedinstvo") of the peoples of Yugoslavia. The Yugoslav Communists saw the tension between these two ideas (the difference endemic to brotherhood and the singleness asserted by unity) as not only productive but a fully reconcilable solution to the challenges of a unified, multinational, and multiethnic Yugoslavia. "Brotherhood and Unity," Sabrina Ramet writes, went from a slogan used during the war to being "refined into a central pillar of the system" (Ramet 2006: 4–5).

Film, and nonfiction film in particular, became one of the vehicles for communicating this core ideological principle. It emerges not just in the films themselves but in the social experiences people had with cinema. Exhibited in all-Yugoslav film festivals and as part of cinema programs, nonfiction film—in particular newsreels, monthly film journals, and documentaries—contributed to this effort to shape a new vision of supranational and national identity in the formative years of Yugoslavia following World War II.

The dynamic between the supranational and the national is at the heart of the Yugoslav postwar nonfiction film project. But how it gets negotiated from the mid-1940s to the early 1950s is neither stable nor straightforwardly aligned with state policy. Because of this, a study of films made during this period can teach us several key lessons about nonfiction film, its history, and its role in Yugoslavia. First, such study contributes to efforts to theorize the specificity and multiplicity of nonfiction film forms across production contexts by opening to analysis the nonfiction media ideologies of producers and critics—that is, what genres were seen as appropriate for communicating what kinds of ideological messages. Second, because nonfiction film was both a privileged and sophisticated space for communicating a core tenet of the Yugoslav project, providing new material for scholars of Yugoslav history and for scholars of nations and nationalism will aid in understanding how such ambivalences unravel and explode, as they did in Yugoslavia when it broke up in the late 1980s and early 1990s. Third, and most broadly, the Yugoslav case elucidates what I am conceiving as a documentary imaginary.

Documentary imaginary is a concept that has begun to circulate in documentary studies. My argument is that this case study reveals the extent to which a political ethics of documentary always can and has depended significantly on a combination of the textual and the extratextual. This step relies on two assumptions: First, that the documentary imaginary maintains a significant political-ethical component, that the judgments people make about, in this case, social documentaries are primarily driven by political-ethical questions. That is not to say that aesthetic components are always mined for their political-ethical value or that the regimes collapse into one another. Rather, it is to assert that viewers are concerned with how films deal with established hierarchical relationships and how, in so doing, they establish relations with others (and I mean this both in terms of how the filmmakers are understood to relate to the people in their films and the subject-object relations they enact for spectators). The second issue is that this imaginary is shaped by textual and extratextual considerations, which I come to in the next section.

Following the logic of my objects of analysis—primarily newsreels and monthly film journals—I have structured this essay by opening with long shots and gradually moving thematically to tighter ones.[2] I will begin by establishing the space of theoretical intervention—the larger idea of documentary imaginary and how a Peircean semiotics can provide tools for specifying the experience in a given context. I will then demonstrate how the Yugoslav postwar nonfiction film project sought to project, model, and instill brotherhood and unity at a range of textual and extratextual levels. And I conclude with the recognition that, while remaining effectively ambiguous, the framework nevertheless establishes the terms of the sociopolitical conversation.

The Documentary Imaginary

The last fifteen to twenty years have seen incredible growth in the audience size, funding potential, and (purported) influence of political documentaries. Increasingly, we have the opportunity to see political documentaries in theaters, financially successful films such as *Fahrenheit 9/11, Born into Brothels, An Inconvenient Truth*, or Laura Poitras's *Citizen Four*. Most people who decide to spend their time watching an almost two-hour documentary on Edward Snowden (in whatever format or location) will be somewhat familiar with the story. Perhaps they have read about the film before viewing, perhaps they do so afterward, or perhaps they interrupt their viewing to do some research. They may choose to learn more about Poitras's history with Snowden and about her activities since those initial meetings. Or they may go back and read Glenn Greenwald's initial articles and more about Greenwald. People may be paying attention to the role played in pro-

---

2. Siegfried Kracauer likewise sees shot types as a potential model for historiography ([1969] 2013: 105).

ducing the film by Jeff Skoll and Participant Media, by Steven Soderbergh, or even take an interest in Harvey Weinstein's promotion (an interest whose focus has likely changed since the film's release in 2014!). And many take a keen interest in the *method* of the film: the process by which it gets made, the means by which information is obtained, and the treatment of subjects in the film.

Paratextual and extratextual information of this type (information that is in addition to critical responses to the film) is weighed in relation to people's judgments on the topics, themes, and their formal articulation in the film. Questions such as: How should I account for the focus on Snowden himself, and how he's shot within the space of the Hong Kong hotel room, in relation to his argument about him *not* being the story? What's the balance between visual and verbal information in this film? How do I align the depth and complexity of the verbal in relation to what I already know? What are the implications of these long takes? How *historical* of a film is this? Answers to these kinds of questions, which vary in type and degree of sophistication, combine with information accrued about the production, distribution, marketing, critical response, and exhibition context to form people's political-ethical judgments about documentaries (I do not think this works the same way for fiction films).[3]

It is not difficult to imagine why this is taking place in the information age. But nonfiction film has long aimed to shape subjectivities and, in turn, build citizenries by projecting, modeling, and instilling new visions of collectivity. Nonfiction film shapes social imaginaries by communicating, as Charles Taylor writes, "the ways people imagine their social existence, how they fit together with others, . . . the expectations that are normally met, and the deeper normative notions and images that underlie these expectations." They are neither theories nor simply ideas but "common understanding that makes possible common practices" (2004: 23). These imaginary relations are shaped by the combination of their articulation in representations and their reinforcement in everyday practice.

Taylor's concept works so well for documentary, especially in contexts of public viewing, because his understanding of the social imaginary necessitates the interrelation of materiality and discursivity, of text and reception. The exhibition space of documentary film (and therefore the social experience of viewing) reinforces the sense of collectivity (collectives on-screen or imagined potentially mirroring viewing collectives), and

3. For a related take on the topic, see Carroll 1983.

its performativity sustains the potential of its undoing (its presentational and highly rhetorical qualities challenge any naive representationalist belief in the power of images to unproblematically represent things). For Taylor, the combination of understanding and activity produces a different level of knowing. The images, narratives, and modes of address, in this case, are inextricable from their contexts of production and circulation. The performativity of this effort is overt even if it is not always verbal. The approach enables us to see the multitude of ways that this core, transformative, fundamental understanding—this new tenet of social imaginary—gets articulated through nonfiction film.

Whereas Taylor's concept establishes a broad experiential and epistemological framework for understanding engagements with nonfiction film, and the concept of documentary imaginary specifies the questions that are sparked by experiences with nonfiction film, recent work in anthropology, film studies, media studies, and art history on the complex taxonomy of signs developed by Charles Saunders Peirce offers a complementary approach. Work on Peirce's concept of the indexical sign, in particular, provides tools for marking the specificity not just of nonfiction film language and the chronotopic logics it employs but of how the dynamic of immediacy and mediation governs nonfiction media aesthetics.

Indexicality as Trace and Deixis

Scholars of documentary have a history of analyzing how various (and shifting) semiotic strategies work to buttress the truth claims of a given film or set of films. Indexicality is acknowledged as a crucial support for such assertions—the material connection between the photographic sign projected on-screen and the object in the real world serving as guarantor of truth. But is the referential indexicality of film studies—the emphasis on physical trace between the object viewed on-screen and the object in the real world—sufficient for understanding the engagement documentary viewers have with documentary images? And if not, is there another way of theorizing indexicality that accounts for the breadth of what falls under Peirce's notion of the index; the diversity of ways films reference, speak, and listen to the real world; and the changing media landscape? In this way, indexicality could retain its critical potential and currency by speaking to the kind of work artists produce while accounting for their (and their audiences') increasing understanding of the labor that goes into producing truth and referencing the real.

As is well-known, Peirce developed a complex taxonomy of signs that sought to account for what he understood as the dynamism of both speech and interpretation. Whereas Ferdinand de Saussure emphasizes the arbitrariness of the link between signifier and signified, Peirce offers a typology of relations that identify the ways in which the sign can stand for an object. Peirce identifies three sign functions—icon, index, and symbol—that make meaning possible. He was, as W. J. T. Mitchell writes, "not interested in classifying signs by their singular manifestations, such as 'words and images,' but by their *sign function*, which depends upon the way they make meaning" (2015: 45). The index, his second class of signs, is likely the most multifaceted, distinguished by the way it speaks to the singularity of the referenced object and serving primarily as an assurance of its existence rather than testifying to the nature or content of the object. On the one hand, indices specify signs that are physically modified by their objects (footprints, masks, weathervanes) so that they share a physical *connection* to that object. On the other, they refer to the deixis or "shifter" ("this," "here," "now," "I," "you"), Roman Jakobson's term for the category of linguistic signs that signifies *spatiotemporal presence* even as it remains hollow (i.e., it is only meaningful once the referent is supplied) (1984: 41–58).

The definition of the index as trace has been thought of as applicable to photography, whereby the photograph has an existential bond with an object that leaves its imprint on light-sensitive material ("they are in certain respects exactly like the objects they represent" [Peirce 1932: 159]). Photographs also merge index with icon (and often symbol), their images resembling the objects themselves. In so doing, the image's iconicity relies on the index, depending upon the fact that it was "physically forced to correspond point by point to nature," in this case, the object photographed (159). Cinema's basis in photography and projection sustains and even extends this claim; light carries the embedded information directly to a screen (which viewers then engage), thus maintaining this physical connection.

If the index as trace upholds an alignment with iconicity, index as deixis partakes of the symbolic order. It emphasizes not just existence but presence and immediacy, underscoring the contingency of the linguistic articulation. Whereas the index as trace has a rich history of elaboration in film studies, the index as deixis has received considerably less consideration. But the deixis's assertion of "this" or "here" speaks to the direction of attentivity so central to the management of the cinematic gaze. Christian Metz describes how the image *actualizes* a real for the viewer, a quality he identifies as an "index of actualization." For example, "a close-up of a revolver does not mean 'revolver' (a purely lexical unit), but . . . 'Here is a revolver!'" For Metz, even a straightforward cinematic image corresponds to a sentence rather than a word. It does so less by the "quantity of its meaning . . . than by its *assertive* status" (1974: 67; emphasis added). Whereas Metz's conception emphasizes the present moment and the index's power as a cultural and semiotic force, it is interesting to note that Metz uses precisely a presentational sentence containing a deictic ("Here is . . .") to illustrate this "assertive" status. If the index as trace speaks to the historicity of the photographic image, the index as deixis marks the enunciative moment itself as critical to the establishment of spatial and temporal context. In this way, it speaks to the multiple temporalities these different indexical claims instantiate.

This idea of deictic index as indicator and as symbol is also realized in the way in which, in addition to the index of actualization, the deictic brings to the fore the limit of the frame itself. As Mary Ann Doane specifies in relation to cinema, the deictic demarcates the borders of cinematic space. In so doing, it isolates a space for aesthetics, in turn creating expectations in viewers of aesthetic activity (2007: 138–40). This combination of various indexical claims and expectations is what drives Doane's argument that the index is today potentially "*the* primary indicator of cinematic specificity"—even in the digital age (129). It is the dialectic of the index as trace and index as deixis that so powerfully sustains it as a force in cinema. The index as trace or imprint on a photograph *endures*, testifying to the reality of its existence at some point in time. The index as deixis actualized through cinematic strategies marks the *temporal* moment of actualizing the real, testifying to the immediacy of the viewing experience. And the index as deixis that demarcates the borders of the frame highlights the "hereness" or "thereness" of space, testifying to cinematic spatiality. This combination produces an assurance and intensity, explaining the index's theoretical value for conceiving cinematic ontology while still accounting for the dynamics of the interpretive moment.

Doane's focus on the index of actualization subtends her understanding of cinematic ontology. But specifying the experiences of nonfiction film in general and those of Yugoslav postwar nonfiction film in particular requires additions to the semiotic architecture, additions that return us to questions raised by the concept of the documentary imaginary. Film viewers in Slovenia, Macedonia, Montenegro, Croatia, Serbia, and Bosnia and Herzegovina encountered these films as part of film programs. Most often, they were seen together with a fiction feature and an animated short.

But they were also seen in special screenings, in traditional cinemas or other designated spaces, or in mobile cinema programs (Tadic 2011: 5). For the first time, Yugoslav citizens saw themselves on-screen, and, for the first time, they saw themselves addressed as both Yugoslav and national republic citizens. Moreover, the films were often introduced and ideologically framed by a live speaker. As such, these spaces were highly presentational and performative. What we see, riffing off Metz, is not simply the index of actualization that insists, "Here is a laboring, youthful Yugoslav body." Rather, that index is framed by a voice beyond that voice that says, "Here is a program which contains, among other things, images of laboring Yugoslav bodies." Thus, in what follows, I delineate the various levels or orders of indexing that take place through viewers' experiences with Yugoslav nonfiction film, moving from words and images through narrational structures, programmatic structures, and extratextual encounters. The goal is to account for what and how this programmatic order indexes so as to come to terms with how Yugoslav nonfiction film communicates the essential ambivalence of the postwar era—an ambivalence pivotal to the documentary imaginary of the period.

Bodies of Films, Their Institutional Contexts, and Dominant Themes

Based on research at the Yugoslav film archive (the federal film archive), the *Filmske Novosti* federal newsreel archive, and the individual national archives in Serbia, Montenegro, Macedonia, Croatia, Slovenia, and Bosnia and Herzegovina, I have identified the period 1945–51 as the first phase of the Yugoslav postwar nonfiction film project.[4] This phase was driven by efforts toward unity and conciliation, and was organized during a period of administrative control. However, whereas Gertrude Robinson (1977) in her work on mass communications and both Daniel Goulding ([1985] 2002) and Radenko Rankovich (2004) in their work on Yugoslav film define the period by a centralized administrative structure, they leave out nonfiction film. In producing newsreels and documentaries, administrative power operated dialectically, with control in the hands of both federal agen-

4. The archives are as follows: Macedonian Kinoteka, Skopje, Macedonia; Montenegrin Cinematheque, Podgorica, Montenegro; Yugoslav Kinoteka, Belgrade, Serbia; Filmske Novosti, Belgrade, Serbia; Slovenian Film Archive, Ljubljana, Slovenia; Croatian Film Archives and Croatian State Archives, Zagreb, Croatia; and the National Film Archives of Bosnia and Herzegovina, Sarajevo, Bosnia and Herzegovina.

cies as well as those at the republic or national level, presupposing and entailing the desire for supranational and national identity.

Like many new regimes, the Yugoslav Communists in the immediate postwar era turned to nonfiction film in an effort to unify and edify the citizenry (Malitsky 2014). The *Filmske Novosti* (*Filmed News*) federal newsreel was established on October 20, 1944, even before liberation. In the early years, its institutional location changed frequently. It was initially termed the Film Unit and located within the Supreme Headquarters of the Yugoslav National Liberation Army. Shortly after liberation in 1945, the State Film Company assumed control over the production and distribution of the newsreels. A year later, *Filmske Novosti* became a separate division within the Federal Enterprise for Production and Distribution of films (Zvezda Films). It was based in Belgrade, Serbia, but maintained branches in the individual republics. In 1950, however, the organizational structure was changed, and it was placed under the auspices of the Committee for Cinematography of the government of the Federal People's Republic of Yugoslavia, as Central Filmed News Studio. Here the government directly controlled the content, organization, and technical aspects of the productions (Tadic 2011: 6–7; Goulding [1985] 2002; Volk 1986).

The issues were produced weekly, for the most part, and included between five and eight stories. The number of stories per issue began to drop in 1948–49, when the average became four or five. They also produced special monthly issues, which focused on a single topic and had more of a documentary feel.

The dominant themes of this federal newsreel were the primary concerns of the period. Coming out of World War II, with its brutal occupation and its mass killings at the hands of Germans, including their own citizens, the Partisans and their leader Josip Broz Tito faced the fundamental perplexity that many revolutionary leaders face. They had to create a sense of newness that marked the moment of revolution as transformative while appropriating an old authority capable of providing the stability they needed to realize their vision.[5] The Yugoslav context transforms the way in which this dynamic typically functions in critical ways. Like most postrevolutionary parties, the Yugoslav Communists relied on the authority associated with institutions, recognizable public spaces, certain local, national, and regional

5. See the introduction to Malitsky 2014 for the applicability of the concept for thinking about cinema and nation-building and Arendt 1963: 31–32 for a broader articulation of the postrevolutionary dynamic.

traditions, et cetera, to solidify its status as rulers. At the same time, however, emerging from the chaos of World War II, the Communists recognized that their goal of supranational stability depended not only on appropriating old authority but also marking themselves as distinct from the previous regimes' inherent instability. This is one of the dominant rhetorical moves made in the initial years after the war and the prevailing argument of the first years of the *Filmske Novosti* newsreel. The Partisans argue, through varying degrees of explicitness, that the fractiousness resulting from the monarchist government of the Kingdom of Yugoslavia's privileging of Serbia over the other nationalities is what caused the kingdom to be vulnerable and occupiable. Unity is the only way to preserve security. We, they claim, are the only ones who can truly represent unity, since we did not support one nationality/national movement over another during the war. Thus, what was unique about the Yugoslav nation-state building project during these initial years was that its primary enemy was not so much the previous ruling class and its cohorts but the separatists who sought to break up the country along national boundaries. They saw nonfiction film, and the newsreel in particular, as uniquely equipped to project this unifying aspect of the nation-building project.

The third story of issue no. 3 (1945) provides an explicit example. It begins with a youth parade in Zagreb, followed by a Communist Youth Organization meeting. At that meeting, a Serbian girl insists that the conflicts during the war between Serbs and Croats need to be forgotten. She remarks that "it is time to move on," a somewhat shocking call given how recent the conflicts were but one aligned not only with the long-term goals of the Communist Party but also with its short-term interests prior to a national election.

Unity along national lines among members of the kingdom is echoed in the assertion of unity along class lines. Multiple times Tito refers directly to the "unity of peasants, workers, and honest intelligence." This is the phrase Tito used to accompany his position that there are no more bourgeois— only "citizens working physically and intellectually." The claim was both ideological and practical, aiming to account for the extraordinary loss of skilled workers, professionals, and intellectuals during World War II and the party's concern not to alienate those who remained.

The third dominant theme is that of unity behind leadership. Whereas during the initial episodes of 1945, Tito is referenced relatively infrequently, by the middle of the 1945 (especially by issue no. 5) the references to Tito increase exponentially, and we first hear the phrase "Tito's Yugoslavia." Tito is referenced in banners and street names, as well as signs on bridges, buildings, and trains. The election was forthcoming, and there was clearly an explicit attempt to situate Tito as the omnipresent figure—dominant throughout the republic. Indeed, the visualization of his authority changed as the dynamics between brotherhood and unity shifted.

Bodies On-Screen

In 1945 and 1946, *Filmske Novosti* visualized unity through an array of speeches, celebrations, marches, and tributes/memorials. By 1947, the inaugural year of the first five-year plan, the image of laboring Yugoslav bodies began to represent the new supranational unity with its transnational cooperation and ability to transform social and geographical space. It is no surprise, given the devastating effect of World War II on both the landscape and the built infrastructure, that this subject became the space of supranational unity and transformation (Figure 1).

Three aspects of the effort to represent laboring bodies in the initial years of the *Filmske Novosti* strike me as significant, some of which are evident from these images. First, there is a considerable emphasis on laboring youth, even if they are framed as part of an effort toward broader intergenerational cooperation. But rather than highlighting the sacrifices they are making and connecting them to larger sociopolitical developments, their labor is seen as social, communal, and playful. This makes sense given the attention to the Belgrade-Zagreb highway (the first phase of the massive Brotherhood and Unity Highway) that the volunteer youth labor brigades and the Yugoslav People's Army were building. Sequences set on this site often formally and tonally match stories of youth summer camps shown in the individual republics' monthly film journals. And they are explicitly linked to a youth "physical culture" that promotes exercise as a requirement for one to be able to do one's laboring duty. The overall message is of cooperation, joyfulness, and youthful sexuality and vibrancy instead of sacrifice (Figure 2).

Second, in addition to emphasizing the social, pleasurable elements of collective labor and leisure, the newsreel issue marks itself as distinct from related traditions by calling attention to nonmechanized labor. We see bodies engaging tools and the land much more so than a productivist aesthetic that highlights the relationship between individuals and machines—a tendency much more central to both the Cuban and Soviet traditions.

Third, related to but complicating this emphasis on skilled, organic

Figure 1 Youth brigades building the Brotherhood and Unity Highway (*Filmske Novosti* no. 134, 1948).

Figure 2 Youth brigades combining leisure and labor (*Filmske Novosti* no. 134, 1948).

laboring bodies is the focus on the utter transformation of the land. If landscape painting traditionally chose not to show human bodies so as to demonstrate nature's "labor," these films celebrate humans' capacity for completely rebuilding the natural world. The natural world could be shaped to fit new multinational demands—creating a new supranational body with new internal networks of connection.

By 1947, most film activity was still based in Belgrade, Serbia. The government wanted to expand and develop production and so knew that they needed to train cinema workers. In 1947, they opened the Yugoslav School for Film Directing and Acting as well as technical schools for cinema not only in Belgrade but also in Zagreb. During the same period, they reorganized the relationship between federal and national production. Republic committees and commissions were now in charge of theaters in their regions as well as the production of documentary and educational/informational films (Goulding [1985] 2002: 11). They reported not to the federal ministries but consulted their republic's ministries of education and culture. In 1946–47, the Federal Film Agency had each republic begin to produce its own monthly film journals, both recognizing that the *Filmske Novosti* did not have the capacity for such coverage and asserting the value of the local production of nonfiction film as news. These monthly film journals were created to provide broader and deeper coverage of local events and to provide a training ground for documentary workers. Fiction films and *Filmske Novosti* continued to be overseen at the federal level.

Many of the dominant themes from the *Filmske Novosti* continued over into the monthly film journals, which maintained a focus on unity through labor and visualized citizens transforming the natural world. Youth brigades remained central, though they worked less on transnational projects than toward individual regional goals. As to be expected, each monthly highlighted its region's specific industrial and agricultural developments. In doing so, each called attention to the processes of industrial and agricultural production, linking the extraction of natural resources, their transformation into products, and their circulation throughout (and beyond) the country in a Marxist lesson on political economy. This argument was made visually—rarely was the process of production described in detail. Detail was left for data—yields of tobacco in Bosnia, tonnage of ships produced in Croatia, kilowatts of hydroelectric power produced in Macedonia, and results of competition across many societal domains in each republic. These images thus referred not to the singularity of past events but to classes or types of events.

At the same time, however, the monthlies also saw significant varia-tion across republics. At times, this was clearly a result of different contexts. For example, Croatia focused more on industrial production than Montene-gro since it was a more industrially advanced republic. But other times, the reason behind a choice was less apparent. Bosnian monthlies highlighted national and federal leadership less than any other example, whereas Mon-tenegrin monthlies included the most historical material. It is not clear why this was the case.

Cultural specificity, including language, is certainly highlighted in the issues. In Macedonia, the emphasis is on the plural, as Albanian and Roma traditions are celebrated alongside local Macedonian culture. The monthly journals consistently call attention to the fact that, for the first time, Mace-donian children will be able to study in their own language—and that this opportunity is provided for minority children. Here we see the respect for minority nationalities that Tito insisted on. It is used to provide evidence for one of the foundational promises of brotherhood and unity—that the new order replaces the "three-named people" concept (Serbs-Croats-Slovenes) that dominated royalist thinking with an inclusive multinational and multieth-nic vision. In Montenegrin monthlies, national culture involved building up a culture industry through training programs and the growth of museums and galleries. Local customs are celebrated at times, but it is not an issue of contention in the same way. Croatian monthlies, on the other hand, evince a slight de-emphasis on cultural specificity in favor of industrial moderniza-tion. When cultural specificity does emerge, it is most commonly in Dalma-tian folk traditions such as lacework. In each example, we see nonfiction film and the nation achieving homologous status through their respective identities as media—realized through viewers' spectatorial relations with cinema.

All the monthly film journals—Montenegrin, Serbian, Macedonian, Bosnian, Slovenian, and Croatian—emphasize national unity, but they use different strategies to make the point. Macedonian monthlies are much more verbal in their celebration of national unity. And industrial develop-ment, especially with Macedonians' reputation as builders, takes a much more central role in the effort to project a national imaginary. In Montene-gro, national unity is articulated in two ways—first through reference to national landscape (rocky mountains and rushing streams) and second with reference to history through literary narratives or painting traditions. Slovenian films work similarly, highlighting the national association with the alpine and the activities associated with it. In Croatia, the nation is visualized less through iconic landscape images and more through democratic traditions—detailed coverage of voting for members of Congress (the Sabor)—and peasant traditions. But increasingly, the cultural activities that get the most attention are those that relate to industrial concerns. For example, nautical traditions are given increased attention as they redevelop their ports and expand their shipbuilding enterprises.

This emphasis on unity over brotherhood in monthly film journals' visions of labor was hardly totalizing. Both the federal *Filmske Novosti* newsreel and the monthly film journals highlight skilled labor and connect it to national traditions. Whether it is Macedonians' bricklaying skills, Montenegrins' stonework, or Dalmatians' lacework, the national working body reasserts itself through the focus on craftsmanship, on individual national skills, and traditions.

In addition to these themes and the forms through which they are articulated, the monthlies in each context frequently address explicitly *Yugoslav* themes, reminding citizens (less often in Montenegro than in the other republics) that their national identity is to be understood in relation to their role as Yugoslav citizens. But as we will see, the dynamic between the national and the supranational is given high priority. To understand how this dynamic was asserted and experienced, we need to turn to an array of extratextual factors.

Bodies behind the Camera

Film theory has taught us to be highly conscious of the ways that spectators occupy positions of power, most frequently through their audiovisual alignments with the camera's viewing position. Whether it is the psychosexual dynamics of the classical Hollywood cinema or the political-ethical struggles in which we often find ourselves viewing documentaries, "the voice" of the film, as Bill Nichols argues, is central to shaping a host of imaginary relations, often grounded on the specifics of the "look" (1983).

Despite numerous disingenuous claims otherwise, documentaries do not come to us with pretenses of being objective windows on the world (though of course there are varying claims to less partiality and greater rigor). Documentaries and newsreels make explicit arguments about the world, and their institutional affiliations are usually plain to see. Bodies behind the camera—individuals, teams, and institutions—consistently call attention to their own organizing vision, especially in contexts such as Yugoslavia in the postwar period. They use narration as structuring systems, consciously shaping the meaning of images through juxtaposition, intertitles, and, at times, voice-over. In Croatia, beginning in 1947, they began to structure film monthlies in a way that demonstrated processes of production—from usage back to industrial production and then back to natural resources—aiming to shape not only what information about industrial progress Croatian citizens had but also how they understood the social relationships involved in production.[6] Issue no. 7 (1947) contains a story titled "Harvests" that emphasizes the modernization of grain harvesting, showing the separate steps, explaining what was done with the surplus, and even listing both the number of machines in operation and the number needed for the achievement of the Five-Year Plan. We get a related but even more clearly structured example in issue no. 4 (1948) on the timber industry. The story begins with the familiar rhetoric of old and new, wherein manual labor is replaced by machine labor, demonstrated in the forest with the felling of trees. The timber is then moved to the mills, where it is refined and prepared for its next stage—local factories where workers build furniture. The repetition of this logic across issues and the Marxist-Leninist lesson behind it is plain to see and touches numerous spheres of production.[7]

But whereas the organization of material points to a body or voice shaping meaning, the actual bodies and positions of individuals matter as well. Back in 1929, Dziga Vertov famously called attention to the potentially troubling role of cinematic labor when he asserted that the "man with a movie camera" was a good/useful laborer like any other. Instead of being on the side of wastefulness, obfuscation, false dreams, and useless services, nonfiction film directors were productive laborers, helping people under-

6. Salome Skvirsky locates this type of work as well as others that highlight chronologically ordered labor and that produce a finished product in a larger multimedia genre in her excellent work *The Process Genre* (2020).

7. Interestingly, in the essay "About Our Film Monthly," which was written in 1950 but came out of a conference on the Croatian film monthly in 1949, the writer (not identified but clearly someone in a leadership position in Croatian Cinema) critiques the *pregleds* (monthlies) as not going into enough depth, political and personal, about the issues. What we end up with, he argues, "didn't match the reality, meaning it was only the pale image of reality, I would say the falsified image of reality" (13). Although pleased with much of the development of the series, the writer decries the lack of focus on individual faces and individual stories. For sure this is evidence of the effort (here not achieved) to imbue nonfiction film with Socialist Realist ideals and aesthetics. Commission for Agitation and Propaganda of the Central Committee of the CP (Croatian branch), box 12; 3.3.4.6 fond 1220; 1945–1954.

stand the truth of everyday Soviet reality while remaining invulnerable to criticisms that they are artists or intelligentsia.

Yugoslav nonfiction filmmakers were likewise presented as productive laborers and could be seen as the third group in Tito's famous division of labor into "workers, peasants, and honest intelligence." But in addition to being visible as textual organizers and class representatives, these filmmakers were national representatives as well. Many worked on *Filmske Novosti* and their republic's monthly journals but also collaborated on documentaries and fiction film projects across borders. Velimir Stojanovic is one prime example. Stojanovic was born in Pristina, Serbia (now Kosovo), in 1921 and went to film school in Dubrovnik, Croatia, prior to the war. He worked in the army during the war and later directed two documentaries in Serbia for Avala Films in 1950 and 1951. At that point, he went to Montenegro, where he and the Montenegrin writer Ratko Djurovic teamed up to make the most important films of the period in Montenegro, establishing what the leading expert on Montenegrin film, Gojko Kastratovic, calls the Montenegrin Documentary School, a style that is "largely Mediterranean, but a bit off" (pers. comm., October 2014).[8] After his time in Montenegro in the 1950s, Stojanovic continued his career across Yugoslavia, working extensively in Serbia and occasionally in Bosnia until his early death in 1959. This kind of movement and these various collaborations were common, encouraged, and reflected newsreels' efforts to locate culture in supranational space, continually highlighting artistic collaboration and exchange. Perhaps most importantly, collaborations across personnel and agencies were announced loudly and often. For example, many of the early Montenegrin monthlies reported in their title sequences that Croatia's Jadran Films had cooperated in processing the film. Bosna Film was slightly more ambivalent about their own independence but still called attention to it. They pointed to the fact that Lovcen Film (Montenegro) and Jadran Film (Croatia) assisted in processing their early issues. But they also announced in issue no. 21 (1949), "This is the first monthly to be entirely produced and processed by Bosna film."

Evidence of this desire to celebrate the supranational dimension likewise appeared in newspapers, where articles emphasized the multinational makeup of documentary production crews. This is also true for fiction film production. In regard to the first major fiction film production, *In the Mountains of Yugoslavia*, film historian Petar Volk writes, the "participation of all

---

8. See Kastratovic 1999.

Yugoslav nations had to be visible, and the role of the Communist Party and its leadership had to be emphasized" (1986: 10). That is not to say that all audiences heard that message or that the nonfiction industry articulated themselves the way, for example, Hollywood has always made itself part of the story. But it is to say that there was a conscious effort to make these collaborations knowable. Brotherhood and unity, the central pillar of the system, became a way of imagining the occupational directive of the bodies behind the screen, and that meant a movement across and between regions of the country.

Institutional Bodies and Programmatic Structure

This desire for, and ambivalence of, the supranational and the national that is legible in the activity of bodies behind the camera is likewise evident in the institutions for whom the film workers labored. In the initial postwar years, nonfiction film was produced largely in Belgrade, Serbia, but also in Zagreb, Croatia, where the Independent State of Croatia had produced a series of documentary/educational films on public health prior to and during the war. *Filmske Novosti*, to remind, was founded immediately after the war, developed offices in each of the republics while maintaining a base in Belgrade, and was under the control of Zvezda Film. The State Film Company was in charge of fiction film and was connected to the government and political leadership both through the Ministry of Education and through the Propaganda Department of the Central Committee of the Communist Party of Yugoslavia. It established an import and distribution company, but the Central Committee regulated all activity on the distribution of films, including rental prices to theaters. The republics were given the movie theaters that belonged to the State Film Company free of charge and paid 10 percent post-tax income to the state for cinema development, but the federal government still controlled fiction film production and distribution (Volk 1986: 465–89).

To be sure, in 1947, most fiction and nonfiction film activity was still based in Belgrade. But in addition to opening film schools in Belgrade and Zagreb, around this time the Central Committee also reorganized their institutional structure and production process, especially regarding nonfiction film. The republic committees and commissions were put in charge of theaters in their regions as well as the production of documentary and educational/informational films, about which they consulted their own republic's ministries of education and culture (465–89).

Within this structure, fiction and nonfiction film were treated differently: the republics were allowed to maintain control over film monthlies
and documentaries, but fiction films were entirely controlled at the federal
level. Perhaps unsurprisingly, this organizational structure was echoed at
the level of the structure of the film programs themselves, which likewise
communicated brotherhood and unity. During this period, citizens would
most often sit down to a *Filmske Novosti* (federal newsreel), a monthly film
journal (republic newsreel), potentially a short documentary (produced at
either the federal or national level), and a feature film. Thus, even when the
dynamic between the supranational and the national was not asserted ver-
bally, its significance came through the programmatic system. The presentational and performative exhibition space and the textual and extratextual
thematic assertions of brotherhood and unity indexed at different orders.
But they combined to assert the primacy of this "pillar of the system."[9]

Bodies of Authority

One of the most surprising aspects of Yugoslav postwar nonfiction
film was the lack of continuity in personnel, style, and narration for the federal newsreel. This was not necessarily the case for the individual national
monthly newsreel issues, but it is significant that it appears with the federal
newsreel. At one level, it runs counter to the project's broader goals of uni-
fication articulated clearly in a set of guidelines and goals established following a newsreel workers and management conference that took place in
1947. At another level, it counters our common understandings of the literal
and symbolic "voice" of the newsreel. Especially in those contexts where
governments are trying to build new film industries, we expect the newsreel
to serve as a unifying force with the voice-over narration as the symbolic
epicenter. In the Yugoslav case, there are twin and interrelated forces driving the discontinuity, each of which relates to the larger supranation-building
project—basic pragmatic concerns and a wariness to project a centralized
authority. One was the cooperation across the republic; the other was the
Communist Party itself.

One of the reasons for discontinuity in personnel is certainly because

---

9. Although it extends the period under consideration in this essay, the Pula Film Festival
also points to this effort to assert brotherhood and unity. Pula, which began in 1954, was
the hugely popular and celebrated all-Yugoslav film festival, and it worked hard to ensure
that each republic was represented and its work celebrated.

Filmske Novosti was a new institution, and, as is common practice, it served as a training ground for film professionals (as did the monthly film journals).[10] This fluctuation and particular confluence of film workers likely contributed to the stylistic discontinuity of the issues. While the overall structure did not change much during the initial years, the introductions, credits, form of titling, and visual approach underwent continual redesign. We see a host of new wipe transitions in episode 20 (1945), the emergence of shorter stories at the end of 1945 and early 1946, strange musical experiments in episode 26 (1946) with a shift back to standard classical fare by episode 53 (1946), and a striking use of tracking shots by episode 74 (1947). Topically, in 1945, especially early 1945, most of the issues focused on a particular nation. A typical example would be an issue centered on Slovenia with various liberation celebrations, highlights of the national landscape, and awards for war heroes and cultural figures. Toward the end of the year, we begin to see issues that coordinate stories from the various nations in one issue. Thus, the issues lose some aesthetic continuity as they become more supranationally inclusive.

But it is at the level of narration that we see the logics of this discontinuity emerge and where we can begin to see how it aligns with the previous (supra)nation-building efforts I have discussed. The narration of the *Filmske Novosti* newsreel not only changed from nation to nation but maintained little stability across and within issues. By episode 51 (1946), for example, we see a shift from narration with considerable intensity to one that is more subdued and holds a Macedonian accent. In other words, there were multiple narrators speaking the different languages required for viewers to understand—but even they were not stable over time. Similarly, there were often multiple narrators for individual stories. This seems to reinforce the notion that the *Filmske Novosti* sought to undermine the idea of centrality itself—refusing the possibility of a stable narrational *national* or *supranational* authority. This type of address buttresses the way in which the aesthetics and rhetoric of the issues aim to create a particular imaginary

10. In the initial postwar period, the most experienced filmmakers were those in Croatia who trained with the Ustashe prior to and during the war. Many, like Kosta Hlavaty and Branko Marjanovic, retained prominent positions and claimed they were not doing political work. Rather, they were protecting inventory and personnel while working for Hrvatski Slikopis, the main state film production company at the time. During this period, they made newsreels, short culture films, short live actions, documentaries, public health films, and educational films. Commission for Agitation and Propaganda of the Central Committee of the CP (Croatian branch), box 12; 3.3.

geography of the country. In their effort to assert an authority consistent with an emphasis on brotherhood, they project decentralized geography.

But that is not to say that the unity does not reemerge in the guise of leadership. If a legible structure or center comes across, it is perhaps grounded in the figure of the leader, Marshal Tito, whose presence across all the nations in the *Filmske Novosti* and in the monthly film journals (with the exception of Bosnia) increases dramatically starting in 1946. At this time, we see in the *Filmske Novosti* a great effort to locate him physically across the country, to avoid a direct association of Tito with a home, and power, in Belgrade. It is perhaps in the sequences covering "the Relay of Youth" (Stafeta Mladesti) that this effort crystallizes. Starting in 1945, each region in Yugoslavia held a symbolic relay race in which young people carried batons as a symbolic birthday pledge to Tito. After moving through the cities and towns of each region, youth brought the *stafeta* to Belgrade to present to Tito on May 25, Tito's official birthday and the Day of Youth. By 1950, more than a million children were participating in the event, which lasted over a month. The process was covered both in *Filmske Novosti* issues as well as in the monthly journal issues, and it served a variety of purposes. It asserted brotherhood and unity across Yugoslavia, and it aligned those principles with subservience to leadership. It identified youth as the synecdoche of the nation and as aligned with Tito himself. And the efforts to "cover" this mobile relay served as visual tours of the modernization and natural beauty the national filmmakers aimed to showcase: thriving factories, decimated villages coming back to life, mountain streams, snowcapped mountains, and dense forests. Concluding these sequences in Belgrade, with Tito, we thus see that it is the body and personage of Tito that, logically, subsumes and resolves the ambivalence of the (supra) nation-building project, as articulated through nonfiction film. We end up with what Nevena Dakovic describes as a "Tito-centered moveable feast" (pers. comm., June 2007), or what I would describe as a mobile radiality, with Marshal Tito's figure, image, and name marking the only possible center—the center of authority, stability, and unity.

Bringing together the multiple ways that brotherhood and unity get articulated in this nonfiction film project allows us to recognize how the effort to shape the social imaginaries of Yugoslav citizens in the initial postwar years requires a consideration of the experiences of cinema that government officials, filmmakers, film producers, distributors, and exhibitors created. The ever-shifting balance between socialist revolution, with its manifestation in Yugoslav supranational identity, and the individual national identities is at the core of the nonfiction film project. Its ambivalence and irresolvability are knowable through the multiple engagements people have with this project—evident from the themes of the films as well as the extra-textual knowledge that the film industry took pains to communicate to citizens. The documentary or nonfiction film imaginary they sought to project, model, and instill was neither hidden nor strategically implicit. As in the documentaries themselves, the labor that went into these efforts to build the country, to build the nonfiction film industry, and to establish this relation between the viewing subject and his or her brave new world was legible on its various surfaces. And citizens' responses to these efforts to instill a desire for a layered identity certainly entailed recognition not just of the identarian dynamics in play but the extraordinary stakes involved in this effort.

Conclusion

Throughout this essay, I have sought to demonstrate the various levels or orders of indexing that takes place through viewers' experiences with Yugoslav nonfiction film (and in the process, implicitly, point to this approach's value in thinking about other nonfiction forms and situations). Words and images index one meaning, narrational structures index another, programmatic structures index another, and textual encounters beyond the film text and exhibition context index yet another. Together, they build up into an nth-order indexicality that indicates to audiences how nonfiction film articulates the relation between federal and national levels of identity and activity. But how viewers felt about those experiences depends on their own position with regard to supranational and national identity.

Yugoslav citizens in the postwar period were living in a highly politicized space and coming off a brutal war at a moment when speech was taking on increased political valences. Nowhere is this more true than around the issue of nations, their autonomy, and leadership. The combination of brotherhood and unity slogans, thematics, overt narration, and programmatic structures works to cement it as a dominant idea in the social fabric, despite its accompanying ambivalence and irresolvability. Its force comes from the fact that it is a dynamic, a ratio, and a constantly shifting one at that. In this way, it becomes a master-signifier (pivotal political words that rally citizens but are signifiers without signifieds) in part through these films

(Žižek 1989: 93). It is a malleable signifier whose strength comes from the *and*. There just needs to be some brotherhood and some unity. The point, of course, is not that people necessarily or fully buy into the specificity of the individual ideological arguments. What is important is that they recognize that these are the terms of the conversation and that those terms get established through their experiences with nonfiction film—as a text, as a cinematic experience within a larger film program, and as part of an industry that imagines and creates its own collectivity. Nonfiction film puts the performative element of this effort on display.

The principle of brotherhood and unity is realizable as a visualized collective activity (isn't watching a film program a version of participating in brotherhood and unity?). It is an idea shaping relations with internal and external citizens. And it is a political principle shaping policy decisions. It both absorbs and resolves social conflict, even as its solutions vary and as its resolutions remain temporary. Moreover, it is telling that nonfiction film was the space where the dynamic seemed to hold most effectively— fiction film was controlled almost entirely at the federal level (too much unity), whereas education was controlled mostly at the national level (too much brotherhood). For Slavoj Žižek, master-signifiers work not because they contain some preexisting, complete, transcendental, and totalizing meaning but because they are empty. The signifier brotherhood and unity thus marks the specificity of the Yugoslav revolutionary project (distinguishing it from all outside efforts) and its internal indeterminacy and flexibility. Its force comes from the fact that we see it in all its textual specificity, experience it in all its materiality, and yet . . . we still cannot say quite what it is.

References

Arendt, Hannah. 1963. *On Revolution*. Westport, CT: Greenwood.

Carroll, Noel. 1983. "From Real to Reel: Entangled in Nonfiction Film." *Philosophic Exchange* 14, no. 1: 1–42.

Commission for Agitation and Propaganda of the Central Committee of the CP (Croatian branch), box 12; 3.3.4.6 fond 1220; 1945–1954.

Doane, Mary Ann. 2007. "The Indexical and the Concept of Medium Specificity." *differences* 18, no. 1: 128–52.

Goulding, Daniel. (1985) 2002. *Liberated Cinema: The Yugoslav Experience, 1945–2001*. Bloomington: Indiana University Press.

Haug, Hilde Katrine. 2012. *Creating a Socialist Yugoslavia: Tito, Communist Leadership and the National Question*. London: I. B. Tauris.

Jakobson, Roman. 1984. *Russian and Slavic Grammar*. New York: Mouton.

Kastratovic, Gojko. 1999. *Crnogorska kinematografija i filmovi o Crnoj Gori* (Montenegrin cinematography and films about Montenegro). Podgorica: Lovcen Library.

Kracauer, Siegfried. (1969) 2013. *History: The Last Things before the Last.* Princeton, NJ: Markus Wiener.

Malitsky, Joshua. 2014. *Post-Revolution Nonfiction Film: Building the Soviet and Cuban Nations.* Bloomington: Indiana University Press.

Metz, Christian. 1974. *Film Language: A Semiotics of the Cinema,* translated by Michael Taylor. New York: Oxford University Press.

Mitchell, W. J. T. 2015. *Image Science: Iconology, Visual Culture, and Media Aesthetics.* Chicago: University of Chicago Press.

Nichols, Bill. 1983. "The Voice of Documentary." *Film Quarterly* 36, no. 3: 17–30.

Peirce, Charles Sanders. 1932. *Collected Papers of Charles Sanders Peirce.* Vol. 2, edited by Charles Hartshorne and Paul Weiss. Cambridge, MA: Harvard University Press.

Ramet, Sabrina. 2006. *The Three Yugoslavias: State-Building and Legitimation, 1918–2005.* Bloomington: Indiana University Press.

Rankovich, Radenko. 2004. *Organization of the Yugoslav Cinematography in Administrative Management Period.* Novi Sad: Zvezda Film.

Robinson, Gertrude. 1977. *Tito's Maverick Media: The Politics of Mass Communication in Yugoslavia.* Urbana-Champaign: University of Illinois Press.

Skvirsky, Salome. 2020. *The Process Genre.* Durham, NC: Duke University Press.

Tadic, Darko. 2011. "Yugoslav Propaganda Film: Early Works, 1945–1952." *Journal of Film and Video* 63, no. 3: 3–12.

Taylor, Charles. 2004. *Modern Social Imaginaries.* Durham, NC: Duke University Press.

Volk, Petar. 1986. *Istorija jugoslovenskog filma* (History of Yugoslav film). Belgrade, Yugoslavia: Institut za Film.

Wachtel, Andrew. 1998. *Making a Nation, Breaking a Nation: Literature and Cultural Politics in Yugoslavia.* Palo Alto, CA: Stanford University Press.

Žižek, Slavoj. 1989. *The Sublime Object of Ideology.* New York: Verso.

The World Union of Documentary and the Early Cold War

Alice Lovejoy

A photograph taken in June 1947 at the Brussels International Film Festival captures the earliest and perhaps most hopeful moment in the brief history of the World Union of Documentary (WUD), an association that aimed to articulate a common purpose for postwar documentary and to facilitate the international exchange of films, professionals, and knowledge in the field. Gathered behind a luncheon table are many of documentary's interwar luminaries. Standing third from the left is Belgian filmmaker Henri

This essay draws on the exceptionally rich World Union of Documentary-Association Internationale des Documentaristes Collection, assembled by Bert Hogenkamp and Miryam van Lier and housed at the Joris Ivens Archive in Nijmegen, the Netherlands, as well as on sources from the British Film Institute and the Czech National Film Archive. I am grateful to the staff at all three archives for their assistance, and to Hogenkamp and André Stufkens, director of the European Foundation Joris Ivens, for their generous guidance during my research. Many thanks as well to Daniel Morgan for generative comments and edits and to Nataša Ďurovičová, Paula Rabinowitz, and Katie Trumpener for their readings of earlier versions of this essay. Unless otherwise noted, all translations are my own.

boundary 2 49:1 (2022)   DOI 10.1215/01903659-9615445   ©2022 by Duke University Press

Figure 1 World Union of Documentary founding meeting in Brussels, June 1947. Standing left to right: Geoffrey Smith, Edgar Anstey, Henri Storck, Jean Painlevé, Joris Ivens, Theodor Balk, Gaston Bouthoul, Ralph Bond. Seated left to right: Iris Barry, Basil Wright, Jiří Lehovec, Jerzy Toeplitz, Paul Rotha. Credit: Coll. Joris Ivens Archives / European Foundation Joris Ivens, Nijmegen

Storck, who, with socialist politician Pierre (Piet) Vermeylen and André Thiri-fays, hosted the meetings; the three men had also cofounded the Brussels festival and the Belgian Cinémathèque. To Storck's right are Geoffrey Smith of South Africa and Edgar Anstey, representing the British Documentary Movement with Ralph Bond, John Grierson, Basil Wright, and Paul Rotha. To Storck's left is French scientific filmmaker Jean Painlevé, who was joined in Brussels by his compatriots Jean Grémillon and Cinémathèque française cofounder Henri Langlois.

Iris Barry, founder of the MoMA film library, sits at the photograph's bottom left. Next to her are Wright, Czech documentarian Jiří Lehovec (for-merly of the Czechoslovak avant-garde group Left Front, or Levá Fronta), Jerzy Toeplitz, a former member of the Polish avant-garde group START (the Society for the Promotion of Film Art, or Stowarzyszenie Miłośników

Filmu Artystycznego), and, at the end of the row, Rotha. Standing behind Rotha are, from the right, Bond, Gaston Bouthoul (cofounder of the Institut français de polémologie) and, wearing glasses, Yugoslav doctor and journalist Teodor Balk. A veteran of the International Brigades and the newly minted chief of the Yugoslav state film company's documentary section (Vojtěchovský 2012: 56), Balk was in Brussels thanks to his friendship with Joris Ivens (standing fourth from the right), the celebrated peripatetic filmmaker whom he had met in Spain and who was, in Toeplitz's recollection, the World Union's "great master," its raison d'être.[1] Ivens was in Brussels fresh off the success of his *Indonesia Calling* (1946) and en route to Prague (Waugh 2016: 355) (Figure 1).

In 1947, it was unremarkable that an association devoted to documentary would have been populated by archivists and festival founders in addition to filmmakers and critics. Before World War II, the emergence of documentary, like that of film festivals and archives, had helped articulate a vision of cinema as cultural, educational, and political (not merely commercial or entertaining), and in the first years after the war, there were reasons to be optimistic about this vision (Hagener 2014: 3; Wasson 2005). Festivals were flourishing, and documentary had gained institutional support in the United Nations. The mode's interwar proponents had also matured and now commanded major institutions and considerable resources. This brought with it obligations. As Ivens stated at the opening of the Brussels meetings, "We all carry a responsibility vis-à-vis the youth in all countries who want to make brave and honest films and who expect us to indicate the path."[2] Yet despite these grand goals and the considerable institutional, human, and financial resources behind them, the World Union lasted barely three years, collapsing in 1950.

The World Union's demise is typically attributed to high politics of the Cold War (MacDonald 2013: 462; Jansen 2004).[3] And the association's brief history does offer a glimpse of the significance, for documentary, of the immediate post–World War II period—a moment that has largely been

---

1. Bert Hogenkamp and Miryam van Lier, interview with Jerzy Toeplitz, 1991. b. 1, f. 9, WUD-AID Collection, Joris Ivens Archives, Nijmegen (hereafter WUD-AID).
2. Union Mondiale du Documentaire: Procès verbal de la première réunion, dimanche 8 juin 1947 à 14:30 à l'Hôtel Astoria à Bruxelles. b. 1, f. 12, WUD-AID.
3. A more nuanced account is offered in Bert Hogenkamp's scholarship, which builds on the research he and Myriam van Lier conducted on the World Union of Documentary and the Association Internationale des Documentaristes.

overlooked in documentary history, dismissed as a point at which the mode lost the financial and popular support it enjoyed during the war, migrated from cinemas, and was sapped of its formal dynamism (Waugh 2016: 333). In Bert Hogenkamp's words, "The common view was this: after the 1930s nothing happened" (2000: xi). However, the World Union's history also lays bare the complex transformations that documentary underwent during the first postwar decade in terms not just of aesthetics, funding, or exhibition but also of geopolitics: the ways in which documentary filmmakers and institutions understood the mode's relationship to the nation, the state, and the *international* sphere. The latter is the focus of this essay, which describes how the World Union's vision of international documentary emerged—and unraveled—in 1947–50 and how this rise and fall was tied to the postwar histories of both film festivals and the peace movement. I focus on Eastern Europe in particular. Not only was the World Union headquartered in this region for most of its existence, the association's history is inextricable from that of Ivens's 1949 omnibus *The First Years* (*Pierwsze lata*), about the East European "new democracies" of Bulgaria, Czechoslovakia, Poland, and Yugoslavia—a film whose history this essay also narrates. Both projects, I argue, were impeded not only by the polarized political atmosphere of the period but also by complex political, administrative, and generational dynamics within the documentary community and the international Left.

• • • •

Already in the early 1930s, documentary's links to the nation were well established. In Britain, the United States, and elsewhere, filmmakers and critics had come to understand the mode as what Jonathan Kahana terms "a cinematic social pedagogy addressed by an individual or corporate author to the citizen of the modern industrial nation-state" (2008: 7). Simultaneously, the idea had taken root that cinema's pedagogical, edifying role might assume international dimensions. Among the most prominent proponents of this idea were the Comintern-sponsored filmmaking and film distribution organizations Mezhrabpomfilm and Prometheusfilm and the League of Nations' International Institute of Intellectual Cooperation, which, Zoë Druick argues, modeled a liberal internationalism for cinema, becoming "a forum for international discourse about cultural film" (2008: 72–73).[4] In the middle of the decade, these liberal and socialist visions

---

4. On the Comintern and visual culture, see Glaser and Lee 2019.

of documentary internationalism found consensus in the antifascist Popular Front (comprised of liberals, socialists, and communists in Europe and North America, yet steered by the Soviet Union), which pioneered a deliberately popular, formally hybrid mode of production that Thomas Waugh dubs the "mise-en-scène" documentary for its reliance on staging. As Waugh writes, "mise-en-scène" documentaries (epitomized by Ivens's own 1937 *The Spanish Earth*) "had the purpose not only of reflecting the world but also of acting upon it, to change it" (2016: 206).[5] This politics and style continued to define documentary during World War II, when—generously sponsored and widely distributed by government agencies such as the American Office of War Information and the British Ministry of Information—the mode reached the apex of its popularity and influence.

As a result, in 1945 documentary's prospects looked good. The postwar world was seemingly in need of the clear-eyed guidance documentarians had long prided themselves in offering, and the United Nations was building an international framework for a range of initiatives that supported practical, cultural, and educational understandings of cinema (Rotha 1966: 30).[6] Documentary was particularly prominent in the United Nations Educational, Scientific, and Cultural Organization (UNESCO), founded in 1946; as Druick writes, UNESCO "was a clear continuation of projects and ideas found in the [League of Nations'] Committee on International Cooperation" (2008: 80). This sense of possibility extended to postwar films themselves. In Waugh's words, "if 'land' was the hallmark of prewar documentary titles . . . 'world' might be seen as the symptomatic post-war equivalent" (2016: 346).

In its conception as both a professional union and a framework for international exchange, the World Union echoed aspects of the League of Nations' and UNESCO's film programs. Similarly, in the spirit of the United Nations, the 1947 Brussels meetings proceeded in a studied balance between the national and international. Attendees reported on local developments in documentary and strategized ways to support its production and distribution. They discussed its scope (in particular its relationship to newsreels, scientific films, and educational films), and they debated aesthetics. Crucially, everyone present agreed that documentary form—which they believed had been pushed to do too much too quickly during the war—needed to change.

5. On Popular Front documentary, see also Kahana 2008.
6. On UN film activities in the early postwar period, see Longo 2015.

There was less agreement about what form this change should take and especially about whether or not the pragmatism of Popular Front documentary was still necessary. In Paul Rotha's words, the central question was if—counter to Popular Front ideals—documentary should simply "present the social or other fact without proposing a solution."[7] Painlevé supported this view, arguing that French documentarians favored "critical and lyrical documentaries like [Eli Lotar's 1946] *Aubervilliers*, which state the existence of a social situation" but "do not offer solutions to the problems they pose."[8] Both the British filmmakers and Balk disagreed, however: according to Balk, problem-solving was a crucial part of Yugoslav cinema, itself "an integral part of the country's reconstruction." Although the meetings ultimately concluded that documentaries *should* offer solutions, this had less to do with the durability of Popular Front conceptions of documentary than it did with a return to origins, for as Waugh describes, the "mise-en-scène" approach had roots both in liberal and social-democratic interwar documentary traditions *and* in socialist realism (2016: 206). Ultimately, it would be between these approaches to documentary—embodied by the World Union's British and East European members, respectively—that the association's fatal disagreements would emerge.

Indeed, the alliances at the emerging association's core were fragile, and discussions about its structure raised sensitive geopolitical questions. Smaller states such as Poland and Czechoslovakia feared underrepresentation, and the question of whether the association would accept individual members or only official national sections was debated extensively before an agreement was reached to form national sections of equal standing. Even more vexing was the association's relationship to the two interwar lodestars of international documentary, the Soviet Union and the United Nations. The former was conspicuously absent from the Brussels meetings: then Soviet Deputy Minister of Cinematography Mikhail Kalatozov had promised that a Soviet representative would be present, but in the end, the country sent no delegates to the Brussels festival. Ivens assured his col-

---

7. Festival mondial du Film, Bruxelles, le 9 juin 1947, séance de 20 h 30. b. 1, f. 12, WUD-AID; Festival mondial du film, Réunion des documentaristes, lundi 9 juin à 14 heures. b. 1, f. 12, WUD-AID.

8. Union Mondiale du Documentaire: Procès verbal de la première réunion, dimanche 8 juin 1947 à 14:30 à l'Hôtel Astoria à Bruxelles. b. 1, f. 12, WUD-AID. Nevertheless, *Aubervilliers* exemplifies a strain of left-wing French documentary described by Steven Ungar as a "response to [Jean] Vigo's 1930 call for a social cinema" (2014: 51).

leagues that the Soviet Union was "following our meetings, as well as our documentary film movement, with great interest."[9]

The United Nations, conversely, was very much present in the person of John Grierson, the veteran British producer often credited with founding the British Documentary Movement. Grierson had recently been named UNESCO's director of mass communications and public information (Druick 2014: 113), and in Brussels he gave a report on the organization's cinematic activities. British documentarians—perhaps bound by what Richard MacDonald terms "the British documentary ethos . . . of the group or unit as the primary creative entity" (2013: 458)—had already publicly adhered to UNESCO's cinematic program, and Grierson intended the World Union to collaborate closely with the UN organization. Thus, in his draft of the Brussels meetings' concluding statement, Ralph Bond declared the World Union's "total participation in UNESCO's entire program."[10] But the meetings' socialist and communist participants dissented. Painlevé noted that Grierson had been invited to Brussels as a filmmaker, not as a UNESCO representative; he argued that the World Union's politics and mission were distinct from UNESCO's (despite their common commitment to assuring an active postwar role for documentary). Painlevé, Toeplitz, Grémillon, Balk, and Ivens requested that Bond's sentence be edited to reflect the World Union's willingness to work with other international organizations as well (such as the communist-affiliated World Federation of Trade Unions): singling out UNESCO, they argued, would help secure the World Union's political viability in Britain but have the opposite effect in the Soviet Union, which would not join UNESCO until 1954.[11]

These edits, accepted under protest by the British documentarians, foretold the World Union's collapse as early as its very first day. The association, it was obvious, encompassed two now-incompatible interwar models of documentary internationalism. Grierson embodied one of these models, a legacy of the British Documentary Movement and the League of Nations: what Martin Stollery describes as a "progressive internationalism" rooted in the overlapping of the 1930s' liberal internationalism and enlightened impe-

9. Festival mondial du Film, Bruxelles, le 9 juin 1947, séance de 20 h 30. b. 1, f. 12, WUD-AID.

10. Festival mondial du Film, Bruxelles, le 9 juin 1947, séance de 20 h 30. b. 1, f. 12, WUD-AID.

11. East European countries, however, had been members of the organization since 1946. On UNESCO and Eastern Europe, see Graham 2006.

rialism, and closely aligned with UNESCO (2006: 1494).[12] The other model, supported by Ivens, representatives of East European countries, Storck, and Painlevé, reflected these figures' hope for a postwar revival of Popular Front documentary. The summer of 1947 was perhaps the last point in the first postwar decade that such hope was imaginable, at least on a global scale: in September, the Cominform (Communist Information Agency) was formed, rejecting the Truman Doctrine and sketching a picture of a world divided into "two camps."[13]

• • • •

Despite these still-nascent tensions, the Brussels meetings ended with the seeds of an institution. A committee (Balk, Ivens, Painlevé, Rotha, Toeplitz) was appointed to draft the World Union's constitution, and a provisional headquarters was established in Paris at Painlevé and Georges Franju's Institute of Scientific Cinema. The association's first congress was planned for Czechoslovakia in 1948.[14] And the Brussels Declaration, presented at a festival press conference by Ivens, Rotha, and Storck, defined documentary's social role ("not only to state the problems exactly, but also to guide the public towards the solution of these problems"), sketched a broad aesthetic direction ("art and technique . . . fused with . . . social purpose"), and outlined the issues with which documentary should engage ("the fight against the enemies of peace and democracy; national, racial and economic oppression and religious intolerance"; "independence of subject peoples"). "Documentary film workers," it concluded, "will collaborate with all international organisations working for the principles enumerated above."[15]

Although the declaration's final sentence glossed over the fractures evident in Brussels, in a practical sense the World Union's construction depended on a series of international organizations, most importantly

12. On this, see also MacDonald 2013.
13. In practice, the divisions between these documentary internationalisms were often less sharply drawn: French and East European documentarians, among them officers of the World Union, actively collaborated with UNESCO throughout the late 1940s. Elmar Klos, for instance, was present in Paris during UNESCO's founding in fall 1946 and, in 1948, made a film for the organization in collaboration with a French cameraman (Lukeš 2011: 171, 175).
14. Festival mondial du Film, Bruxelles, le 9 juin 1947, séance de 20 h 30. b. 1, f. 12, WUD-AID.
15. The Brussels Declaration. b. 1, f. 13, WUD-AID.

film festivals. Many festivals of the period were themselves products of the era of the United Nations (federal in structure, and, as Dudley Andrew has described, intended to "[foster] both equality and difference in artistic expression"), and they provided essential scaffolding for the documentary association (2010: 71). For while the World Union was nominally headquartered in Paris, it existed primarily in correspondence between its far-flung members and in chance or planned meetings at such events. "During the International Conference of Film Trade Unions in Czechoslovakia," Storck wrote to Franju in August 1947, "I ran into some of the founders of the World Union of Documentary. We have decided to meet to discuss what has already been achieved and get up to date on the delegates' goals."[16] A month later, the constitution committee met after the Congress of Scientific and Technical Film in Cannes.[17]

Another festival—Czechoslovakia's International Film Festival, held in the western Bohemian spa town of Mariánské Lázně—served as the backdrop for the association's first congress. This was not initially planned: in Brussels, Jiří Lehovec had proposed a wintertime gathering in the Slovak mountains (bž 1947: 1). However, the international and national political landscape had shifted since Brussels, both with the Cominform's founding and the events of February 1948, when the Communist Party assumed control of the Czechoslovak government. Although the Party had dominated Czechoslovak politics since 1946 (and Czechoslovakia's nationalized film industry since 1945), the takeover upended plans for the congress. Its budget was approved only on the condition that "Slavic documentarians" participate, and its planned location changed frequently throughout the first half of 1948.[18] Sites in the Slovak Tatra Mountains were scouted in January 1948, but in early March, the congress was moved to Prague.[19] At the end of June, Elmar Klos—the head of Short Film (Krátký film), the nonfiction division of Czechoslovakia's nationalized film industry—informed Painlevé

16. Storck to Franju, August 6, 1947. b. 1, f. 17, WUD-AID.
17. Commission de travail pour le constitution de l'Union mondiale du film documentaire, tenue à Cannes les 20, 21, et 22 septembre 1947. b. 1, f. 15, WUD-AID.
18. Zápis o poradě ústředního ředitele a náměstky ze dne 2. března 1948. b. R13/ BII/5P/1K, f. ČFS - Porada náměstků 16.9.1947 - 25.5.1948, UŘ ČSF (unprocessed collection), National Film Archive, Prague (hereafter NFA). As Jindřiška Bláhová has described, the International Film Festival served important diplomatic purposes for Czechoslovakia, and its programming echoed Czechoslovak geopolitics more broadly (Bláhová 2012).
19. J. Valenta to E. Klos, January 16, 1948. b. R10/AI/5P/8K, f. 1947, UŘ ČSF, NFA.

and Langlois that the World Union would meet in Mariánské Lázně in conjunction with the film festival, which alternated between that city and Karlovy
Vary in its first years. "A large number of film workers from all over the world
will be present," he noted, which "will give our Congress's delegates ample
opportunity to meet Festival guests."[20]

Like Brussels and Cannes before it, there were practical reasons to
meet in Mariánské Lázně: many World Union members planned to attend,
and the city had infrastructure for screenings, lodging, and meetings. In
addition, Ivens and Balk were already in Czechoslovakia: Ivens was working
for Czechoslovak State Film on *The First Years*, while the tubercular Balk
was recuperating in the nearby spa town of Karlovy Vary (Vojtěchovský
2012: 57). Yet the decision to hold the congress at one of the country's premier international cultural-political events also underscored that the World
Union's links to film festivals were not just pragmatic, nor were they only
rooted in interwar projects. Hosting the World Union also gave Czechoslovak State Film an international platform on which to showcase its *own*
post-"February" political priorities. For the moment, these priorities were
also rooted in the Popular Front, in which many of the nationalized film
industry's founders had been involved—among them Lubomír Linhart, the
industry's director.

It was thanks to Linhart that Ivens was in Czechoslovakia in the first
place.[21] According to André Stufkens, the concept for *The First Years* was
Linhart's, as was the idea to ask Ivens to direct the film (Stufkens 2016:
472). The two men had met in Moscow in the early 1930s, when Linhart was
working as a film critic for the Czechoslovak Communist Party daily *Red
Evening News* (*Rudý večerník*) and leading the Film-Photo Group of the
Left Front (Waugh 2016: 355).[22] When the Czech lands were occupied by
Nazi Germany, Linhart helped shape underground plans for the film indus-
try's nationalization, and after the war, as the industry's head, he not only
advocated for *The First Years* but traveled with Ivens and his partner Marion
Michelle on their scouting and shooting trips.

In its original conception, Stufkens observes, *The First Years* was
based on American Russian journalist Maurice Hindus's 1947 book *The

20. Klos to Painlevé and Langlois, June 26, 1948, b. 1. f. 15, WUD-AID Collection, Joris
Ivens Archives, Nijmegen.
21. Ivens would work in the region for much of the 1950s—successively in Czechoslovakia, Poland, and East Germany. On this period in the director's oeuvre, see—in addition
to Waugh 2016—Musser 2002 and Hodgin 2016.
22. On Linhart, see Szczepanik and Anděl 2008.

Bright Passage, an account of the "so-called Czech way" and "its attempts to find a balance between the free enterprise in the West and the planned economies of the East, between collectivism and individualism, between evolution and revolution" (2016: 473). The project soon expanded to four sections: one about Bulgaria, one about Czechoslovakia, one about Poland, and one about Yugoslavia (the latter scrapped soon after the 1948 Tito-Stalin split). Each section has a distinct topic and style: in Waugh's description, Bulgaria's is "lyrical," chronicling the modernization of tobacco farming; Czechoslovakia's is "practical," reiterating the nationalist historiography embraced by the country's postwar communist intellectuals (beginning with the Reformation, culminating in "victorious February"); and Poland's is "epic," the story of a war widow working in heavy industry in Silesia (2016: 357–58).

The omnibus format both promised *The First Years* more funding than Czechoslovak State Film alone could provide—each government was to pay for production in its own country and contribute an additional 25 percent to the total budget—and supported the film's geopolitics, which were rooted in the hope that some in the West placed in postwar Eastern Europe as a model for a third-way socialism (355–56).[23] Ivens, in texts written between 1948 and 1950, described *The First Years*' goal as to "reach, touch, and activate Western audiences" about the "People's Democracies" by showing these countries' "high respect for democratic liberties and their common will to defend these liberties against fascism," and thereby foster peace in an increasingly divided world.[24] Understandably, Czechoslovakia's cultural elite was amenable to such interpretations, given the dominant political rhetoric about a "Czechoslovak road to socialism" (Abrams 2004).

All of this was evident in July 1948. On the eighth of the month, Ivens held a press conference in Prague about *The First Years*, and on the seventeenth, the congress opened in Mariánské Lázně with a speech by Vítězslav Nezval (head of the Czechoslovak Ministry of Information's Film Section and, like Linhart, a prominent figure in Czechoslovakia's socialist interwar avant-garde).[25] Nezval commended the delegates' work in light of "the uncertain state of world affairs," in which he pronounced documentary capable of encouraging "cooperation" and "peace," "[bringing] into being a world movement which in the name of truth breaks the bonds of geo-

23. On this vision of Eastern Europe, see Judt 1992.
24. A Short History of the New Democracies Film, June 10, 1949. b. 21, f. 285, WUD-AID.
25. Důležité sdělení redakcím: Tisková konference. b. 21, f. 286, WUD-AID.

graphic and political frontiers." He alluded to the compatibility between post-"February" Czechoslovak cinema's emphasis on "film's function in society" and the World Union's commitment to documentary's practical and social uses. And he drew a comparison between documentary rhetoric about truth and Czechoslovak history, noting that "our own people have made appeal to [the truth] ever since the epoch of Hus"[26]—referring to the fifteenth-century Bohemian religious reformer who, along with his famous dictum "truth shall prevail," was a key means of national legitimization for the Czechoslovak Communist Party in the late 1940s.

• • • •

By all accounts, the congress's five days were congenial and productive. Formal delegations from Belgium, Brazil, Czechoslovakia, France, Britain, Holland, Hungary, Yugoslavia, Poland, and Switzerland as well as observers from Australia, Romania, the United States, and the Soviet Union reported on national developments and discussed the World Union's international and national status. The association's Executive Committee was elected—Wright as chairman, Ivens and Klos as vice presidents, the Brazilian painter Carlos Scliar as treasurer, Toeplitz as secretary—and Warsaw's Film Polski, where Toeplitz was head of documentary film, was designated its new home. Subcommittees were charged with discussing production, distribution, and other matters, and an International Court of Honor (Painlevé, Storck, and critic/theorist Béla Balázs) was elected, charged with ensuring adherence to the Brussels Declaration. The delegates also continued to discuss the issues raised at Brussels. They enlarged the World Union's definition of documentary to four categories (social, scientific, cultural, and experimental), further refined by intended audience (general, specialized, or school), and agreed on a definition of the mode: "the business of recording on celluloid any aspects of reality, interpreted either by factual shooting or by sincere and justifiable reconstruction, so as to appeal either to reason or emotion, for the purposes of stimulating the desire for and the widening of human knowledge and understanding, and of truthfully posing problems and their solutions in the sphere of economics, culture and human relations."[27]

26. First Congress of the World Union of Documentary. BCW/3/23, Basil Wright Files, BFI National Archive Special Collections, London (hereafter, BFI).
27. First Congress of the World Union of Documentary. BCW/3/23, BFI.

If the delegates were hopeful when they left Czechoslovakia, the Cold War remained on everyone's mind. Raymond A. Bech, the Swiss delegate, wrote optimistically that "the Congress demonstrated its firm intention to remain beyond all political considerations, in giving committee posts (and the organization's seat) to personalities from countries that are often distant, if not 'politically opposed.' The seat is located in Warsaw, while the president is none other than English filmmaker Basil Wright" (Bech 1948). Yet Cold War geopolitics *had* found their way into the World Union's governing bodies, which included representatives both from countries whose film industries had been nationalized and from those whose industries had not.[28] A report in the Polish newspaper *Wieczór* (*Evening*) argued that the congress had demonstrated that "where film production is nationalized, there is creative freedom and financial support," whereas "in capitalist countries, films about social issues are made almost exclusively by people on the 'progressive margin'" (Anonymous 1948).[29]

The British delegates at Mariánské Lázně, Basil Wright and Donald Alexander, made a similar assessment in a mid-August article in *Kinematograph Weekly*. Pointed and sarcastic, the article probed the differences between documentary produced by nationalized film industries and by Britain's Central Office of Information (COI, which had no funding of its own, instead relying on ministerial commissions) (Hogenkamp 1999). Alexander and Wright wrote that they had "listened with some envy to the explanation by most of the nationalised countries of how a documentary film already accompanies a feature in every kinema programme." They reserved particular praise for Czechoslovakia's film industry, noting that "the Short Film Corporation comes under the general supervision of the Ministry of Information and makes many of its films at the direct request of Government departments but has very great freedom over the manner in which it executes its work." The results, they wrote, were "imaginative and experimental films which no power on earth could have persuaded some of our more stodgy Government departments to sponsor" (Alexander and Wright 1948: 6).

28. This distinction did not map neatly onto the Iron Curtain; some Western European film industries were also nationalized.
29. Such evaluations of the World Union were common in the East European press: writing on the Brussels meetings, Jiří Lehovec mused that "it was interesting to hear . . . that in countries where film hasn't been nationalized, the creation of [national sections of the World Union] will not be an easy task. . . . From this perspective, Slavic lands have an advantage, for they have already been centralized and planned production is underway" (1947: 1).

Alexander and Wright's article inadvertently placed the World Union at the epicenter of Cold War politics. This was in part an accident of timing: the article was published less than two weeks before the World Congress of Intellectuals met in Wrocław, Poland—a gathering intended, as Melissa Feinberg writes, "to unite scholars and intellectuals from around the world against war" (2017: 35). The Mariánské Lázně and Wrocław congresses, products of their time, had structural similarities: both had national delegates from east and west, both convened in an East European "new democracy," and both aimed to produce a collective statement. But unlike the World Union's meetings in Brussels and Czechoslovakia, the Soviet Union was a central participant in the World Congress of Intellectuals, whose origins were more firmly fixed in early Cold War geopolitics. In Feinberg's words, the congress and the peace movement to which it gave rise were not only anti-war but were also "meant to be a vehicle for mass mobilization against the evils of the West" (32). Ultimately, the British delegates in Wrocław found themselves unable to sign the congress's resolution, which they saw as "promot[ing] one side"—the Soviet—"at the expense of cooperation" (36).

The effects were swiftly seen. A few weeks later, when plans circulated for the September meeting of British Documentary (Britain's section of the World Union), members were surprised to see a series of arrogant, nationalist motions attacking the decisions made in Mariánské Lázně. One proposed "that the constitution of the World Union of Documentary not be ratified unless and until true and patent representation . . . be secured from a wider number of countries, especially the English-speaking countries." Another stated that "in view of the fact that the Documentary movement was started in this country and that the reputation of British documentary stands higher than any other in the world, this meeting refuses to ratify the agreement arrived at by the delegates to the Mariánské Lázně conference, which would place the headquarters in Warsaw and allow one vote to each nation."[30]

As Hogenkamp has described, these motions were orchestrated by Grierson, who in early 1948 had left UNESCO for a position with the COI. Grierson's dismissal from his position as commissioner of Canada's National Film Board, after one of his employees was implicated as a Soviet spy by Russian defector Igor Gouzenko, had made him "extremely wary of

---

30. British Documentary, Members Meeting at 7:30 on Monday, September 13, Order Paper. b. 4, f. 36, WUD-AID.

anything communist"—and by extension anything East European. In the World Congress of Intellectuals' tense aftermath, this fear was doubtless exacerbated by the COI's dependence on British government commissions. And although the motions were ultimately withdrawn as part of a "solution" proposed by Grierson, postponing the ratification of the World Union's constitution to the 1949 Edinburgh congress, it was obvious that as long as the World Union remained tied to Eastern Europe, British involvement would be impossible (Hogenkamp 1999).[31]

The links between the World Union and the peace movement—to this point, ostensibly superficial—were reinforced the following April in Prague at a meeting of the World Union's Executive Committee. Here, a grim tally of the organization's few functioning national sections (Britain and Poland, with Denmark and Czechoslovakia in formation) was followed by a discussion of the Paris Peace Congress of that month. Ivens proposed that the World Union support the congress, in keeping with the "ideological principles of the Brussels Resolution," and those present (Ivens, Klos, and Toeplitz) agreed. But Wright—who, unable to travel to Eastern Europe, was reached by telephone—did not.[32] The gesture, he argued, would "complicate and make difficult the position of the British Section, which must appeal to the British Government and authorities for . . . funds for the organization of the [1949 Edinburgh] Congress."[33] Wright had reason for concern: the Attlee government was so opposed to the Cominform-sponsored World Peace Congress scheduled for the following year in Sheffield, England, that it forced it to move at the last minute to Warsaw (Deery 2002). Nevertheless, Ivens, Klos, Toeplitz, and Scliar (also in absentia) voiced their support of the Peace Congress, an act that officially broke the tenuous links that had bound documentary's liberal and socialist internationalists.

• • • •

By spring 1949, it had become evident that British Documentary would be unable to muster support for the Edinburgh Congress. In its place, planning began for a congress in Denmark, with the Scandinavian country proposing a new model for international documentary. This "practical internationalism"

31. For a detailed discussion of Labour's relationship to British documentary, see Hogenkamp 2000.
32. Wright to Toeplitz, May 22, 1949. b. 3, f. 35, WUD-AID.
33. Le compte rendu de la 3ème réunion du Comité Executif de l'Union Mondiale du Documentaire. b. 1, f. 15, WUD-AID.

born from the "exchange [of] experience and formulat[ion] of common goals" between "representatives from East as well as West" attempted to sidestep politics via pragmatism, and it, too, did not materialize (Anonymous 1949). Yet while the World Union was disappearing from view in parts of Western Europe, it continued to operate in the East, where Ivens still lived and worked. In fact, Czechoslovakia's national section only began to operate in 1949. It was in Prague that hopes for a renewed Popular Front project for international documentary briefly (and belatedly) persisted—and soon floundered.

Like British Documentary, Czechoslovakia's Documentary Film Board served as both the country's branch of the World Union and Czechoslovak State Film's advisory body for documentary. Led by Klos, it met weekly to codify "the meaning of documentary film, documentary methods in film, etc.," to increase domestic production, to select Czechoslovak documentaries for international distribution, to prepare texts for the bulletin the World Union planned to publish, and to suggest films for the association's congresses.[34]

Though the board's inauguration was a rare piece of good news for the World Union, the international association was on unstable ground by 1949, as were Ivens's plans for *The First Years*. At this point, Czechoslovakia's film industry looked markedly different than it had in Mariánské Lázně: it was in this period, Klos recalled, that "the craze for collective organs began," and the industry's leadership was shuffled (quoted in Lukeš 2011: 174). Most troublingly, Linhart had been removed from his position at Czechoslovak State Film in August 1948—just weeks after the World Union's congress—and relegated to the Romanian ambassadorship. The Documentary Film Board nevertheless insisted on its intention to follow the line established at Mariánské Lázně. On September 9, it formally adopted the World Union's definition of documentary and discussed plans for producing long-format films. The inspirations for these were both Soviet and Western: Rotha's 1943 *World of Plenty* and 1947 *The World Is Rich*, a quintessential UNESCO film; Storck and Paul Haesaerts's 1948 *Rubens*; American director Paul Strand's 1942 *Native Land*; French filmmaker Georges Rouquier's 1947 *Farrebique*.[35] The interwar personal networks that undergirded the

---

34. Záznam o schůzi Sboru pro dokumentární film při Filmovém ústavu Čs. státní film dne 9.IX.1949. b. R5/BII/P1/K5 UR CSF 1948–1952, f. Mezinárodní společnost pro dokumentární film, UŘ ČSF, NFA.

35. Záznam o schůzi Sboru pro dokumentární film při Filmovém ústavu Čs. státní film dne 9.IX.1949. b. R5/BII/P1/K5 UR CSF 1948–1952, f. Mezinárodní společnost pro dokumentární film, UŘ ČSF, NFA. On the Rotha films, see MacDonald 2013 and Druick 2011.

World Union likewise remained visible in the board's early activities: Balk, for instance—whose sanatorium stay had transformed into Czechoslovak exile after the August 1948 Tito-Stalin split—visited its meeting on February 24, 1950, where he was introduced as the World Union's representative from "progressive [e.g., Stalinist] Yugoslavia."

By the time of Balk's visit, however, the board's meetings were sparsely attended, as a generational shift saw some of its members begin to move into fiction filmmaking (in Czechoslovakia, documentary was still seen by many as "training" for fiction features).[36] These months also marked the point at which Czechoslovakia responded to Soviet pressure for ideological conformity, the last country in the region to do so. In these early months of Czechoslovak Stalinism, invocations of a "Czechoslovak road to socialism" were replaced with praise for the so-called Soviet model, and agricultural collectivization began—as did the country's show trials. New approaches to film production and culture were also codified. Among these was socialist realism, which was adopted as Czechoslovakia's core "creative method" at the January 1950 meeting of the Czechoslovak Writers Union.[37]

These political shifts were reflected in Czechoslovak documentary. Klos (accused of "Klosism," an epithet obscure even to him) was advised to break with his "bourgeois origins" and briefly demoted to maintaining the archive of Short Film (Lukeš 2011: 177, 48). By late March 1950, it was apparent that the Czechoslovak Documentary Film Board could no longer function as a branch of the World Union in its original conception as an international network and clearinghouse for documentary. On the agenda for a meeting on the twenty-fourth of that month was a discussion of the "possibility of using foreign documentaries domestically." As Klos described, this had an economic logic. Referring to the World Union's "goal of working in mutual understanding between nations to support truthful, progressive films," he noted that it made little sense to go to the expense of producing a film if there was already a suitable foreign title on the topic. He put the issue to discussion, asking the board if foreign filmmakers could, in theory, docu-

36. Záznam o schůzi Sboru pro dokumentární film při Filmovém ústavu Čs. státní film dne 9.IX.1949. b. R5/BII/P1/K5 UR CSF 1948–1952, f. Mezinárodní společnost pro dokumentární film, UŘ ČSF, NFA. Klos himself took this path; in 1963, he codirected the Oscar-winning film *The Shop on Main Street*.
37. In April, this was reflected in the Central Committee's "Resolution regarding the Creative Tasks of Czechoslovak Film: 'Toward High Ideological and Artistic Standards for Czechoslovak Cinema." For a fuller accounting of the institutional and political shifts in Czechoslovak cinema at this moment, see Knapík 2004; Clybor 2011, 2012.

ment life in another nation and, more pointedly, whether or not documentary films could cross the East–West divide of the Cold War.

The filmmakers present expressed different opinions on the matter. A. F. Šulc—a filmmaker and critic working for the Czechoslovak Film Institute (the nationalized film industry's scholarly and archival branch)—argued that dialectical materialism, as a method, "allow[ed] a foreign filmmaker to shoot with similar success at home and abroad." Director Pavel Blumenfeld disagreed, describing a fundamental difference between documentary's function in Eastern and Western Europe, and echoing the debates about documentary aesthetics that occurred in Brussels. "In the West," he argued, "documentary film is a sort of '*j'accuse*' . . . its method is critical realism. In Czechoslovakia, documentary film is a partner in building the state." "My opinion is thus," he concluded: "It would be possible for us [Czechoslovaks] to make documentary films in Eastern European countries after a certain amount of study, for there are common denominators between our states. Western documentarians would encounter nearly insurmountable difficulties here, whether administratively, or, more importantly, because they would not have a sufficiently flexible perspective on the dramatic events of the time."[38]

Blumenfeld's comments display the increasing influence of Zhdanovism—anti-Western and xenophobic—on Czechoslovakia's cinema institutions and culture. Moreover, they illuminate how the model of socialist realism adopted in 1950 altered discourse about documentary. Socialist realism was not new to Czechoslovakia and had been discussed in avant-garde circles since the mid-1930s, a decade when Czechoslovak documentary had been dominated by the popular, practical approaches of the "mise-en-scène" aesthetic. After the war, the same approaches were used in films that were intended to play an active role in rebuilding Czechoslovakia. Blumenfeld, however, suggested that by 1950, the purposes of the "mise-en-scène" aesthetic diverged according to geography: in socialist Eastern Europe, films no longer needed to point out "problems and their solutions" because solutions were already implicit in the "Soviet model." In addition, he suggested that socialist-realist documentary could not also be international(ist). It was, Blumenfeld argued, impossible to produce effective documentary films in a foreign country because the "fundamental demand on documentary film" was "typicization"—a cornerstone of socialist realism

---

38. Záznam o schůzi Sboru pro dokumentární film při Filmovém ústavu Čs. státního filmu dne 24.III.1950. b. R5/BII/P1/K5 UR CSF 1948–1952, f. Mezinárodní společnost pro dokumentární film, UŘ ČSF, NFA.

that implied deep familiarity with a nation's history and social and cultural life. Klos agreed, offering two examples of "the pitfalls that even the most experienced and progressive documentarians encounter in foreign countries": Vasilii Beliaev and Vladimír Vlček's 1950 Soviet-Czechoslovak coproduction *The New Czechoslovakia (Novaia Chekhoslovakiia)*—and Ivens's *The First Years*.[39]

The future of *The First Years* had been in question since Linhart's ouster in August 1948; it was, in Ivens's words, "a kind of illegitimate child," treated by the Czechoslovak film industry "with complete negligence and without any understanding of [its] political importance." In April 1949, moreover, the film's Bulgarian section had been put in jeopardy by officials in Sofia, who accused Ivens of misrepresenting the country by showing it in an agrarian (not industrial) light.[40] Nevertheless, after reshoots, reediting, and considerable diplomacy, the film was completed in November 1949 and premiered in Prague in December (Waugh 2016: 356). It was no surprise that this would be its only screening in Eastern Europe: as Ivens himself had noted, *The First Years* was intended for Western audiences. And when it was shown in Paris in March 1950—just two days after the Documentary Film Board meeting at which Klos criticized it—it met with great acclaim, playing to an enthusiastic crowd of three thousand at the prestigious Salle Pleyel in a screening sponsored by the Union of French Intellectuals and introduced by Jean Painlevé.[41] In the program, strikingly, Ivens is described as vice-president of the World Union of Documentary (see Figure 2).

It is also no surprise that *The First Years* was received more warmly in France than in Eastern Europe, since by 1950 the World Union and the idea of international documentary that it represented were contending not just with the East-West divide of the Truman Doctrine, the Cominform, and the peace movement but also with related conflict between East European communist parties and their sympathetic counterparts in Western Europe. In 1950, the French Communist Party (PCF) and Eastern European "new democracies" were nominally aligned via their allegiance to the Soviet Union, and both the PCF and the East European and Soviet parties had begun excluding and expelling prominent Popular Front figures (Judt 1992:

39. Záznam o schůzi Sboru pro dokumentární film při Filmovém ústavu Čs. státního filmu dne 24.III.1950. b. R5/BII/P1/K5 UR CSF 1948–1952, f. Mezinárodní společnost pro dokumentární film, UŘ ČSF, NFA.
40. A Short History of the New Democracies Film, June 10, 1949. b. 21, f. 285, WUD-AID.
41. Invitation to Salle Pleyel screening. f. 57, Marion Michelle collection, Joris Ivens Archives, Nijmegen.

Figure 2 Invitation to screening of Joris Ivens films, Paris, March 26, 1950. Credit: Coll. Joris Ivens Archives / European Foundation Joris Ivens, Nijmegen

109–11). But this masked disagreements. The PCF (with which Ivens had close relations) considered the institutionalization of socialism in Eastern Europe to be progress for anti-Americanism and anti-imperialism. Yet as we have seen, East European filmmakers disparaged their Western comrades for their alleged inability to comprehend "true" socialist development. At times, these misunderstandings had tragic results—perhaps most famously with Paul Éluard's refusal to defend his surrealist colleague Záviš Kalandra, who was sentenced to death during Czechoslovakia's first show trial and subsequently executed.

Czech filmmaker Hanuš Burger's experiences in 1950 crystallize this fragmentation. Burger's career closely mirrored Ivens's: a Popular Front documentarian, he had volunteered for the United States during World War II (in the Army's Psychological Warfare Division). After the war, he remained in New York, where he worked for the United Nations Film Board.[42] Burger

42. Burger, Alexander Hackenschmied (Hammid), and Herbert Kline codirected the 1939 film *Crisis* (US), about Czechoslovakia after the Munich Agreement. In 1945, Burger directed *Die Todesmühlen*, the American version of which was Billy Wilder's *Death Mills*.

fled the United States in the spring of 1950 after becoming certain that he would be called before the House Un-American Activities Committee (HUAC), which had begun targeting members of the UN Film Board. En route to Prague, awaiting a re-immigration visa, he stopped in Paris, where he was among the crowd at Salle Pleyel on March 26. By his own account, Burger enjoyed the evening with old friends and comrades (Burger 1977). Two months later, however, at a May 19 presentation at the Czechoslovak Documentary Film Board, he recalled the screening as a "great success" that only proved the backwardness of Western European socialism, for "foreign countries in the West, where social progress is delayed, consider as 'progressive' films that have already been surpassed by development here."[43] Burger disparaged the UN Film Board in similar terms, as having succumbed to "political developments" that had "ruined the original calling of the United Nations' common international bodies."[44]

Yet if Burger's rejection of Ivens, like Klos's, underscored the growing schism between the PCF and the East European communist parties, its abruptness also suggests that the gesture was performative—the product of a moment at which many Czechoslovak cultural figures were justifiably afraid of being fired, harassed, arrested, or even executed (with his Romanian exile, Linhart got off comparatively easily). Among the primary victims of Czechoslovakia's show trials were members of the International Brigades, and purges would soon render figures like Burger and Balk personae non gratae. The minutes of the board's meetings were also destined for a specific readership: Czechoslovak State Film's leaders and their ministerial oversight.

A parallel accounting of the World Union's fate in Eastern Europe, in a March 1950 letter from Klos to Toeplitz, supports this interpretation. This letter, written in Czech, is unusual in its archival context: although the two East European members of the World Union's Executive Board frequently

---

43. Záznam o schůzi Sboru pro dokumentární film při Filmovém ústavu Čs. státního filmu dne 19.V.1950. b. R5/BII/P1/K5 UR CSF 1948–1952, f. Mezinárodní společnost pro dokumentární film, UŘ ČSF, NFA.

44. In his memoir, Burger recalls a film about American neocolonialism in Latin America, whose critical voice-over (by screenwriter Joseph Moncure Marsh) was censored by the UNO under American pressure, as the breaking point in his work for the organization (1977: 315–16). As S. E. Graham details, Cold War tensions escalated in UN organizations at the beginning of the 1950s. In UNESCO, these centered on the United States' insistence on the "freedom of international information," which Eastern European delegations correctly interpreted as a means of ensuring a US information program abroad. See Graham 2006: 240–48.

corresponded in their mutually comprehensible mother tongues, Klos wrote not in his typical formal address but rather in the familiar second person. "Dear friend," he began,

> I agree that we must confirm the Party's political standpoint on whether it makes sense to support progressive Western filmmakers through the World Union or whether it is best to put this good idea on ice for now. In that case, however, I would recommend that we find a reason for stopping activities that would give us the opportunity to renew the organization honorably. Perhaps it would be best if a reason could be found in today's political pressure on progressive workers, and in the idea the Union's intervention on their behalf brought about its ban in the West. It makes me sad to abandon a useful and good thing, but today's world atmosphere truly stifles every international activity, and I fear that even in our people's democracies, we will not find backing or friendly reception.

"I hope," he concluded, "that you will find an opportunity to come to Prague in the foreseeable future, and that we will say more in person."[45]

Following the implication that even this strikingly open letter was inadequately candid was a postscript: Ivens, who had planned to return to Prague by early 1950, was still in Paris.[46] As Klos suggested, the time was not right. And by late May 1950, it was not only *The First Years* that was an "orphan," as Ivens also referred to the film (Waugh 2016: 356), but also the World Union, an association inextricably entangled with Cold War geopolitics yet lacking support from either superpower.

. . . .

Klos's criticism of Beliaev and Vlček's *New Czechoslovakia* at the Documentary Film Board's March 1950 meeting suggests a different reason for the World Union's collapse. The film had been reviewed positively in the Soviet Union, and thus Klos's dismissal was unusual, as it implicitly questioned the validity of the "Soviet model" for Czechoslovak documentary.[47]

45. Klos to Toeplitz, March 3, 1950. b. 3, f. 35, WUD-AID.
46. Ivens to Czechoslovak Film Society, January 16, 1948. b. 21, f. 285, WUD-AID.
47. On *The New Czechoslovakia*, see Kopalin 1950. The author criticizes the directors as "carried away by displays of national costumes, traditions, and dances," a factor that may have contributed to the Documentary Film Board's critique. I am grateful to Raisa Sidenova for alerting me to this article and translating it.

Indeed, the rejection hinged on a nationalism that was increasingly evident in the board's discussions and that was rooted in a long-standing Czecho-slovak (primarily Czech) exceptionalism—a tendency to see the country as unique among its Central European neighbors, not least because of its geographic position between East and West. As Klos remarked later in the March 1950 meeting, "Czechs are, as we know, more adaptable to foreign environments, and thus our filmmakers would probably have a better basis from which to learn to see a foreign reality, and to work in a documentary way."[48] A corollary of the notion that Czech(oslovak) filmmakers were excep-tionally sensitive to foreign cultures was the idea that it would be impossible for a foreign filmmaker to accurately document Czechoslovakia.

   With its origins in deeply held identity, this nationalism was not dis-similar to the version that can be found in British Documentary's September 1948 meeting, which held that "the Documentary movement was started in this country and . . . the reputation of British documentary stands higher than any other in the world" and refused to ratify the organization's constitu-tion anywhere else than in Britain. This British nationalism, like the Czech, recalled aspects of interwar and wartime documentary that the Popular Front had attempted to transcend and that the World Union's commitment to internationalism obscured: in the British case, the mode's foundational entwining with imperial structures and politics; in Czechoslovakia, not just exceptionalism but also documentary's articulation of an ethnocentric Czech identity that ignored the country's historic multinationalism.[49] While in the early 1950s, such nationalist rhetoric was protective (of funding and livelihoods), it nevertheless damaged the association.

   These tensions show that although the World Union was undoubt-edly a "victim [of] the Cold War," it was not solely the victim of high politics (Jansen 2004: 4). The conflicts that plagued it never rose to the heights of those surrounding the peace movement, with which the World Union was—to some degree coincidentally—entwined, and both the Soviet Union and the United States maintained their distance from the documentary association. Nor was the World Union's collapse only caused by irreconcil-able conflict between the liberal and socialist models for international docu-

---

48. Záznam o schůzi Sboru pro dokumentární film při Filmovém ústavu Čs. státního filmu dne 24.III.1950. b. R5/BII/P1/K5 UR CSF 1948–1952, f. Mezinárodní společnost pro dokumentární film, UŘ ČSF, NFA.
49. On the links between interwar British documentary and colonialism, see Grieveson 2011. On the national politics of interwar Czechoslovak documentary, see Lovejoy 2015.

mentary that had emerged in the interwar period, allied pragmatically in the 1930s and during the war, and maintained a fragile entente through the first moments of the World Union's existence. Resurgent nationalism within the association's member states was an important third cause. In this sense, in establishing the national as an essential component of the international, the World Union's federalism may have contributed to its downfall.

A fourth explanation for the association's failure comes from Toeplitz himself, who, in conversation with Hogenkamp and Miryam van Lier over forty years later, characterized the World Union as "absolutely divorced from practical reality . . . a kind of bureaucratic organization."[50] The association's archive corroborates this, with the vibrant exchanges about documentary form and politics at Brussels followed almost immediately by preoccupation with organizing and administering national sections, committees, and events. This bespeaks the genuine difficulty of creating an international association via letter (and, more rarely, telephone) in a world barely emerged from a devastating war. Yet it also reaffirms the 1930s' importance to the association's history. For like that decade's film festivals and archives, the World Union was rooted in a vision of cinema as a cultural and social force. It was also created by the same figures who had helped realize this vision—many of whom, after the war, found themselves leading the institutions they had brought to life. Painlevé, for instance, served both in the Institute of Scientific Film and as director general of cinema in France from August 1944 to May 1945. From 1948, Toeplitz—a gifted organizer—was secretary of the World Union and head of Film Polski's documentary department, and president of the International Federation of Film Archives. Klos was the head of Czechoslovakia's Short Film. Taxed by these responsibilities, they were left with little time to devote to initiatives such as the World Union, whose history, absent this time, is largely one of self-justifying bureaucratization. Moreover, in their positions they were subject to pressures of a nature and on a scale that they had not experienced before the war—among them high politics, as both the fate of British Documentary and Klos's letter to Toeplitz make clear.

Yet Klos's letter is significant less for demonstrating that political pressures existed than for its frank accounting of the negotiated relationships that figures like Klos and Toeplitz held with these politics. Often, postwar East European government initiatives with roots in the interwar cultural

---

50. Bert Hogenkamp and Miryam van Lier, interview with Jerzy Toeplitz, 1991. b. 1, f. 9, WUD-AID.

or political avant-garde are disparaged as the logical (Stalinist) endpoint of the avant-garde's socialism or as a mere reflection of their proponents' political ambitions. A similarly simplistic trajectory is often described in East European documentary between the 1920s and the early postwar years, as the mode became increasingly tied to government initiatives: as Mateusz Werner writes of the Polish case, "rebellious experimentation and artistic ambition . . . replaced by political dogmatism and formal conservatism" (2014: 160).

These readings ignore the complex political and historical conditions in which both artists and politicians worked in this period. Indeed, Klos's letter to Toeplitz demonstrates that despite the nationalism evident in the British and Czechoslovak cases, the World Union's primary actors had ambivalent links with their governments. The equation of formal conservatism with Stalinism also does not hold up in light of the fact that, between the 1930s and early 1950s, documentary developed similarly in the East and the West. That is, it was not the Communist Party that determined the move from "experimentation" to "conservatism" but rather documentary's own service to urgent anti-fascist and wartime causes and then to the task of postwar reconstruction—whether reconstruction was envisioned in the sweeping terms of UNESCO films or *The First Years* or in those of the countless more practical titles intended as instruction in new agricultural or industrial techniques and so forth. Such formal strategies, again, were not confined to the East.

The World Union's conviction that the documentary models of the 1930s and 1940s remained appropriate to postwar reconstruction may also have contributed to the association's undoing. For if the World Union's history represents a key moment of transition for documentary, this transition was in part generational, and it would take another half decade for a new group of filmmakers (many of them the products of the institutions—film schools, cinémathèques, etc.—that the 1930s generation had built) to determine what documentary should do next. This included the critical form of observation associated in the West with Free Cinema, direct cinema, and cinéma vérité, and in the East with Poland's Black Series and eventually parts of the Czechoslovak New Wave, Yugoslav Black Wave, and others. These developments occurred in step with the seismic political shift of 1956, when Khrushchev's revelations about Stalin—and later the Soviet invasion of Hungary—destabilized orthodoxies and grand narratives, leading to a form of documentary that, pointedly, did not always seek to offer solutions.

It was in this shifting climate that, in 1955, Toeplitz met Ivens at the

Warsaw Youth Festival, writing soon after to Wright to suggest that it was "high time to bring our old World Union of Documentary Film to life again."[51] Nearly a decade passed before this occurred, and when the Association internationale des documentaristes (International Association of Documentarians, or AID) was formed in 1964 by many of the World Union's protagonists (Ivens, Storck, Grierson, Wright, etc.), it was once again in the context of a film festival: Mannheim. The association was an active intellectual presence for documentary through the mid-1970s, and its later meetings would also take place at festivals, among them Oberhausen, Nyon, and Leipzig, the latter a crucial site for Second and Third World encounters in documentary (Hogenkamp 2006).[52] Indeed, when the AID was created, festivals remained an important and generative space for ideas about cinema and its geographies—for instance, in the Oberhausen Manifesto, drafted in 1962 by twenty-six young German filmmakers and credited with giving rise to the New German Cinema.

Hogenkamp argues that the AID attempted to avoid the World Union's "most glaring mistakes," one of which was permitting East European national sections to participate (because there were more of them, and thus they could outvote their Western counterparts); membership in the AID was on an individual basis (53–54). In this sense, while the project of international documentary did survive the height of the Cold War, the AID was still unable to free itself from Cold War politics. Nor was it able to resolve the tension between the international and national, whose geopolitical economies and institutions remained essential to nonfiction film.

The relationship between the national and the international in documentary has continued to shift, as films are increasingly supported, exhibited, and lent prestige and identity not just by state institutions (cinematography councils, broadcast organs) but also by a range of international organizations that extends far beyond the United Nations. Critical among these are international film festivals, the very bodies that played a pivotal role in the World Union's development and later helped the AID flourish. Festivals have evolved significantly since the postwar moment at which the WUD was founded, when the events offered professionals and enthusiasts the opportunity to view, discuss, and in some cases buy and sell films

51. Toeplitz to Wright, August 11, 1955. b. 1, f. 16, WUD-AID.
52. On Leipzig, see Moine 2018. On Second and Third World interactions in cinema, and especially documentary, of this period, see Djagalov 2020 and Djagalov and Salazkina 2016.

from across the world. Now, festivals are also important sites for financing films, both features and documentaries. For instance, the Bertha Fund of the International Documentary Film Festival Amsterdam supports projects whose directors hail from Africa, Asia, Latin America, the Middle East, and parts of Eastern Europe, adding nuance to the financed films' geographic origins. And while funds like these are, in part, a reflection of contemporary politics—in particular neoliberalism's devastating effects on state support for nonfiction media—they also open a new chapter in the long, entangled history of film festivals and the idea of international documentary.

References

Abrams, Bradley F. 2004. *The Struggle for the Soul of the Nation: Czech Culture and the Rise of Communism*. Lanham, MD: Rowman and Littlefield.

Alexander, Donald, and Basil Wright. 1948. "Documentary Union Can Benefit World's Film Industries." *Kinematograph Weekly* 378, no. 2154, August 12.

Andrew, Dudley. 2010. "Time Zones and Jetlag." In *World Cinemas, Transnational Perspectives*, edited by Nataša Ďurovičová and Kathleen Newman, 59–89. New York: Routledge.

Anonymous. 1948. "Film, oskarża, bronia, ulepsza: Swiatowa unia filmu dokumentalnego radzi w Warszawie." *Wieczór*, no. 332, December 2, n.p.

———. 1949. "World Union Congress in Copenhagen." *Dansk Filmforbunds Bulletin* 3, no. 20, n.p.

Bech, Raymond A. 1948. "Premier congrès de l'Union mondiale du film documentaire." *Les services publics*, August 27, 1948, n.p.

Bláhová, Jindřiška. 2012. "Národni, mezinárodní, globální. Proměny rolí filmového festival v Mariánských Lázních/Karlových Varech, 1946 až 1959." In *Naplánovaná kinematografie: Český filmový průmysl, kulturní politika a státní plánovaní, 1945–1960*, edited by Pavel Skopal, 277–79. Praha: Academia.

Burger, Hanuš. 1977. *Der Frühling war es wert: Erinnerungen*. München: Bertelsmann.

bž. 1947. "Světová unie dokumentaristů ustavena." *Filmové noviny* no. 24, June 14.

Clybor, Shawn. 2011. "Socialist (Sur)Realism: Karel Teige, Ladislav Štoll and the Politics of Communist Culture in Czechoslovakia." *History of Communism in Europe*, no. 2: 143–67.

———. 2012. "Laughter and Hatred Are Neighbors: Adolf Hoffmeister and E. F. Burian in Stalinist Czechoslovakia, 1948–1956." *East European Politics and Societies* 26, no. 3: 589–615.

Deery, Phillip. 2002. "The Dove Flies East: Whitehall, Warsaw and the 1950 World Peace Congress." *Australian Journal of Politics and History* 48, no. 4: 449–68.

Djagalov, Rossen. 2020. *From Internationalism to Postcolonialism: Literature and Cinema between the Second and the Third Worlds*. Montreal: McGill-Queen's University Press.

Djagalov, Rossen, and Masha Salazkina. 2016. "Tashkent '68: A Cinematic Contact Zone." *Slavic Review* 75, no. 2: 279–98.

Druick, Zoë. 2008. "'Reaching the Multimillions': Liberal Internationalism and the Establishment of Documentary Film." In *Inventing Film Studies*, edited by Lee Grieveson and Haidee Wasson, 66–92. Durham, NC: Duke University Press.

———. 2011. "Visualizing the World: The British Documentary at UNESCO." In *The Projection of Britain: A History of the GPO Film Unit*, edited by Scott Anthony and James G. Mansell, 272–80. New York: Palgrave Macmillan.

———. 2014. "Grierson in Canada." In *The Grierson Effect: Tracing Documentary's International Movement*, edited by Zoë Druick and Deane Williams, 105–20. New York: Palgrave Macmillan.

Feinberg, Melissa. 2017. *Curtain of Lies: The Battle over Truth in Stalinist Eastern Europe*. New York: Oxford.

Glaser, Amelia, and Steven S. Lee. 2019. *Comintern Aesthetics*. Toronto: University of Toronto Press.

Graham, S. E. 2006. "The (Real)politiks of Culture: U.S. Cultural Diplomacy in Unesco, 1946–1954." *Diplomatic History* 30, no. 2: 231–51.

Grieveson, Lee. 2011. "The Cinema and the (Common) Wealth of Nations." In *Empire and Film*, edited by Lee Grieveson and Colin MacCabe, 73–113. London: BFI.

Hagener, Malte, ed. 2014. *The Emergence of Film Culture: Knowledge Production, Institution Building, and the Fate of the Avant-Garde in Europe, 1919–1945*. New York: Berghahn Books.

Hodgin, Nick. 2016. "The Cosmopolitan Communist: Joris Ivens, Transnational Filmmaker before Transnationalism?" *Transnational Cinemas* 7, no. 2: 34–49.

Hogenkamp, Bert. 1999. "Definitions and Divisions: The International Documentary Film Movement from 1946 to 1964." *International Documentary Filmfestival Amsterdam 1999 Catalogue*, 160–65. Amsterdam: IDFA.

———. 2000. *Film, Television and the Left in Britain, 1950–1970*. London: Lawrence and Wishart.

———. 2006. "Association Internationale des Documentaristes." In *Encyclopedia of the Documentary Film*, edited by Ian Aitken, 1: 53–54. New York: Routledge.

Jansen, Huub. 2004. "Inventory of the W.U.D.-A.I.D. Collection." Nijmegen: European Foundation Joris Ivens/Municipal Archives Nijmegen.

Judt, Tony. 1992. *Past Imperfect: French Intellectuals, 1944–1956*. Berkeley: University of California Press.

Kahana, Jonathan. 2008. *Intelligence Work: The Politics of American Documentary*. New York: Columbia University Press.

Knapík, Jiří. 2004. Únor a kultura: Sovětizace české kultury 1948–1950. Prague: Nakladatelství Libri.

Kopalin, I. 1950. "Dokumental'nye fil'my iubileinogo goda." *Iskusstvo kino*, no. 1: 20–23.

Lehovec, Jiří. 1947. "Dokumenaristé sněmovali (Původní zpráva z Bruselu)." *Filmové noviny* no. 25, June 21.

Longo, Regina. 2015. "Palimpsests of Power: UNESCO-'Sponsored' Film Production and the Construction of a 'Global Village,' 1948–1953." *Velvet Light Trap* 75: 88–106.

Lovejoy, Alice. 2015. *Army Film and the Avant Garde: Cinema and Experiment in the Czechoslovak Military.* Bloomington: Indiana University Press.

Lukeš, Jan, ed. 2011. *Černobílý snář Elmara Klose.* Praha: Národní filmový archiv.

MacDonald, Richard. 2013. "Evasive Enlightenment: World without End and the Internationalism of Postwar Documentary." *Journal of British Cinema and Television* 10, no. 3: 452–74.

Moine, Caroline. 2018. *Screened Encounters: The Leipzig Documentary Film Festival, 1955–1990,* translated by John Barrett. Oxford: Berghahn Books.

Musser, Charles. 2002. "Utopian Visions in Cold War Documentary: Joris Ivens, Paul Robeson and Song of the Rivers (1954)." *Cinémas: Journal of Film Studies* 12, no. 3: 109–53.

Rotha, Paul. 1966. *Documentary Film.* 3rd ed. London: Faber and Faber.

Stollery, Martin. 2006. "Basil Wright." In *Encyclopedia of the Documentary Film,* edited by Ian Aitken, 3: 1018–20. New York: Routledge.

Stufkens, André. 2016. *Joris Ivens: Filmář světa,* translated by Iva Honsová. Prague: NAMU.

Szczepanik, Petr, and Jaroslav Anděl. 2008. *Cinema All the Time,* translated by Kevin B. Johnson. Prague: Národní filmový archiv.

Ungar, Steven. 2014. "'Toute la misere du monde': Eli Lotar's *Aubervilliers* and a Sense of Place." *Romanic Review* 105, nos. 1–2: 37–51.

Vojtěchovský, Ondřej. 2012. *Z Prahy proti Titovi: jugoslávská prosovětská emigrace v Československu.* Prague: Filozofická fakulta Univerzity Karlovy.

Wasson, Haidee. 2005. *Museum Movies: The Museum of Modern Art and the Birth of Art Cinema.* Berkeley: University of California Press.

Waugh, Thomas. 2016. *The Conscience of Cinema: The Works of Joris Ivens, 1912–1989.* Amsterdam: Amsterdam University Press.

Werner, Mateusz. 2014. "A Rebellion à la polonaise." In *The Struggle for Form: Perspectives on Polish Avant-Garde Film, 1916–1989,* edited by Kamila Kuc and Michael O'Pray, 155–62. New York: Wallflower.

Archival Collections

Basil Wright Files. British Film Institute National Archive Special Collections, London.

Ustřední ředitelsvi ČSF (UŘ ČSF) (unprocessed collection). National Film Archive, Prague.

World Union of Documentary–Association Internationale des Documentaristes (WUD-AID) Collection. Joris Ivens Archives, Nijmegen.

New Media, Neo-Media:
The Brief Life of Socialist Television in Ghana

Jennifer Blaylock

... all the familiar landmarks of my thought—*our* thought, the thought that bears the stamp of our age and our geography—breaking up all the ordered surfaces and all the planes with which we are accustomed to tame the wild profusion of existing things. . . . In the wonderment of this taxonomy, the thing we apprehend in one great leap, the thing that, by means of the fable, is demonstrated as the exotic charm of another system of thought, is the limitation of our own, the stark impossibility of thinking *that*.

—Michel Foucault, *The Order of Things: An Archaeology of the Human Sciences*

Portions of this essay were first presented as part of the Society for Cinema and Media Studies Conference panel "The Beginnings and Ends of New Media." I am grateful for the comments and feedback given, especially from fellow panelists Andrew Lison, Kyle Stine, and Paul Benzon. I am also thankful for Daniel Morgan's skillful editorial work.

boundary 2 49:1 (2022)   DOI 10.1215/01903659-9615459   ©2022 by Duke University Press

Michel Foucault begins his 1966 "Archaeology of the Human Sciences" with an account of an intellectual sensation he felt after reading Jorge Luis Borges's "The Analytical Language of John Wilkins." Confronting alterity in Borges's speculative fiction, for it was a fictional Chinese encyclopedia that provocatively ordered animals in inconceivable ways, the structures of meaning Foucault took as stable—a constant and immovable force—began to dissipate. Thus, Foucault begins his detailed archaeology of Western thought from the sixteenth century to the twentieth century with an acknowledgment that the precarity of that intellectual tradition is the result of "the stamp" not only of temporal but also geographic specificity.

Media archaeology, deriving its methodology in part from Foucault, is a critical practice that excavates media pasts in order to recontextualize the media present and their possible futures (Huhtamo and Parikka 2011: 28). Like Borges's illusory Chinese encyclopedia, the unearthed discarded media object in the hands of the media archaeologist destabilizes the presumed order of things. In the case of media archaeology, this is an assumption of the inevitability of the media of the present. In other words, "the stark impossibility of thinking that" about our contemporary media demonstrates "the limitation of our own" suppositions about what media have been, are, and what they can become. By exhuming the failed and forgotten media oddities of the past, media archaeologists reject teleological histories that celebrate the newest media as the most advanced in favor of histories of media that dwell in the speculation of what was and is potentially possible (Huhtamo and Parikka 2011: 3).[1]

Still, it would seem media archaeologists have been too preoccupied with time. In their pursuit of the "always already new" (Gitelman 2008), they tend to set aside questions about the impact that provenance has on the old new media they uncover. As a result, media archaeologies have often begun and ended in the West. Underneath this tendency to focus on new media in Euro-American contexts is the principle that media are new when their material components become tangible, or when they are first dreamed up and patented. The focus on novelty years, media transitions—the so-called moments of medial identity crises—in the West reifies a particular narrative of media history.

However, media are always becoming. The distribution of media systems across the globe and the use of technologies in imaginative new ways

1. Specifically, Siegfried Zielinski, whose archaeologies, as deeply historical as they are, are forward thinking and future oriented.

allow for the continuous reinvention of media. Not only do use-centered his-tories of media affirm the social construction of technology, they also insist that human creativity and innovation are found beyond the Silicon Valleys of our media pasts (Edgerton 2007; Mavhunga 2017). I want to make the case that to know the contours of the present mediatic moment, and perhaps those of the future as well, media archaeology might consider new media geographies as much as alternative media timelines. What do the histories of new media in the Global South show about worldwide discourses of new media, which often remain latent in contemporary media archaeologies that focus on the usual Western sites of new media production and their suc-cessful white male inventor-entrepreneurs? By focusing on the short-lived experiment in socialist television, which characterized the birth of Ghana Television in the mid-1960s, I will attempt a start.

In general, it is only since the "global turn" in television studies in the 1990s and early 2000s that the field to focus on television histories outside industrialized Western nations (Parks and Kumar 2003: 6). Most sub-Saharan television scholarship today focuses on mass media after structural adjustment and the wave of media privatization that swept the continent in the 1990s, leaving the history of African television during its ini-tial years still understudied.[2] This early period where it is discussed is char-acterized by an initial period of poor access and technological lag. In the year 1960, UNESCO reported that only five countries in Africa had at least one television per one thousand people, while in Europe there were twenty-four and in North America fourteen (UNESCO 1963). Additionally, summa-ries of the origins of African television have suggested that television was nothing more than a parting gift from former colonial powers (Berwanger 1995: 310; "Africa, Sub-Saharan" 2004: 45). Yet this picture can be mislead-ing. The relatively small numbers of television receivers in Africa during the mid-twentieth century should not diminish the work that African broadcast-ers were doing to bring the new medium to the citizens of their countries. Nor does the role of foreign governments and transnational corporations in the establishment of African television mean that African broadcasters were importing media technologies indiscriminately.

Unlike the origins of radio and cinema in Ghana, which were initi-ated under British colonial rule, the first official Ghanaian television broad-cast on July 31, 1965, came out of a radical time when Africans across

2. With the exception of Oluyinka Esan's detailed history of Nigerian television in *Nigerian Television: Fifty Years of Television in Africa* (2009).

the continent were boldly and creatively inventing systems of governance intended to contest imperialism and racial inequality. Alongside the formation of the new state, television was seen as a new medium that would help realize the African socialism promoted by the first prime minister of Ghana, Kwame Nkrumah. Yet with the February 24, 1966, coup d'état, only seven months after programming began, Nkrumah was overthrown, and Ghanaian socialist television came to an end. Contemporary institutional histories of Ghana Broadcasting Corporation (GBC) omit the influence of Nkrumah's style of African socialism on Ghana Television's founding, emphasizing instead the long-standing educational mission of GBC (Mahama 2015; see also "The Humble Beginning of GBC" 2015). In this essay, I suggest that we read the first seven months of Ghanaian television as an Afrofuturist segment of Ghana's media past and as a counternarrative to the enduring colonial discourse that positions Africa as the passive receiver of new media machines. Focusing on work done by Shirley Graham Du Bois, the first director of Ghana Television, this media history establishes how television was invented in Ghana as a revolutionary alternative to the capitalist alienation of an implicitly white, Western technology. The detailed account of Du Bois's theories of television underlines the centrality of race in global discourses of the new medium.

Transnational Entanglements

The inauguration of Ghana Television happened at four o'clock in the afternoon on July 31, 1965, as thousands of individuals came to GBC to celebrate the first television transmission (see Figures 1–4). Parliamentarians, diplomats, chiefs, and other distinguished guests attended the "simple but very impressive" ninety-minute ceremony, while countless other Ghanaians watched live from television sets across the country (*Ghana Radio* 1965b: 12). Nkrumah's speech to inaugurate Ghana Television celebrated the day but also negotiated a tension that characterized both the development of television in Ghana and the country's own political situation in the 1960s. Choosing to remain unaligned during the Cold War, Nkrumah's Convention People's Party (CPP) government increasingly appeared more socialist as the decade wore on. His attack on Western capitalism in his 1965 book *Neo-colonialism: The Last Stage of Imperialism* strained Ghana's relationship with the United States, England, and other capitalist countries. And yet television was established over seven years through an assortment of transnational economic and political relationships, which in some cases

Figures 1 and 2 Large crowds gathered at GBC for the inauguration of Ghana Television. Courtesy of Information Services Department, Photo Library, Accra, Ghana.

Figure 3 President Kwame Nkrumah giving his inaugural address. Seated to his right is his wife, Fatimah Nkrumah. Seated behind Fatimah Nkrumah, in Kente cloth, is director of television, Shirley Graham Du Bois. Courtesy of Information Services Department, Photo Library, Accra, Ghana.

Figure 4 Members of Parliament, ministers, chiefs, and others in their seats at the inaugural ceremony of Ghana TV. Courtesy of Information Services Department, Photo Library, Accra, Ghana.

resembled the neocolonial dependencies Nkrumah despised. With the use of British equipment, help from Canadian expertise, and a Japanese industrial partnership, it was necessary for Nkrumah to acknowledge these international associates at the inauguration.

After a brief introduction on the origins of Ghana television, Nkrumah thanked the Canadian government for being "so generous" with their "equipment and personnel" (Nkrumah 1965: 1). He then expressed his gratitude to the British electronics company Marconi, who "assisted in no small measure" with the construction of Ghana's television transmitters and the television studio complex (1). A delegation of three, led by B. N. MacLarty, a consulting engineer from Marconi, sat in the audience to receive his thanks (*Daily Graphic* 1965b: 3). Nkrumah also went on to acknowledge the Japanese Sanyo Corporation, who were partners with the Ghanaian government in establishing a local television factory in Tema, before thanking the many Ghanaian staff involved in making television a reality despite the "sceptics [who] declared that the establishment of a truly indigenous Television Service, organised and staffed by Ghanaians was an impossible task" (Nkrumah 1965: 1–2). Yet, Nkrumah's earlier acknowledgement of international assistance suggests that Ghana television was hardly "indigenous." The heavy involvement of international collaborators meant that neocolonial entanglements—especially British interests—were bound up within the history of Ghana's new medium. The discussion of the emergence of African media industries has focused on the legacy of former colonial empires because of influences like those of Marconi in the history of Ghana Television, but Nkrumah would navigate a Cold War policy of nonalignment by developing partnerships with capitalist and communist countries alike.[3]

Following Ghanaian independence on March 6, 1957, there was some talk among Ghanaians of starting a national television service, but most of this was only exploratory. Toward the end of 1958, two British electronic equipment companies, Marconi Co., Ltd. of London and W. G. Pye & Co. Ltd. of Cambridge, began lobbying the Ghanaian government to

3. For instance, Nkrumah pursued negotiations with Kaiser Industries and Edgar Kaiser to build his signature infrastructural development project, the Akosombo Dam, despite the doubts of some of his advisors. Financial support from the World Bank, the United States, and Britain had to be negotiated since Ghana remained unaligned, but Nkrumah increasingly drew closer relationships with the Eastern bloc. Kaiser had to convince Nkrumah to soften his anti-imperial rhetoric to sustain the United States' economic support for the project. See Miescher 2014 for a detailed account of how Nkrumah pursued a type of African socialism that remained nonaligned.

start a national television service. In April 1959, the Ghanaian government accepted a joint proposal from the two companies for limited television coverage of the royal visit to Accra scheduled for November 1959.[4] The scheme was designed as a trial run, which would come to an end after the royal visit. Around fifty television receivers would be made available to the government with additional receivers available for hire during the demonstration. The royal visit was to be aired live with a three-hour recap in the evenings ("Supply" 1959: 631). In presenting the proposal to Parliament, the minister of education and information, Kofi Baako, explained, "Although the experiment will be limited to Accra I hope that it will give people here some idea of what television is like. As a result I believe hon. members will be interested when later on I bring before them my proposals for the establishment of a national television service" (631). Baako emphasized that it would not "in any way commit the Government to any particular system of television," but he hoped it would give the Ghanaian government enough background information so that they would be able to solve, on their own, any problems that may arise (631). When the royal visit was postponed to early 1961, the arrangements were canceled. As an alternative event, Baako invited Ghanaian ministers, foreign dignitaries, and members of the press to a small reception at the Broadcasting House on September 21, 1959, in honor of Founder's Day. There, Ghanaian broadcasting engineers demonstrated a closed-circuit television system that had been set up by Marconi for training purposes.

The early efforts by Marconi to woo Ghanaian officials had G. W. Marshall, the UK trade commissioner in Accra, convinced that British companies would win any bid that was solicited. On October 24, 1959, he gathered and sent a detailed intelligence report about the development of Ghanaian television to A. B. Savage at the Board of Trade in London. The report made clear England's vested economic interests in the development of Ghana television, seeing it as an opportunity to sell program material and transmitting and receiving equipment and give technical advice. With

4. The relationship between British royalty and new media spectacle in Africa has a long tradition. Film screenings by the Bantu Educational Kinema Experiment in Tanganyika, Nyasaland, Northern Rhodesia, Kenya, and Uganda concluded with the British national anthem and an image of the king (Rice 2011: 137). The planned television demonstration, even if it would have brought the royals into Ghanaian homes, would not provide the intimacy that André Bazin attributes to the broadcast of Queen Elizabeth's coronation when it entered domestic spaces across Europe because the symbol of the Crown was used to promote British superiority and white supremacy in African colonies (2014).

a shared national language and the long association between the British Broadcasting Corporation, GBC, and Marconi, Marshall assumed British companies would be more attractive partners. Believing in the superiority of their own television model, Marshall also presumed that the Ghanaian government would pursue state control over a commercial television system through legislation similar to the United Kingdom's Television Act.

Any challenges that British companies would have in winning the television contract with the Ghanaian government were taken to be largely practical. Marshall noted that the greatest difficulties a British company would have would be finding the technicians needed to operate the service, the training of Ghanaian personnel, and acquiring a supply of programs with suitable African content. He wrote, "Programmes will have to have a good proportion of African content (i.e. film material with white faces would not do for all of the time). This means that much of the programmes will have to be prepared on the African Continent, although in the beginning sound pro- gramme material will probably be in considerable use."[5] Marshall's report on the development of a Ghanaian national television station assumes that whichever company won a government contract would have significant con- trol over the station. For Marshall, good will efforts toward training African staff and creating film material with Black faces instead of white ones were a cosmetic necessity to win the bid.

Not only would GBC eventually accept British equipment, entering an agreement with Marconi, they also welcomed numerous consultants and experts from England and abroad. The Canadian government, in par- ticular, became an important resource and influence on Ghana Television, especially during the early days of its development. As Baako explained in an address to Parliament, the ministry "sought advice as to the prob- lems involved in television from the Government of Canada" because it "is a developing country, like ourselves in many ways, and may be able to help us to decide how best to go about the complex process of intro- ducing a television service" ("Supply" 1959: 631). Dealing with an English- speaking country that was not a former colonial ruler allowed Ghanaians, at least in theory, to avoid appearing to fall into a neocolonial relationship with Britain.

Following the successful consultation work of Canadian Broadcast-

5. G. W. Marshall to A. B. Savage, October 24, 1959, GHA 382/6, Dominions Office, and Commonwealth Relations and Foreign and Commonwealth Offices 1959–1960, The National Archives, Kew, United Kingdom.

ing Corporation (CBC) employees A. L. Pidgeon and J. L. Marshall on the establishment of a Ghanaian international radio broadcast, Ghana invited two more consultants from the CBC to advise on the development of a television system. On November 6, 1959, R. D. Cahoon and S. R. Kennedy arrived in Ghana to make their recommendations. Cahoon and Kennedy were tasked with several items: to evaluate several proposals submitted to the Ghanaian government by equipment manufacturers and suppliers, to prepare a report on the best implementation practices while noting what risks Ghana might need to mitigate against, and, lastly, to provide recommendations for the organizational structure of the new department. The Ghanaian government stressed that they had already decided to establish a state-owned television service that would be integrated within the GBC. They also insisted that the Ghana television service should be "African in content and not simply a reflection of television services in other countries" (Cahoon and Kennedy 1959). In other words, Ghana wanted a unique television system, not the wholesale adoption of a BBC (or CBC) model like Marshall had predicted.

After a month of research, on December 11, 1959, Cahoon and Kennedy filed their report, and the Ghanaian government largely accepted the proposal. However, there were some minor changes. Where the Canadian report suggested offsetting costs by allowing commercial content, Ghana decided to make their television system commercial free. Additionally, in an effort to make "television for everyone," instead of installing only three transmitters in the southern and central parts of the country and waiting to broadcast to the northern part of Ghana in a second stage, a northern relay station was added to ensure that television would be beamed to nearly two-thirds of the country upon its inauguration ([Du Bois] 1964: 7).

Following the acceptance of Cahoon and Kennedy's report, close ties with Canada continued. Under the Technical Assistance Agreement between Canada and Ghana, Frank Goodship and Wes Harvison, also from the CBC, arrived in late 1961 to assist with the development of a television training school—what would be the first institution of its kind in sub-Saharan Africa. During 1962, the school was constructed at the GBC Broadcasting House and outfitted with television equipment, though it was not until January 28, 1963, that the minister of information and broadcasting, L. R. Abavana, officially opened it (*Ghana Radio Review* 1963b: 4). Goodship was in charge of training the television production staff and advised on all aspects of television programming, while Harvison trained technical staff (*Ghana Radio Review* 1964: cover). In early 1964, four more CBC employees would become instructors at the television school: Harry Heywood, a technical adviser; Pier Castonguay, television program adviser and production training officer; Harry Makin, film manager and news cameramen and film personnel manager; and Burns Stewart, a news training officer (*Ghana Radio Review* 1964: cover).

The initial pupils at the television school were mostly culled from the ranks of Radio Ghana employees, and later from the Photography Division of the Information Services Department.[6] After six months of basic training, twenty-four trainees from the Ghana Television School—twelve producers and twelve technicians—were sent to Canada for further studies and on-the-job training (*30 Eventful Years* 1965: 20). Several Ghana Television students took courses at the Ryerson Institute of Technology in Toronto before practical assignments at the CBC (*Ghana Radio Review* 1963c: cover). By 1965, when television began, fifty Ghana Television men and women had been trained in Canada (*30 Eventful Years* 1965: 20).

In addition to training television staff, there were efforts to prepare Ghanaian teachers to use television as an educational tool in the classroom. At the Educational Television Seminar, held at the Accra Television Training School, September 2–13, 1963, thirty Ghanaian secondary school and Teacher Training College teachers were encouraged to develop teaching materials for the school broadcasting (*Ghana Radio Review* 1963d: cover). The seminar was primarily designed "to emphasise the educational values of Television" (*Ghana Radio Review* 1963a: 7). Seminar instructors included two educational television experts from the United Kingdom:

6. On the February 21, 1966, C. C. Lokko wrote a long letter to Shirley Graham Du Bois about the loss of talented Information Services Department (ISD) officers to television. These staff members that were trained by ISD applied for positions at Ghana Television without passing their applications through ISD. One employee, R. M. Adu, apparently applied for a job at Ghana Television without telling his superiors at ISD to avoid a post to Northern Ghana. C. C. Lokko wrote, "I only wish the various constituent organisations within the Ministry of Information would come to some working agreement to halt, at least, the rapid movement—I am almost tempted to say, drain!—of staff which can be quite embarrassing to departmental plans and programmes sometimes" (C. C. Lokko to Shirley Graham Du Bois, "Ghana TV," February 21, 1966. MC 476 Box 44.15, Shirley Graham Du Bois Papers, Schlesinger Library, Radcliffe Institute, Harvard University). Shirley Graham Du Bois wrote back with complete support, but it is certain that given her closeness with Nkrumah, Ghana Television was given certain privileges over other Ministry of Information departments (Shirley Graham Du Bois, "Ghana TV," February 22, 1966. MC 476 Box 44.13, Shirley Graham Du Bois Papers, Schlesinger Library, Radcliffe Institute, Harvard University).

Charlotte Reid, a language instructor, and Tony Gibson, the director of the Centre for Educational Television Overseas (CETO). Also participating in the opening day's program was Dr. Joseph Coleman de Graft and Shirley Graham Du Bois, the second wife of W. E. B. Du Bois and future director of Ghana Television (*Ghana Radio Review* 1963a: 7).

The Du Boises had defected to Ghana in the early 1960s to escape political restrictions in the United States for their involvement in the Communist Party. W. E. B. Du Bois's radicalization later in life has often been attributed to Shirley Graham Du Bois's beguiling leftist influence (Horne 2000: 31). However, as Gerald Horne writes, "The idea that a weak-minded Du Bois was seduced into joining the party does not do justice to him and, perhaps, overstates Graham's powers of political persuasion. On the other hand, it would be naïve to underestimate her dynamic influence on him, particularly her ability to bring him into radical circles that he otherwise avoided" (32). On her bidding, W. E. B. Du Bois joined her on a world tour that included a trip to the Soviet Union shortly after the success of Sputnik, as well as to China, which the United States government still prohibited its citizens to visit. Their voyage perturbed the United States, resulting in the couple's passports being revoked and solidifying their resolve to live abroad. With an invitation from Kwame Nkrumah, they chose to make their home in Accra and became Ghanaian citizens. For the Du Boises, and a number of other international Black Marxist thinkers who composed Nkrumah's intellectual circle (notably George Padmore and C. L. R. James), there was a consensus that capitalism was inextricable from global white supremacy, and therefore the need to forge a new Pan-African economic future was imperative.

Shortly after W. E. B. Du Bois's death, Nkrumah appointed Shirley Graham Du Bois as the director of Ghana Television. On February 1, 1964, she became director of what she later described as "Ghana's 'non-existent' Television."[7] Her first fifteen months, she recounted, "went into constructing, organizing, planning, training personelle and all the other activities necessary for building television in an ambitious, but un-developed country."[8]

---

7. Shirley Graham Du Bois to Mikhail Kotov, "Correspondence 1965," November 7, 1965. MC 476 Box 18.15, Shirley Graham Du Bois Papers, Schlesinger Library, Radcliffe Institute, Harvard University.
8. Shirley Graham Du Bois to Mikhail Kotov, "Correspondence 1965," November 7, 1965. MC 476 Box 18.15, Shirley Graham Du Bois Papers, Schlesinger Library, Radcliffe Institute, Harvard University.

With little background in television, before her appointment, Du Bois was sent by the Ghanaian government to study television systems in Great Britain, France, Italy, the German Democratic Republic, Czechoslovakia, and Japan before returning to invent, as she put it, "a *specifically Ghanaian* approach to Television organization and programing" ([Du Bois] 1964: 9).

Her trip began in England on October 28, 1963, and ended in early December in Italy. In London, Du Bois visited CETO, the same organization that was responsible for the Educational Television Seminar she participated in back in September 1963. CETO was a nonprofit organization founded in 1962 to promote the use of television as a tool for education in developing countries (Lawler 1965: 359). Funded in part by the Ford Foundation, the organization researched the needs of developing nations, offered advice on how to implement educational television programming, and provided their own educational content and graphics that came customizable for producers in overseas countries (Lawler 1965: 360). On her visit, Du Bois sat in on a CETO-produced lesson on cartography. In it, an Indian teacher used a map of India to give a televised lecture for a class in New Delhi. Despite the material being geared for an Indian classroom, Du Bois saw potential: "The various pieces and illustrations used to explain map making could just as easily apply to a map of Ghana."[9] Responding to the capacities of the medium, she was excited by the potential to use television to broadcast such visual aids to "hundreds of viewing centers at the same time!"[10]

This was the type of translation work Du Bois would do throughout her trip. In each of the places she visited, she took stock of how the country was approaching television in order to appropriate methods that would work in a Ghanaian context. In Italy, she visited the Telescuola Centre in Rome and came away speaking highly of the novel Italian approach to reducing illiteracy. At the Telescuola studio, she observed the production of the classroom lesson where an instructor gave a history lesson to eight students seated at desks in a classroom setting, a lesson that was then broadcast to hundreds of television schools in nearby towns. After two

---

9. Shirley Graham Du Bois, "Report on Television Survey," December 15, 1963, 1. MC 476 Box 44.7, Shirley Graham Du Bois Papers, Schlesinger Library, Radcliffe Institute, Harvard University.
10. Shirley Graham Du Bois, "Report on Television Survey," December 15, 1963, 1–2. MC 476 Box 44.7, Shirley Graham Du Bois Papers, Schlesinger Library, Radcliffe Institute, Harvard University.

days at the studio, Du Bois, along with five other observers from different countries, traveled to viewing centers to see the children who received the broadcast lessons. She also viewed an adult education program called *It's Never Too Late*. The Telescuola model would become extremely important to the development of television in Ghana, as Du Bois borrowed the idea of using monitors at viewing centers to interpret televisual lessons for adult audiences. She wrote, "One senses immediately that this approach to television teaching has the simplicity and directness which is needed to combat illiteracy anywhere. Many of the methods used in Italy can very well be applied to Ghana."[11]

Following Ghana's policy of nonalignment, Du Bois also examined Czechoslovakia's use of television for education. Similar to efforts in Western Europe, the Eastern Bloc considered educational television a critical tool in social transformation, modernization, and development. School television programs were seen across Europe as a means to accelerate learning in low-performing school districts. Television systems under Soviet authority were even developed through transnational collaborations with television systems in Western Europe (Imre 2016: 13; see also Gumbert 2014). Anikó Imre argues that there was a shared pre–Cold War "ethos of public service broadcasting" across Europe that saw national television as possessing a "government-led mission to inform and educate while promoting nationalism" (17). In Hungary, for example, where almost a third of the population had not obtained an eighth-grade education, television promised to offer a new means of adult education (45).

In Czechoslovakia, Du Bois met with representatives from the Ministry of Education and Culture—which administered television, radio, theater, and film departments—but she was most impressed with her visit to the famous Kudlov Film and Puppet Studio, where she remarked on the importance of imagination for both puppetry and television. Du Bois was delighted by the inventor of the puppets and director of the studio, Madam Tyrlova, writing, "first of all, [she] loves children and understands them (which is not always the same). And she also knows that something of the child lingers in grown-ups—if only the imagination can be stirred and the fancy set free. Her puppet films are for all people whose hearts would be young. . . . In this Film and Puppet Studio the imagination, so important for television, reigns

11. Shirley Graham Du Bois, "Report on Television Survey," December 15, 1963, 13. MC 476 Box 44.7, Shirley Graham Du Bois Papers, Schlesinger Library, Radcliffe Institute, Harvard University.

Figure 5 Puppets at the Japan Broadcasting Corporation studios in Japan. Ghana T.V.: Trip to Japan, 1964. MC476 DuBois PD.84, Shirley Graham Du Bois Papers, Schlesinger Library, Radcliffe Institute, Harvard University.

supreme."[12] Du Bois's love of puppetry would inspire her again when she observed the use of puppets for educational television programming during her subsequent visit to Japan (Figure 5). Puppets, Du Bois claimed, gave Ghana a solution to the problem of retaining "young pupils [*sic*] full attention throughout a television lesson."[13] Indeed, GBC would go on to incorporate puppets into their educational television repertoire in late 1966.[14]

Following her trip to Europe, Du Bois organized a twenty-day trip to

12. See Shirley Graham Du Bois, "Report on Television Survey," December 15, 1963, 12. MC 476 Box 44.7, Shirley Graham Du Bois Papers, Schlesinger Library, Radcliffe Institute, Harvard University.
13. Shirley Graham Du Bois, "Radio Report to Japan," Tokyo, March 14, 1964. MC 476 Box 44.18, Shirley Graham Du Bois Papers, Schlesinger Library, Radcliffe Institute, Harvard University.
14. Ghana Television Puppet Theatre, with the comedian puppet Kofi Brokeman, could be seen at 6 p.m. every Wednesday from December 1966 to at least July 1968 (*Ghana Radio* 1967: cover).

Japan to study television in a non-European context. She was accompanied by Alex Quarmyne, deputy director of television, and Jacob Dentu, director of engineering. From February 24 to March 15, 1964, the small Ghanaian cadre visited numerous electronic factories and Japanese television stations. On February 27, for example, the group visited the Japan Broadcasting Corporation's (NHK's) Technical Research Laboratories, where they "examined the Separate Luminance Color camera," which was later used to broadcast in color parts of the 1964 Olympic Games in Japan and, as Du Bois put it in her report of the trip, "may well revolutionise television everywhere."[15] Quarmyne and Dentu also picked up programming ideas from the NHK, adopting how they assigned personnel to productions and drew up their production schedules (Quarmyne, pers. comm., July 13, 2017).

On their visit to Nippon Television Network Corporation on March 3, the group was given a tour of the studio and a color-television demonstration. After her visit, Du Bois became convinced that Ghana Television should begin in color. Given that color television was still only used in the United States and Japan at the time, this was a bold statement. She argued that the beauty that color television could afford was amplified by the impact it would have in moving Ghana forward to take their "place in the foremost ranks" of global communications technology ([Du Bois] 1964: 17). Du Bois also felt that the vibrancy of Africa could not adequately be represented in black and white: "Its bright sunshine, rich foliage, tropical flowers, blue skies, skin coloring, golden seashores and vivid clothing—all cry out for color."[16] Color television thus offered the means to celebrate more fully Black African identity. It could directly confront global racial hierarchies reinforced by ideologies about media diffusion, which projected Africans as late adopters, while also making visible the brightness of African culture.

While Canadian and European television experts emphatically stated that the cost of starting Ghanaian television service in color would be too prohibitive, in Japan Du Bois found manufacturers who understood the symbolic power color television could play in shifting global attitudes toward the new nation. In a memorandum to the Ghanaian minister of information and

15. Shirley Graham Du Bois, "Radio Report to Japan," Tokyo, March 14, 1964. MC 476 Box 44.18, Shirley Graham Du Bois Papers, Schlesinger Library, Radcliffe Institute, Harvard University.
16. Shirley Graham Du Bois, "Radio Report to Japan," Tokyo, March 14, 1964. MC 476 Box 44.18, Shirley Graham Du Bois Papers, Schlesinger Library, Radcliffe Institute, Harvard University.

broadcasting, she emphasized Sanyo Electric's willingness to help Ghana Television start in color. According to Du Bois, T. lue, president of Sanyo Electric Company, said, "If Ghana becomes the first country in the world to *start television in color*—it will seize a psychological leadership which will be world-wide. Think of the impact this would have on Europe! And the standard it would set for Africa! I'd like to see it done—and I promise you every possible assistance."[17] Matsutaro Shoriki also assured her, "You can have color television if you really want it, plan for it and work for it!"[18]

Impressed by Japan's improvements upon American television equipment, and their success at shipping electronics to the United States, Du Bois saw a partnership with Japanese manufacturers as an attractive alternative to economic relationships with European or American television manufacturers.[19] To explore possible relationships, the Ghanaian group visited Sanyo Electric, where they were given a warm welcome and thorough tour (Figures 6 and 7). Du Bois wrote, "We learned why your companies can produce equipment of high quality to sell cheaper than similar equipment produced in other countries: You take unskilled workers, train and educate them and give them the opportunity to join the ranks of skilled workers. Through cooperative effort the workers earning capacity is increased. Ghana, where most of its workers are unskilled, can learn from you."[20] Captivated by the training of workers in Japan's factories, Du Bois began brokering a deal with Sanyo Electric to open a factory for radio and television assembly in Ghana. An agreement with Japanese electronics companies, she thought, offered Ghana a means to avoid a neocolonial relationship like that which shaded their work with Marconi. Eventually a deal would be made to form a company that would be equally financed by the Ghanaian government and three Japanese companies—Sanyo, Marubeni-Iida, and

17. Shirley Graham Du Bois to Minister of Information and Broadcasting – Memorandum, "Ghana TV," March 16, 1964. MC 476 Box 44.13, Shirley Graham Du Bois Papers, Schlesinger Library, Radcliffe Institute, Harvard University.

18. Shirley Graham Du Bois, "Radio Report to Japan," Tokyo, March 14, 1964. MC 476 Box 44.18, Shirley Graham Du Bois Papers, Schlesinger Library, Radcliffe Institute, Harvard University.

19. Shirley Graham Du Bois, "Radio Report to Japan," Tokyo, March 14, 1964. MC 476 Box 44.18, Shirley Graham Du Bois Papers, Schlesinger Library, Radcliffe Institute, Harvard University.

20. Shirley Graham Du Bois, "Radio Report to Japan," Tokyo, March 14, 1964. MC 476 Box 44.18, Shirley Graham Du Bois Papers, Schlesinger Library, Radcliffe Institute, Harvard University.

Figure 6 Visit to Tokyo Sanyo Electric. "Ghana T.V.: Trip to Japan," 1964. MC476 DuBois PD.83, Shirley Graham Du Bois Papers, Schlesinger Library, Radcliffe Institute, Harvard University.

Nichimen Jitsugyo. The establishment of Ghana Sanyo Electrical Manufacturing Corporation was signed into effect on December 8, 1964.[21]

    The effects of this relationship were significant, although they would be curtailed by the political deposition of Nkrumah's government less than two years later. On May 7, 1965, Nkrumah broke ground in Tema on the Sanyo radio and television factory that cost the Ghanaian government approximately 36,000 pounds (*New Ashanti Times* 1965: 12). Yet the factory would not produce televisions until April 1966—shortly after the February 22 coup d'état.[22] In a July 4, 1966, letter to Du Bois, K. Funabashi reported

21. William Baidoe-Ansah to Shirley Graham Du Bois, "Trip to Japan, 1964; includes clippings, itineraries, correspondence, lists, receipts, report," December 9, 1964. MC 476 Box 44.18, Shirley Graham Du Bois Papers, Schlesinger Library, Radcliffe Institute, Harvard University.
22. K. Funabashi to Shirley Graham Du Bois, "Correspondence 1966," July 4, 1966. MC 476 Box 19.4, Shirley Graham Du Bois Papers, Schlesinger Library, Radcliffe Institute, Harvard University.

Figure 7 Tour of the factory. "Ghana T.V.: Trip to Japan," 1964. MC476 DuBois PD.86, Shirley Graham Du Bois Papers, Schlesinger Library, Radcliffe Institute, Harvard University.

that the Ghana Sanyo Electrical Manufacturing Corporation was able to sell six hundred of the television sets they had produced since April and that production had reached three hundred units a month in June.[23] However, under the National Liberation Council (NLC), the new military government would roll back support for state-owned industries, a concern Funabashi expressed: "As for business, it became very much harder without you as a matter of course."[24] Funabashi informed Du Bois that the new government proposed to cancel the provision in their agreement that gave Ghana Sanyo the exclusive right to manufacture and sell televisions in Ghana.[25] Even as

23. K. Funabashi to Shirley Graham Du Bois, "Correspondence 1966," July 4, 1966. MC 476 Box 19.4, Shirley Graham Du Bois Papers, Schlesinger Library, Radcliffe Institute, Harvard University.
24. K. Funabashi to Shirley Graham Du Bois, "Correspondence 1966," July 4, 1966. MC 476 Box 19.4, Shirley Graham Du Bois Papers, Schlesinger Library, Radcliffe Institute, Harvard University.
25. K. Funabashi to Shirley Graham Du Bois, "Correspondence 1966," July 4, 1966. MC 476 Box 19.4, Shirley Graham Du Bois Papers, Schlesinger Library, Radcliffe Institute, Harvard University.

Ghana decided to adopt free-market economic policies, Funabashi naively remained optimistic, "The future of Ghana Sanyo is not hopeless however it will not be easy either."[26] In the end, without the economic protections of the state, the Ghana Sanyo factory—Du Bois's "baby"—would quietly close without lament.[27]

In the Black Radical Tradition

This history may suggest that Ghana television was the result of a familiar narrative of technology transfer—where new media are created elsewhere by experts, designers, and engineers and dispersed to Africa as charity, along with a hyperbolic discourse about how these technologies will transform underdeveloped countries on the continent. However, Nkrumah proposed an alternate vision in his speech to inaugurate Ghana television: "Our Television Service should be African in its outlook; and in its content," and "should remain geared to the needs of Ghana and Africa." Drawing on precolonial communication systems to justify different types of distribution methods, and making visible Black African expertise, Ghana Television located the newness of new media technologies in their adaption, implementation, and use.

Nkrumah's sentiment was echoed in the writings of Shirley Graham Du Bois. With the publication of *This Is Ghana Television* in 1965, she solidified her theorization of the new medium. In it, she argues that television is a weapon in the struggle for African unity against imperialism, colonialism, and neocolonialism—and that its ammunition is Ghanaian, African, and socialist content ([Du Bois] 1964: 5). Drawing on the discourses of international communications prevalent at the time, Du Bois articulated the power of television to transform living conditions, health, and agricultural practices. (In a claim reminiscent of contemporary enthusiasm for the power of mobile phones in developing countries, she at one point exclaimed to a crowd of GBC employees, "Television can save lives!"[28]) However, the educational

---

26. K. Funabashi to Shirley Graham Du Bois, "Correspondence 1966," July 4, 1966. MC 476 Box 19.4, Shirley Graham Du Bois Papers, Schlesinger Library, Radcliffe Institute, Harvard University.

27. William Baidoe-Ansah to Shirley Graham Du Bois, "Trip to Japan, 1964; includes clippings, itineraries, correspondence, lists, receipts, report," December 9, 1964. MC 476 Box 44.18, Shirley Graham Du Bois Papers, Schlesinger Library, Radcliffe Institute, Harvard University.

28. From a speech delivered to television workers on January 8, 1965 (Du Bois 1965: 4).

potentials for television were not limited to teaching science, health, and hygiene, or new agricultural methods. For Du Bois, television was political, and she insisted that it be used to prepare "Ghanaian children for service in a dynamic, forward-looking socialist state" (1964: 22). Television also had the power to unite; it would send out "its beams of light as a unifying force for all Africa" (22).

It was thus not only television content that was geared toward Ghana and Africa. Ghanaians would be able to resituate the new medium as a continuation of indigenous media systems by linking Ghanaian television to a history of precolonial African communication systems. Nkrumah likened the Ghana Broadcasting Service to ɔkyeafoɔ, the skilled orators who draw on traditional proverbs, royal history, and poetry to translate and interpret the will of the Asantehene (the Ashanti king) (1965). Du Bois would likewise situate Ghana Television within an indigenous media history: "Television in Ghana will be the heir to a long tradition of journalism that goes back to the talking drums which have been used to transmit and receive messages for several hundreds of years" (1964: 28). The talking drums, which were used to communicate from village to village, became the call signal for Ghana radio and television (Smith 1970: 106) and were incorporated into the Ghana Broadcasting logo. Visitors to GBC were, and are still today, greeted by "the proverbial 'gong-gong' beater standing elegantly on the green turf in the middle of the compound" (*30 Eventful Years* 1965: 5). Those who tuned in to Radio Ghana's *Farm Forum* on Sunday evening would hear Kwadwo Osae, the town crier of Aburi in Akwapim, "intone the call sign" using a double flanged bell (*Ghana Radio Review* 1965d: cover). Local broadcast systems, like the talking drum, the town crier, and even the ɔkyeafoɔ shaped the way television was used and adapted by Ghanaians in the 1960s to share information, educate, and explain and translate government policy to the people. In this way, television and radio were not just incoming technologies from abroad but were remade in Ghana within the *longue dureé* of indigenous media (Mavhunga 2017: 14).

Besides being a noncommercial television system, Ghana Television's emphasis on using viewing centers as a means of set distribution denoted a significantly different conception of television. At a basic infrastructural level, the government instituted numerous official public viewing centers, especially in those parts of the country that were further from urban Accra (*Ghanaian Times* 1965). Television receivers were set up in schools and in chiefs' palaces. During the day, the televisions at schools were for classroom use, but in the evenings they were open to the public (Quarmyne, pers. comm., July 13, 2017). At official television viewing centers, "monitors," modeled in part on traditional African storytellers, were employed to translate English content into local languages, thus combining "one of the oldest traditions of Ghana with this newest scientific invention" ([Du Bois] 1964: 15).[29]

Ghana was not the only place that public television viewing centers were used. It was a practice that recalled, for example, the way the British colonial administration in the 1940s brought educational content to rural communities for communal consumption through mobile cinema vans and shares some similarity with calls for the development of information communication technology community centers to bridge the digital divide in the early 2000s. More proximately, the French télé-club of the 1950s was a notable model of collective television reception, as villagers would congregate at schools to watch national broadcasts, discuss programming, and give feedback to producers—a model that was influential on UNESCO's approach to the promotion of television in developing nations (Wagman 2012). Indeed, a 1961 UNESCO document suggested that group viewing was essential for ensuring that television in Africa reached "those sections of the population for whom educational television is particularly designed" (UNESCO 1961). By 1964, there were community viewing centers in Kenya, Nigeria, Uganda, and fifteen community television centers in Sierra Leone (UNESCO 1964).

Communal viewing extended into domestic spaces in Ghana, as people with private receivers would welcome their neighbors into their homes to watch television. The tendency to share family possessions with one's community, of which collective television viewing is an example, has been described by Ghanaian philosopher Kwame Gyekye as Akan humanism. "Akan thought," he writes, "sees humans as originally born into a human society (onipa kurom), and therefore as social beings from the outset" (1995: 155). Because humans are naturally social, it is essential to Akan thought to guarantee the well-being of each member of their society. Nkrumah would draw on these African values to articulate what he saw as a particularly African idea of socialism. In his 1964 book, Consciencism, he argues for enacting a uniquely African style of economic socialism (rather than adopting the socialism of the USSR or China) that was rooted in pre-

29. They also recall the role of the cinema commentator that accompanied mobile cinema vans. The commentator would translate films into local languages and explain government policies to film audiences.

colonial African social systems which valued collectives, cooperatives, and asset sharing.

Quarmyne recounted that his brother, who lived in Kaneshie, "encouraged anybody in the neighborhood who wanted to watch television to come to his house. He later had to stop, because his furniture was all broken" (pers. comm., July 13, 2017). To preemptively try to manage the ruckus that hordes of excited children might cause, the *Ghanaian Times* warned children "not to be too noisy" while watching television in a neighbor's house (quoted in Merya 1965). However, Martin Loh would leave his window open so that neighbors could come and watch. As a television producer, he liked to hear his neighbors' chatter and would use their comments "to realign" his "own thinking about things" he was producing (pers. comm., August 18, 2017).

This practice was found not only in Ghana. Nigerians had a similar tendency to share television access with neighbors. In *Nigerian Television*, Oluyinka Esan shows that "neighbours maintained an open-door policy, and often, family resources such as radio, and, later, television, were placed at the disposal of all" (2009: 40). Communal television viewing, Esan argues, was the result of "transporting to urban living, a rural mindset that respected communal living and sharing of assets" (40). Esan concludes that even though television in Nigeria was a "modern artefact," it was adapted and used in "still largely traditional societies" and as such, Nigerian television was both a domestic medium and a "group/public medium" (41).

The radical force of Ghanaian television was that it was expected to be communally shared both at official viewing centers and in the homes of private individuals.[30] It was, as Esan observes, both a domestic and pub-

---

30. It bears noting that the communal viewing at official television centers did not always result in the access to the medium that Ghana Television employees imagined. Shortly after the start of television, the *Ghana Radio and Television Times* reported that citizens had been complaining about problems with access. These problems included claims that sets were locked up or turned off before the end of broadcast; sets turned toward the wall when programming other than music was being broadcast so that music could be played to attract customers for the sale of drinks; the public not being allowed in when important people visited centers; and "big men" allegedly removing sets and moving them into their own homes. Enterprising individuals were, apparently, able to monetize state assets by transforming community centers into drinking spots, and the control of access to "communal" television sets became important assets to establish and maintain local power structures (*Ghana Radio* 1965c: 2). Warnings in the *Ghana Radio and Television Times* about the illegality of removing television sets from viewing centers continued from October 1, 1965, to January 21, 1966.

lic medium. This is quite different from the way television was advertised to consumers in capitalist democracies. As Raymond Williams noted in his seminal work on television, the privatized set sold a consumer product to the masses but was never a *mass* medium. In the United States and Europe, Williams noticed that earlier public technologies, like the railways and city lighting, were being replaced by new private technologies which were "at-once mobile"—connected to the desire to go out and see new places—"and a home-centered way of living." He calls this tendency "mobile privatization" ([1974] 2003: 19–20) and argues for treating television broadcasts as a social product of this trend.

Yet, Williams also stresses that television might have turned out otherwise (23). When television was new, many people experienced it outside of the home in public commercial spaces like taverns, department stores, and even buses.[31] John Logie Baird publicly demonstrated his experimental television system in England at Selfridge's Department Store in the 1920s (Aldridge 2012: 15–17). In the 1950s, people in Mexico City congregated in the streets to watch televisions in shop windows (Bonilla 2019), and in Japan, televisions were placed at railway stations and in parks, offering open-air television for urbanites (Yoshimi 2003: 463). Television, as Milly Buonanno argues, was an initially public medium that had to be domesticated (2008: 14). Even after television became the dominant domestic amusement in homes across the world, it always had non-domestic varieties—in bars, schools, and shopping areas. Television's "slipperiness," its ability to adapt in different social spaces, is part of what defines the medium. Anna McCarthy has thus argued that the physical space of television reception, which compresses global images within local processes, is critical for defining the medium (2001: 13). Local values and television viewing practices establish television anew in each location. Akan humanism, African socialism, and indigenous media practices all contributed to the unique formation of the medium in Ghana.

In this context, the first seven months of Ghanaian television offer a glimpse of a distinctive televisual alternative that drew on imaginaries of precolonial African social relations oriented toward a liberated pan-African future. Nkrumah's political vision—for African socialism and a United States of Africa—and Du Bois's television system were futurological projects. In his

---

31. William Boddy notes that only 6,500 television sets were sold in 1946 and were mostly used in taverns and the homes of media professionals. According to Lynn Spigel, a television receiver was installed in a California bus line in 1950 (Boddy 1998: 131; Spigel 1992: 196).

work on Afrofuturism, Kodwo Eshun identifies the collapse of the "planned utopias of African socialism" when Nkrumah was overthrown as influencing a disenchantment with futurism (2003: 288). But before the coup d'état, African counterfutures were not only possible but central to Pan-Africanism, a political project television's arrival on the continent helped herald. In a *Ghana Radio and Television Times* article, a correspondent offers a prophetic revelation of the future of television in Africa. Television can, according to the article, "present the stark problems of countries still oppressed and the appalling apathy of others neglected"; it can depict the distinct cultural diversity of the continent while also highlighting Africans' "common denominator as one continent one people" and promote African Unity; and it can provide a means to see "through the intrigues and maneouvres of colonists and their agents" (1965a: 5). Notably, the article begins with the adage, "to see is to believe," highlighting television as a visionary medium (5). By conjuring its own images of Africa, Ghanaian television could dispel an Africa whose only future existed through Euro-American mimicry. African culture was activated to imagine technological futures that would actualize values like universal liberty, equality, and prosperity, which, during the colonial period, had been espoused by colonial powers but were never intended to extend to those they colonized. The visual work of television could make the possible actual: "With pride, we learn in vivid terms, through the medium of television, the facts of potential Africa" (5). Throughout the article, a future-conditional *can* does the work of proclaiming a liberated Afrofuture made possible by television.

An important part of television's role in building Afrofutures was visualizing the existence of African engineers, expertise, and technological aptitude. Before the inauguration of television, Nkrumah visited GBC to explain to broadcasting employees why he decided to set up a television system in Ghana: he had traveled all over Africa and had not seen one Black cameraman. In addition, the programs were all being produced by European staff and were not geared toward the uplift of the continent. According to Loh, Nkrumah "wanted Ghana Television to be different." He wanted Ghana to "develop television programs that would make our country feel proud of themselves" and to inspire its citizens "to be as good any nation of the world" (pers. comm., August 18, 2017). Part of this pride would come from the visibility of a television station run by all Black technicians, directors, broadcasters, and editors. It would be a new television model in terms of mode of production, the content of what was shown, and the way it was experienced by the general public.

The power that Black men and women in front *and* behind the television camera imparted was not lost on Du Bois. In a January 8, 1965, speech, she described Ghana Television as "the first indigenous Television System in Africa—indigenous in that the content of our programmes will come out of Ghana and Africa—indigenous in that our System will be manned in all its extended parts by Ghanaians or by workers from Sister African States" (1965). In the introduction to *This Is Ghana Television*, Du Bois asserts that the invention of Ghanaian television defied "experts"—here coded as white foreigners—and their predictions about the possibility of a "young African country's" ability to "develop its own original television" with "its own trained Ghanaian engineers, producers," and "cameramen." As an African American political activist who closely followed the civil rights movement in the United States, she was very aware of the radical implications of the formation of an all-Black television station in the year 1965. William Gardner Smith, a prominent African American journalist and novelist who was invited to Accra to help organize the television news department, was "struck by the visible signs of black sovereignty: the black ministers, heads of corporations, managers of big department stores, customs officials, bank clerks, salesmen, and the producers, directors, technicians, and journalists at the radio and television studios" (1970: 96). Thus, what made Ghana Television different was not just African programs telling African stories but also the powerful statement that Ghanaian ownership and command over "the best equipment money can buy . . . in studios second to none" signaled to the world ([Du Bois] 1964: 3).

The Beginning of the End

Nowhere was the importance of Black technological ability more apparent than in the preparations for and the broadcast of the Organization of African Unity's African Summit Conference, only three months after the inauguration of Ghanaian television. "Hardly had we begun," Shirley Graham Du Bois wrote to a friend in the USSR, "than we were faced with preparing for a supreme test—coverage of the African Summit Conference, along with presentation of programs which would involve all the independent African States."[32] The Organization of African Unity (OAU) was founded

---

32. Shirley Graham Du Bois to Mikhail Kotov, "Correspondence 1965," November 7, 1965. MC 476 Box 18.15, Shirley Graham Du Bois Papers, Schlesinger Library, Radcliffe Institute, Harvard University.

two years earlier, on May 25, 1963, to promote the emancipation of all African countries and work toward joining all of Africa under one union. By the 1965 conference, Nkrumah hoped that the organization would resolve to become one "United States of Africa." At the African Summit, Ghana Television would have the chance to prove itself as a fully independent African television station and demonstrate its commitment to advancing the principles of socialism and Pan-Africanism to an international audience.

All over Accra, improvements were made for this important event. In less than a year, a $24 million state house and a twelve-story hotel block containing sixty deluxe three-room suites to house the visiting African dignitaries were constructed (Sanders 1966: 138–46). Ghana's modern splendors were everywhere on display. One enterprising neon company made "a huge, blazing map of Africa" and erected it "overlooking the road coming in from the Air Port" in order to welcome arriving African dignitaries. The sign was notably "designed, manufactured and erected . . . by Ghanaians in 14 days" (*Daily Graphic* 1965a: 4). Describing the sign, Du Bois wrote to a friend, "I have heard the boast that this is the largest neon sign in the world. Remembering neon signs in New York City, I don't know about that. But this map stands out alone against the black sky and certainly is impressive."[33] It was, quite literally, a sign of African participation in global modernity. New technologies, in particular, were central to projecting a confident, modern, African state, and Ghana Television would have an important role to play on this international stage. As Nkrumah said at the inauguration of television, "All who are employed in our Television Service and our Sound Broadcasting Service have a unique opportunity . . . to play a vital role in the development of Ghana . . . and create in the minds of our people, through television and broadcasting, an awareness of the benefits to Ghana of modern science and technology" (1965: 6).

Promoting Pan-Africanism was a central task of the new television station, and the televised broadcast of the OAU meeting was critical for fulfilling that mission. There were two television studios set aside at the conference to interview the heads of state about "their commitment to African unity and the emancipation of Africa" (Loh, pers. comm., August 18, 2017). This engagement was part of an effort by Nkrumah to use television as a means to demonstrate the capabilities of independent Africans, to break

33. Shirley Graham Du Bois to Berny, "Correspondence 1965," November 21, 1965. MC 476 Box 18.15, Shirley Graham Du Bois Papers, Schlesinger Library, Radcliffe Institute, Harvard University.

the colonial mentality that presumed that technology could only be wielded by white men. But the crew was also encouraged to casually converse with leaders when the opportunity availed itself. Many of the dignitaries were interested in television and engaged staff in discussions about the medium. As Loh described, "Some of them had television already, but they were just showing films from France. . . . They hadn't developed their own indigenous programs to meet the demands of the day." Ghana Television staff asked many questions, and an informal exchange on the state of African television and engineering in different parts of the continent developed (pers. comm., August 18, 2017).

Nkrumah took a personal interest in Ghana Television's preparations for the conference. He requested that Loh, who had been tasked with directing the OAU conference coverage, meet him in his office at Flagstaff House to discuss broadcast plans. Nkrumah gave him a lecture about his expectations for Africa and what he wanted the visiting African leaders to gain from the conference. Loh, only twenty-six at the time, remembered that Nkrumah was emphatic that "his vision of African independence and redemption" would "fire on" even after the leaders headed home. Nkrumah insisted that Ghana Television had a duty to demonstrate to the other heads of state "that we as Africans can manage these things and do them well." Loh explained the feeling of responsibility that he and other Ghana Television employees experienced at the time: "We didn't have any foreign experts supporting us, helping us anymore. We were on our own; we were on our feet. We must show that we can do it. And at an important function like that . . . we couldn't fail" (pers. comm., August 18, 2017).

In addition to covering all the open sessions of the conference live, Ghana Television collected and presented, for the edification of the African leaders and their delegations, programs from every independent African country participating in the conference.[34] They also produced a summary and analysis of the proceedings for special news programs. Notably, television personality Sam Morris hosted a show called *Today at the Conference* every evening after the proceedings. In addition, entertainment programs highlighted a pan-African solidarity with African Americans and the African diaspora more broadly.[35] For the opening ceremony, Ghana invited

34. Shirley Graham Du Bois to Berny, "Correspondence 1965," November 21, 1965. MC 476 Box 18.15, Shirley Graham Du Bois Papers, Schlesinger Library, Radcliffe Institute, Harvard University.
35. The artistic presence of the African diaspora was also felt at the conference through the fine arts. For instance, in addition to being featured on Ghana Television, African

international stars—Josephine Baker from Paris and Mariam Makoba from New York—to perform as "special entertainers."[36] Despite describing them as "temperamental dames,"[37] Du Bois declared Baker's performance in particular "a tremendous success."[38] On October 24, during the Sunday conference hiatus, Ghana Television featured a "special OAU audience participation programme with famous Ghanaian comedian Bob Cole, the blind composer-vocalist Dokyi Appenteng, an African theater troupe, and the Black Star Line highlife band." Later in the evening, the internationally recognized *Hamile* (1965), a Ghana Film Industry Corporation adaptation of *Hamlet*, was screened with an introduction by Genoveva Marais.[39] To close the night, Du Bois read a poem by her late husband called "Ghana Calls" with charcoal illustrations by African American artist Herman Bailey (*Ghana Radio* 1965e: 14). The entertainment programs effectively presented pan-African unity through its diverse presentation of global Black excellence.

To make sure that the visiting African dignitaries saw Ghana Television's productions, television sets were mounted along the main corridor connecting the hotel where the leaders were staying to the main conference hall (pers. comm., August 18, 2017). There were three cameras in the main hall, two in the on-site studios, and one outside the convention hall to interview people on the street. "We virtually moved GBC to that place," recalls Loh. The televisions distributed around the conference grounds not

---

American artist Herman Bailey also had an art exhibition for his work during the Organization of African Unity's African Summit Conference. See Shirley Graham Du Bois to Vivian Schuyler Key, "Ghana TV," October 14, 1966. MC 476 Box 44.13, Shirley Graham Du Bois Papers, Schlesinger Library, Radcliffe Institute, Harvard University.

36. Shirley Graham Du Bois to Berny, "Correspondence 1965," November 21, 1965. MC 476 Box 18.15, Shirley Graham Du Bois Papers, Schlesinger Library, Radcliffe Institute, Harvard University.

37. Shirley Graham Du Bois to Berny, "Correspondence 1965," November 21, 1965. MC 476 Box 18.15, Shirley Graham Du Bois Papers, Schlesinger Library, Radcliffe Institute, Harvard University.

38. Shirley G. Du Bois to Josephine Baker, "Correspondence 1965," November 14, 1965. MC 476 Box 18.15, Shirley Graham Du Bois Papers, Schlesinger Library, Radcliffe Institute, Harvard University.

39. The film was written by Terry Bishop, a British expatriate, and was produced by the Ghanaian writer, Joe de Graft. It stared Kofi Middleton-Mends as Hamile/Hamlet, Mary Yirenkyi as Habiba/Ophelia, and Ernest Abbequaye as Abrahim/Polonius. As Camela Garritano puts it in her exceptional book on Ghanaian film, "The Africanizing of Shakespeare by well-educated members of the African elite was meant to demonstrate Africa's civility and humanity" (Garritano 2013: 52).

only presented what Ghana—and, by extension, Africa—was capable of, it also broadcast a diverse array of African cultures through the newest mass media communication system. As Loh put it, African leaders "would watch all these productions of African concepts" that announced to the viewer, "'You are in Africa, these are Africans!'" The aim was that the heads of state would be able to "believe in themselves" (pers. comm., August 18, 2017).

Ghana Television's coverage of the OAU meeting was considered a success. Nkrumah personally came to GBC to congratulate the crew and nominated each of them for a raise. Du Bois was also impressed. "Television did me proud!"[40] she wrote to friends and family; Ghana Television "won praise for itself"[41] and "established itself as the first real African Television Service on the continent."[42]

During the next four months, Ghana Television settled on a weekly program that focused on education and continued to expand the number of programs it broadcast. On weekdays, children's programming began at 6:00 p.m., followed by educational programs like *I Will Speak English* and the news, before nightly entertainment shows. Educational programs included topics like public health, agriculture and fisheries, homemaking and maternal health, and cultural heritage. The most popular programs, on Saturday and Sunday, were those that featured live performances by Ghanaian musicians and the Sunday soccer match at the Accra Stadium. On Monday, January 31, 1966, educational programming expanded to include morning educational broadcasts with secondary school lessons at 10 a.m. and technical school lessons at 10:45 a.m.

The height of success Ghanaian socialist television celebrated after the OAU conference seemed like a distant dream on the morning of the February 24 coup d'état. Television announcer Samilia Karji described being woken by gunshots on that morning. The broadcasting flats, where GBC employees were housed, were located next to the president's offices at Flagstaff House and the Accra police living quarters, two locations tar-

40. Shirley Graham Du Bois to Berny, "Correspondence 1965," November 21, 1965. MC 476 Box 18.15, Shirley Graham Du Bois Papers, Schlesinger Library, Radcliffe Institute, Harvard University.

41. Shirley Graham Du Bois to Mikhail Kotov, "Correspondence 1965," November 7, 1965. MC 476 Box 18.15, Shirley Graham Du Bois Papers, Schlesinger Library, Radcliffe Institute, Harvard University.

42. Shirley G. Du Bois to E. Ablade Glover, "Correspondence 1965," October 28, 1965. MC 476 Box 18.15, Shirley Graham Du Bois Papers, Schlesinger Library, Radcliffe Institute, Harvard University.

geted by the NLC military. To avoid being harassed and assaulted by the military, GBC employees painted the letters G-B-C on the outside of their homes (pers. comm., July 18, 2017). Du Bois was put under house arrest until her lawyer negotiated permission from the new military government for her to leave Ghana on March 12, 1966.[43] On the morning of the coup, Quarmyne was on his ham radio, as he often was during his time off. He had made contact with a man in England when he heard in the background a radio broadcast from GBC announcing the overthrow of Nkrumah's government. Shocked, Quarmyne reported the news to his radio contact in England. The Englishman called the British authorities, and the news broke internationally that the Convention People's Party had fallen (pers. comm., July 13, 2017). Nkrumah, who was out of the country at the time, had been overthrown, and Ghanaian socialism ended.

The socialist status of television was bound up in the political transformation of the state after the coup d'état, though how much it changed is itself part of its contested legacy. Socialism had rarely overtly entered the content of Ghana Television, except in some documentaries and news programs, complicating the realization of Du Bois's project. The news magazine program *Ghana '65* featured occasional episodes like "The Role of the Press in Socialist Ghana" and "The Role of the Co-operative Movement in Socialist Ghana," and Loh remembers producing documentaries on the significance of grassroots African socialism in cooperatives (pers. comm., August 18, 2017). Other former Ghana Television employees have denied that Ghana Television was socialist, and GBC's institutional histories have removed Nkrumah's assertions about the socialist goals of Ghana Television from the history of television's founding.[44] In a speech that launched the eightieth anniversary celebrations of GBC, the GBC board chairman transformed Nkrumah's famous words—"Television will be used to supplement our educational programme and to foster a lively interest in the world around us. It will not cater to cheap entertainment nor commercialism. Its paramount objective will be education in the broadest and purest sense. Television must assist in the Socialist transformation of Ghana" (1965: 3)—in

43. T. K. Impraim to Shirley Graham Du Bois, "Correspondence 1966," March 12, 1966. MC 476 Box 19.1, Shirley Graham Du Bois Papers, Schlesinger Library, Radcliffe Institute, Harvard University.

44. Quarmyne and Smilia Karji objected to claims that Ghana Television was socialist, while Loh heartily affirmed its socialism. The ideology of Du Bois and the state only minimally shaped content allowing multiple perspectives on what Ghana Television was like during this era (Karji, pers. comm., July 18, 2017; Loh, pers. comm., August 18, 2017; Quarmyne, pers. comm., July 13, 2017).

paraphrase. In the tribute, listeners now heard a different vision: "Ghana Television was to supplement the country's educational programmes and foster a lively interest in the world around the people at the time. Its paramount objective was to provide public education in its broadest and purest sense without any element of commercialization" (Asante 2015: 18). In a related television documentary made to commemorate the first eighty years of GBC, Nkrumah's language is again reworded: "The basic aim of Ghana Television would be to supplement Ghana's educational programme and to foster an interest in world affairs. It would not cater for cheap entertainment and communication" (Mahama 2015). While the phrase parallels the language of the first two sentences of the Nkrumah's speech, this time, in addition to leaving out television's role in the socialist transformation of Ghana, the word *commercialism* has been changed to *communication*, further removing Ghana Television from its socialist origins. The change was significant since GBC commercialized their content shortly after the 1966 coup d'état.

Socialist television in Ghana had mediated two seemingly divergent ambitions: to produce a radically novel African socialist media system that would promote empowering images made by and for Africans and to ensure that Ghana television met modern global standards. It was the latter ambition that allowed subsequent accounts of GBC to emphasize the continuity of the organization over the rupture following the 1966 coup d'état. The socialist origins of Ghana Television may now be treated as little more than a false start in GBC's institutional narrative of technological advancement, but the first seven months of Ghana Television is an example of a media system explicitly designed to oppose—at the level of content *and* production—the dominant assumptions about the capitalist domesticity of the medium and its implicit whiteness.

New Media Afrofutures

If Afrofuturism were a methodological approach to media studies, it would share some characteristics with media archaeology. Both excavate the past to critique a narrative of scientific and technological progress that has been central to the history of Western Enlightenment. Both are interested in excavating the history of "old" technologies. A driving force of Afrofuturist thinking across the Black Atlantic has been, according to Ytasha Womack, "to unearth the missing history of people of African descent and their roles in science, technology, and science fiction" (2013: loc 233 of 2265). Accordingly, Afrofuturism is about the enunciation of an African past, one that Hegel famously denied, in order to engineer a liberated Black future.

Afrofuturists draw on the long history of science, technology, and innovation in Africa to push the limits of what is conceivable for Black technological futures. Like steam punk, whose nineteenth-century steam-engine-powered alternative worlds have been evoked as a symbol of the "media-archaeological spirit of thinking the new and the old in parallel lines," Afrofuturism also thinks the old and new in tandem (Parikka 2012: loc 171 of 4641). In the case of Ghana Television, there was an intentional reworking—a remediation—of older African media (talking drums, double flanged bell) to imagine a new television system. Media archaeology, especially as an artistic practice, also invokes alternative histories to "offer critical insights into the assumed-natural state" of various media (Parikka 2012: loc 3110 of 4641).

The crucial difference between the two is that Afrofuturism makes a commitment to contemporary racial justice central to its engagements with the past and its projections of the future. If "media archaeology has been interested in excavating the past in order to understand the present and the future" (Parikka 2012: loc 171 of 4641), Afrofuturism time-travels to change the present. As Kodwo Eshun writes, "Afrofuturism may be characterized as a program for recovering the histories of counter-futures created in a century hostile to Afro-diasporic projection and as a space within which the critical work of manufacturing tools capable of intervention within the current political dispensation may be undertaken" (2003: 301). In other words, the technologies of Afrofuturism are unambiguously politically engaged.

Shirley Graham Du Bois, without describing herself as a media archaeologist or Afrofuturist, nevertheless identified and retooled African media and cultural practice to fabricate a new media system that would undo the symbolic work that media technologies have historically done to entrench white supremacy. While some contemporary media archaeologists project upon media technologies a nonhuman alterity that excuses their human theorists from acknowledging the racial politics embedded within media (Ernst 2011), an Afrofuturist media archaeology would make the racial politics of new media technology and its use explicit. Thus, by manufacturing television through a process of indigenization, television was remade in Ghana for the advancement of a more equitable Black future.

The Afrofuturist and media archaeological project of Ghana Television demonstrates the imaginative process in which media are constantly made and remade through use outside of the presumed centers of innovation in ways that demand historical attention. As long as the "new" is tied to the formation of the material components of media objects, instead of in the interpretive reading, translation, and application of that material within cultural-historical contexts—especially those within new media geographies that have been neglected—it will be impossible to separate the "new" in *new media* from the double "neo" in *neocolonialism* and *neoliberalism*. The geography of media archaeology makes the racial politics of media history fundamental to media theory and to understanding contemporary global media.[45] In a moment when, as Mark Fisher puts it, "capitalism seamlessly occupies the horizons of the thinkable" (2009: 8), turning toward the emergence of television in Ghana shows that the failure of more familiar media innovators, like those in Silicon Valley, to move beyond a techno-Darwinist survival of the newest and fittest stems from an absence of genuine and radical imagination. The Afrofuturist project of Ghanaian television to actively disentangle new media technologies from racial capitalism offers an optimistic reminder that media technology that resists the neoliberal "mobile privatization" can still be invented.

References

"Africa, Sub-Saharan." 2004. In *Encyclopedia of Television*, edited by Horace Newcomb, 45–47. 2nd ed. New York: Taylor and Francis.

Aldridge, Mark. 2012. *The Birth of British Television: A History*. London: Palgrave Macmillan.

Asante, Richard Kwame. 2015. "Speech Delivered by Mr. Richard Kwame Asante—Board Chairman at the Launch of GBC's 80th Anniversary Celebrations." In *GBC Anniversary Edition: 80 Years of Dependable Broadcasting: Evolving into the Digital Age*, 18–19. Accra: GBC Publications Department.

Bazin, André. 2014. "A Contribution to an Erotologie of Television." In *André Bazin's New Media*, edited by Dudley Andrew, 105–15. Berkeley: University of California Press.

Berwanger, Dietrich. 1995. "The Third World." In *Television: An International History*,

---

45. For instance, it is not hard to see the shift in contemporary international development discourse from supporting community information and communication technology centers to their support for educational applications for individually owned mobile devices in the early 2000s as a move away from the support of public infrastructure to that of mobile phone privatization.

edited by Anthony Smith and Richard Paterson, 188–200. Oxford: Oxford University Press.

Boddy, William. 1998. "The Amateur, the Housewife, and the Salesroom Floor: Promoting Postwar US Television." *International Journal of Cultural Studies* 1, no. 1: 129–42.

Bonilla, Laura Camila Ramírez. 2019. "Television Reception and Technological Convergence in the 1950s: The Case of Mexico City." In *The Future of Television: Convergence of Content and Technology*. London: IntechOpen. https://www .intechopen.com/chapters/64718.

Buonanno, Milly. 2008. *The Age of Television: Experiences and Theories*. Bristol: Intellect Books.

Cahoon, R. D., and S. R. Kennedy. 1959. *Recommendations on the Establishment of Television Service in Ghana*. Accra: Government Printer.

Daily Graphic. 1965a. Advertisement. October 30, 1965.

———. 1965b. "Marconi Delegation to Watch TV Opening." July 29, 1965.

[Du Bois, Shirley Graham]. 1964. *This Is Ghana Television*. Tema: State Publishing Corporation.

Du Bois, Shirley Graham. 1965. "T.V. in Ghana." *The Spark*, March 12, 1965, 4–5.

Edgerton, David. 2007. *The Shock of the Old: Technology and Global History since 1900*. Oxford: Oxford University Press.

Ernst, Wolfgang. 2011. "Media Archaeography: Method and Machine versus History and Narrative Media." In *Media Archaeology: Approaches, Applications, and Implications*, edited by Erkki Huhtamo and Jussi Parikka, 239–55. Berkeley: University of California Press.

Esan, Oluyinka. 2009. *Nigerian Television: Fifty Years of Television in Africa*. Princeton, NJ: AMV.

Eshun, Kodwo. 2003. "Further Considerations on Afrofuturism." *CR: The New Centennial Review* 3, no. 2: 287–302.

Fisher, Mark. 2009. *Capitalist Realism: Is There No Alternative?* Winchester, UK: Zero Books.

Foucault, Michel. 1970. *The Order of Things: An Archaeology of the Human Sciences*. New York: Random House.

Garritano, Camela. 2013. *African Video Movies and Global Desires: A Ghanaian History*. Athens: Ohio University Press.

Ghana Radio Review and TV Times. 1963a. "TV Training for Teachers." 4, no. 27, August 30, 1963.

———. 1963b. "What Is Television?" 4, no. 4, March 22, 1963.

———. 1963c. 4, no. 20, July 12, 1963.

———. 1963d. 4, no. 28, September 6, 1963.

———. 1964. 5, no. 8, April 17, 1964.

———. 1965a. "The Role of TV in a Developing Africa." 6, no. 35, October 22, 1965.

———. 1965b. "TV Day." 6, no. 24, August 6, 1965.

————. 1965c. "Viewpoint: TV Sets & Communal Viewing." 6, no. 31, September 24, 1965.

————. 1965d. 6, no. 18, June 25, 1965.

————. 1965e. 6, no. 35, October 22, 1965.

————. 1967. 8, no. 28, September 1, 1967.

Ghanaian Times. 1965. "TV Viewing Centres to be Set Up." July 10, 1965.

Gitelman, Lisa. 2008. *Always Already New: Media, History, and the Data of Culture.* Cambridge, MA: MIT Press.

Gumbert, Heather L. 2014. *Envisioning Socialism: Television and the Cold War in the German Democratic Republic.* Ann Arbor: University of Michigan Press.

Gyekye, Kwame. 1995. *An Essay on African Philosophical Thought: The Akan Conceptual Scheme.* Philadelphia: Temple University Press.

Horne, Gerald. 2000. *Race Woman: The Lives of Shirley Graham Du Bois.* New York: New York University Press.

Huhtamo, Erkki, and Jussi Parikka. 2011. "Introduction: An Archaeology of Media Archaeology." In *Media Archaeology: Approaches, Applications, and Implications*, edited by Erkki Huhtamo and Jussi Parikka, 1–24. Berkeley: University of California Press.

"The Humble Beginning of GBC." 2015. In *GBC Anniversary Edition: 80 Years of Dependable Broadcasting: Evolving into the Digital Age*, 9–13. Accra: GBC Publications Department.

Imre, Anikó. 2016. *TV Socialism.* Durham, NC: Duke University Press.

Lawler, L. J. 1965. "Television's Educational Role in the Developing Commonwealth." *Journal of the Royal Society of Arts* 113, no. 5105: 352–66.

Mahama, Abibata, dir. 2015. *A Documentary on GBC at 80.* Accra: GTV, September 12, 2015.

Mavhunga, Clapperton Chakanetsa. 2017. "Introduction: What Do Science, Technology, and Innovation Mean from Africa?" In *What Do Science, Technology, and Innovation Mean from Africa?*, edited by Clapperton Chakanetsa Mavhunga, 1–28. Cambridge, MA: MIT Press.

McCarthy, Anna. 2001. *Ambient Television: Visual Culture and Public Space.* Durham, NC: Duke University Press.

Merya, Auntie. 1965. "Ghana Television Begins Tomorrow." *Ghanaian Times*, July 30, 1965.

Miescher, Stephan F. 2014. "'Nkrumah's Baby': The Akosombo Dam and the Dream of Development in Ghana, 1952–1966." *Water History* 6: 341–66.

New Ashanti Times. 1965. "Seven Days More for Ghana Television." July 24, 1965.

Nkrumah, Kwame. 1965. "Inauguration of Ghana Television Service." July 31, 1965. ADM 5/4/238, Public Records and Archives Administration Department, Accra, Ghana.

Parikka, Jussi. 2012. *What Is Media Archaeology?* Malden, MA: Polity.

Parks, Lisa, and Shanti Kumar. 2003. *Planet TV: A Global Television Reader.* New York: New York University Press.

Rice, Tom. 2011. "From the Inside: The Colonial Film Unit and the Beginning of the End." In *Film and the End of Empire*, edited by Lee Grieveson and Colin MacCabe, 135–53. London: BFI.

Sanders, Charles L. 1966. "Kwame Nkrumah: The Fall of a Messiah." *Ebony* 21, no. 11: 138–46.

Smith, William Gardner. 1970. *Return to Black America.* Englewood Cliffs, NJ: Prentice-Hall.

Spigel, Lynn. 1992. *Make Room for TV: Television and the Family Ideal in Postwar America.* Chicago: University of Chicago Press.

"Supply: Committee—Broadcasting and Printing." 1959. *Ghana Parliamentary Debates, Official Report*, Vol. 16, No. 15, Thursday, July 16, 1959.

30 Eventful Years of Broadcasting in Ghana. 1965. Accra: Government Printer.

UNESCO. 1961. "Television on the African Continent." Programme and meeting document for "Meeting on Educational Broadcasting in Tropical Africa" Conference. United Nations Educational, Scientific and Cultural Organization, September 6, 1961. https://unesdoc.unesco.org/ark:/48223/pf0000144689.locale=en.

———. 1963. *Statistics on Radio and Television, 1950–1960.* Paris: UNESCO.

———. 1964. "Television in African Countries." Programme and meeting document for "Meeting on the Introduction and Development of Television in Africa" Conference. United Nations Educational, Scientific and Cultural Organization, September 1, 1964. https://unesdoc.unesco.org/ark:/48223/pf0000178441.locale=en.

Wagman, Ira. 2012. "Télé-clubs and European Television History Beyond the Screen." *Journal of European Television History and Culture* 1, no. 2: 118–28.

Williams, Raymond. (1974) 2003. *Television: Technology and Cultural Form.* London: Routledge.

Womack, Ytasha. 2013. *Afrofuturism: The World of Black Sci-Fi and Fantasy Culture.* Chicago: Lawrence Hill Books.

Yoshimi, Shunya. 2003. "Television and Nationalism: Historical Change in the National Domestic TV Formation of Postwar Japan." *European Journal of Cultural Studies* 6, no. 4: 459–87.

Utopia in a Package? Digital Media Piracy and the Politics of Entertainment in Cuba

Laura-Zoë Humphreys

Cuba's Pirate Modernity

One sweltering evening in August 2014, some young Cuban film-maker friends of mine and I waited to place an order at a pizzeria in Havana's middle-class neighborhood of Vedado. Much to my annoyance, the cafeteria's TV was in violent competition with that of the locale next to it, as both establishments pumped out conflicting *reggaetón* beats at high volumes. Scenes such as these became increasingly common after 2010, when Raúl Castro's government first announced plans to expand the categories in which individuals could apply to work as small business owners, or *cuentapropistas*, in an effort to shift several thousand workers from the state sector to the private.[1] Four years later, a whole array of new restau-

---

1. For the initial state announcement of plans to shift workers from the state sector to the private, see "Pronunciamiento de la Central de Trabajadores de Cuba," *Granma*, September 13, 2020, http://www.granma.cu/granmad/2010/09/13/nacional/artic01.html. Official plans for economic reform, the Lineamientos de la Política Economíca y Social, were approved in May 2011.

boundary 2 49:1 (2022)   DOI 10.1215/01903659-9615473   © 2022 by Duke University Press

rants and bars dotted the urban landscape, serving a still small but growing class of Cubans with a little extra money on hand. To add to the new attractions, almost all of these establishments boasted their own television sets, which broadcast to their customers the sounds of music videos supplied through another flourishing new business: the *paquete semanal*, or weekly package, one terabyte of pirated digital media distributed across the island by hard drive and flash drive on a weekly basis with daily updates, which included contents ranging from international news magazines to South Korean television dramas and popular music, Cuban American reality TV shows, and new forms of national cultural production, such as advertising and PDF magazines. Not really expecting an answer, I wondered aloud about the new ubiquity of televisions in the city's small businesses. "It's what they think is modern," one of my friends shrugged, clearly less than convinced.

The relationship between media and modernity has long been an issue of concern in media archaeology. Citing Noël Burch, Thomas Elsaesser contends that a key argument that linked new film history to the project of media archaeology is the idea that "it could have been otherwise" (2004: 81; see also Parikka 2012: 13). In other words, media archaeology sets out to recover forgotten media pasts and to write against teleological accounts of technical progress (Sengupta 2021: 4). Yet the difficulty with much of this work, as Rakesh Sengupta, Dan Morgan in the introduction to this special issue, and the authors of the essays gathered here make clear, is that media archaeology has prioritized time over space and focused on Euro-American media histories. When Euro-American media practices are taken as the unquestioned norm, the particular confluence of digital technologies, hand-to-hand media exchange, and media piracy that characterized the sudden increased availability of global entertainment and information in Cuba can only be presented as an eccentric and exotic curiosity or as a failed copy of a digital modernity to be found elsewhere, namely in the Global North. This was exhibited, for instance, by the numerous headlines by Western journalists that touted the *paquete* as Cuba's Netflix, Hulu, or Spotify or as Cuba's version of the internet.[2]

2. The following are only a few of the more high-profile international press reports on the *paquete*: Silvia Ayuso, "Netflix Contra El 'paquete' Cubano," *El país*, February 15, 2015, http://internacional.elpais.com/internacional/2015/02/15/actualidad/1423981072_014165 .html; Johnny Harris, "This Is Cuba's Netflix, Hulu and Spotify—All without the Internet," *Vox*, September 21, 2015, https://www.vox.com/videos/2017/11/16/16658322/cuba -paquete-internet-netflix; Miguel Helft, "No Internet? No Problem: Inside Cuba's Tech

What such views ignore is how alternate media histories and practices in places such as Cuba can lead to different understandings of key questions in media studies, including the politics and perceptions of copyright and entertainment and their links to modernity. Ravi Sundaram (1999, 2009a, 2009b), for instance, describes the pervasive nonlegal practices of copying and distribution through which many citizens in India and other locations in the Global South obtain media as leading to what he calls a "pirate" or "recycled" modernity. In many parts of the world, Sundaram and other scholars point out, piracy provides citizens with their most reliable access to the latest in world technology, entertainment, and information, promising experiences of speed and global connectivity from which they are otherwise marginalized. At the same time, such practices come into conflict with international intellectual property laws, which, driven by Euro-American interests, rapidly expanded in the late twentieth and early twenty-first centuries, leading to new confrontations between citizens and governments and subjecting populations with alternate conceptions of property and creativity or without the economic means to purchase sanctioned goods to moralizing accusations of theft and inauthenticity.[3] New forms of digital media copying and distribution in Cuba hold out similar promises of access, but the dilemmas such practices pose have been interpreted differently. As my friend's dismissal of *reggaetón* music videos suggests, debates over the *paquete* in Cuba have largely revolved around concerns about the *quality* of the content distributed through digital media piracy and not with ethics, suggesting how alternate histories of media and intellectual property can give rise to competing interpretations of piracy and its social and political consequences.

Revolution," *Forbes*, July 1, 2015, http://www.forbes.com/sites/miguelhelft/2015/07/01/no-internet-no-problem-inside-cubas-tech-revolution/; Sarah Kessler, "In Cuba, an Underground Network Armed with USB Drives Does the Work of Google and YouTube," *Fast Company*, July 7, 2015, http://www.fastcompany.com/3048163/in-cuba-an-underground-network-armed-with-usb-drives-does-the-work-of-google-and-youtube.

3. For work that tracks the expansion of intellectual property law in the twentieth and twenty-first centuries and challenges commonplace moral assumptions about profit, theft, and copyright, see, for instance, Coleman 2013; Lobato 2008 and 2014; and Lobato and Thomas 2015. Ethnographic work in the Global South has been particularly fruitful to these debates, demonstrating how Euro-American enforced concepts of copyright often work to further marginalize populations with alternate conceptions of property and creativity or without the economic resources to gain access to legally sanctioned goods. For work in this vein, see, for example, Dent 2012; Eckstein and Schwarz 2014; Karaganis 2011; Larkin 2004; Thomas 2016; Wong 2014.

In this essay, I explore how the legacy of state socialism gave distinctive shape to experiences and perceptions of digital media piracy.[4] This research combines archival and textual analysis with ethnographic fieldwork conducted with *paquete* creators and distributors, cultural producers, and consumers in the summers of 2014 and 2015, when the *paquete* had just reached the height of its influence and the debates about it acutely revealed fissures and tensions in Cuban media practices and ideologies. While it is often assumed that piracy exists in tension with local governments, I show how the socialist state's own contentious relationship to international intellectual property law, citizens' increasing resistance to state censorship, and ongoing attachment to the aesthetic and social values established under socialism both fostered hopes that piracy might enable new freedoms and raised suspicions that such practices could ultimately support state power. As scholars of media piracy have pointed out, ethical evaluations and the classification of diverse practices of copying and distributing media as piracy do not precede but rather are an effect of intellectual property law and efforts at enforcement (Karaganis 2011: 2; Lobato and Thomas 2015). The Cuban state's ratification of international intellectual property agreements in the 1990s meant that most Cubans with whom I spoke understood the *paquete* as piracy. Yet the state's historic and ongoing contravention of copyright also provided them with a discourse through which to legitimate practices of copying and challenge global discourses that equate the protection of intellectual property with morality and piracy with theft.

At the same time, the ongoing influence of socialist aesthetic discourses in Cuba also meant that many Cubans did not see access to global

---

4. A short analysis of this research was previously published as an extended blog post (Humphreys 2017b). For further research on the dynamics and consequences of digital media piracy and transnational entertainment genres in Cuba, see Humphreys 2020, in which I examine how copy places for pirated media transformed urban sociality in Havana and how these forms of sociability were disrupted by COVID-19, and Humphreys 2021, in which I explore how K-pop, whose influx to the island was facilitated by the *paquete* and related digital media piracy, appealed to Cuban youth by fostering fantasies of becoming enterprising individuals through neoliberal solidarity. For other analyses of digital media piracy and the *paquete* in Cuba, see Arcos 2015; Boudreault-Fournier 2017; Farrell 2019; Köhn 2019; Pertierra 2012; Reyes 2017; Rodríguez 2016. To this body of research, this essay contributes an examination of how the legacy of state socialism, including debates over intellectual property, commercial entertainment, and the role of art within socialism, shaped the production and reception of the *paquete* and the forms of media distribution and cultural production it enabled.

media flows as a simple good. The *paquete* shifted control over distribution in a large-scale fashion out of the hands of the state for the first time since the onset of the Cuban Revolution in 1959, facilitating widespread circulation of both global entertainment genres and new forms of local cultural production, including advertising, that were often distinctly consumerist. While both foreign and Cuban observers celebrated the *paquete* for circumventing state control over media distribution and the island's limited infrastructure in order to gain access to global media flows, even those Cubans most critical of state censorship sometimes worried about what effects the genres circulated through piracy might have on citizens' tastes and social values. And in a final twist, some Cubans argued that it was the socialist state itself that stood to gain the most from the *paquete*'s distractions.

The emergence of the *paquete* generated enormous excitement not only within Cuba but also abroad, with observers celebrating the phenomenon as the work of a tech-savvy and entrepreneurial generation agilely skirting technological and state-imposed limitations to usher in a "new" Cuba. While this is certainly part of the story, such accounts overlook how the *paquete* and reactions to it on the island were shaped by earlier practices of media piracy and long-standing debates on the island over the social role of art and media. Here, I instead show how new forms of media entrepreneurialism converged with the aesthetic and social values established under socialism in sometimes unexpected ways, as citizens turned to media piracy to reimagine social life in the midst of intensified economic reforms and contested relations with the United States.

Films That Make You Think: Building a Socialist Modernity

Hungarian dissident Miklós Haraszti (1988) once suggested that many Eastern European intellectuals were initially seduced by state socialism because it promised artists the opportunity of making avant-garde art for the masses. A similar romance can be seen at work in the first decade of the Cuban Revolution. While censorship was a concern from the start, many Cuban intellectuals who stayed in Cuba recall the 1960s as an exciting moment when the nationalization of artistic production, distribution, and exhibition gave artists new prominence and aesthetic experimentation ruled. Left-leaning intellectuals from around the world traveled to Cuba to take part in and bear witness to the new socialist revolution, which both foreign and Cuban artists hoped would succeed in combining political commitment with artistic freedom and experimentation. In the 2010s, these aspirations and, in particular, the arguments forwarded by the artists and intellectuals associated with the state film institute, the Instituto Cubano del Arte e Industria Cinematográficos (ICAIC, Cuban Institute of Cinematographic Art and Industry), continued to fuel contemporary debates over media and aesthetics even as many cultural workers and citizens questioned the elitism of early revolutionary discourse about the arts. I begin, then, by outlining the ICAIC filmmakers' efforts in the 1960s to create a modernist socialist art that would resist the stupefying effects of both capitalist media and Soviet socialist realism.

One of the first acts of the new government after the triumph of the revolution in 1959 was to establish the ICAIC. Soon thereafter, the state set about nationalizing movie theaters and distributors on the island, granting the ICAIC and other state institutions enormous influence over cinema production, distribution, and exhibition. These policies demonstrate both the importance the socialist state granted cinema and the political capital enjoyed by the ICAIC's original founders, especially its long-time director, Alfredo Guevara. Drawing on his personal relationship with Fidel Castro, Guevara worked with the ICAIC filmmakers to advocate for a critical, experimental, and modernist cinema even as he himself engaged in censorship.

In spite of their own fondness for at least a certain brand of Hollywood, in the early 1960s, the ICAIC filmmakers pushed for a rupture with the commercial American and Latin American cinema that had previously dominated Cuban screens. Criticisms of American media often linked ideological colonization to aesthetic form. In a 1969 article, Guevara contended that the United States had blocked the development of Latin American nations' "intellectual autonomy" by taking over major media industries and provoking an "invasion of comics, radionovelas, and telenovelas" whose "themes" and "simplifying, facile, [and] schematic language have served through many years to condition not only the taste but also the reader, radio-listener, and spectator's capacity for comprehension." This, in turn, led to the "imposition of a way of seeing life . . . an absolute cultural alienation and a pathological rupture with reality," Guevara concluded ([1969] 1998: 41–42).

Even after the official declaration of the socialist nature of the Cuban Revolution in 1961, however, the ICAIC filmmakers also dismissed what they viewed as the efforts of some cultural functionaries to impose Soviet-style socialist realism. In a debate over the ICAIC's exhibition policies in 1963 with Blas Roca, an important functionary in the revolutionary government who had previously served as the leader of the prerevolutionary Partido Socialista Popular (PSP, Popular Socialist Party), Guevara argued that socialist realism treated characters as "abstract archetypes . . . who could compete in their falsehood and lack of realism with . . . the standard image of supermen." Equating Soviet art with Hollywood, he concluded that socialist realism transformed art into an "arte opio," or an "opium art," which would in turn "reduce the public into a mass of 'babies' to whom maternal nurses administer[ed] the perfectly prepared and sterilized ideological baby food" ([1963] 2006: 171–73). For Guevara and the ICAIC filmmakers, then, like US cultural imperialism before it, Soviet socialist realism ensured that the masses remained intellectually dependent and disengaged with reality.

A truly revolutionary film culture, the ICAIC filmmakers contended, must instead aim to create spectators who were at once capable of independent thought and committed to the revolution. As I have argued elsewhere (Humphreys 2019: 32–34), this goal both drew on and modified ideals key to the liberal imaginary. In the 1960s, Cuban intellectuals rejected not only free market competition but also liberal ideals of autonomy. Depictions of the artist or intellectual as speaking truth to power, they maintained, served as a mask for a system that allowed criticism only insofar as it fell short of threatening the dominant capitalist order. The revolutionary intellectual must instead work from a position of commitment to society and the revolution. At the same time, however, Cuban intellectuals insisted on the importance of criticism and public debate in the new society. In a debate over freedom of expression that took place in 1961, Fidel Castro famously established the boundaries of art with an oft-cited phrase: "dentro de la Revolución, todo; contra la Revolución, nada" (within the revolution, everything; against the revolution, nothing) ([1961] 1980: 12–15). In a performative play on this phrase, the ICAIC filmmakers and other intellectuals argued for "crítica desde adentro" (criticism from within) the revolution, a strategy through which they believed citizens would keep society moving toward the future utopia by addressing current social and political errors and shortcomings.

The task of the arts, according to this model, was to create critical but loyal revolutionary subjects by exposing spectators to the best of world cinema, fostering aesthetic experimentation and cultivating what I have described as modernist allegories (Humphreys 2017a, 2019). Inspired by international new cinema movements and the theories and art practices of German playwright Bertolt Brecht and Soviet filmmaker Sergei Eisenstein, Cuban filmmakers worked to strike a balance between conveying socialist meanings and prompting spectators to reach their own conclusions. Employing modernist aesthetic techniques and open endings, early revolutionary Cuban films such as Julio García Espinosa's *Aventuras de Juan Quin Quin* (*Adventures of Juan Quin Quin*; 1966) and Tomás Gutiérrez Alea's *Memorias del subdesarrollo* (*Memories of Underdevelopment*; 1968) aimed both to incorporate socialist meanings and to avoid a didactic delivery, with the goal of ensuring that spectators had to work out the meaning of films for themselves. By challenging spectators to grapple with modernist aesthetic forms, so went the theory, Cuban films would train spectators to become socialist new men and women who thought for themselves instead of a mass of "babies" taking orders from on high.

Tuning in to the World:
Media Piracy in Cuba from the 1960s to the 1990s

The trouble with this vision of an alternative socialist modernity, as one of my Cuban friends put it, was that intellectuals sometimes forgot "the beauty of entertainment." Even in the heady early days of the revolution, filmmakers and other artists worked to refunction popular genres to new revolutionary goals.[5] The intervening decades, meanwhile, saw a series of attempts to merge nationalist, auteurist, and modernist sensibilities with popular genres. But from the late 1960s and into the 1970s, many forms of foreign and especially Anglo-Saxon popular culture were met with increasing state censure. In this context, nonlegal practices of media copying and distribution became the primary means through which citizens accessed global media flows from which they were otherwise barred by state censorship, limited economic and technological resources, and the US embargo.

Many of the Cuban intellectuals with whom I spoke traced contemporary forms of digital media piracy to citizens' earlier efforts to circumvent state censorship of American and British music.[6] From the beginning of the revolution, Cuban political leaders linked these pop culture trends to homo-

---

5. Julio García Espinosa's *Aventuras de Juan Quin Quin* (1966), for instance, refunctioned classic Hollywood genres such as the western and the adventure film through modernist and Brechtian aesthetic tactics, thereby working to deliver entertainment and to spark spectators' critical reflection. See García Espinosa 1975.

6. In addition to the secondary sources cited here, information about the history of media piracy in Cuba was obtained through informal conversations and interviews with Gustavo Arcos, Victor Fowler, Dean Luis Reyes, and other Cuban friends who shared their personal experiences of piracy with me and who I leave anonymous here to protect their identities.

sexuality, gender deviance, and other forms of behavior deemed criminal. For example, in 1963, Fidel Castro equated juvenile delinquency with Elvis Presley and Western fashion trends, arguing that "all of them are relatives: the lumpen, the lazy, the *elvispresliano*, the guy who wears jeans [*el pitusa*]" (quoted in Guerra 2012: 246). Media deplored men who wore their hair long and women who donned short skirts, while state television and radio stations censored the Beatles and other foreign rock music. In spite of these sanctions, however, throughout these decades, youth continued to hunger for the latest in American and world culture. Indeed, the 1970s, widely recalled as one of the periods of greatest state censorship on the island, has also become synonymous with the illicit pleasures of listening to the Beatles and other foreign music. Albums were brought to the island by foreigners or Cubans with the privilege of traveling abroad, then further distributed on makeshift copies or cassettes. Many Cubans also gained access to foreign music by tuning in to radio stations broadcast out of Florida.

The arrival first of VHS and later DVD greatly facilitated the spread of informal media distribution on the island. Up until 2008, it was illegal in Cuba to sell or purchase VHS players, personal computers, DVD players, or cell phones. Nonetheless, state officials often turned a blind eye to the acquisition of these technologies and, even prior to their official legalization, most Cubans did not view their ownership as particularly controversial.[7] Those who belonged to cultural institutions and had the opportunity to travel obtained licenses to import VCR or DVD players and computers from abroad; others purchased these technologies through the informal economy where they were supplied, among other means, by sailors who smuggled them by ship into the country. Equally illegal but tolerated *bancos de video* (video rental collections kept either in vendors' homes or delivered door to door), meanwhile, kept Cubans supplied with a steady stock of pirated films and television series.

In the early 1990s, new sources of informal media distribution came into play. As part of an attempt to appeal to foreign tourism in the wake of the collapse of the Soviet Union—and the economic crisis that ensued—the state broadcast a package of satellite channels for visiting foreigners from the top of Havana's landmark hotel, La Habana Libre. Cubans in the areas nearby quickly devised ways to access this transmission, then, in later years, began hacking the satellite signals of direct broadcast providers, such as DIRECTV

---

7. See Pertierra 2009 for an account of the everyday acquisition and perception of DVD players and other appliances prior to their legalization in 2008.

and DISH. Users camouflaged satellite dishes on balconies or rooftops with plants, water tanks, and other methods and paid local technicians for access codes that would allow receiver cards to descramble signals.

Improvised satellite connections were more heavily pursued than VHS and DVD circulation, with the state periodically carrying out raids and imposing heavy fines and even jail sentences on technicians. It thus seems likely that at least part of the pleasure—as well as the anxiety—generated by these informal methods of media copying and distribution in Cuba was derived from their illicit status. Still, most Cubans viewed such tactics across the decades as a means of keeping up with and tuning in to global trends rather than as a deliberately oppositional act. One older friend of mine, for instance, recalled her Beatlemania in the 1960s as a harmless pastime. Reminiscing about how she and her high school friends in Santiago de Cuba would meet up at the home of whoever had managed to get their hands on a new pirated album, she insisted that these gatherings were "healthy," taking care to note that they typically didn't involve alcohol or drugs. Listening to or coming into possession of this music was a way of proving that you were up to date, she explained, of experiencing "what there was in the rest of the world, beyond the national." Besides, she concluded, Cubans had long been steeped in Anglo-Saxon culture; this was just a continuation of that abiding fascination.[8]

The state's own contentious relationship to intellectual property regimes also helped to justify such consumption. In keeping with socialist practices, in the 1960s the Cuban state disregarded the Spanish-derived law pertaining to intellectual copyright in the country, favoring instead the free copying and distribution of books and other cultural products. In 1967, for instance, Fidel Castro ordered foreign books needed in schools to be copied with no compensation provided to publishers (Moore 2006: 76). The revolutionary government finally established a new copyright law in 1977, but this law continued to grant the state broad leeway in the use of works while restricting the rights of authors to the receipt of their wages as state employees.

---

8. Data collected by other authors suggest similar conclusions. One interviewee cited by Robin Moore (2006: 140) observed that the same political leaders responsible for banning rock music on the radio and television often brought back this music from abroad for their children, who would in turn copy it for friends. Similarly, Lillian Guerra (2012: 252–54) reports that many young people felt no incongruity between being committed to the revolution and listening to rock music.

These policies began to change in the 1980s. As Cuban musicians acquired international fame in the late 1970s and a 1988 amendment to the US embargo made it possible for artists to earn royalties in that country, a number of Cuban artists joined foreign copyright societies such as the Spanish Sociedad General de Autores y Editores (SGAE) in order to collect earnings abroad. In 1986, the Cuban state established its own copyright collecting agency, the Agencia Cubana de Derecho de Autor Musical (ACDAM), and, in 1994, the SGAE opened up an office in Havana to facilitate interactions with their growing Cuban clientele. In the 1990s, meanwhile, Cuba made further adjustments to its national copyright law, working to bring it in line with international standards as part of an effort to attract foreign investment following the collapse of the Soviet Union. In the Uruguay Round of the General Agreement on Tariffs and Trade (GATT) culminating in 1994, ratification of the Agreement on Trade-Related Aspects of Intellectual Property Rights (TRIPS) was established as a prerequisite for membership in the World Trade Organization (WTO) as a result of intense lobbying by the United States government at the behest of its music, film, software, and pharmaceutical corporations and against vocal criticisms about the potential impact of TRIPS on developing and Global South nations. In 1995, Cuba thus became a signatory of TRIPS when it joined the WTO, and in 1996, it signed on to the Berne Convention. The ACDAM subsequently entered into agreements with collection societies around the world and, along with other agencies and institutions on the island, has been active in efforts to educate Cuban artists, institutions, and small businesses in copyright law.[9]

Ironically, however, in spite of the state's official entry into these international intellectual property rights agreements, as a result of Cuba's financial crisis in the 1990s, state institutions themselves became ever more dependent on media piracy. Faced with an absence of funds with which to pay for the rights to use media from other countries, the ICAIC and state television filled out their programming with pirated copies of American films and television shows. As Benigno Iglesis, then head of programming at the ICAIC, explained to me in 2008, "because the United States has shown

---

9. For histories of intellectual property law in Cuba, see Hernández-Reguant 2004; Moore 2006: 75–77. Information about the activities of the SGAE and the ACDAM were obtained through interviews with Darci Fernández, head of the SGAE's Cuban office, Havana, June 18, 2014, and Leonel Elias Perna, vice president of operations at ACDAM, Havana, June 26, 2014.

so much aggression towards Cuba, Cuba has allowed itself the privilege of not paying for rights to American films. We can't do this with films from other countries."

The *Paquete*: Piracy Goes Digital

Thanks to citizens' informal practices of media copying and distribution and the state's own practices of contravening copyright, then, by the beginning of the twenty-first century Cubans were just as avid consumers of American and other foreign media as they had been in the 1950s. The *paquete* greatly contributed to this dynamic, mobilizing digital technologies and an elaborate system of distribution to compensate for new forms of information isolation.

As has been well documented, throughout the early twenty-first century, Cuba has consistently had one of the lowest rates of internet penetration in the world. According to official Cuban government statistics, in 2009, only 2.9 percent of the population had regular access to the internet, while a marginally higher percentage of the population—5.8 percent—had access to email (ONE 2010). Access has steadily improved since then. In 2013, a long-anticipated fiber-optic cable connecting Cuba to Venezuela was finally pronounced active, replacing the slow and outdated satellite services on which Cuba had previously depended. In July 2015, the state telecommunications company, ETECSA, launched Wi-Fi hot spots in city neighborhoods and parks across the island. And in December 2018, ETECSA rolled out a new 3G, then 4G, data service for smartphones.

Even with these improvements, however, in practice, online activities remained limited throughout the 2010s. Up until 2018, in order to get online, Cubans not only had to struggle to secure smartphones or tablets and computers, which they frequently obtained through relatives or friends abroad, but also had to make time to travel to parks with Wi-Fi services. Many complained about the discomfort involved in surfing the net or video chatting with loved ones from public park benches in often sweltering heat. New access to 3G and 4G data services through smartphones radically improved this situation, allowing Cubans to access internet and SNS services from locations they chose for the first time. At 10 CUC (roughly US$10) for 1 GB of data, however, these services were nonetheless prohibitively expensive for most Cubans. The Cubans I spoke with in the winter of 2020 were primarily using cell phone data packages to keep up with friends, relatives, and chat groups within Cuba and abroad using WhatsApp, since this application consumes less data than other services. They also occasionally consulted the internet for information and obtained music videos using applications such as VidMate, which permits users to access and download videos hosted by sites such as YouTube. While technically feasible, most avoided more intensive and hence more costly online activities such as streaming or torrenting video.

Nonetheless, by the time I first visited Cuba in 2003, Cubans were already getting around the island's limited internet access by circulating everything from foreign news reports to local independent films over flash drives and hard drives. The *paquete* built on and vastly expanded the capacity of this and previous forms of media piracy on the island, making the products of piracy available to a far broader swathe of citizens than were previously able to take advantage of such strategies. As with previous forms of media piracy, much of the romance of the *paquete* rested in its illicit status, even as those who were involved in its operations or consumed its products generally did not frame their activities as oppositional. Demonstrating the excitement that the *paquete*'s nonlegal status itself provoked, when I first began ethnographic fieldwork on the phenomenon in the summer of 2014, rumors abounded as to its origins. Many of my Cuban friends and interlocutors speculated that materials were recorded through DIRECTV or DISH satellite connections. Others argued that information technicians downloaded the information at their state workplaces overnight. One friend mused that perhaps this was why the internet connection at the ICAIC, where she worked, was so often so painfully slow. Still others suggested that the *paquete* was delivered by hand by "mules" who travel back and forth from Miami and other locations to transport consumer goods for sale on the island, insisting that no internet connection on the island was fast enough to transmit the amount of data involved.

Whatever their theory, everyone was convinced that I would never get to the root of it. "Nadie lo sabe ni te lo van a decir" (Nobody knows nor will they tell you), one young man who made a living reselling the *paquete* and its contents told me when I asked him where he thought it came from. Gustavo Arcos, a film critic who was active in debates over the paquete on the island, joked, "The big mystery of the country right now is not how to solve the economy, but rather how the *paquete* is made" (pers. comm., May 25, 2015). Nonetheless, I was able to follow tips back up the chain of distribution to two individuals who claimed at that time to be among those at its source: Dany (pers. comm., May 31, 2015), a student who in 2015 was in his fourth year in engineering at the CUJAE (Cuba's engineering and architecture school) and who compiled one version of the *paquete*; and Elio (pers. comm., July 2, 2014), who went by the name of "El Transporta2or," in reference to the 2002 French action film *Le transporteur*, and was a self-styled "music promoter" responsible for collecting music videos and audio for Dany's paquete.[10] I interviewed both at their respective modest apartments in Centro Habana, a low income, centrally located neighborhood in Havana. While at Dany's home, I also spoke informally with two other individuals employed in his business: Dany's friend, Yusmey, and Alberto, a middle-aged man who worked as a "messenger" for the *paquete*.

While both Dany and El Transporta2or evaded some sensitive questions, they also clarified important aspects of the *paquete*'s operations. According to them, at that time, Dany's *paquete* was one of three *matrices*, or original sources, on the island. Every *matriz* employed several individuals, each of whom was responsible for collecting different types of information. Dany and El Transporta2or either refused to say or perhaps didn't quite know themselves how the individuals involved obtained all their data, but it soon became clear that at least some of the rumors were true. Some of the *paquete*'s materials were evidently recorded off illegal satellite connections and then edited to remove the original advertisements, a fact that was evident because, during our interview, a satellite feed was running continuously in the top corner of Dany's computer screen. Dany and Yusmey also claimed that they downloaded YouTube videos and other materials using

---

10. *Le Transporteur* tells the story of an ex–Special Forces operator who transports goods—human or otherwise—for a living, making a point of never looking in the packages he is given or asking for the names of the people who hire him. Elio's chosen pseudonym thus reinforced the mystery that surrounded the *paquete*, particularly in its early years. Elio and Dany both went public shortly after I spoke with them, giving interviews to foreign magazines and news sources ranging from *Forbes* to *Vox* (see note 4) and, in the case of Elio, even appearing in a Cuban-produced play that toured abroad. In 2014 and 2015, those who were involved in the production of the other two main sources for the *paquete* were far more reluctant to discuss their work with foreigners. In subsequent years, however, they too have become at least cautiously more open about their practices, collaborating with Cuban artist Nestor Siré and American artists Julia Weist in the creation of a 64-terabyte server that compiles fifty-two weeks of the *paquete* from August 2016 to August 2017. For a description of this project, see https://queensmuseum.org/2017/01/julia-weist.

connections at nearby hotels, showing me their ETECSA internet access cards to prove this.

As one of my interlocutors put it, the information gathered by the *paqueteros* included "algo para todos los gustos" (something for everyone). Carefully sorted and organized into folders designed to facilitate the user's navigation of materials, from 2014 to 2020 a typical *paquete* incorporated weekly listings from Revolíco, a Cuban classified advertisements website; antivirus software; video games; national and international sports and news; the latest Cuban and world releases and classic movies and TV shows; and national and international music videos, including a healthy dose of *reggaetón*. Miami-based reality TV shows such as *Caso cerrado* or South Korean and Turkish television dramas were among some of the *paquete*'s most popular content. Indeed, these genres exploded in popularity on the island between 2012 and 2019, thanks in part to their distribution through the *paquete*.

Dany's version of the *paquete* also contained a section titled "Interesantes" (interesting), which was further subdivided into folders on topics ranging from "chisme y farandula" (gossip and celebrity news) to "tu peinado" (your hairstyle). In the versions of Dany's *paquete* I reviewed while chatting with him in 2015, this section also included a subfolder titled "ahora si tu negocio va a prosperar" (now your business will prosper), which contained YouTube videos on topics ranging from cooking shows illustrating how to make salmon portabella mushroom burgers to instructions on how to start your own beauty salon. Suggesting how the *paquete* both responded to and played a key role in the economic reforms underway on the island, Dany and Yusmey told me that this section was designed to help those Cubans who had started up their own small businesses. Also tucked into "Interesantes" was another subfolder containing PDF versions of international magazines and a new array of magazines made in Cuba, to which I will return later.

In 2015, this information was collected by central *paqueteros* such as Dany over the course of the week and compiled into a final version on Sundays, which was then copied onto multiple hard drives, all carefully labeled with their final destination (Figure 1). On Mondays, messengers such as Alberto delivered these hard drives to the homes of major clients in Havana and to interprovincial bus drivers, who for a small fee transported them to resellers located across the island. These resellers paid anywhere from 10 to 20 CUC per week for the *paquete*, then sold it either in its entirety or in smaller portions to end users. Emphasizing the fact that part of the

Figure 1 Copying the *paquete* at its source on to hard drives for distribution throughout Cuba. Each hard drive is labeled with the town or region to which it is destined. Photo by Laura-Zoë Humphreys.

attractiveness of the *paquete* was its promise of speed and contemporaneity, in its early years, prices for end users decreased over the course of the week, ranging from 3 to 1 CUC for a full *paquete*. In later years, the central *paqueteros* added a daily update service, supplying redistributors with the latest episodes of television series or telenovelas of interest the morning after they aired abroad.

Those involved in the resale and distribution of the *paquete*, meanwhile, sought roundabout ways to legalize their activities. One young man who sold the *paquete* out of his living room in Vedado, for instance, held a state license for computer services. Signs outside his apartment building and his apartment door made clear what these services consisted of, openly advertising the availability of the *paquete*, video games, and TV series, and advising clients to arrive with their flash drives or internal or external hard drives (Figure 2). The fact that this reseller could publicize his services makes clear how the *paquete* sat in a legal gray zone, neither officially condoned nor actively persecuted. The diversity of clients he served also demonstrated how the *paquete* quickly became a mundane and everyday part of life in Cuba. Over the course of the time that I spent with him, his clients ranged from a middle-aged man looking to copy the entirety of

Figure 2 A sign outside a second-story apartment in Havana advertises "Digital Information." The vendor specializes in the resale of the *paquete*. Photo by Laura-Zoë Humphreys.

"Revolíco" to a young boy accompanied by his father who came in search of a new video game.

Not only did the *paquete* grow out of previous informal media distribution practices on the island, as previously mentioned, it also continued to intersect with them. Many of those who participated in the redistribution of the *paquete* were more specialized, depending not only on the *paquete* but also on their own or others' collections for the audiovisual content they sold. Mario, for example, became involved in piracy when he realized that his passion for collecting television series could be rendered lucrative. By 2007, when he first began selling episodes or seasons of the shows that he had collected, he told me, he owned over two thousand DVDs, which he subsequently transferred to hard drives. He purchased the *paquete* on a weekly basis to supplement his own archive, copying only the folders containing television shows, downloading Spanish subtitles when these weren't included in the data in the *paquete*, and maintaining an extensive catalog with images and descriptions of the television series in his possession.

Prospective clients could go to his home to purchase individual episodes for a few cents or an entire season of a series for 1 CUC; for regular clients or for purchases over 10 CUC, Mario would come to you, hard drives in hand. Mario's passion for the television series he collected also added value to his services, as he was always happy to provide detailed accounts of individual series or offer recommendations. Other distributors acquired reputations among Cuban artists for their ability to hunt down hard-to-locate foreign and art films and documentaries. Finally, a handful of distributors earned reputations for their extensive collections, coming to serve as nodal points for information by selling not only directly to consumers but also to other distributors. By 2020, it was common practice, for instance, for distributors with more limited information storage capacities to visit larger distributors in order to purchase television series or films that had been requested by clients. While pricing was such that the distributors further down the chain generally lost money on this exchange, their hope was that they would recover this investment by selling the content to other customers and by maintaining the loyalty of the client who had issued the initial request.

As should be clear from this description, the large-scale information transfers involved in the creation and distribution of the *paquete* depended on the development in the 2010s of cheaper hard drives and flash drives with increased storage capacities. At his sales point in 2015, for instance, Dany worked with a large PC hooked up to eight four-terabyte hard drives. Clients were themselves often in possession of ever larger capacity flash drives and hard drives, whose contents they regularly erased to make room for more data. Toward the end of the 2010s, DVDs increasingly played only a marginal role: while some older clients continued to prefer this format as a means of saving copies of their favorite films or series while leaving flash drives free for other uses, many clients and vendors increasingly operated exclusively with flash drives and hard drives. Nonetheless, DVDs arguably played an important role in the origins of the *paquete*. Most of the *paqueteros* and intellectuals with whom I spoke argued that the *paquete* began in an organized fashion in 2010, when Raúl Castro's government inadvertently legalized media piracy by handing out small business licenses for the sale of DVDs yet neglected to specify whether vendors had to comply with copyright laws.

In 2015, the folders dedicated to films and series included in the *paquete* were clearly designed with these vendors in mind, incorporating both video files and printable DVD jackets, as well as what was known as "combos": four to six films compressed into a single file that were sold as one disk. One young couple who operated a DVD business explained that they often added their own touches to this material to improve its quality, making sure that subtitles were in synch with image tracks, adding menus to facilitate customer navigation, producing their own combos to ensure that files were not too compressed, and finishing off every DVD jacket with their own invented company logo. A much smaller number of vendors, meanwhile, specialized in music videos, selecting the best videos from the *paquete* and their own archives, and then compiling them onto disks sold either through other vendors or at their own points of sale. As with the scene with which I began this essay, these music video compilations were what many restaurants, bars, and cafeterias purchased to play on television sets in their establishments.

Pirate Productions: Between the State and the Market

Throughout the 2010s, the *paquete* thus rapidly became integral to Cuba's media ecosystem, providing those involved in its distribution, as many insisted to me, not with an excess amount of money but with "enough to live" (Dany and Alberto, pers. comm., May 21, 2018). As the above discussion already begins to suggest, the *paquete*, like previous forms of media piracy in Cuba, also sat precariously between the illicit and the tolerated. Both the *paqueteros* and a new generation of cultural producers, who made use of the *paquete* to create novel content, were careful to cultivate this status. Promoting their products as a means of democratizing access to global media flows, they worked to transform Cubans into modern entrepreneurs and consumers, while also insisting on their alignment with the state and earlier socialist aesthetic projects.

As with cinema in the early decades of the revolution, the Cuban state nationalized the production and delivery of television on the island. Yet whereas the filmmakers and other artists associated with the ICAIC earned a reputation in Cuba for striving to maintain at least a margin for aesthetic experimentation and social criticism, state television was long regarded as censored, aesthetically limited, and, perhaps most damningly of all, boring. The *paqueteros* in turn built on state television's poor reputation to justify media piracy. In arguments that resonate with strategies deployed in efforts to commercialize television around the world, the *paqueteros* presented the *paquete* as both a more democratic and a more appealing alternative to state television.[11] Referring to the *paquete* as a "televisión artesanal" (DIY television), Alberto argued that the "advantage of the *paquete* is that it has a variety of programs, from which you can choose according to your own personal tastes." He continued, "It's not like the government's television, where if you don't like the programming, you still have to watch it."

Even as they insisted on their difference from state-controlled media

---

11. Arguments for commercializing Indian television in the mid-1970s through the mid-1980s also, for instance, often relied on arguments that this would create a more democratic and pleasurable alternative that, unlike state television, catered to viewers' preferences (Mazzarella 2012).

outlets, however, the *paqueteros* strove to remain within the bounds of what they anticipated would be tolerated by state officials. While controversial materials could be obtained unofficially through those who redistribute the *paquete*, the *paqueteros* repeatedly insisted to anyone who cared to listen that they monitored all data carefully in order to ensure that "nada de porno ni de política" (neither porn nor politics or, in other words, works that could be considered an attack on the Cuban state) were included in the *paquete*'s offerings. As Alberto commented to me, "nosotros mismos nos censuramos" (we censor ourselves) (Dany and Alberto, pers. comm., May 21, 2018). The state's own changing approach to international intellectual copyright laws also helped to legitimize the *paquete*. Most of the Cubans with whom I spoke viewed the *paquete* as piracy, reflecting a growing awareness of and concern about the ethics and consequences of such practices. Leonel Elias Perna, vice president of operations at the ACDAM, for instance, insisted on the vulnerable position in which institutionalized tolerance of these practices placed Cuban artists. "How are we going to defend Cuban rights abroad if at home our institutions are violating copyright?" he asked (pers. comm., June 2014).

Nonetheless, even Perna, who, given his position, had reason to subscribe to international discourses advocating for the protection of intellectual property, defended piracy. He himself, Perna noted, wouldn't have been able to obtain the knowledge about the arts that he had were it not for the state's policy of freely distributing artistic works in the early decades of the revolution. The high prices of CDs and DVDs, combined with low salaries in Cuba, he continued, meant that piracy was the only means through which Cubans were able to access cultural works. Others were similarly ambivalent about piracy. When I asked *paqueteros* and other Cubans for their thoughts on such practices, a number acknowledged that piracy might pose a problem for artists. But they also defended nonlegal practices of copying on the grounds of access and, in many cases, through the precedent set by the state. "Piracy? What piracy? Piracy here is *oficial*" (official, or state-sanctioned), was a frequent response to my queries.

As in much of the Global South, moreover, piracy in fact had mixed effects on the work of local cultural producers. Some Cuban filmmakers objected to the rampant piracy of their work, but some began handing over copies of their films to the *paqueteros*. Cooperating with media pirates, they found, was the only way to control the quality of their work in contexts where films otherwise risked being pirated in unfinished versions. Other artists turned piracy to their advantage. Several resellers of the *paquete* told me that *reggaetón* musicians provided *paqueteros* with copies of their music and music videos, using piracy as a means of promoting their work in the hopes of attracting Cubans to concerts where the musicians made the bulk of their revenue. This strategy was even immortalized in a 2013 song and music video titled "El paquete" by a woman *reggaetón* artist, La Diosa. The repeated refrain of La Diosa's song insists that to be "pegao" (hot), one has to "sale en el paquete" (come out in the package), suggesting that the road to local and even global fame lay through media piracy rather than in spite of it.[12]

Lending credence to such claims, the *paquete* also gave rise to new forms of cultural production on the island. A number of young artists and entrepreneurs took advantage of the *paquete*'s distribution network to produce their own PDF magazines on themes ranging from popular culture to sports and fashion. The most successful of these was *Vistar*, a new "revista de farandula," or celebrity magazine modeled after *Rolling Stone*. Legally registered with a publisher in the Dominican Republic to skirt restrictions on independent publications in Cuba, as of 2020, *Vistar* was circulating in PDF format on the island via the *paquete* and was also available for download via a website and Facebook page. In addition to these distribution tactics, one of the magazine's biggest claims to novelty was its inclusion of all branches of Cuban art, from the popular to the elite. As its then twenty-eight-year-old founder and cultural director, Robin Pedraja, told me in 2014, the magazine highlighted the "best of what happens every month in every branch of Cuban culture," including features on Cuba's national ballet, reviews of recent Cuban films, two-page layouts dedicated to the work of young Cuban graphic designers, reports on Vin Diesel and the other American stars who took to traveling to the island for work or for pleasure between 2014 and 2017, in what proved to be only a momentary thaw in relations between Cuba and the United States, and interviews with Cuban *reggaetón* musicians (pers. comm., June 26, 2014).

Vistar's inclusion of *reggaetón* in particular allowed its producers to lay claim to a radical and democratic inclusivity. Since it first became popular in Cuba in the early 2000s, *reggaetón* has repeatedly sparked controversy for its celebration of consumption and sex, and it was often banned

---

12. La Diosa, "El paquete," https://www.youtube.com/watch?v=3rcZlGiwh-M.

from state media outlets.[13] "This is the first time that this sort of report is appearing in Cuba," Pedraja told me of the magazine's regular coverage of *reggaetón*. "[State] media doesn't treat *reggaetón* as part of Cuban culture, in spite of the fact that many people follow it." Like the *paqueteros*, however, the producers behind *Vistar* also worked to align themselves with the state—or, at the very least, with certain elements of the state. Confirming how Alfredo Guevara and the ICAIC filmmakers came to emblematize a form of state-sanctioned criticism and aesthetic experimentation in the 2010s, the *Vistar* team frequently invoked them to justify their own work. An editorial celebrating the one-year anniversary of *Vistar*, for instance, defended the magazine's inclusion of *reggaetón* and other commercial entertainment genres as follows: "In the words of Alfredo Guevara, who always criticized those who considered the beautiful illegitimate: not everything substantive needs to be ugly, nor everything that is aesthetically pleasing, banal" (*"Vistar"* 2015: 7).[14]

Such arguments are not entirely specious. With its focus on Cuban cultural production, *Vistar* was an important and innovative platform for continuing the efforts of earlier generations to promote the nation's arts. By incorporating reports on popular arts such as *reggaetón* side by side with reviews of the national ballet and cinema, *Vistar* arguably both subscribed to and pushed at the boundaries of the essentially bourgeois hierarchy of taste established under socialism. Indeed, it seems likely that the magazine's attention to popular genres helped to fuel distribution of news about more elite arts, whose inclusion in turn helped to legitimize the magazine in the eyes of the island's political and cultural hierarchy. Finally, like the ICAIC filmmakers before them, and in spite of their claims to the contrary, the *Vistar* team was not satisfied to respond to actually existing tastes but rather actively attempted to shape them.

It is here, however, that the goals and strategies of the early ICAIC filmmakers and those adopted by the *Vistar* team part ways. Whereas early revolutionary Cuban filmmakers favored modernist and experimental aesthetics as a means of producing socialist citizens who could think for themselves, the producers behind *Vistar* aimed to refashion Cubans into taste-

13. For analyses of how *reggaetón*'s aesthetics and its embrace of consumption, sex, and Black racial identities sit uncomfortably with official revolutionary discourses, see, for instance, Boudreault-Fournier 2008; Gámez Torres 2012.
14. Copies of *Vistar* can be downloaded at https://vistarmagazine.com/ (accessed February 17, 2020).

ful and effective entrepreneurs and consumers. This difference is most explicit in the *Vistar* team's attempts to give shape to a new advertising industry on the island. After fading out in the early 1960s, advertising saw a brief resurgence in Cuba during the 1990s. During this period, however, its use was restricted to large state-private co-ventures. Advertising professionals, meanwhile, were employed by the state and worked under strict guidelines that limited the celebration of consumption and forbade targeting consumers along the lines of class, race, or gender (Hernández-Reguant 2002).

Thanks to the *paquete*, private Cuban entrepreneurs instead began hiring professionals to design publicity for their businesses, while the task of creating these advertisements was taken over by independent cultural producers. For their part, the team behind *Vistar*, which was funded through the sale of advertising services to local businesses, made it their mission to educate the Cuban population in the art and aesthetics of advertising. As Pedraja told me, convincing business owners of the usefulness of advertising was no easy task: "A lot of people want to start their own business, but they don't realize the power that advertising has. One of the objectives of the magazine is to give advertising the importance that it has in the rest of the world. We face a double challenge: First, [we have] to make [business owners] understand that they need advertising. Second, once they have understood this, they tend to want a picture of their place and that's it." Pedraja, who had spent six months working in an advertising firm in Jamaica, explained that the staff at *Vistar* instead "search for a concept for each of these advertisements: what is it that fuels your business, that defines it?"

Vistar's approach to advertising can be seen in one of the magazine's ad campaigns for a new tapas bar by the name of Encuentro (Encounter). One of the first ads for the location shows a translucent green hookah beside a plate of roasted vegetables and a glass of white wine. Black letters at the top of the ad announce, "Encuentro: Bar de tapas y hookahs" (Encounter: Tapas and hookah bar) (Figure 3).[15] An ad for the same business published in the magazine a year later demonstrates how the *Vistar* team attempted to play with imagery while conserving the central concept associated with the business. This second ad both highlights the bar's specialization in hookahs and tapas and plays with its name: the image shows a fashionably dressed, attractive, woman seated on a yellow couch, red

15. This advertisement can be found in *Vistar*, no. 1 (April 2014): 10.

Figures 3 and 4 2014 and 2015 ads for a new private bar,
Encuentro, created by *Vistar* advertising team.

hookah pipe in hand, looking expectantly upwards at a man walking toward
her (Figure 4).[16]

In the 1990s, state-managed advertising attempted to negotiate the
contradictions between official socialism and that decade's openings to
the global market by discouraging an excess emphasis on consumption or
class difference. This image, by contrast, bespeaks luxury and privilege in
the frame of a romantic "encounter" about to occur. Notably, the models in
this ad (as in many of *Vistar*'s other advertisements) are white, suggesting
how, from the 1990s into renewed economic reform in the 2010s, privilege
continued to be bound up with racism in spite of official claims that the revolution had long since put an end to discrimination.

Utopia in a Package or the Freedom to Be Vulgar?

It would be easy to dismiss the *paqueteros'* and new cultural producers' appeals to continuity with earlier revolutionary artistic projects as cyni-
cal. When I first asked one *paquetero* why he was working in the business,
he emphasized his own economic needs. Yet the moment I began recording
our interview, he spoke of his ambitions to "educate and inform [Cubans]
about what is happening in the world, while also entertaining them." This latter statement clearly reframed the *paquetero*'s earlier, more personal expla-

16. This advertisement can be found in *Vistar*, no. 14 (May 2015): 33.

nation, casting his private business into a project in line with long-standing Cuban state views that art should be socially useful. To entirely dismiss such rhetorical maneuvers, however, would be to ignore the hold that the socialist legacy continued to have on many Cubans well into the twenty-first century. In the mid-2010s, lingering attachments to the social and aesthetic values established under the revolution combined with a growing resistance to state censorship shaped responses to the *paquete*, leading to sometimes surprising assessments of the *paquete*'s social and political consequences.

Following the collapse of the Soviet Union, the Cuban state worked to contain political dissatisfaction in part by allowing it to have an outlet— within limits—in the arts. This strategic relaxation of state censorship can be seen in official responses to the *paquete*. Reassured, no doubt, by the *paqueteros*' efforts to monitor the materials circulated through the *paquete*, in debates that broke out in 2014, state officials argued against censoring the new business. Abel Prieto, who served as minister of culture from 1997 to 2012 and again beginning in 2016, cautioned that censoring the *paquete* would only further fuel its circulation. "We already know what happens when we prohibit things," he commented during a 2014 meeting of Cuban artists and cultural functionaries.[17] Nonetheless, Prieto and other intellectuals were also vocal in their concerns about the effects the *paquete* and the new foreign and domestic entertainment genres whose circulation it enabled might have on the population. "One of the traps of these new forms of cultural consumption," Prieto observed in a public debate over the *paquete*, "is that they give the impression that the individual is choosing what he wants to consume, when these selections are made according to paradigms that are imposed."

Comments by other intellectuals made even more transparent how state and intellectual resistance to the *paquete* built on long-standing arguments about the pernicious effects of capitalist globalization and US cultural imperialism. "It would be more precise to say that it offers the 'freedom to see what others place in the *paquete*,'" noted Cuban film critic Rolando Pérez Betancourt (2014) in an editorial published in the state newspaper, *Granma*. "The *paquete* . . . speaks to humanity's need to arm itself critically against a world-become-store-display which, via the globalization of the so-called cultural industry, converts politics and ideology . . . into a support for its mercantilism." In an attempt to regain control over cultural consumption

17. "Abel Prieto se refiere al Paquete Semanal," *OnCubaNews*, July 6, 2014, https://www.youtube.com/watch?v=nZOD32LR6wE.

while satisfying new demands for media, the state created an "official" version of the *paquete*, "La mochila" ("The Suitcase"), a compilation of media selected by state cultural institutions and distributed for free through the island's Joven clubs de computación (youth computer clubs).[18] This project once again bespeaks the state's willingness to treat intellectual copyright loosely; it is unclear whether those behind the *mochila* paid royalties for the use of the foreign and national media included, while the format itself facilitated further copying. The *mochila* was also largely unsuccessful, incapable of competing with the rapid and wide-scale distribution system and the diversity of content selection offered by the *paquete*.

For more liberal intellectuals, by contrast, the popularity of the *paquete* was indeed a clear sign of citizens' growing frustrations with the "imposition of cultural paradigms"—but by the socialist state rather than by the global culture industry or the *paqueteros*. Echoing and amplifying filmmakers' arguments in the 1960s that certain cultural functionaries were infantilizing spectators, these intellectuals dismissed Prieto's and others' concerns as paternalistic. "Children aren't going to throw themselves out of buildings because they watch Superman cartoons," author Victor Fowler observed wryly. "Consumers aren't that banal—this is an enormous error made by the cultural elite" (quoted in Recio 2014). The real reason behind political leaders' concern over the *paquete*, insisted Arcos, was their fear of losing control over the media. "In Cuba, which is a totalitarian country controlled by a rigid ideological system that governs all the media, technological change is like Pandora's box," he commented. "Out comes everything that is bad, but in this case, it's bad for the state. For the citizen, it's a huge advantage" (pers. comm., May 25, 2015). Film analyst Dean Luis Reyes proposed an alternative to the restoration of state control over media distribution. By encouraging artists to contribute to and intervene in the *paquete* itself, he argued, Cubans might yet witness the creation of a "socialist utopia," one that would be "free of bureaucracy, censorship, and the policing of thought" and allow "room for everything from the most banal to the most vanguardist" (2014).

Yet as Reyes's comment already suggests, even those intellectuals who supported the *paquete* did not seem to think that all the genres

---

18. For an early article on the *mochila* project, see Bosch Taquechel 2015. An official website for the *mochila* can be found here: http://mochilablog.cubava.cu/acerca-de/ (accessed February 17, 2020).

whose circulation it facilitated were good for citizens—or, perhaps more to the point, good for all citizens. One film critic with whom I spoke argued that older generations had been better equipped by school and family to consume popular culture with a critical eye, such that they could enjoy "violent video games" or "bad movies" without having them shape their values or affect their behavior. But the decay of the Cuban education system in recent years, he worried, meant that today's youth no longer possessed this same capacity for discernment. "The educational system that we have in Cuba now is contributing to an immense gap in knowledge, a lot of vulgarity, really, and a loss of values," he told me. "So, when teenagers see a music video of a *reggaetónero* singing lyrics that are vulgar, violent, and sexist, using bad words and poor grammar, surrounded by women, they'll take that singer as their model" (pers. comm., May 25, 2015). Many of my friends echoed such concerns, complaining about what they saw as *reggaetón*'s lack of quality, its sexism, and its glorification of consumption.

Such reactions arguably reflect the preferences of an elite distanced from and suspicious of popular taste. Indeed, state officials and intellectuals were most critical of *reggaetón*, Miami-based and Latin American reality TV shows, and South Korean popular culture—in other words, the Global South genres largely associated with youth, Afro-Cubans, the lower classes, and women. Yet even those behind the *paquete* sometimes expressed concerns about the influence it might exercise over citizens. When I asked *paqueteros* whether or not they thought the government might eventually attempt to block their operations, they resorted to arguments that resonated with Alfredo Guevara's earlier dismissals of Hollywood and Soviet socialist realism as the opiate of the masses. "This is like a drug," Alberto explained. "It stops people from thinking about their problems" (pers. comm., May 31, 2015). Dany echoed this assessment, noting that the *paquete* kept people "entretenido y tranquilo" (entertained and quiet). These responses suggest the hold that socialist aesthetic discourses and ideals still have on many citizens, along with their growing suspicion that the state may have its own reasons for tolerating media piracy.

Revolutionary Aesthetics, Reprised

Aesthetics, argues Terry Eagleton, has always been a "double-edged concept" (1990: 28). Attempts to establish social and political order through appeals to the senses, values, habits, and the body hold out the possibility of creating a community of citizens linked through fellow feeling rather than by obedience to an external authority. Viewed more cynically, however, this ideal is based on the internalization of an external authority so effective that citizens mistake their subjugation for self-determination. While Eagleton's argument refers to the transition from authoritarianism to liberal democracy in a Euro-American context, it nonetheless sheds light on the socialist history of media in Cuba and how this legacy has shaped the dilemmas and possibilities presented by digital media piracy. Early revolutionary aspirations to popularize experimental and modernist aesthetics promised to transform Cubans into a collective of critical, self-governing citizens united in the pursuit of socialism for the betterment of all, but they also subjected citizens' tastes and desires to the authority of cultural elites. The *paquete*, by contrast, was welcomed by many as a means of shifting media distribution out of the state's control. Yet this new freedom came at the expense of training Cubans in commodity aesthetics in ways that many feared would only further promote the racism, sexism, and consumerism that the revolution promised to do away with but never really did. More surprisingly, long-standing criticisms of popular entertainment on the island fueled concerns that the *paquete* and its offerings were a facile distraction that refocused citizens' attention away from pressing economic problems and political limitations, thereby shoring up the authority of the state. The deliberate efforts by the *paqueteros* and new cultural producers to align themselves with the state, and to restrict contents to what they themselves sometimes dismissed as "puro esparcimiento banal" (banal, light, distraction), give reason to these concerns. While more research is needed to analyze what uses and meanings Cubans make of the *paquete*, related digital media piracy, and the international entertainment genres whose circulation these practices have enabled in Cuba, as the aftermath of transition in so many formerly socialist states has amply demonstrated, private enterprise and discourses of individual choice evidently can coexist with authoritarian state power.

In this context, perhaps hope rests in what Eagleton describes as the excess of the aesthetic—the idea that deep-seated desires and habits may sometimes resist attempts to harness them to specific political or economic projects. Just as in the early decades of the revolution the state's efforts to control citizens' media consumption ran up against Cubans' ongoing interests in and efforts to continue tapping into the global media that they had always consumed, in the twenty-first century new entertainment genres and opportunities for independent entrepreneurship mixed with values and habits shaped by the revolution in ways that might yet have a similarly unpredictable outcome. What is certain is that, in a context where entertainment increasingly represents not only welcome distraction but also economic opportunity and rebellion against state censorship, the new generation of cultural producers and distributors who turned piracy into a business, and the many Cubans who take advantage of their offerings, will not abandon its attractions—whatever use they may make of its pleasures.

References

Arcos, Gustavo. 2015. "Gustavo Arcos sobre el paquetfix (o el consumo audiovisual en Cuba)." *El cine es cortar.* August 19, 2015. https://www.elcineescortar .com/2015/08/19/el-paquete-semanal-y-el-consumo-audiovisual-en-cuba/.

Bosch Taquechel, Loraine. 2015. "Mi Mochila: Un Paquete Al Estilo de Joven Club." *Soy Cuba.* March 4, 2015. https://jmanuelr.cubava.cu/2015/03/06/mi-mochila -un-paquete-al-estilo-de-joven-club/.

Boudreault-Fournier, Alexandrine. 2008. "Positioning the New *Reggaetón* Stars in Cuba: From Home-Based Recording Studios to Alternative Narratives." *Journal of Latin American and Caribbean Anthropology* 13, no. 2: 336–60.

———. 2017. "The Fortune of Scarcity: Digital Music Circulation in Cuba." In *The Routledge Companion to Digital Ethnography*, edited by Larissa Hjorth, Heather Horst, Anne Galloway, and Genevieve Bell, 344–53. New York: Routledge.

Castro Ruíz, Fidel. (1961) 1980. "Palabras a los intelectuales." In *Revolución, letras, arte*, 3–33. La Habana: Editorial Letras Cubanas.

Coleman, Gabriella. 2013. *Coding Freedom: The Ethics and Aesthetics of Hacking.* Princeton, NJ: Princeton University Press.

Dent, Alexander. 2012. "Piracy, Circulatory Legitimacy, and Neoliberal Subjectivity in Brazil." *Cultural Anthropology* 27, no. 1: 28–49.

Eagleton, Terry. 1990. *The Ideology of the Aesthetic.* Malden, MA: Blackwell Publishers.

Eckstein, Lars, and Anja Schwarz, eds. 2014. *Postcolonial Piracy: Media Distribution and Cultural Production in the Global South.* London: Bloomsbury.

Elsaesser, Thomas. 2004. "The New Film History as Media Archaeology." *Cinémas: revue d'études cinématographiques/Cinémas: Journal of Film Studies* 14, no. 2–3: 75–117.

Farrell, Michelle Leigh. 2019. "Piracy, Access, and Production in Cuba's Media Distribution Platform *El Paquete Semanal*: The Case of *MiHabana TV*." *A contra corriente* 16, no. 3: 403–26.

Gámez Torres, Nora. 2012. "Hearing the Change: Reggaetón and Emergent Values in Contemporary Cuba." *Latin American Music Review* 33, no. 2: 227–60.

García Espinosa, Julia. 1975. "A propósito de *Aventuras de Juan Quin Quin*." In *Cine y revolución en Cuba*, 157–60. Barcelona: Editorial Fontamara.

Guerra, Lillian. 2012. *Visions of Power in Cuba: Revolution, Redemption, and Resistance, 1959–1971*. Chapel Hill: University of North Carolina Press.

Guevara, Alfredo. (1963) 2006. "Alfredo Guevara responde a las 'Aclaraciones.'" In *Polémicas culturales de los 60*, edited by Graziella Pogolotti, 169–74. Havana: Letras Cubanas.

———. (1969) 1998. "El cine cubano: instrumento de la descolonización." *Cine cubano*, no. 140: 41–43.

Haraszti, Miklós. 1988. *The Velvet Prison: Artists under State Socialism*. London: I. B. Tauris.

Hernández-Reguant, Ariana. 2002. *Radio Taino and the Globalization of the Cuban Culture Industries*. PhD diss., University of Chicago.

———. 2004. "Copyrighting Che: Art and Authorship under Cuban Late Socialism." *Public Culture* 16, no. 1: 1–29.

Humphreys, Laura-Zoë. 2017a. "Paranoid Readings and Ambivalent Allegories in Cuban Cinema." *Social Text* 35, no. 3: 17–40.

———. 2017b. "Utopia in a Package? Digital Media Piracy and the Politics of Entertainment in Cuba." Hot Spots series, *Fieldsights*, March 23, 2017. https://culanth.org/fieldsights/utopia-in-a-package-digital-media-piracy-and-the-politics-of-entertainment-in-cuba.

———. 2019. *Fidel between the Lines: Paranoia and Ambivalence in Late Socialist Cuban Cinema*. Durham, NC: Duke University Press.

———. 2020. "Copying and COVID-19 in Havana, Cuba." *Mediapolis: A Journal of Cities and Culture*, June 16, 2020.

———. 2021. "Loving Idols: K-pop and the Limits of Neoliberal Solidarity in Cuba." *International Journal of Cultural Studies* 24 no. 6: 1009–26.

Karaganis, Joe, ed. 2011. *Media Piracy in Emerging Economies*. Social Science Research Council. https://www.ssrc.org/publications/view/media-piracy-in-emerging-economies/.

Köhn, Steffen. 2019. "Unpacking El Paquete: The Poetics and Politics of Cuba's Offline Data-Sharing Network." *Digital Culture and Society* 5, no. 1: 105–24.

Larkin, Brian. 2004. "Degraded Images, Distorted Sounds: Nigerian Video and the Infrastructure of Piracy." *Public Culture* 16, no. 1: 289–314.

Lobato, Ramon. 2008. "The Six Faces of Piracy: Global Distribution from Below." In *The Business of Entertainment, Vol. 1: Movies*, edited by R. C. Sickels, 15–36. Westport, CT: Greenwood.

———. 2014. "The Paradoxes of Piracy." In *Postcolonial Piracy: Media Distribution and Cultural Production in the Global South*, 121–33. London: Bloomsbury.

Lobato, Ramon, and Julian Thomas. 2015. *The Informal Media Economy*. Cambridge: Polity.

Mazzarella, William. 2012. "'Reality Must Improve': The Perversity of Expertise and the Belatedness of Indian Development Television." *Global Media and Communication* 8, no. 3: 215–41.

Moore, Robin. 2006. *Music and Revolution: Cultural Change in Socialist Cuba*. Berkeley: University of California Press.

Oficina Nacional de Estadisticas (ONE). 2010. "Tecnologías de la información y las comunicaciones: Uso y aceso en Cuba, enero–diciembre 2009." September. https://docplayer.es/41586149-Tecnologias-de-la-informacion-y-las -comunicaciones-uso-y-acceso-en-cuba-enero-diciembre-2009.html.

Parikka, Jussi. 2012. *What Is Media Archaeology?* Cambridge: Polity.

Pérez Betancourt, Rolando. 2014. "Del paquete y otras visitaciones." *Granma*, September 18, 2014. http://www.granma.cu/opinion/2014-09-18/del-paquete-y -otras-visitaciones.

Pertierra, Anna Cristina. 2009. "Private Pleasures: Watching Videos in Post-Soviet Cuba." *International Journal of Cultural Studies* 12, no. 2: 113–30.

———. 2012. "If They Show *Prison Break* in the United States on a Wednesday, by Thursday It Is Here: Mobile Media Networks in 21st Century Cuba." *Television and New Media* 13, no. 5: 399–414.

Recio, Milena. 2014. "¡Qué Paquete (Semanal)! Diálogo múltiple durante el Ania Pino in Memoriam." *Catalejo: el blog de Temas*. December 3, 2014. http:// cubacoraje.blogspot.com/2014/12/que-paquete-semanal.html.

Reyes, Dean Luis. 2014. "Intervención de Dean Luis Reyes en el foro sobre consumo cultural en Cuba." *Cine Cubano, La pupila insomne*. November 4, 2014. https://cinecubanolapupilainsomne.wordpress.com/2014/11/04/intervencion -de-dean-luis-reyes-en-el-foro-sobre-consumo-cultural-en-cuba/.

———. 2017. "Las políticas culturales del Paquete Semanal." *On Cuba News*, January 12, 2017. https://oncubanews.com/opinion/columnas/republica-de -imagenes/las-politicas-culturales-del-paquete-semanal/.

Rodríguez, Fidel A. 2016. "Cuba: Videos to the Left—Circumvention Practices and Audiovisual Ecologies." In *Geoblocking and Global Video Culture*, edited by Ramon Lobato and James Meese, 178–88. Amsterdam: Institute of Network Cultures.

Sengupta, Rakesh. 2021. "Towards a Decolonial Media Archaeology: The Absent Archive of Screenwriting History and the Obsolete *Munshi*." *Theory, Culture and Society* 38, no. 1: 3–26.

Sundaram, Ravi. 1999. "Recycling Modernity: Pirate Electronic Cultures in India." *Third Text* 47: 59–65.

———. 2009a. *Pirate Modernity: Delhi's Media Urbanism*. New York: Routledge.

———. 2009b. "Revisiting the Pirate Kingdom." *Third Text* 23, no. 3: 335–45.
Thomas, Kedron. 2016. *Regulating Style: Intellectual Property Law and the Business of Fashion in Guatemala*. Oakland: University of California Press.
"*Vistar*: Un año de cultura y farándula." 2015. *Vistar* 12 (March): 7.
Wong, Winnie Won Yin. 2013. *Van Gogh on Demand: China and the Readymade*. Chicago: University of Chicago Press.

Suppositionality, Virtuality, and Chinese Cinema

Jason McGrath

In summer 2015, the computer-animated 3D film *Monkey King: Hero Is Back* (*Xiyouji zhi dasheng guilai*; dir. Tian Xiaofeng) was a sensation in China, quickly surpassing DreamWork's *Kungfu Panda II* from 2011 to become the highest-grossing animated film ever in the country. Promoted with the slogan "This Is an Era that Calls for Heroes!" the film itself was treated as a patriotic hero of sorts (Zhu 2015), asserting Chinese cinema's ability to dominate the domestic box office by retelling stories from the Chinese narrative tradition while also measuring up to the latest technological wizardry of Hollywood in an age of computer-generated imagery (CGI) and 3D production and exhibition.

In China as elsewhere, the digital had begun to transform thinking about cinema by the beginning of the century. In a 2001 article, prominent Chinese film critic and scholar Chen Xihe (2001) exulted in the "post-filmic" world augured by digital cinematography. In that now-canonized essay (Ding 2002: 720–36), Chen hailed computer imagery for providing cinematic expression with a "genuine freedom" in which cinema no longer rests

boundary 2 49:1 (2022)   DOI 10.1215/01903659-9615487   ©2022 by Duke University Press

on a foundation of realism: "Digital imagery leads to the collapse of Bazin's ontological theory of the image. As the digital image seizes the primary role in production, in fact any image at all becomes possible" (Chen 2001: 86). Thus, "verisimilitude is no longer the goal," and post-filmic cinema will be guided not by photographic realism but instead by what Chen called the "virtual realism" of the artificial image (87).

Of course, Chen's maximal claim for the rupture presented by digital cinema was far from unique. Many Western film and media theorists made similar claims, either embracing digital cinema as liberating or lamenting it for sounding the death knell of film as we knew it. What interests me here is not another rehearsal of the various stances on digital cinema—ranging from premature nostalgia for analog film as the lost love object to the techno-utopian anticipation of the digitally enabled fulfillment of a "myth of total cinema" (Bazin [1946] 1967) through technologies like 3D IMAX or virtual reality goggles.[1] Rather, I am interested in the question of how Chen's enthusiasm conveys the sense of a new beginning for Chinese popular cinema as it continues its uphill struggle, dating back to its earliest years, for market position along what Michael Raine (2014) calls the "geopolitical incline" constituted by a global imbalance of power in favor of Hollywood. Given a long-standing anxiety that film, as a fundamentally realist system of representation, poorly matches a Chinese aesthetic tradition that had long favored the stylized, expressionistic, or symbolic over the mimetic, the apparent freeing of cinema from its so-called indexical ontological link to reality—making it instead, as Lev Manovich put it, "a subgenre of painting" (2001: 295)—suggests that Chinese aesthetic and narrative traditions might find new life in the transformed medium of cinema in the digital age.

Such an effort raises questions that echo long-standing—even clichéd—Chinese cultural debates over Westernization versus the preservation of Chinese cultural uniqueness. The director of *Monkey King: Hero Is Back* insisted, "We don't need to follow the mindset of the West, especially that of Hollywood," and Ying Zhu (2015) has credited the film's success with renewing a long-standing goal to create a unique national style

---

1. I refer to André Bazin's idea that the ultimate aspiration of cinema's inventors and filmmakers was to create "a perfect illusion of the outside world in sound, color, and relief." Of course, when it comes to much CGI and virtual reality, the Bazinian notion is perverted in the sense that the ideal he described was "a total and complete representation of *reality*" (emphasis mine), not an imaginary virtual world of fantasy ([1946] 1967: 20).

of animation "rooted in the Chinese fine arts tradition." However, Zhu her-self notes that there are plenty of visible Western influences on the film's look, as had been true of Chinese animation since it began in the 1920s. Thus, the ostensible Chineseness that is asserted—constituting a strate-gic essentialism meant to capture the patriotic domestic audience and pos-sibly even appeal to foreign audiences with its exoticism—is very much a relative one. In her recent authoritative study of Chinese animation from the 1940s to the 1970s, Daisy Yan Du (2019) shows how even during periods of ascendance of a "national style" in Chinese animation, an international style always continued to develop alongside it. And so, even though ani-mation and CGI provide a painterly alternative to the photographic realism of live-action cinema, providing Chinese filmmakers a new palette of pos-sibilities for giving contemporary form to traditional Chinese narratives, the results inevitably incorporate elements from international cinema aesthet-ics while also neglecting or fundamentally transforming some aspects of China's pre-twentieth-century arts.

Here I will explore the theoretical implications of the remediation of the Chinese artistic and narrative tradition in contemporary animation and CGI cinema along two related vectors. The first concerns an aesthetics of presence in which the possibilities of digital cinema, including both anima-tion and CGI effects composited with live-action cinema, are employed to give the characters and settings of fantastical Chinese narratives unprec-edentedly vivid visual expression. The second is what Du has labeled an aesthetics of absence, which she uses in particular to describe the com-positional use of empty or negative space in traditional Chinese literati ink paintings and the form of "national style" in animation that drew upon that tradition (2019: 131).

I will expand the idea of a culturally specific aesthetics of absence to a discussion of the *suppositionality* of Chinese operatic performance—in which much of a fictional diegesis is supposed or posited rather than being mimetically depicted—a concept that sheds light on how fictional worlds are cocreated by actors and audiences. Suppositionality turns absence into a tool for that imaginative effort. Suppositional performance, as we will see, was explicitly rejected by early Chinese film theorists as one of the aspects of traditional drama that was incompatible with the ontological realism of cinema as a photographic medium; things in the story world that used to be gestured to suppositionally could now be filmed directly. Like-wise, because fantastical fictional worlds have found ever more vivid rep-resentation through cel animation and, later, computer imaging, the virtual realism of those media would seem to counter a suppositional aesthetics of absence. I will argue, however, that the concept of suppositionality not only helps us to evaluate how contemporary Chinese blockbusters remediate premodern cultural narratives in new ways but also provides a measure for analyzing the growing phenomenon of composited performances, in which either actors interact with CGI creatures and sets absent during the original performance (for example, the boy and the tiger in Ang Lee's *The Life of Pi* [2012]), or fictional characters themselves are composites of a human actor and a CGI-animated creature (such as Andy Serkis as Gollum in Peter Jackson's *Lord of the Rings* trilogy [2001–2003]). Such film practices present unprecedented circumstances for actors and audiences in their mutually interdependent labors of imagining the story world, and the concept of suppositionality returns to relevance as a way of grappling theoretically with the new situation.

My discussion of suppositionality and virtuality is based partly on an intriguing slippage between the two terms in Chinese, and the relationship I will trace between the two phenomena serves to illustrate that the history of modern Chinese film and drama is not a clean progression from the traditional/suppositional to the modern/realist and then on to the postmodern/virtual. It also calls into question the medium essentialism that is implied by arguments for a fundamental rupture between analog film and digital cinema. Tom Gunning has suggested that rather than assuming any singular essence to the medium of film or any singular key to its relation to reality, we should instead recognize that "cinema has never been one thing. It has always been a point of intersection, a braiding together of diverse strands," including constantly shifting relations to and borrowings from other media and narrative arts (2007: 36). Among the diverse strands that contemporary Chinese digital entertainment cinema braids together are not just stories, images, and characters from premodern Chinese fiction and drama but also the legacy of a suppositional performance style that has new relevance in an age of motion-capture acting and composited mise-en-scène, in which, as Lisa Bode has put it in a key recent study, "in the increasing integration of live action and animation, and the changing relationship between figure and ground this entails, screen performance has become even more important as a conduit for belief" (2017: 185). The tradition of suppositional performance in Chinese opera assumes new relevance in the context of the frequent erasure of the boundary between live action and animation in the viewing experience of contemporary cinema.

Monkey King: Hero Is Back and Chinese Shadow Play

Monkey King: Hero Is Back is only one of the latest among count-less adaptations of the classic sixteenth-century Chinese vernacular novel *Journey to the West.*[2] The novel is based very loosely on the historical fig-ure Xuanzang (AD 602–664), a Chinese monk who journeyed to India dur-ing the early Tang Dynasty to bring Buddhist scriptures and religious icons back to China. In the novel, the monk has three fantastical companions for his journey—a human-pig hybrid, a river ogre, and, most famously, Sun Wukong, an immortal monkey with magical powers to transform his body.[3] A total of one hundred chapters narrate these characters' origin stories and then trace their journey through numerous fantastical kingdoms in which they encounter various obstacles and supernatural enemies. Due to the novel's sheer length, its many film and television adaptations necessar-ily focus only on a particular section—either one of the episodic adven-tures the travelers encountered on their journey or else the backstory of Sun Wukong as the Monkey King or Great Sage Equal to Heaven, who had defied, battled, and finally been subdued by the celestial bureaucracy (led ultimately by the Buddha himself), leading to his imprisonment under a mountain for five hundred years until finally he was freed by the Bodhisat-tva Guanyin in return for agreeing to serve as a bodyguard for the monk's pilgrimage to India.

Monkey King: Hero Is Back mostly depicts events not found in the original novel, reimagining the pilgrim monk as a mischievous orphaned boy monk in training named Jiang Liu'er, who more or less accidentally participates in the freeing of the Monkey King from his imprisonment under a mountain just as an army of mountain trolls are attacking the boy's own village. After a brief recounting of the backstory of Sun Wukong's imprison-ment and of how Jiang Liu'er came to be orphaned, the main story of the film begins with the boy coming upon a shadow puppet show in his village, where the performance is none other than the story of the Monkey King causing the havoc in heaven that led to his imprisonment (Figure 1).

2. The novel is said to have been written by Wu Cheng'en, though this is in dispute. English editions include the popular abridged version translated by Arthur Waley called simply *Monkey* (1961) and the authoritative full translation by Anthony C. Yu, titled *The Journey to the West* and published in four volumes originally in 1977–1983 and in revised and updated form in 2012.
3. For a study of how the figure of Sun Wukong has been adapted in various historical and cultural contexts, see Sun 2018.

Figure 1 Shadow puppet screen in *Monkey King: Hero Is Back* (2015).

For a few moments, during which the movie screen coincides with the shadow puppetry screen, the scene slyly jumbles past and present both diegetically and nondiegetically. Within the story, we have the odd fact that the boy watches a shadow play about the very Monkey King with whom he is about to have an adventure. He is in fact already a "fan" of his soon-to-be co-protagonist, even carrying around a little Sun Wukong doll throughout the movie. At the same time, in referencing shadow puppetry in its opening sequence, *Hero Is Back* makes a subtle nod to the origins of Chinese cinema as well as a possible thread for an indigenous aesthetic of the moving image. An early name for cinema in China had been *yingxi* (shadow play), originally a shortening of "Western shadow play" or "electric shadow play"—names which demonstrate that cinema's prehistory, the ways in which it was situated with reference to pre-cinematic traditions of both fictional narration and optical entertainment, varied from culture to culture in ways that could not help but affect its later development in those contexts.[4] Locating Chinese cinema's prehistory in traditional shadow play has

---

4. For a thorough study of pre-cinematic technologies in the West, see Mannoni 2000. Of course, pre-cinematic optical entertainments also were shared across cultures; Mannoni notes that when Claudio Grimaldi introduced the magic lantern to China in 1669, "the Chinese were fascinated by all aspects of optics: certainly they already knew of the kaleidoscope, magic mirrors, and shadow shows" (71).

long been a way that Chinese cineastes have countered the anxiety that film may be an ineluctably foreign art form (Zhang 1999: 33; Huang 2014: 13). Indeed, Chris Berry and Mary Farquhar have identified more broadly a long-standing "shadow opera" mode of filmmaking in China that includes genres from Chinese opera films to martial arts cinema to the *yangbanxi* or revolutionary model performance films of the Cultural Revolution—a cinematic lineage that distinguishes itself from the "realist mode" of Chinese filmmaking that conforms more to mainstream Western cinema aesthetics (2006: 47–74). Thus, in referencing shadow puppetry as an audio-visual narrative entertainment that helps to constitute a distinctively Chinese genealogy of cinema, *Hero Is Back* positions both itself and its contemporary Chinese audiences within a national imaginary that simultaneously helps constitute and is partially constituted *by* its cinema (Berry 2000).

Suppositionality and the Ontology of Film

In China, the relations between cinema and drama, particularly indigenous Chinese dramatic forms, were fraught from the beginning. Chinese film critics of the 1920s were careful to assert cinema's difference from and superiority to theater, in large part by rejecting the stylized aesthetics of traditional opera in favor of the ostensible realism of cinema. Gu Kenfu, in an essay now canonized as possibly the earliest work of Chinese film theory—the preface to the first issue of *Shadowplay Magazine* (*Yingxi zazhi*; also know in English as the *Motion Picture Review*) in 1921—championed cinema as "sketched from life" and therefore the most "verisimilar" of any form of drama ([1921] 2003: 6).[5] He made his case in particular against Beijing (Peking) opera by contrasting photographic realism with the artifice of operatic *suppositionality*, with its gestures such as "empty-handedly closing a door" (6).

Suppositionality is the usual English translation of the Chinese *jia-dingxing*, meaning the positing of the fictional world by inviting the audience to *suppose* it rather than by mimetically *showing* it. Ran Changjian, chair of the Department of Directing at the National Academy of Chinese Theatre Arts in Beijing, describes the overall effect this way: "If the artistic view of suppositionality is followed, the limited space of the stage is turned into a limitless aesthetic space, in which every element of the imagination

---

5. All translations are my own unless otherwise indicated. I have discussed Gu Kenfu's essay more fully in McGrath 2013.

can be performed at will, making the narrow stage an entire heaven and earth where the spirit can roam freely" (2007: 79). What is "supposed" in Chinese drama is an entire array of elements of the story world that are not directly visible but instead indirectly suggested by conventions, including pantomime, stylized performance cues, and metonymic props. A typical example of the suppositionality of traditional Chinese drama is the opera technique known as *tangma*, in which riding a horse is represented by the performer going through a series of poses and dancing motions while holding a stylized riding crop. The performance is meant to signify the spirit of horseback riding without any need of directly representing an actual horse or even a verisimilar "riding" motion that would be identifiable to audiences not schooled in the relevant operatic conventions.[6] What cues the audience to imagine or suppose the story action of horse riding, rather than to experience the illusion that they are seeing it, is the expressive body and voice of the opera performer, aided by makeup, costume, and minimal props. As Ran puts it, Chinese opera "employs suppositional actions to bring the audience into the realm of the imagination" (83).[7]

Early Chinese film theory explicitly rejected the model of suppositionality in favor of realism. The suppositional horse-riding technique, for example, was among those directly criticized by Gu Kenfu in 1921. Ridiculing the fakeness of the traditional opera poses, he notes that actually *being able to ride* a horse is a skill that must be learned by film actors, since instead of *symbolizing* such an activity, they must actually *do* it in the service of cinema's superior realism. Other activities that Gu asserts must be actually performed in films rather than just symbolically represented include swimming, paddling a boat, driving a car, and even flying an airplane. Besides such elements of performance, Gu notes that films feature

6. Colin Mackerras describes the stage of traditional Chinese theater thus: "The stage on which the performance takes place is square and faces the audience on three sides. It is fairly bare, with a carpet and usually a table and two chairs of traditional style. There is a curtain at the back, but not at the front. Actors enter on stage right and exit on the left" (2016: 43). Sets of traditional drama performances became significantly more elaborate in the twentieth century.

7. A fascinating variation occurs in the famous Beijing opera *At the Crossroads* (*San cha kou*), in a scene in which two characters pantomime trying to swordfight each other in an entirely darkened room in which neither can see his opponent (resulting in what amounts to a slapstick routine in which they keep barely missing each other without knowing exactly where the other is). Here what is "supposed" is not something that cannot be seen but rather *that something cannot be seen* when in fact it can be, as the stage remains lit during the performance.

"real mountains, water, trees, and houses" ([1921] 2003: 6). Since the reality of these is captured directly by photography, the verisimilitude (*bizhen*) that Gu Kenfu champions here is at least in large part the sort of ontological or indexical photographic realism we are familiar with from Western film theorists such as André Bazin ([1945] 1967) and Siegfried Kracauer (1960). Whereas in traditional opera a chair on the stage may serve to represent a mountain, for example, a film can show us an actual mountain. Peter Wollen, in his classic discussion of "the semiology of the cinema," made a similar point that symbolic rhetoric "may still hold good in the Chinese theatre where a complicated code is used to express, say, weeping," but in the kind of realist performance preferred in cinema, "to show one is weeping, one must weep" ([1969] 1972: 146–47).

Opera Film, Animation, and a Chinese Film Aesthetic

The hailing of cinema's realism as superior to Chinese drama evinced broader concerns over a fundamental mismatch between the technology of film and the mainstream of the Chinese aesthetic tradition—such concerns themselves being a subset of an even broader anxiety in the late nineteenth and early twentieth centuries over the perceived failure of China to meet the demands of an increasingly global modernity. The tension between indigenous drama and imported film aesthetics perhaps came into sharpest relief in the case of the Chinese opera film genre. Indeed, despite the ostensible mismatch between traditional opera and cinema, opera films have constituted many of the key "firsts" in Chinese film history, including first film (*Dingjun Mountain* [*Dingjun Shan*]; dir. Ren Qingtai, 1905), first sound film (*Sing-song Girl Red Peony* [*Genü Hong Mudan*]; dir. Zhang Shichuan, 1931), and first color film (*Eternal Regret* [*Shengsi hen*]; dir. Fei Mu, 1948). The genre inevitably raises the larger questions of, first, whether Chinese cinema should adhere to the realist mode of Western mainstream cinema or develop its own comparatively stylized, nonrealist mode in keeping with the supposed autochthonous Chinese aesthetic; and second, how the ostensible intrinsic realism of the photographic medium could be adapted to the needs of a nonrealist regime of representation.

These questions motivated a 1942 essay by Fei Mu—the great Chinese film auteur of the 1930s–1940s who would direct the first Chinese color film mentioned above—on how to "cinematize traditional opera" (2003). He summarized the problem as follows: "The primary performance mode of cinema is an absolute realism; how then can matters be easily settled when it encounters something as surreal as Chinese opera?" (273). Unlike Gu Kenfu, Fei Mu did not reject tradition but rather held out pre-modern Chinese literati painting—with its expressionist, stylized form—as both an example of an indigenous Chinese aesthetic in opposition to cinema's realism and as the kind of model that filmmakers would have to be inspired by if they wanted to preserve the sensibility of Chinese opera. In this view, China should not simply play an impossible-to-win game of catch-up with the West, enacting the kind of rejection of all Chinese tradition that had been advocated by Chinese modern intellectuals since the May Fourth Movement of the 1910s–1920s. Instead, Chinese tradition itself should be remediated and kept alive through an indigenous cinema, thereby quite possibly realizing a comparative advantage in competing with the West for the domestic audience. As Fei Mu put it, "Given the strong interest in the Beijing opera so loved by the Chinese people, the film adaptation of traditional drama has its commercial value; at the same time, it has quite a bit of interest from the perspective of 'developing national essence'" (272).

Indeed, the opera film genre itself demands that Gu Kenfu's eagerness to embrace the imported realist aesthetic of film be countered by those such as Fei Mu who are concerned with using film to preserve and remediate China's aesthetic traditions. Weihong Bao has described the opposition and yet interdependence of the suppositional or subjunctive (*xuni*) and the mimetic (*moni*) as "a key problem in the making of opera film, a central locus of anxiety in the politics of medium specificity when Chinese opera, deemed symbolic and suppositional, confronts its mimetic supplement" (2010: 257)—that is, the world captured through the realism of live-action photography. In attempting to give cinematic form a uniquely Chinese imprint, Fei Mu, in both his opera films and his non-opera films, sought to maintain what he called a certain "atmosphere" or "air" in his mise-en-scène and cinematography ([1934] 2002)—which Victor Fan has interpreted as being based on "the presence of an absence" (2015: 136–41).[8] Indeed, in Fei Mu's masterpiece *Spring in a Small Town* (*Xiao cheng zhi chun*, 1948), the entire story revolves around a constitutive absence—namely the passionate mutual love between two characters who nonetheless are unable ever to consummate it due to social propriety. (In that way, it is a clear pre-

8. Fan writes that Fei Mu's distinctive "air" (*kongqi*) "crystalizes the presence of an affect that is in fact absent," or, "the main theme is made present by means of its absence" (2015: 133, 134). See also pp. 140–41 for a discussion of "the presence of an absence" in Bazin's theory.

decessor to Wong Kar-wai's *In the Mood for Love* [2000].) Fei Mu uses techniques such as dissolve cuts to create odd ellipses not just between but *within* scenes of intense but suppressed emotion as a way of negatively representing the impossible desires that flow under the narrative and give it its remarkable power.

Such a negative or apophatic mode of representation recalls the Chinese literati landscape paintings that Fei Mu recommended as a model for Chinese filmmakers—the same "aesthetics of absence" that Daisy Yan Du has recently named as the basis of the "national style" of Chinese animation. Making use of blank spaces, such paintings can, in Fei Mu's words, "fill the page with smoke and clouds and, with an occasional few light brushstrokes, transmit the charm of mountains, waters, flowers, and birds, all without bothering with verisimilitude" ([1942] 2003: 272). As with his earlier comments regarding "atmosphere," here Fei Mu argues for a Chinese cinematic style based partly on omission or absence, in keeping with the less-is-more aesthetic of suppositionality. In other words, even the realist medium of cinema can become suppositionally suggestive by putting emphasis not on the profilmic material reality but on what can be represented only partially or indirectly.

In contrast to such a subtractive approach, in which some abstract form of suppositionality seems still to be operative, more mainstream approaches to Chinese cinema fully embraced realist representation, whether photographic or virtual. But this had its own challenges. Particularly in the case of many popular stories with premodern sources (whether drama or vernacular fiction), filmmakers had to find a way to artificially represent fantastical things that could not be captured through normal live-action photography, and thereby to construct a "mimetic supplement" that relies on modern technologies allowing a virtual or perceptual realism of the moving image that may go well beyond any profilmic material reality. Just as in the West the divide between cinematic realism and formalism has been traced to the early cinematic realism of the Lumière actualities as contrasted with the trick photography of Méliès, in China as well the drive to realism was balanced by a willingness to exploit the plasticity of the film image to create fanciful adaptations of traditional tales through special effects. This could be accomplished through sleights of hand in editing, photography, and props. Importantly, it was also achieved through the use of animation as an alternative to live-action photography as the basis for the filmic image.

It is no accident that such formal techniques would be deployed especially in film adaptations of the fantastical episodes of *Journey to the*

West. A recently rediscovered film, *Cave of the Silken Web* (*Pan si dong*; dir. Dan Duyu, 1927), for example, depicts an episode in which the Buddhist pilgrim and his companions are threatened by a group of flesh-eating spider spirits disguised as attractive women. Substitution splices resulting in a Méliès-style stop-trick effect are used to show the metamorphosis of the women (played by human actors) back into spiders (large, elaborately constructed props with wriggling legs). The film was only one of a number of hugely popular Chinese films of the late 1920s that featured martial arts, visual effects, and often supernatural themes.[9]

Later, China's first feature-length animated film, *Princess Iron Fan* (*Tie shan gongzhu*; dir. Wan Laiming and Wan Guchang, 1941), gave another episode from *Journey to the West* a vivid, unprecedented cinematic expression. With animation, long before the shift from celluloid film to digital video, the ostensible "indexical" ontological realism of the film image—its material, existential tie to a profilmic material reality—already appears to be irrelevant. In fact, however, *Princess Iron Fan* complicates this picture through its use of rotoscoping. Rotoscoping—or the hand tracing of live action footage as a basis for animated drawings—was invented by Max Fleischer in 1915 and used in his pioneering animation series *Out of the Inkwell* (1918–1927) and then later in dance sequences for his Popeye and Betty Boop cartoons in the 1930s (which were familiar to audiences in Shanghai). Walt Disney adopted the practice for his 1937 film *Snow White and the Seven Dwarfs*, which, after it was exhibited in Shanghai in 1938, "triggered the creation of *Princess Iron Fan*," according to Du (2019: 22). Made by the Wan brothers—the founders of Chinese animation and makers of several of its masterpieces—*Princess Iron Fan* "strictly adhered to the procedure of rotoscoping" (51) to create its strikingly dynamic images (Figure 2). Rotoscoping was felt to be especially effective in realistically depicting motion, thus making cartoons seem more perceptually convincing. The technique also means that the resulting animation did not achieve a purely "virtual" realism but rather retained at least a secondhand indexical tie to material reality. Nonetheless, an animated feature like *Princess Iron Fan* presented a unique opportunity to lay claim to a distinctively Chinese aesthetic in cinema. Despite their borrowing of the technique of rotoscoping from the West, the Wan brothers insisted they wanted "to create a unique

9. Such films were thought to have negative impacts by the Republican-era government and were banned by the early 1930s. For more information on the martial arts film craze of the late 1920s, see Zhang 2005: 199–243 and Bao 2014: 39–90.

Figure 2 Sun Wukong in *Princess Iron Fan* (1941).

cinematic art of the East" and "to use traditional Chinese art to delineate the characters' demeanor, costumes, and gestures in *Princess Iron Fan*" (quoted in Du 2019: 48).

After the establishment of the People's Republic of China in 1949, an international style of animation continued to develop, influenced now by Soviet exchanges in addition to techniques already borrowed from Disney, but the Chinese national style of animation also began to be more systematically promoted and explored beginning in 1956 (Farquhar 1993; Du 2019: 114–51; Macdonald 2016: 78–104). The film credited with starting this trend, *The Arrogant General* (*Jiao'ao de jiangjun*, sometimes translated as *The Proud General* or *The Conceited General*; dir. Te Wei, 1956), drew heavily from Chinese opera, including its colors, costumes, makeup, character types, backgrounds, and, most importantly for our discussion, character movements. Opera teachers were invited into the studio to aid in this process, and the entire enterprise explicitly embraced opera as a "road to national style" (Macdonald 2016: 91–92). Other animated films during this period, such as the pioneering *Little Tadpoles Look for Mama* (*Xiao kedou zhao mama*; dir. Te Wei, 1960) by the same director, appeared as animated traditional Chinese ink paintings, including the same technique of *liubai*—leaving signifying blank spaces in an aesthetics of absence—that Fei Mu had named as inspiring his films.

The culminating achievement of Mao-era animation was once again an adaptation of *Journey to the West*, the two-part film *Uproar in Heaven* (*Danao tiangong*) released in 1961 and 1964 and directed by the same Wan brothers who had made *Princess Iron Fan*. The film retained many elements from operatic versions of the story, including music, setting design, and characterization. The music, for example, was provided by the music group of the Beijing Opera Academy of Shanghai, and, just as in Beijing opera, percussive sounds were orchestrated with the motions of the animated characters, including the punctuation of fluid movements with moments of static poses or *liangxiang* (Figure 3). Most importantly, the hero, Sun Wukong himself, was in part "a stylized adaptation," as Sean Macdonald puts it, "of the opera character (including makeup and wardrobe)" (2016: 23).

In such classics of Chinese animation, then, the filmmakers endeavored to retain the aesthetics of traditional opera within the new medium. We may even see the movements of the characters—insofar as they are based on opera—as retaining echoes of the suppositional performance style. Nonetheless, the protean possibilities of animation to depict anything the artistic director can imagine allowed for animated films adapted from *Journey to the West* to represent myriad things that were only "supposed" in traditional opera. Settings and beings—including all kinds of creatures and demons encountered by the pilgrims—that would have been imagined in the story world of an opera performance but not actually present on the stage could now be given vivid perceptual form through animation: the suppositional aesthetics of absence gives way to the virtual aesthetics of presence.

From the Suppositional to the Virtual

The line between these, however, may not be so sharp, not least due to the interesting slippage in Chinese between the terms used for *suppositionality* and *virtuality*. The standard word for *virtual* in Chinese is *xuni*, as in *virtual reality* (*xuni xianshi* or *xuni shijing*), *virtual sex* (*xuni xingjiao*), or the "virtual realism" (*xuni xianshizhuyi*) of digital cinema that Chen had celebrated. However, *xuni(xing)* also can mean "suppositional" or "subjunctive" and has been applied to traditional Chinese drama aesthetics in a similar way as *jiading(xing)*. Some scholars, such as Min Tian (2016: 494) and Haiping Yan (2003: 66), have translated *xuni* directly as "suppositional" in

Figure 3 Sun Wukong in *Uproar in Heaven* (1961, 1964).

relation to Chinese opera.[10] Weihong Bao, on the other hand, maintains a distinction between the "suppositionality" (*jiadingxing*) of operatic conventions in general and the "subjunctive" (*xuni*) nature of specifically the bodily performance of actors (2010: 257). Writing in Chinese, Ran Changjian (2007: 83) similarly associates *xuni* with the "performance form" and *jiadingxing* with the art of the theater more broadly. He argues that "*xuni* implies relying on the imagination to carry out a transformative operation on the thing observed, so that things are represented through both omission and presence." He then quotes an oft cited formula by Ming dynasty intellectual Wang Jide that exhorts theater artists to "value truth [*shi*] in conception and artificiality [*xu*] in presentation."[11] Ran emphasizes that in tradi-

10. The latter source actually gives the Chinese as *xuyixing* and translates it as "suppositionality," but I have confirmed with the author that this was a typographical error and was intended to be *xunixing*.
11. Or, as the existing published English translation renders it, "It is crucial that plays are truthful in conception but ethereal in expression" (Wang [1623] 2002: 64). The original

tional drama, presence/realism (*shi*) and absence/suppositionality (*xu*) work together to create the story world, concluding that "where there is omission there is *xu*, and where there is presence there is *shi*" or realism (83). Taking as an example the *tangma* or horse-riding performance that the 1920s film critic Gu Kenfu had ridiculed, the realism or *shi* is provided only by the immediate presence of the performers—perhaps a few actors in military costumes with riding crops—but their "suppositional [or subjunctive: *xuni*] movements can not only represent galloping war horses but express a thousand soldiers and ten thousand horses crossing a thousand mountains and ten thousand waters" (83). Suppositionality obviously requires the active imagination of the audience, an imagination activated by the actors' performances and enabled rather than limited by the subtractive element of the representation.

The complexity of the meaning of *xu*—the implications of which can range from the abstract or fictional nature of conventionalized opera performance to the "falseness" or artificiality of a purely illusory virtual image—helps to explain how *xuni* could be translated variously as "suppositional" or "virtual." Even the aesthetic of suppositionality on the Chinese stage is not limited to traditional dramatic forms; in the 1980s, for example, when a new avant-garde theater scene emerged in Beijing, artists and critics revived the concept and connected it to ideas of modernist avant-garde drama artists ranging from Bertolt Brecht to Vsevolod Meyerhold. In a study of Nobel Prize–winning Chinese playwright Gao Xingjian, Quah Sy Ren notes his following of both Meyerhold's idea of "stylization" and the Chinese concept of suppositionality: "They envision a theatre which blatantly reveals the fact that it is not a mechanical reflection of reality, but aspires to invoke the audience's imagination with its formal representation" (2001: 172). The idea of suppositionality thus was incorporated comfortably into a modernist aesthetic for the resurgent Beijing theater avant-garde of the 1980s, which must be read at least in part as a reaction against the strictures of socialist realism in the context of post–Cultural Revolution China.

Just as suppositionality is not limited to the pre-modern in Chinese aesthetic practices, virtuality of course is not limited to the (post)modern, either in China or the West. Traditional Chinese shadow play, for example, as in the traditional shadow puppetry of other locales such as Java, creates virtual moving images by means of shadows cast on a screen by actual

---

Chinese is *chu zhi gui shi, yong zhi gui xu. Xu*, the first character of *xuni*, has an ancient history in Chinese aesthetics, philosophy, and religion, with meanings including void, emptiness, vacant, abstract, artificial, false, deceitful, nominal, and fictional.

moving objects. In traditional shadow play in China, the virtual images of the play's characters would function in a way similar to live actors in traditional opera, in that their movements and voices would facilitate the imagining of an entire fictional world that remained largely suppositional, given the limits of what could be projected onto a shadow-play screen. With modern technology, of course, virtual moving images could aspire to a greater realism. In the nineteenth-century West, the invention of a variety of optical devices (the phenakistoscope, zoetrope, flip books, and so on) demonstrated a fascination with virtual, often moving, images enabled by technology well before the appearance of cinema. These were, not surprisingly, also objects of fascination in China. Insofar as virtuality is concerned with creating visual illusions, it is fundamentally unlike the suppositionality in Chinese opera, which is concerned with positing imaginary objects, beings, and events that precisely are *not* visible. Suppositionality engages the imagination; virtuality tricks the senses.

Indeed, the relationship between suppositionality and virtuality prompts us to ponder the status of what we might call the mise-en-scène of the imagination in suppositional narration. It would be a mistake to think of the suppositional elements of "traditional" Chinese opera performances as necessarily prompting individual acts of concentrated visual imagination to fill out the fictional space; we need not posit that the "supposed" parts of the story are imagined in a literal way by individual spectators—as if they squint their eyes, focus their minds, and endeavor to mentally hallucinate the elements of the story (a tiger, a mountain, etc.) that are not directly represented on the stage. Rather, performers and spectators alike share in a broader cultural imagination in which those elements of the story are supposed to exist, so that their effects in the narrative have a powerful fictional realism whether or not they are envisioned in any verisimilar detail by individual spectators. At the same time, it is inevitable that people's imaginations will be conditioned by the visual interpretations they *have* seen—for example, any reader of the novel *Journey to the West* from the Qing dynasty to the present would likely have mental images spurred not by the novel alone but also by how they have seen a character like Sun Wukong (the Monkey King) depicted in shadow puppetry, opera performance, or indeed cinema, whether live-action or animated.

When these narratives are virtually materialized in the contemporary era through the immediacy of digital cinema, it is not simply that what had been suppositionally imagined by the performer and the spectator is now actualized in a convincingly detailed visual image. More precisely, a long-standing element of the cultural imaginary is both granted a new visual expression and inserted into a historically new phenomenological experience through the immediacy of the mechanically moving image. The cultural heritage is thus remediated and posited anew in the transformed mediascape of the present, one that literalizes what had often in the past been suppositional while also transforming that past in a fundamental way for current and possibly succeeding generations. That is, the collective cultural imagination is potentially transformed—much in the way that James Whale's 1931 *Frankenstein* made it impossible to disentangle the cultural imagination of Frankenstein's monster from Boris Karloff's image.

The Live Actor vs. the Synthespean

It is beyond the scope of this essay to survey the dozens—indeed, more likely hundreds—of film and television adaptations of *Journey to the West*, in Taiwan and Hong Kong in addition to mainland China. They have ranged from special effects–enhanced live-action films such as the Shaw Brothers' 1966 *Monkey Goes West* (*Xiyouji*) to the Stephen Chow adaptation *Journey to the West: Conquering the Demons* (*Xiyou: jiang mo pian*; 2013), in which the characters are mainly real actors shot in live-action photography, with CGI used for monsters as well as Sun Wukong in his most extreme transformations. The metamorphosis in that film of Sun Wukong's image from live-action performance to CGI is striking, and significant for the present discussion, as the physical comedy of the actor Huang Bo, who captures well the sense of humor and mischief of the traditional Sun Wukong, gives way to a spectacular yet generic computer-animated ape figure during the film's climax. While in the earlier scenes Huang Bo manages to keep the audience's gaze focused on his expressive body, the CGI image gestures toward a conventionalized global stereotype of an enraged, almost airbrushed-looking cartoon gorilla very similar to Hollywood's King Kong (Figure 4). With this particular use of CGI, one cannot help but feel that the body's expressiveness, not to mention the specificity of the Chinese narrative tradition, has been lost.

This observation brings us again to a fundamental difference between suppositionality, which is supposed to have underpinned the aesthetic of traditional Chinese drama, and virtuality, or the new aesthetic of post-celluloid, CGI-constituted or composited cinema. What Chen called the "virtual realism" of the latter often involves a particular form of posthuman representation, in that the human figure is shouldered aside in the movie

Figure 4 (l-r) Sun Wukong as played by Huang Bo in *Journey to the West: Conquering the Demons*; metamorphosis into giant CGI monkey in same film; Hollywood's *King Kong* (2005).

frame in favor of spectacular digital creatures. This marginalization of the photographed human body by a digital figure is well illustrated through a comparison of the tiger-fighting scenes of the Cultural Revolution model opera film *Taking Tiger Mountain by Strategy* (*Zhiqu Weihu Shan*; dir. Xie Tieli, 1970) and Tsui Hark's 2014 remake, *The Taking of Tiger Mountain*. The Beijing opera-based version of the scene (which recalls the famous "Wu Song fights a tiger" incident in the Ming dynasty vernacular novel *The Water Margin* [*Shuihuzhuan*]), despite having a much more elaborate set than would appear on a traditional opera stage, nonetheless remains focused throughout on the bodily performance of Yang Zirong, the human hero of the story. At the scene's beginning, he is represented as riding his horse in the operatic *tangma* tradition mentioned earlier, the body motions and use of a stylized tasseled whip suppositionally indicating the activity even though there is no horse on the screen (although a horse neighing is briefly heard on the soundtrack). As the scene progresses, the tiger as well (aside from a similar offscreen roar that is heard on the soundtrack) is indicated only suppositionally through the bodily reactions of Yang Zirong to the threat as he draws his gun and ultimately shoots the still-unseen animal (Figure 5). In Tsui Hark's version of the scene, in contrast, an effort seems to have been made to recruit the virtual tiger from *The Life of Pi* to replace Yang Zirong as the star of the scene. As in Ang Lee's movie, the tiger is a composited image that, in a manner analogous to rotoscoping, is built partly out of motion capture of live-action footage of tigers, so that an indexical trace remains in the digital image. Nonetheless, the scene has to accomplish what Kristen Whissel notes is common in the construction of digital creatures in contemporary cinema, which is to somehow render through computer code an image that paradoxically seems imbued with vital, even

Figure 5 Tiger-fighting scene in *Taking Tiger Mountain by Strategy* (1970).

deadly organic life (2014: 91–130). The tiger dominates the screen and steals the scene as a virtual actor or "synthespian" (North 2008: 148–78). The viewer, in the latest manifestation of the "aesthetic of astonishment" that dates back to the earliest cinema (Gunning 1999), simultaneously marvels at the spectacle of a tiger known to be a digital creation and suspends disbelief enough to be jolted by the fictional danger that the tiger poses to Yang Zirong. The unique dynamic here is that the suppositional opera performance is replaced by the composited virtual spectacle of an actor interacting with a digital creature that was in fact added only in postproduction. In such an instance, suppositionality thus remains *in the moment of performance*. For example, in *The Taking of Tiger Mountain*, the live-action actor fighting off the tiger—itself actually a "synthespian" to be added to the shot later—must appear to be looking at an animal not actually there at the moment of performance. The actor therefore must employ the equivalent of the traditional Chinese opera technique of making the audience believe the

Figure 6 Tiger-fighting scene in *The Taking of Tiger Mountain* (2014).

actor is seeing something even if it is not actually there.[12] The suppositionality now is one-sided, however, since what had been imaginatively supposed by the performer—in this case, the tiger—is instead realized in a profuse display of virtual, perceptual realism that becomes the main attraction for the viewer; whereas the human actor was the central figure of the scene in *Taking Tiger Mountain by Strategy*, the CGI tiger steals the scene in *The Taking of Tiger Mountain* (Figure 6).

Suppositionality thus provides a culturally specific tool for approaching the kind of performance required in today's CGI-laden blockbusters, a subject of immediate concern to scholars of film acting. In her study of screen performance and special effects, Lisa Bode (2017) argues that motion-capture (mo-cap) performance, for example, is not a good match for the type of "internal acting" that often has been celebrated as most appro-

12. As Xing Fan explains, "One basic eye technique, *tishen* (literally 'holding the attention'), also called *dingshen* (literally 'focusing the attention) or *lingshen* (literally 'leading the attention'), is performed by focusing the eyes on one object without blinking and holding the gaze for a short while. Performers do not necessarily need to really see anything; the goal is to make the audience believe they do" (2016: 103). Of course, such performances also occurred in analog cinema; for example, closer shots of one character for a scene with two or more might be filmed when the actor's counterpart(s) are not even on the set or are played by doubles or even offscreen stand-in objects, as is often the case with CGI scenes.

priate for film, whether in the switch from a "histrionic" to a "verisimilar" performance style in the early Biograph films of D. W. Griffith (Pearson 1992) or the influence of Stanislavski and "method" acting in later Hollywood cinema. A similar discourse of "internal" or "interior" acting (*neixin biaoyan*) arose in China by the 1920s to distinguish the type of performance called for in cinema compared to traditional drama (McGrath 2013: 405–6). However, Bode argues that today a very different style of performance may be better suited to motion- or performance-capture acting: the actor's body, after all, is covered in sensors and is performing against a blue or green screen, with a plethora of digital effects to later alter the actor's appearance and the environment, including any creatures or objects with which the fictional character is supposed to be interacting. Bode cites performance-capture actor Sean Aita's assertion that an "outside-in" performance style is actually better suited to such acting (2017: 38): the actor assumes a pose, gesture, or expression, and that triggers the internal emotion rather than the other way around (just as some cognitive science and neuroplasticity research tells us that if we practice smiling, it can actually make us happier). Moreover, since "the actor's body and face are conduits for our belief," the success of that performance will be essential to selling the audience on the virtual reality created around the actor in postproduction: "the actor's corporeality and embodiment of being co-present also play a key part in authenticating these sensory illusions," thus making mo-cap a form of "biologically grounded digital realism" (163, 180, 42). In that context, a cultural tradition of suppositional opera performance may actually be a useful tool for the type of acting needed for the virtual realism of CGI cinema, similar to black-box theater in the West, which mostly lacks sets, costumes, or props but instead "relies largely on the actor to bring a world to palpable life for the audience's imagination solely through performance" (178).[13]

Of course, despite any similarities between the style of acting called for in suppositional Chinese opera performance or black-box theater performance on the one hand and CGI mo-cap performance on the other, there is a profound shift *for the audience* from an aesthetics of absence to an aesthetics of presence. As Bode notes, on the bare stage of black-box theater, the belief of the audience depends on the actors and script. If the actor introduces an imaginary animate or inanimate object into the

---

13. According to Bode, "actors who now work in greenscreen environments for film, when talking about the training that is most relevant to this task, often refer to black-box theater" (2017: 178).

fictional space, "they only become 'real' if all actors working in the fictional space agree to their being 'present' and respond to them as if they are so. This presence is built cooperatively and exists in a shared imaginary space between audiences and actors" (182). In contrast, in acting destined for CGI compositing, all the elements of the scene that are "invisible and immaterial" to the performers "will be brought into vivid visualization by the time the audience encounters them onscreen" (183). In the context of contemporary CGI film adaptations of fictions from the Chinese tradition, then, *for the viewer*, digital virtuality supplants not just the photographic realism of earlier cinema but also the culturally specific aesthetics of absence of suppositional opera performance. At the same time, *for the actor*, suppositionality factors into performance to a far greater degree than had been the case in analog cinema.

Animation and Digital Effects Styles in China

Julie Turnock (2015) has argued that in constructing a cinematic world through a composited mise-en-scène, whether based in CGI or pre-digital special effects, two contrasting trends have been evident for decades. The first is a strongly photorealist aesthetic that can be seen in the effects of innovators such as George Lucas, whose original *Star Wars* (1977) did not simply seek to emulate in special effects the way we see things in "real life" but, more specifically, "endeavored to match the look of the dominant style of live-action cinematography in the 1970s" (Turnock 2015: 10). Similarly, in the current era of CGI blockbusters, such an approach has "the goal of making the digital animation look as much like live-action photographic aesthetics as possible" (268). As Dan North put it in another recent study, "When we see, onscreen, an impossible event happening in 'photorealistic' CGI, we are invited into the fantasy that it has actually been recorded photographically, and thus that it has taken place in the real world" (2008: 12). This kind of CGI thus will try to reproduce not just the colors, textures, lighting, and so on of the real world but also such photographic markers as plausible camera movements, motion blur, lens flares, the graininess of specific film stocks, and the like.

The alternative aesthetic to such photorealist effects, according to Turnock, is an "aggressively animated look" that approaches "the world of the movie as more flexible and designable" (2015: 264, 269). Revising Bazin, she summarizes the difference as between "those who put their faith in the optical" and "those who put their faith in animation," understood broadly as an image that does not seem to claim any photographic/indexical link to the real world (267). While noting that the distinction is a matter of emphasis rather than being mutually exclusive, Turnock nonetheless believes that "most contemporary effects-driven films can fit fairly comfortably into one tendency or the other" (269). In the context of the West, at least, we can speculate that this distinction in aesthetic preferences may even manifest itself generationally between younger "digital natives" and older "digital immigrants" (Prensky 2001). To those with strong cinematic memories of Stanley Kubrick's *2001: A Space Odyssey* (1968) or the original *Star Wars*, for example, the later *Star Wars* "prequel trilogy" of 1999–2005 may have seemed like a step *back* in special effects, as instead of a photorealism achieved in part by the use of real three-dimensional models, there was a sometimes-cartoonish quality to the obviously computer-generated images of the later films. However, for a generation raised from the earliest age on video games as well as CGI cinema, the obviously animated look may be less off-putting; "Cool graphics!" is as satisfying a response as "It looks so real!"

Returning to the topic of CGI blockbusters from China with Turnock's key distinction in mind, it is perhaps unsurprising that there appears to be a very clear tendency toward the animation aesthetic rather than the photorealist aesthetic. Putting aside the obvious case of fully animated films such as *Monkey King: Hero Is Back*, hugely commercially successful films that composite their worlds through a combination of live-action photography and CGI tend toward a fantastical mise-en-scène that does not pretend to have been realistically photographed rather than graphically constructed. Stephen Chow, for example, in major international blockbusters such as *Shaolin Soccer* (*Shaolin zuqiu*, 2001), *Kung Fu Hustle* (*Gonfu*, 2004), the aforementioned *Journey to the West: Conquering the Demons*, and most recently *The Mermaid* (*Meirenyu*, 2016), has created an original blend of cartoonish action with live-action photography that also seems to have strongly influenced such Western films as *Scott Pilgrim vs. the World* (Edgar Wright, 2010). Tsui Hark's previously mentioned *The Taking of Tiger Mountain*—which, as with Chow's latter-career films and so many other blockbusters from the region these days, is a coproduction of Hong Kong and mainland Chinese studios—similarly embodies what Turnock identifies as the animation aesthetic in CGI. It manipulates space and time in extremely stylized ways, including camera movements that are obviously virtual, "impossible" camera positions, and changes in speed that freeze or extend dramatic moments. Turnock includes such techniques within the animation tendency in CGI—citing, for example, *The Matrix* (the Wachowski siblings, 1999), in which "the action freezes in midair while the [virtual] camera swirls around the actors, bullets flying all the while" and "effects objects are presented from camera angles with no possible human perspective" (Turnock 2015: 269). Stephen Prince elaborates on these techniques with reference to their later use in films such as *300* (Zack Snyder, 2006), concluding that "the abrupt zooms and speed ramps give the shot a hyperkinetic quality, a herky-jerky, spasmodic energy, a degree of artifice so pronounced that the viewer is forced to take notice" (Prince 2012: 91). His emphasis on the obviousness of the artifice in such scenes shows precisely why they fit into the animation tendency rather than the photorealist tendency in the use of CGI. The film narration does not expect us to indulge in the pretense that the film shows events that might have been photographed in the "real" world but instead flaunts the constructed nature of its graphics. Such moments abound in *The Taking of Tiger Mountain*—for example, in an early battle scene in which the action periodically goes into extra slow motion, putting the characters into near stasis in action while the (virtual) camera tracks in and out or revolves around them, all to emphasize dramatic moments in which bullets are seen flying through the air or blood spurting from a soldier who has just been struck by one.

Conclusion

The suppositional elements of stories from the Chinese narrative tradition—from early modern novels of the late imperial period to the "model operas" of Mao's Cultural Revolution—have been given unprecedentedly vivid visual form in contemporary CGI cinema. Moreover, the fully realized, CGI- and often 3D-enabled visualization of fantastical scenes from traditional stories such as *Journey to the West*, though jettisoning, for the audience, the suppositional aspect of Chinese opera, nonetheless generally do not pursue an aesthetic of photorealism, in which the image, however computer-generated, still pretends to retain the realist ontology of the photographic image. Instead, many Chinese filmmakers embrace what Chen celebrated as the genuine freedom of the "post-filmic" world in which ontological realism and verisimilitude are abandoned, and instead "any image at all becomes possible" (2001: 86). This freedom may allow for a more expressionist approach to predominate over a realist one.

At the same time, such a virtual realism makes the Chinese narrative tradition more globally accessible and therefore affords at least the possibility for Chinese blockbusters to compete for a global audience. While an uninitiated Western spectator would likely be baffled by an actual Beijing opera performance (even if line translations were provided), the same spectator would have little problem following the story of *Monkey King: Hero Is Back*. Moreover, Hollywood itself, which had been relatively indifferent to its Chinese spectators in its early years, is now hyperaware that the Chinese audience increasingly dwarfs the North American one, and that Chinese film aesthetics are themselves worthy of imitation.[14]

During the final credits of *Monkey King: Hero Is Back*, the youthful Jiang Liu'er appears to sit to watch another traditional shadow-puppet show alongside his guardian monk. But when a troll figure from the just-ended movie sits down beside him, Liu'er turns to hand him a pair of 3D glasses, so that it turns out the show they are set to watch apparently is not a shadow play after all but a contemporary 3D digital film like the one just ended (Figure 7). The shot thus stages a humorous collapsing of temporalities of the moving image as well as an implied continuity from a traditional dramatic form (shadow puppetry) through early Chinese cinema (called "shadowplay" in its early years) and on to contemporary digital cinema (with 3D glasses). The "shadows" are now programmed on computers, but the virtual moving images still seek to assert a distinctive Chinese identity that can be inserted into a global circulation of cultural narratives and aesthetic techniques that today is far less one-sided than it was throughout most of the period of analog cinema.

Aside from questions of Chinese cinema's role in that global circulation as well as its relation to "traditional" aesthetics, we can speculate on the implications of the idea of suppositionality to the medium of cinema more generally. Let us return to Ran Changjian's point that even in traditional Chinese drama, realism and suppositionality—material and ethereal, *shi* and *xu*—were not mutually exclusive but, on the contrary, mutually imbricated in creating the overall fictional and aesthetic effect. While our consideration of the concept of suppositionality in relation to virtuality points to crucial differences between traditional drama and analog film—as well as between both of those and the computer-generated moving image—we should not reach facile conclusions of material determinism or medium specificity that

14. For example, *The Matrix* and the many Hollywood action films that followed are widely acknowledged to be indebted to Hong Kong martial arts cinema for much of their action-film aesthetics. For a thorough discussion of how China is changing today's Hollywood, see Kokas 2017.

Figure 7 Final credits of *Monkey King: Hero Is Back* (2015).

overstate these differences. Returning to Gunning's metaphor of cinema as "a braiding together of diverse strands," not just Chinese cinema but cinema in general always has intertwined threads of both presence and absence, of actual being before the camera and of the omitted, the suppositional, the imagined—from offscreen space to editing ellipses to eyeline matches or reaction shots that may actually have been performed in the absence of their fictional objects. The fictional worlds of cinema require both presence and absence, but the ways they are generated and related to each other have varied in response not just to the technology of the medium but to culture, audience, and global commerce. As the international film industry shifts its market focus to Asia at around the same time that digital cinema transforms film aesthetics, Chinese film artists and audiences will shape the possibilities for the future of the medium while bringing to bear artistic and cultural discourses that predate the medium itself.

References

Bao, Weihong. 2010. "The Politics of Remediation: Mise-en-scène and the Subjunctive Body in Chinese Opera Film." *Opera Quarterly. Performance + Theory + History* 26, no. 2–3: 256–90.

———. 2014. *Fiery Cinema: The Emergence of an Affective Medium in China, 1915–1945.* Minneapolis: University of Minnesota Press.

Bazin, André. (1945) 1967. "The Ontology of the Photographic Image." In *What Is Cinema?*, by André Bazin, 1:9–16. Berkeley: University of California Press.

———. (1946) 1967. "The Myth of Total Cinema." In *What Is Cinema?*, by Bazin, 1:17–22. Berkeley: University of California Press.

Berry, Chris. 2000. "If China Can Say No, Can China Make Movies? Or, Do Movies Make China? Rethinking National Cinema and National Agency." In *Modern Chinese Literary and Cultural Studies in the Age of Theory: Reimagining a Field*, edited by Rey Chow, 159–80. Durham, NC: Duke University Press.

Berry, Chris, and Mary Farquhar. 2006. *China on Screen: Cinema and Nation*. New York: Columbia University Press.

Bode, Lisa. 2017. *Making Believe: Screen Performance and Special Effects in Popular Cinema*. New Brunswick, NJ: Rutgers University Press.

Chen Xihe. 2001. "Xuni xianshizhuyi he houdianying lilun" (Virtual realism and post-filmic theory). *Dangdai dianying* (Contemporary cinema), no. 2: 84–88.

Ding Yaping, ed. 2002. *Bainian Zhongguo dianying lilun wenxuan* (Selected works of one hundred years of Chinese film theory). Vol. 2. Beijing: Wenhua yishu chubanshe.

Du, Daisy Yan. 2019. *Animated Encounters: Transnational Movements of Chinese Animation, 1940s–1970s*. Honolulu: University of Hawai'i Press.

Fan, Victor. 2015. *Cinema Approaching Reality: Locating Chinese Film Theory*. Minneapolis: University of Minnesota Press.

Fan, Xing. 2016. "Dance in Traditional Asian Theatre: II. China." In *The Routledge Handbook of Asian Theatre*, edited by Siyuan Liu, 101–5. London: Routledge.

Farquhar, Mary. 1993. "Monks and Monkey: A Study of 'National Style' in Chinese Animation." *Animation Journal* 1, no. 2: 5–27.

Fei Mu. (1934) 2002. "Lue tan 'kongqi'" (On "atmosphere"). In *20 Shiji Zhongguo dianying lilun wenxuan* [Selected works of twentieth century Chinese film theory], edited by Luo Yijun, 1:216–17. Beijing: Zhongguo dianying chubanshe.

———. (1942) 2003. "Guanyu jiu ju dianyinghua" (On the question of cinematizing traditional opera). In *20 Shiji Zhongguo dianying lilun wenxuan*, edited by Luo Yijun, 1:271–74.

Gu Kenfu. (1921) 2003. "*Yingxi zazhi* fakanci" (Introducing *Shadowplay Magazine*). In *20 Shiji Zhongguo dianying lilun wenxuan*, edited by Luo Yijun, 1:3–10.

Gunning, Tom. 1999. "An Aesthetic of Astonishment: Early Film and the (In)Credulous Spectator." In *Film Theory and Criticism: Introductory Readings*, edited by Leo Braudy and Marshall Cohen, 818–32. Oxford: Oxford University Press.

———. 2007. "Moving Away from the Index: Cinema and the Impression of Reality." *Differences: A Journal of Feminist Cultural Studies* 18, no. 1: 29–52.

Huang Xuelei. 2014. *Shanghai Filmmaking: Crossing Borders, Connecting to the Globe, 1922–1938*. London: Brill.

Kokas, Aynne. 2017. *Hollywood Made in China*. Berkeley: University of California Press.

Kracauer, Siegfried. 1960. *Theory of Film: The Redemption of Physical Reality.* Princeton, NJ: Princeton University Press.

Macdonald, Sean. 2016. *Animation in China: History, Aesthetics, Media.* London: Routledge.

Mackerras, Colin. 2016. "Traditional Chinese Theatre." In *The Routledge Handbook of Asian Theatre*, edited by Siyuan Liu, 31–50. London: Routledge.

Mannoni, Laurent. 2000. *The Great Art of Light and Shadow: An Archaeology of the Cinema.* Exeter: University of Exeter Press.

Manovich, Lev. 2001. *The Language of New Media.* Cambridge, MA: MIT Press.

McGrath, Jason. 2013. "Acting Real: Cinema, Stage, and the Modernity of Performance in Chinese Silent Film." In *The Oxford Handbook of Chinese Cinemas*, edited by Carlos Rojas and Eileen Cheng-yin Chow, 401–20. Oxford: Oxford University Press.

North, Dan. 2008. *Performing Illusions: Cinema, Special Effects and the Virtual Actor.* London: Wallflower.

Pearson, Roberta A. 1992. *Eloquent Gestures: The Transformation of Performance Style in the Griffith Biograph Films.* Berkeley: University of California Press.

Prensky, Marc. 2001. "Digital Natives, Digital Immigrants." *On the Horizon* 9, no. 5: 1–6.

Prince, Stephen. 2012. *Digital Visual Effects in Cinema: The Seduction of Reality.* New Brunswick, NJ: Rutgers University Press.

Raine, Michael. 2014. "Adaptation as 'Transcultural Mimesis' in Japanese Cinema." In *The Oxford Handbook of Japanese Cinema*, edited by Daisuke Miyao, 101–23. Oxford: Oxford University Press.

Ran Changjian. 2007. "Biaoyizhuyi xiju" (Expressionistic drama). *Zhongguo xiqu xueyuan xuebao* (Journal of the National Academy of Chinese Theatre Arts) 28, no. 2: 77–84.

Ren, Quah Sy. 2001. "Space and Suppositionality in Gao Xingjian's Theatre." In *Soul of Chaos: Critical Perspectives on Gao Xingjian*, edited by Kwok-Kan Tam, 157–200. Hong Kong: Chinese University Press.

Sun, Hongmei. 2018. *Transforming Monkey: Adaptation and Representation of a Chinese Epic.* Seattle: University of Washington Press.

Tian, Min. 2016. "Traditional Asian Performance in Modern and Contemporary Times: III. China." In *The Routledge Handbook of Asian Theatre*, edited by Siyuan Liu, 491–95. London: Routledge.

Turnock, Julie A. 2015. *Plastic Reality: Special Effects, Technology, and the Emergence of 1970s Blockbuster Aesthetics.* New York: Columbia University Press.

Waley, Arthur. 1961. *Monkey.* London: Penguin Books.

Wang Jide. (1623) 2002. "From *Qu Lü.*" In *Chinese Theories of Theater and Performance from Confucius to the Present*, edited and translated by Faye Chunfang Fei, 61–65. Ann Arbor: University of Michigan Press.

Whissel, Kristen. 2014. *Spectacular Digital Effects: CGI and Contemporary Cinema*. Durham, NC: Duke University Press.

Wollen, Peter. (1969) 1972. *Signs and Meanings in the Cinema*. Bloomington: Indiana University Press.

Yan, Haiping. 2003. "Theatricality in Classical Chinese Drama." In *Theatricality*, edited by Tracy C. Davis and Thomas Postlewait, 65–89. Cambridge: Cambridge University Press.

Yu, Anthony C. (1977–1983) 2012. *The Journey to the West*. 4 vols. Chicago: University of Chicago Press.

Zhang Zhen. 1999. "Teahouse, Shadowplay, Bricolage: 'Laborer's Love' and the Question of Early Chinese Cinema." In *Cinema and Urban Culture in Shanghai, 1922–1943*, edited by Yingjin Zhang, 27–50. Stanford, CA: Stanford University Press.

———. 2005. *An Amorous History of the Silver Screen: Shanghai Cinema, 1896–1937*. Chicago: University of Chicago Press.

Zhu, Ying. 2015. "Has Chinese Film Finally Produced a Real Hero?" *ChinaFile*, August 18, 2015. http://www.chinafile.com/reporting-opinion/culture/has-chinese-film-finally-produced-real-hero.

Contributors

Weihong Bao is associate professor of film and media at UC Berkeley. She is the author of *Fiery Films: The Emergence of an Affective Medium in China, 1915–1945* and is currently working on a new book, "Background Matters: The Art of Environment in Modern China." She coedits the *Journal of Chinese Cinemas* and the Film Theory in Media History book series published by Amsterdam University Press.

Jennifer Blaylock is visiting assistant professor in cinema studies at Oberlin College. Her research has appeared in the *Journal of African Cinemas* and *Screen*.

Hannah Frank (1984–2017) was assistant professor of film studies at the University of North Carolina Wilmington. Her book, *Frame by Frame: A Materialist Aesthetics of Animated Cartoons*, was published in 2019.

Laura-Zoë Humphreys is assistant professor in the Department of Communication at Tulane University. Her research focuses on cinema and censorship, media piracy and urban place-making, media ethnography, and post/socialism. She is the author of *Fidel between the Lines: Paranoia and Ambivalence in Late Socialist Cuban Cinema*. Her work has also appeared in *Social Text* and the *International Journal of Cultural Studies*.

Alice Lovejoy is associate professor in the Department of Cultural Studies and Comparative Literature and the Moving Image Studies Program at the University of Minnesota Twin Cities and a former editor at *Film Comment*. She is the author of *Army Film and the Avant Garde: Cinema and Experiment in the Czechoslovak Military* (2015).

Rochona Majumdar is associate professor in the Departments of South Asian Languages and Civilizations and Cinema and Media Studies at the University of Chicago. She is the author of *Marriage and Modernity: Family Values in the Colonial Bengal*

boundary 2 49:1 (2022)   DOI 10.1215/01903659-615501   © 2022 by Duke University Press

(2009), *Writing Postcolonial History* (2010), and *Art Cinema and India's Forgotten Futures: Film and History in the Postcolony* (2021).

Joshua Malitsky is associate professor of cinema and media studies at Indiana University. He is the author of *Post-Revolution Nonfiction Film* and the editor of *A Companion to Documentary Film History*. He is working on two book projects: "(Supra) national Geographical Imaginaries," which explores Yugoslav nonfiction film after World War II, and "The Documentary Moment," which focuses on the contemporary critical studies of documentary media.

Jason McGrath is associate professor of modern Chinese literature and film in the Department of Asian and Middle Eastern Studies at the University of Minnesota–Twin Cities, where he also serves on the graduate faculty of the Moving Image Studies Program. He is the author of *Postsocialist Modernity: Chinese Cinema, Literature, and Criticism in the Market Age*.

Daniel Morgan is professor of cinema and media studies at the University of Chicago. He is author of *Late Godard and the Possibilities of Cinema* (2012), *The Lure of the Image: Epistemic Fantasies of the Moving Camera* (2021), and numerous articles on the history of film and media theory.

Keep up to date on new scholarship

Issue alerts are a great way to stay current on all the cutting-edge scholarship from your favorite Duke University Press journals. This free service delivers tables of contents directly to your inbox, informing you of the latest groundbreaking work as soon as it is published.

To sign up for issue alerts:

1. Visit **dukeu.press/register** and register for an account. You do not need to provide a customer number.

2. After registering, visit **dukeu.press/alerts**.

3. Go to "Latest Issue Alerts" and click on "Add Alerts."

4. Select as many publications as you would like from the pop-up window and click "Add Alerts."

Printed and bound by CPI Group (UK) Ltd, Croydon, CR0 4YY

13/04/2025

14656478-0002